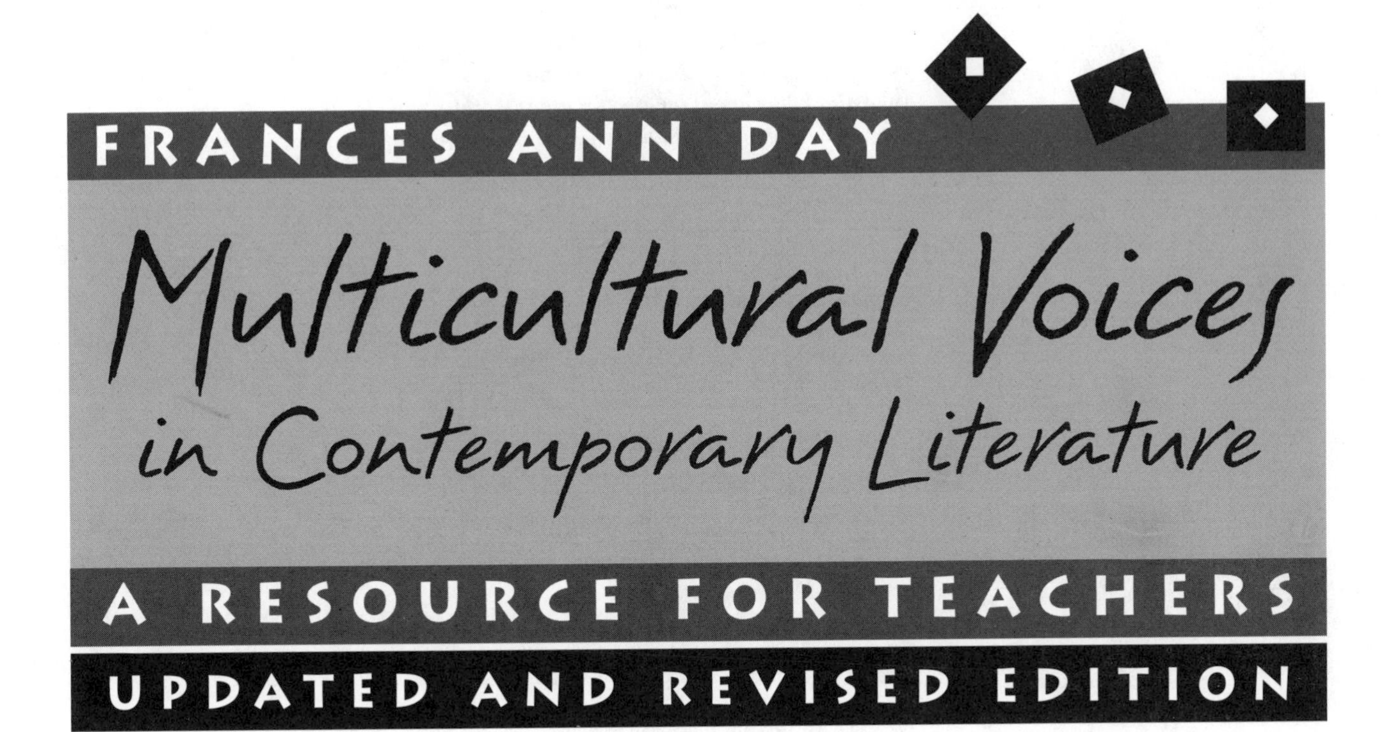

HEINEMANN • PORTSMOUTH, NH

This book is dedicated to my companion, Roxanna,
And to my kindred otherlings,
Who also know about being silenced, invisible.
Who also know about being on the outside.
Who also know about longing for a just world.
May our differences soon be perceived for the beauty they hold,
And our contributions welcomed with respect.

Heinemann
A division of Reed Elsevier Inc.
361 Hanover Street
Portsmouth, NH 03801-3912
http://www.heinemann.com

Offices and agents throughout the world

The first version of this book was written while the author was on sabbatical leave from the Cherry Creek School District in Englewood, Colorado. Frances Ann Day is the sole author of the book, the contents of which do not necessarily reflect the views of the Cherry Creek School District.

We would like to thank those who have given their permission to include material in this book. Every effort has been made to identify the publisher and date in the lists of works published by the forty authors highlighted in this book.

The guidelines listed on page 3–5 were adapted from *Guidelines for Selecting Bias-Free Textbooks and Storybooks,* Council on Interracial Books for Children, New York, NY.

Library of Congress Cataloging-in-Publication Data
Day, Frances Ann.
Multicultural voices in contemporary literature : a resource for teachers / Frances Ann Day. —2nd ed.
p. cm.
Includes bibliographical references and indexes.
ISBN 0-325-00130-8 (alk. paper)
1. Children's literature, American—Minority authors—Study and teaching. 2. Pluralism (Social sciences)—Study and teaching. 3. Ethnic groups in literature—Study and teaching. 4. Ethnicity in literature—Study and teaching. 5. Children—United States—Books and reading. I. Title.
PS153.M56D38 1999
810.9'9282'08693—dc21
99-29447
CIP

Editor: William Varner
Text design: Gwen Frankfeldt
Cover design: Gwen Frankfeldt
Cover quilt: Designed and hand-crafted by Andrea Bursaw

Printed in the United States of America on acid-free paper
03 02 01 EB 2 3 4 5

Contents

Acknowledgments v

PART ONE ◆ AN OVERVIEW

Why This Guide? 1
Evaluating Children's Books for Bias 3

PART TWO ◆ THE AUTHORS AND THEIR STORIES

RUDOLFO ALFONSO ANAYA: Mexican American 9
GEORGE ANCONA: Mexican American 15
SHONTO BEGAY: Navajo 23
ANILÚ BERNARDO: Cuban American 27
IGNATIA BROKER: Ojibway/Chippewa 30
JOSEPH BRUCHAC: Abenaki, English, and Slovak 32
JEANNETTE FRANKLIN CAINES: Black American 42
DIA CHA: Hmong American 46
SOOK NYUL CHOI: Korean American 48
BARBARA COHEN: Jewish American 53
PAT CUMMINGS: African American 66
VIVIAN SHELDON EPSTEIN: Humanist 73
NANCY GARDEN: German Italian American 78
CARMEN LOMAS GARZA: Chicana 83
NIKKI YOLANDA GIOVANNI: Black American 86
ELOISE GREENFIELD: African American 89
VIRGINIA HAMILTON: African American 99
JOYCE HANSEN: African American 115

MINFONG HO: Overseas Chinese 121
JOHANNA HURWITZ: Jewish American 127
JOY NOZOMI KOGAWA: Japanese Canadian 134
JEANNE M. LEE: Chinese American 137
GEORGE LITTLECHILD: Plains Cree Canadian 142
BETTE BAO LORD: Chinese American 148
SHARON BELL MATHIS: African American 150
PATRICIA C. MCKISSACK: African American 154
NICHOLASA MOHR: Puerto Rican American 168
MIN PAEK: Korean American 174
JOHANNA REISS: Jewish American 176
FAITH RINGGOLD: African American 179
SANDRA SCOPPETTONE: Italian American 183
VIRGINIA DRIVING HAWK SNEVE: Lakota 187
YOSHIKO UCHIDA: Japanese American 191
MAI VO-DINH: Vietnamese American 204
ALICE WALKER: African AmerIndian 208
MILDRED PITTS WALTER: African American 212
YOKO KAWASHIMA WATKINS: Japanese American 224
CAMILLE YARBROUGH: African American 228
PAUL YEE: Chinese Canadian 232
LAURENCE YEP: Chinese American 237

PART THREE • APPENDICES

1. Assessment Plan 257
2. Optional Activities 260
3. Author Birthdays 263
4. Multicultural Calendar 264
5. Resources for Educators, Librarians, and Parents 265

INDEXES

1. Illustrator Index 266
2. Title Index 268
3. Subject Index 271

Acknowledgments

My heartfelt thanks to Roxanna.

A very special thank you to the authors and illustrators represented in this book; their kindness, support, insight, and humor have made this journey a warm and fascinating one. With special appreciation of Yoshiko Uchida (1921–1992), an extraordinary person and writer.

My gratitude goes to Alma Flor Ada, Isabel Campoy, judith, Florence M. Hongo, Rosemary Hurtado, Sally Hurtado, Bev Jo, Carolyn Jones, Yoko Kawashima Watkins, Edith King, Nekita Lamour, Lyn Miller-Lachmann, Harriet Rohmer, Isis, Margo Sargent, Linda Strega, and Sandy Tate.

I am grateful to Children's Book Press, Del Sol Books, Inc., Arte Público Press and the other publishers who generously responded to requests for review materials and other information. Thanks also to all the educators, librarians, and others who responded so enthusiastically to the first edition of this book and encouraged me to continue my work. The librarians and staff at the Sonoma County Library are to be commended for their patience, expertise, and caring responses to many questions and requests for information. And finally, thank you to my colleagues who have envisioned a world that truly nourishes the heart, mind, and spirit of every young person.

Why This Guide?

There is something very special about getting to know the person behind the words and illustrations in a book. When we identify with an author, we are much more excited about reading and more likely to extend this interest into our writing. As we get inside an author's head, we learn to read as a writer, watching for the author's possible intentions in writing the piece, the message the author is trying to convey, and the background the author needed to create the piece. We develop the ability to perceive the piece within the context of the author's complete body of work. Having a sense of who the author is enables us to gain more sophisticated meaning from the text and to feel a stronger connection with the printed word. Reading authors as well as books allows us to establish a magical reader/writer bond that provides us not only with a richer literary experience but also a deeper understanding of ourselves and others.

Multicultural Voices in Contemporary Literature celebrates the lives and works of forty inspiring multicultural authors and illustrators. Intended to be used as a resource guide, it provides educators, librarians, and parents with information about writers and artists whose backgrounds and works reflect the diversity of our society. With it, readers will discover fine multicultural literature and deepen and broaden new and established sensitivities to writing styles, language subtleties, and world views.

The information for the biographical sketches was compiled through personal and telephone interviews, written questionnaires, and/or research of secondary sources. In keeping with the philosophy of respecting the individual perspectives and experiences of every person, each of the authors and illustrators self-identified her or his cultural group.

This second edition of *Multicultural Voices in Contemporary Literature* features a number of revisions and updates: We have added the voices of new authors, updated the biographical profiles, added reviews and activities for over 120 new books, and expanded the resource list for educators, librarians, and parents.

The five appendices at the end of this guide:

- Suggest a plan for assessing multicultural programs;
- Offer suggestions for additional activities;
- List the birthdays of the authors and illustrators so that each unit might be further personalized;
- Supply a calendar of multicultural events, holidays, and special days;
- Provide information about additional resources for educators, librarians, and parents.

In addition, a comprehensive subject index is available for use in planning story sessions and units of study. Themes, curricular areas, genres, and topics are included to facilitate infusing literature across the curriculum.

A variety of options are provided so that readers may adapt the material in this guide to fit their individual teaching and learning styles, curriculum requirements, and educational goals. Readers are invited to assess the objectives they have for youngsters and then select any appropriate approach(es) to meet these goals. For example, *Multicultural Voices in Contemporary Literature* may be used as a:

- Classroom, library, and home guide to study a particular author;
- Resource to integrate new authors/works into an established curriculum;
- Tool to encourage youngsters to select and plan the author units and activities they choose to study;
- Reference for identifying individual books for use as a part of the total literature program.

In any and all of these approaches, the emphasis is on exposing young people to works of excellence, nurturing their responses to a variety of literature, and most of all, enjoying the works of fine writers and artists. The material in this book is designed to encourage people of all ages to learn more about the multiplicity of beliefs, experiences, lifestyles, and communities within each cultural group and to reach a more complete understanding of the complexities and commonalities of the human experience. This guide was written with a love of good books, respect for the diversity of all peoples, and hope for the future of all living beings on earth.

Evaluating Children's Books for Bias*

Both in school and out, young children are exposed to racist, anti-Semitic, sexist, classist, ageist, ableist, homophobic and size-oppressive attitudes. These attitudes—expressed repeatedly in books and other media—gradually distort their perceptions until stereotypes and myths are accepted as reality. It is often difficult for an educator, librarian, or parent to persuade young people to question society's attitudes. *But if youngsters are taught how to detect bias in books,* they may incorporate this awareness into their worldview. Although the complexities involved in appraising the intangibles present in the literary arts cannot be encompassed in a checklist, the following guidelines are offered as a starting point in the evaluation of books from a pluralistic perspective.

1. Omission: In spite of the fact that many excellent multicultural books are finally being published, omission continues to be one of the biggest problems in literature for young readers today. Exclusion is one of the most insidious and painful forms of bias; a group may be excluded from an entire collection, or from the books selected for use in a particular library, school district, school, or classroom. The implicit message is that the group does not exist, is insignificant, or has made no contributions to society. Erasure is destructive not only to the group(s) involved but to the larger society.

* Adapted from *Guidelines for Selecting Bias-Free Textbooks and Storybooks,* Council on Interracial Books for Children, New York, NY. Other resources consulted were: "Criteria for Analyzing Books on Asian Americans," unpublished paper by Florence H. Hongo (copyright pending); and *How to Tell the Difference: A Guide to Evaluating Children's Books for Anti-Indian Bias* by Beverly Slapin, Doris Seale, & Rosemary Gonzales. Oyate, 1996. For additional guidelines, see the resources listed in Appendix 5 on page 265.

2. Illustrations: *Stereotypes.* A stereotype is an over-simplified generalization about a particular group which usually carries derogatory implications. Stereotypes may be blatant or subtle. Check for depictions that demean or ridicule characters because of their race, gender, age, ability, appearance, size, religion, sexual orientation, socioeconomic class, or native language.

Tokenism. Is one person from the group presented as having admirable qualities while all the others of the group are stereotyped? In illustrations, do people of color look just like whites except for being tinted or colored in? Do all people from parallel cultures look stereotypically alike or are they depicted as genuine individuals with distinctive features?

Who Is Doing What? Do the illustrations depict people of color in subservient and passive roles or in leadership and action roles? Are males the active doers and females the inactive observers?

3. Check the Story Line: Bias may be expressed in blatant or subtle ways. Check for the following forms of subtle, implicit bias:

Standards for Success. Does it take the white male behavior standards for a person of color or a female to "get ahead"? Is "making it" in the dominant white society projected as the only ideal? To gain acceptance and approval, do people of color and females have to exhibit extraordinary qualities?

Resolution of Problems. How are problems conceived, presented, and resolved in the story? Are people of color considered to be "the problem"? Are the conditions facing oppressed groups represented as related to an unjust society? Does the story line encourage passive acceptance or active resistance? Are problems faced by people from parallel cultures resolved through the benevolent intervention of a white, able-bodied, middle-class male?

Role of Females. Are the achievements of girls and women based on their own initiative and work, or are achievements due to their appearance or to their relationships with males? Are females of all ages presented as problem solvers with a life of their own, or is their role in the story only as a support of male characters? Is it assumed that female characters will marry and that this is their only or major interest in life? Is there an emphasis on describing the physical appearance of female characters? Are positive female characters portrayed as "beautiful" and negative female characters portrayed as "unattractive"? Are older females portrayed in a negative manner? Are older unmarried females ridiculed and assumed to be bitter, unfulfilled, or boring? Are the images of females of all ages prettified? Are they afraid of mice, spiders, or snakes? Do they have to be rescued by a male character?

4. Authenticity: Check for inaccuracy and inappropriateness in the depiction of cultures and lifestyles. Are they oversimplified or do they offer genuine insight into the character? Check for quaint, cutesy, or exotic depictions. Is the portrayal of each group authentic? For example, are Native people from one group shown wearing the hair styles, clothing, or jewelry of another tribe? Does the book portray diversity among Asian Americans or are they all lumped together, ignoring differences in ethnicity, time of immigration, generations of life in the United States, and location of origin as well as the fact that some groups have been in conflict with each other at various times over thousands of years? Are recent immigrants and people from the same ethnic group who were born in the United States portrayed in the same manner? Are the issues facing lesbians subsumed under those facing gay men resulting in distortion, erasure, and/or marginalization?

5. Relationships Between People: Do the white males possess the power, take the leadership roles, and make the important decisions? Do females, people of color, lesbians, gays, elderly, or disabled people function in essentially supporting, subservient roles? Do girls and women have strong friendships with each other or do they depend on males to define them?

6. Heroines/Heroes: Whose interest is the hero/heroine serving? For many years, books showed only "safe" heroes—those who avoided serious conflict with the white, male, able-bodied, heterosexual establishment. Heroines and heroes should be defined according to the concepts of and struggles for justice appropriate to their group. When heroes/heroines from parallel cultures do appear, are they admired for the same qualities that have made establishment heroes famous or because what they have done has benefited the establishment?

7. Consider the Effects on a Child's Self-Image: Are norms established that limit any child's aspirations and self-concept? For example, Asian Americans should not be portrayed as model minorities. Are fat people portrayed in negative ways? Every person from every culture should be portrayed as an individual with unique strengths, weaknesses, interests, lifestyles, and beliefs.

8. Author's or Illustrator's Background: Analyze the biographical data available about the author and illustrator. What qualifies the author or illustrator to deal with the subject? If they are not a member of the group they are depicting, is there anything in their background that would specifically recommend them as creators of the book? There has been considerable debate recently regarding what has been termed *cultural thievery.* Is it ethical for mainstream writers to appropriate the literature of parallel cultures? Many people think it is impossible to write authentically from a perspective one has never experienced personally. People who have been silenced in the past do not take kindly to someone else trying to tell their story now that those stories are finally being recognized as significant. The publishing industry is still a world filled with scarcity: if an established European American author submits a manuscript for a story representing another culture, will there be room for emerging writers from that culture to compete? These important issues and related questions are addressed in a special issue on Multicultural Literature in the March/April 1995 issue of *Horn Book,* as well as in other journals and books.

9. Author's or Illustrator's Perspective: In the past, children's books were written by authors who were white, members of the middle class, heterosexual, able-bodied, and Christian, with one result being that a narrow Eurocentric perspective has dominated children's literature in the United States. For example, the abolitionists featured in the past were the white members of the Underground Railroad, when in actuality, most abolitionists were African Americans. Watch for books that present multiple perspectives. Does the total collection present many world views? Are readers encouraged to consider a situation from several perspectives?

10. Language: Examples of offensive terms include: "savage," "primitive," "conniving," "lazy," "superstitious," "treacherous," "wily," "crafty," "inscrutable," "docile," "backward," "bitter," "barren," "squaw," "papoose," and "Indian givers." Consider the effect of the use of the color *white* as the ultimate in beauty, cleanliness, or virtue (*angel* food); and the color *black* or use of "dark" as evil, dirty, or menacing (*devil's* food). Watch for sexist language that excludes or in any way demeans females. The generic use of the words *man* and *he* were accepted in the past but their use today is outmoded. The following examples show how sexist language can be avoided: ancestors instead of forefathers; humankind instead of mankind; firefighters instead of firemen; synthetic instead of manmade; chair or chairperson instead of chairman; and she/he instead of he.

11. Copyright Date: Books on minority themes—often hastily conceived—suddenly began appearing in the mid- and late 1960s. Most of these books were written by white authors, edited by white editors, and published by white publishers. They often reflected a white, middle-class, mainstream point of view. Not until the early 1970s did the children's book world begin to even remotely reflect the realities of a pluralistic society. The copyright date may be *one* clue as to how likely the book is to be overtly biased, although a recent copyright date is no guarantee of the book's authenticity. Conversely, *do not throw out all the books with old copyright dates!* Use these guidelines to examine each one. Use the biased books as teaching tools with your students and colleagues.

The Authors and Their Stories

Rudolfo Alfonso Anaya

Mexican American (1937–)

Birthday: October 30
Contact: Susan Bergholz
17 West 10th Street, # 5
New York, New York 10011

"Our challenge is to incorporate into the curriculum all the voices of our country. . . . You shortchange your students and you misrepresent the true nature of their country if you don't introduce them to all the communities who have comprised the history of this country. To deny your students a view into these different worlds is to deny them tools for the future." *("The Censorship of Neglect" in* The Anaya Reader, *p. 412)*

Books by Rudolfo Anaya

The Adventures of Juan Chicaspatas. **Arte Público Press, 1985.**

Alburquerque. **University of New Mexico Press, 1992; Warner Books, 1992.**

The Anaya Reader. **Warner Books, 1995.**

Aztlán: Essays on the Chicano Homeland. **Co-edited with Francisco Lomeli. Bilingual Press, 1984; University of New Mexico Press, 1991.**

Bless Me, Ultima. **Warner Books, 1993.**

Cuentos Chicanos: A Short Story Anthology. **Co-edited with Antonio Márquez. University of New Mexico Press, 1984.**

Cuentos: Tales From the Hispanic Southwest. **Illustrated by Jamie Valdez. The Museum of New Mexico Press, 1980.**

Farolitos for Abuelo. **Hyperion, 1999.**

Farolitos of Christmas. **Illustrated by Edward Gonzales. Hyperion Books for Children, 1995; 1998.**

Farolitos Limited. **Hyperion, 1997.**

First Tortilla. **Hyperion, forthcoming.**

Heart of Aztlán. **University of New Mexico Press, 1988.**

Jalamanta: A Message from the Desert. **Warner Books, 1996.**

The Legend of La Llorona. **Tonatiuh-Quinto Sol, 1984.**

Maya's Children: The Story of La Llorona. **Hyperion, 1997.**

Rio Grande Fall. **Warner Books, 1996.**

Shaman Winter. **Warner, 2000.**

The Silence of the Llano. **Tonatiuh-Quinto Sol, 1982.**

Tierra: Contemporary Fiction of New Mexico. **Editor. Cinco Puntos Press, 1989.**

Tortuga. **University of New Mexico Press, 1988.**

Voces: Anthology of New Mexican Writers. **Editor. University of New Mexico Press, 1987.**

Zia Summer. **Warner Books, 1995.**

Rudolfo Anaya, the highly acclaimed author of *Bless Me, Ultima,* was born October 30, 1937, in Pastura, a village lying south of Santa Rosa in eastern New Mexico. When he was a baby, his parents sat him on a rug on the floor. They placed a variety of items around him—saddle, pencil, paper, etc. He crawled to the pencil and paper. He has continued to follow this interest in writing to this day.

Anaya was a very curious child; his mother noticed that he always asked a lot of questions and she knew that he was destined to follow an unfamiliar path. He grew up speaking Spanish at home so when he started school, the transition from a Spanish-speaking world to an English-speaking one resulted in a period of adjustment. Although schoolwork was not difficult for Anaya, he soon realized that he was different and that he had a unique way of perceiving the world.

Anaya's family moved to Santa Rosa when he was a small child and to Albuquerque when he was fifteen. Subsequently, he suffered a spinal injury when he dove into an irrigation ditch and endured an extended stay in a hospital. When he returned home, he was walking with a cane. (He later wrote *Tortuga,* based loosely on this experience.) During his convalescence, he learned to hide his pain, to live within; he learned the true meaning of loneliness. Later, he eloquently expressed this pain and loneliness in his writing.

Anaya attended high school in Albuquerque where discrimination made life difficult for his people. There were no Mexican American teachers and the literature and history of his people were not a part of the curriculum. This widespread omission of information about his heritage understandably resulted in feelings of alienation in the young student as it did in many of his peers. Even during his undergraduate days at the University of New Mexico, there was no mention of Mexican history or art. Indeed, he was still corrected for allowing his Spanish accent to show.

Anaya wrote poetry and prose to assuage the pain, loneliness, and alienation. He struggled for seven years to write his first novel, *Bless Me, Ultima* which became one of the first Chicano bestsellers. The book was awarded the prestigious Premio Quinto Sol Award for the best novel written by a Chicano in 1972. Since then, Anaya has written many other books, poems, plays, articles, and screenplays.

Today, Rudolfo Anaya is considered one of the leading Latino novelists in the United States. After teaching junior and senior high school, he taught creative writing at the University of New Mexico. Later, as a full professor of English, he specialized in Chicano literature. He recently retired after many years of teaching to devote his energies to writing, lecturing, editing, and traveling.

- **Collection of short stories, essays, plays, and excerpts from novels**

Grades 12–Adult

The Anaya Reader

This important collection contains four outstanding essays about the omission of Chicano/a literature, history, and culture in the curriculum: "An American Chicano in King Arthur's Court," "Take the Tortillas Out of Your Poetry," "On the Education of Hispanic Children," and "The Censorship of Neglect."

Suggestions for the Classroom

1. These four essays are highly recommended for all educators, librarians, and parents. People who have been working in the field of multicultural education will be heartened by Anaya's words, and those who are undecided will gain insight into the agenda behind policies that routinely exclude the work of some of our country's best writers and teach children to be ashamed of their heritage. Excerpts might be included in the rationale for grant proposals, changes in curriculum, and initiation of policy changes.

2. The short stories, plays, and excerpts from novels might be used with advanced high school students. Note: "The Silence of the Llano" is a disturbing piece about death, grieving, child neglect, and rape. It ends with a foreboding hint of impending family rape, described in the foreword as "a re-creation of a traditional tale of incest."

Bless Me, Ultima

Premio Quinto Sol Literary Award

- **Career aspirations**
- **Death**
- **Dreams**
- ***Curanderas***

This best-selling novel depicts the maturation of Antonio Marez, a boy growing up in Guadalupe, a small New Mexico farm village. Seven-year-old Antonio narrates (in flashback form) this story of his relationship with his spiritual guide, Ultima, a *curandera* (healer). He struggles with spirituality, confused about the teachings of the Catholic Church, and with his discovery of a genuine spirituality and legitimate morality outside the church, in nature. The book deals with a wide variety of subjects drawn together with intense force. Antonio struggles to understand good and evil, to establish his identity, to conquer childhood fears, and to find his way in his family, school, and community. Throughout the novel, Antonio's trials are balanced with his association with Ultima. She allows him to participate in her life-affirming practices of healing and stabilizing negative forces. Although the novel details only two years in Antonio's life, he changes and grows in profound ways. The skillful crossweaving of social, cultural, and psychological levels of action result in a very powerful book. Available in Spanish edition: *Bendiceme, Ultima.*

Ages 13 up

Suggestions for the Classroom

1. What was Ultima's philosophy? Invite youngsters to respond in writing to the *curanderismo* practiced by Ultima. Examine her role in the community and her influence on Antonio. What did he learn from her? What was her teaching style?

2. Antonio had many questions about spirituality. Discuss his conflicts and the role Antonio's dreams played in helping sort out his confusions.

3. Antonio witnessed four deaths. Discuss each of the losses that Antonio experienced (include his brothers). In writing, analyze Antonio's reactions to one or more of these losses.

4. Discuss the ways in which Antonio's rural *Chicanitoness* impacted his life. How was his life different from an urban European American boy's life?

5. This is Rudolfo Anaya's first book; he struggled for seven years to write it. Why was it such a significant book for him? For Latino literature? For literature for young adults?

Cuentos Chicanos: A Short Story Anthology

- **Short stories**

The twenty-one short stories in this collection offer highly personalized visions of the world presented in styles that range from oral narratives to experimentation with stream-of-consciousness. From tragic to light-hearted, cynical to exuberant, these stories are distinguished by their diversity and vitality. The collection beautifully captures the dimensions, subtleties, nuances, and paradoxes of Chicano life and culture. A short story by Rudolfo Anaya is included.

Ages 13 up

Suggestions for the Classroom

1. Invite youngsters to work in small groups. Each group might select a different story to present to the class. Encourage creativity in the ways in which the stories are presented. Examples: skits, storytelling, filmstrips, pantomime, debate, visual arts, music, etc.

2. Invite youngsters to create a mural that includes images from each story.

3. Read and discuss additional books and stories by the writers represented in the anthology.

- **Folk tales**
- **Southwest**
- **Bilingual (Spanish)**

Ages 8 up

Cuentos: Tales from the Hispanic Southwest

Twenty-three tales of magic, myth, legend, and the events of everyday life in the Latino/a villages of New Mexico and southern Colorado were selected and adapted in Spanish and then retold in English. Rich traditions, values, customs, and wisdom flow through this collection of *cuentos*. A glossary of regional, archaic, and idiomatic words is included.

Suggestions for the Classroom

1. These stories lend themselves to storytelling, dramatization, writing, and visual art. Invite youngsters to create a mural based on the stories in this collection.

2. Invite individuals or small groups to choose a tale and lead a discussion related to that story.

3. Here is an excellent opportunity for language sharing. Invite youngsters who know Spanish to read parts of stories alternating with others reading the English translation.

- **Tradition and change**
- **Christmas**
- **Grandfathers**
- **Illness**

Ages 7 up

The Farolitos of Christmas

Tomás Rivera Mexican American Children's Book Award

Luz's *abuelo* (grandfather) is ill and unable to make the traditional *luminarias* (small bonfires) for Christmas Eve so the *pastores* (shepherds) can see to perform their annual songs and stories. Luz solves the problem by designing *farolitos* (small lanterns) made out of brown paper bags and candles. The family happily makes dozens of them and uses them to line the path to the road. This beautifully illustrated book presents a positive image of a young Mexican American girl who is a risk-taker and who shows ingenuity in solving problems. Glossary included.

Suggestions for the Classroom

1. Luz used her problem-solving skills to help her family. Invite youngsters to create a journal entry she might have written a few days after she designed the farolitos.

2. Themes and topics for discussion and writing include: tradition and change; intergenerational relationships, cooperation among family members, risk-taking, problem solving; and celebration of holidays.

3. Invite youngsters who do not understand Spanish to learn the Spanish words in the glossary and to use these words in their written responses to the book.

4. Rudolfo Anaya has written another book featuring the characters in this book: *Farolitos for Abuelo.*

The Heart of Aztlán

- **Technology**
- **Moving**
- **Newcomers**
- **Leadership**

This is a compelling novel about the adjustments the Chavez family must make when they move from the rural community of Guadalupe to the barrio of Barelos in Albuquerque. As they set out in search of a new future for their family, they encounter unforeseen changes that challenge their adaptability, threaten their lives, and shake them to their very core. Mythological themes, rich symbolism, and the sense of a shared communal soul combine with an inspiring social message to leave the reader with a feeling of hope. An emphatic portrayal of people dispossessed of their heritage and struggling to survive in an alien culture, this philosophical novel draws inspiration from the myth of Aztlán, the mythological place of the Aztecs.

Ages 13 up

Suggestions for the Classroom

1. Themes and topics for discussion and writing include: the sacredness of the earth; the enslavement of people by the giants of technology and industry; people dispossessed of their heritage and struggling to survive in an alien environment; and clashes between urban and rural, political and religious, and poverty and wealth.

2. Discuss and/or write about the symbolism in the book (such as the water tank, the cave spring, the supermarket).

3. Each character responded individually to the hostile urban environment. Invite youngsters to choose a character and write about her/his personal growth and moral development in the book.

4. Analyze the obstacles the Chavez family faced in their new location. Invite youngsters to make recommendations for improving society so that life is fair for everyone.

Maya's Children: The Story of La Llorona

- **La Llorona**
- **Immortality**

"La Llorona," the legendary tale from Latin America about the crying woman who searches for her children along rivers, lakes, and lonely roads, is retold by Anaya in a tender, evocative style. Modifying the most frightening aspects of the original story in which La Llorona takes the life of her children, Anaya has created a version appropriate for young children. Señor Tiempo, jealous of Maya's immortality, deceives her and takes her children away. Youngsters of all backgrounds will be interested in this tale that most Latino/a children have heard in at least one of its many versions.

Ages 5 up

Suggestions for the Classroom

1. In the Author's Note, Anaya provides background information about La Llorona. He also discusses the reasons for the changes he made to the tale. Educators, librarians, and parents will enjoy discussing his ideas about adapting myths and folktales for the very young.

2. Older children will enjoy researching and comparing/contrasting several versions of this tale.

3. For another story about La Llorona, read *Prietita and the Ghost Woman / Prietita y la Llorona* by Gloria Anzaldúa.

- **Hospitals**
- **Paralysis**
- **Illness**
- **Autobiographical fiction**
- **Euthanasia**

Tortuga

Before Columbus Foundation American Book Award

Patterned on the mythic journey motif of classical literature, *Tortuga* is the first-person story of a paralyzed sixteen-year-old boy's quest for wellness and understanding. The novel takes place in a hospital for young people and traces Tortuga's recovery from a near-fatal accident. (The novel is loosely autobiographical.) Tortuga (turtle) is the nickname given the boy by his peers because his body is encased in a shell-like cast. The novel has numerous themes and a great deal of symbolism. One of the most important themes is that physical health is inextricably fused with emotional and spiritual well-being. Tortuga symbolizes the "magic mountain" near the hospital as well as the protagonist's body cast and his psychological shell. Tortuga's literal journey ends with him leaving the hospital on crutches to return home. The male characters in this complex book are developed more fully than the female characters. *Tortuga* is under contract to Helen Landridge, a small British independent filmmaking company.

Mature 13-year olds up, with teacher guidance. Strong language.

Suggestions for the Classroom

1. Analyze the connections among Anaya's three books, *Bless Me, Ultima, Heart of Aztlán, and Tortuga,* including the curative powers of water, the elderly sages, the role of dreams and nightmares, the mythic themes and narratives, and the fantastic imagery and symbolism. Compare the powers of the golden carp, the cave spring, and the Tortuga waters.

2. Examine the use of symbolism: Tortuga (turtle), butterfly, Filomon, Ismelda, Salomon, the blue guitar, etc.

3. Tortuga left the hospital cradling the blue guitar, having discovered his mystical destiny as a singer. Invite interested youngsters to compose a song Tortuga might have sung as a message of hope when he returned home.

4. Some reviewers were critical of the one-dimensional portrayal of the female characters in the book as either idealizations or undesirables. After analyzing the characterization of each female character, invite youngsters to write a paragraph about one of them. Share and discuss.

George Ancona

Marina Ancona

Mexican American (1929–)

Birthday: December 4
Contact: Lothrop, Lee & Shepard
1350 Avenue of the Americas
New York, New York 10019

"Discovering the world of books was a revelation, because I could work with what was inside of me. I could explore my own feelings, my own curiosities. . . . It was a freedom, a discovery, and a search: the right to search for myself and what I wanted to say with my life and what I wanted to do." (The Multicolored Mirror, *p. 60)*

Books by George Ancona

WRITTEN AND PHOTOGRAPHED

And What Do You Do? **Dutton, 1976.**

Aquarium. **Clarion, 1991.**

Bananas: From Manolo to Margie. **Clarion, 1982; 1990.**

Barrio: Jose's Neighborhood. **Harcourt, 1998.**

Cutters, Carvers and the Cathedral. **Lothrop, 1995.**

Dancing Is. **Dutton, 1981.**

Earth Daughter: Alicia of Ácoma Pueblo. **Simon & Schuster, 1995.**

Fiesta Fireworks. **Lothrop, 1998.**

Fiesta U. S. A. **(English and Spanish editions). Lodestar Books, 1995.**

Freighters. **Crowell, 1985.**

The Golden Lion Tamarin Comes Home. **Macmillan, 1994.**

Growing Older. **Dutton, 1978.**

Helping Out. **Clarion, 1985.**

I Feel. **Dutton, 1978.**

It's a Baby. **Dutton, 1979.**

Man and Mustang. **Macmillan, 1992.**

Mayeros: A Yucatec Maya Family. **Lothrop, 1997.**

Monster Movers. **Dutton, 1984.**

Monster on Wheels. **Dutton, 1974.**

My Camera. **Crown, 1992.**

Pablo Remembers: The Fiesta of the Day of the Dead. **Lothrop, 1993.**

The Piñata Maker / El Piñatero. **Harcourt, 1994.**

Powwow. **Harcourt, 1993.**

Ricardo's Day. **Scholastic, 1994.**

Riverkeeper. **Macmillan, 1989.**

Sheepdog. **Lothrop, 1985.**

Teamwork. **Crowell, 1983.**

Turtle Watch. **Macmillan, 1987.**

BOOKS PHOTOGRAPHED BY GEORGE ANCONA

The American Family Farm **by Joan Anderson. Harcourt, 1989.**

Balance It **by Howard Smith. Four Winds, 1982.**

Being Adopted **by Maxine Rosenberg. Lothrop, 1984.**

Being a Twin, Having a Twin **by Maxine Rosenberg. Lothrop, 1985.**

Bodies **by Barbara Brenner. Dutton, 1973.**

Brothers and Sisters **by Maxine Rosenberg. Clarion, 1991.**

Caras **by Barbara Brenner, Spanish by Alma Flor Ada. Dutton, 1977.**

Christmas on the Prairie **by Joan Anderson. Clarion, 1985.**

City! New York **by Shirley Climo. Macmillan, 1990.**

City! San Francisco **by Shirley Climo. Macmillan, 1990.**

City! Washington, D. C. **by Shirley Climo. Macmillan, 1991.**

Dolphins at Grassy Key **by Marcia Seligson. Macmillan, 1989.**

Earth Keepers **by Joan Anderson. Gulliver Green/Harcourt, 1993.**

Faces **by Barbara Brenner. Dutton, 1970.**

Finding a Way **by Maxine Rosenberg. Lothrop, 1988.**

Finding Your First Job **by Sue Alexander. Dutton, 1980.**

The First Thanksgiving Feast **by Joan Anderson, 1984.**

French Pioneers **by Joan Anderson. Lodestar, 1989.**

From Map to Museum **by Joan Anderson. Morrow, 1988.**

The Glorious Fourth in Prairietown **by Joan Anderson. Morrow, 1986.**

Grandpa Had a Windmill, Grandma Had a Churn **by Louise Jackson. Parents, 1977.**

Handtalk: An ABC of Finger Spelling and Sign Language **by Remy Charlip and Mary Beth Miller. Four Winds Press, 1974.**

Handtalk Birthday: A Number and Story Book in Sign Language **by Remy Charlip and Mary Beth Miller. Four Winds Press, 1987.**

Handtalk School **with Mary Beth Miller. Four Winds Press, 1991.**

Handtalk Zoo **with Mary Beth Miller. Four Winds Press, 1989.**

Harry's Helicopter **by Joan Anderson. Morrow, 1990.**

Jackpot of the Beagle Brigade **by Sam and Beryl Epstein. Macmillan, 1987.**

Joshua's Westward Journal **by Joan Anderson. Morrow, 1987.**

Just Beyond Reach **by Bonnie Larkin Nims. Scholastic, 1992.**

Living in Two Worlds **by Maxine Rosenberg. Lothrop, 1986.**

Making a New Home in America **by Maxine Rosenberg. Lothrop, 1986.**

Mom Can't See Me **by Sally Hobart Alexander. Macmillan, 1990.**

Mom's Best Friend **by Sally Hobart Alexander. Macmillan, 1992.**

My Feet Do **by Jean Holzenthaler. Dutton, 1979.**

My Friend Leslie **by Maxine Rosenberg. Lothrop, 1983.**

My New Baby-Sitter **by Christine Loomis. Morrow, 1991.**

My Special Friend **by Floreva G. Cohen. Board of Jewish Education, 1986.**

Over Here It's Different: Carolina's Story **by Mildred Leinweber Dawson. Macmillan, 1993.**

Over on the River **by Louise A. Jackson. Parents Press, 1980.**

Pioneer Children of Appalachia **by Joan Anderson. Clarion, 1986.**

Richie's Rocket **by Joan Anderson. Morrow, 1993.**

Sally's Submarine **by Joan Anderson. Morrow, 1995.**

A Snake Lover's Diary **by Barbara Brenner. Dutton, 1970.**

Twins on Toes **by Joan Anderson. Lodestar, 1993.**

A Williamsburg Household **by Joan Anderson. Clarion, 1988.**

George Ancona is the highly regarded photographer and author of over seventy books for young readers. The son of Mexican parents from small villages in the Yucatan, he grew up in Coney Island. He has enjoyed a long and distinguished career in a variety of art related fields, embarking on his work in children's literature in 1970. Since then, Ancona has become one of the most respected names in the field.

Born in New York City, he was named Jorge Efraín and was called George except by his family who called him Jorgito. Ancona's family, who spoke Spanish at home, moved to Coney Island by the time he was ready to start school. He feels that the hours spent exploring the docks of the East River prepared him for his wanderlust years. He was filled with wonder and awe at the sights and sounds of the ships, and often his imagination took flight. As a teenager, he sketched and painted the boat wrecks, tugboats, barges, and oil tanks along the Coney Island Creek. He recalls being a quiet child, sitting for hours by the creek, doing wood cuts.

Ancona's career as a designer started in high school when he helped design the yearbook, made posters for school events and competitions, and attended art classes at the Brooklyn Museum. It was there that he met and showed his work to Rufino Tamayo, the celebrated Mexican painter, who invited him to Mexico. After graduation, Ancona took a bus to Mexico City where Señor Tamayo arranged for him to attend the Academia de San Carlos, the leading art school in Mexico.

Back in New York, Ancona entered the Art Students' League on scholarship and worked at the *New York Times, Esquire, Apparel Arts, Seventeen,* and NBC Television and Radio Networks. During his spare time, he collaborated with a friend to make his first film, *The Gift.* Next he made a documentary of the South Bronx. When he was thirty years old, he moved into the world of freelancing, producing films for "Sesame Street" and working on documentaries and industrial films in Brazil, Pakistan, Hong Kong, and Japan. His work filming a children's series titled "Big Blue Marble" took him to Iceland, Tunisia, and Switzerland.

Ancona's introduction to children's books came when his friend, Barbara Brenner, invited him to illustrate with photographs a book she had written. The publication of *Faces* in 1970 was the beginning of a new direction for Ancona, one that has proven to be very satisfying and successful. His next step was to write the text for a book of his photographs. This was an exciting challenge because he had never studied writing. To his delight, he has found that by combining words with his pictures, he can enhance the meaning of his stories.

Fulfilling his childhood dreams of traveling and exploring new places, Ancona's research has taken him to Honduras, Brazil, Mexico, and many other places. His unique work has been recognized for the wide range of topics explored and the fascinating text and breathtaking photography. For more information about George Ancona, see *Contemporary Authors,* Volume 19; *Something About the Author Autobiography Series,* Volume 18; *Something About the Author,* Volume 12; and *The Multicolored Mirror: Cultural Substance in Literature for Children and Young Adults* edited by Merri V. Lindgren.

Earth Daughter: Alicia of Ácoma Pueblo

- **Ácoma**
- **Biography**
- **Pottery**
- **New Mexico**

With exuberance and joy, George Ancona celebrates the lives and pottery of the Ácoma people of New Mexico. Beautiful photographs and engaging text follow Alicia Histia as she learns the art of pottery making from her family. For generations the people of Ácoma Pueblo have been making pottery which is known for its beauty and unique designs. The design, photographs, and story in this book are exceptionally appealing. Alicia is a well-rounded person, interested in a variety of subjects and activities. Her family is portrayed in a friendly way, wearing jeans, t-shirts, and turquoise jewelry . The closeness the Ácoma people have with Mother Earth is lovingly portrayed. Ancona's sensitive book helps combat stereotypes of the Pueblo people as well as of females. Alicia not only plans to be a lawyer *and* follow the family traditions but is not afraid of snakes, a misunderstood, much-maligned creature. This is a lovely, engaging book that will replace some of the stereotypical materials that were published in the past.

Ages 7–12

Suggestions for the Classroom

1. Follow the steps involved in creating pottery. "Working with clay is a slow process. It cannot be rushed; clay doesn't want you to be angry with it." Discuss.

2. Alicia plans to follow her dream of being both a potter and a lawyer. Discuss her varied interests and aspirations.

3. Reread and discuss the words in the glossary and the notes from the author providing background information about the Ácoma people.

- Day of the Dead
- Las Posadas
- Los Matachines
- Three Kings' Day

Fiesta U. S. A.

George Ancona's vibrant photographs and warm text pay tribute to four fiestas. On November 2, we go to San Francisco where we join the Day of the Dead procession that commemorates people who have died. Next we go to Albuquerque, New Mexico where we join the procession of Las Posadas, which takes place during the nine days before Christmas. Our next stop is in the tiny village of El Rancho in northern New Mexico where we learn about Los Matachines. The Matachines represent the arrival in Mexico of Hernán Cortés, the Spanish conqueror of the Aztecs. On January 6, our last stop is in East Harlem in New York City for Three Kings' Day. Twelve days after Christmas, La Fiesta de los Reyes Magos celebrates the three kings who came bearing gifts for the baby Jesus. Spanish edition available.

Ages 7–12

Suggestions for the Classroom

1. This book might be read in four sittings with discussion and activities following each. Or the section featuring each fiesta might be read during the appropriate time of year to celebrate that event.

2. Discuss the role these fiestas play in bringing the community together, preserving traditions, and providing an opportunity to have fun.

3. Discuss the ways in which these fiestas help children of immigrants understand a bit of what it was like for their parents and/or grandparents growing up in the old country.

- Deafness
- Sign language

Handtalk: An ABC of Finger Spelling and Sign Language

School Library Journal *Best Book of the Year*

American Institute of Graphic Arts 50 Books of the Year

Kirkus Choice *100 Books Recommended for Libraries*

American Library Association Notable Book of the Year

Child Study Association Children's Book of the Year

Handtalk Birthday: A Number and Story Book in Sign Language

New York Times *Best Illustrated Children's Book Award*

Handtalk School

Handtalk Zoo

These four exuberant books provide information on sign language and finger spelling. Clear color photographs record conversations in American Sign Language among multiracial groups of children and adults. Two kinds of sign language are featured: finger spelling in which words are formed letter by letter with the fingers, and signing in which signs are made with one or two hands combined with facial expressions and body language. Each of these joyous books provides an interesting journey in creative expression. The multicultural cast of characters and the lighthearted, humorous facial expressions and subject matter will demystify sign language.

All Ages

Suggestions for the Classroom

1. Hearing youngsters will be interested to learn that anyone can use sign language to communicate with deaf and hearing impaired people as well as for talking from far away without shouting, from behind closed windows, and even under water.

2. Many young people are interested in learning sign language. The first book in this series introduces the signs for each letter of the alphabet as well as a word for each letter of the alphabet.

Mom Can't See Me

Notable Children's Book in the Field of Social Studies

Mom's Best Friend

- **Blindness**
- **Guide dogs**
- **Death of an animal companion**

In *Mom Can't See Me,* nine-year-old Leslie discusses the many ways in which her blind mother, Sally Hobart Alexander, leads an active and rich life. The sequel, *Mom's Best Friend,* details the changes the family experiences after the death of the author's first guide dog, Marit. The entire family mourns the loss of their beloved animal companion. But for Alexander, Marit's death means curtailed mobility as well as heartache. So she returns to The Seeing Eye where she found Marit twelve years before, for another guide dog. The death of the beloved family member is handled with sensitivity, acknowledging the intensity and complexities of the grieving process. These are stereotype-breaking books that feature a blind person who is independent, resourceful, playful, and creative.

Ages 6–10

Suggestions for the Classroom

1. These books will prompt discussions about the importance of being sensitive to people who are blind as well as those with other differences. Leslie confides that not everyone understands about having a blind mother and she wishes they did. She explains the insensitivity of laughing at jokes that call someone blind when they don't understand something.

2. Discuss the author's many interests: camping, tap dancing, playing the piano, swimming, volunteering at her daughter's school, and writing books. How do these books help break the stereotypes of blind people?

3. Youngsters will be interested in discussing and writing about the complicated training process for guide dogs and the many skills the dogs must possess.

Over Here It's Different: Carolina's Story

- **Dominican Republic**
- **Immigration**
- **Newcomers**
- **Moving**
- **Gender roles**

The experiences of an eleven-year-old girl who emigrated from the Dominican Republic to New York City when she was seven are related in text and photographs. Eleven-year-old Carolina Liranzo reflects on the many changes she has encountered during the past four years and discusses the two worlds she lives in. She misses aspects of her earlier life and realizes that someday she may want to go back to live in the Dominican Republic. At first the adjustment to the noisy, crowded, cold city and new language was difficult and Carolina was homesick. But after four years, she is quick to point out all the advantages of her new home. Her school experience has been a positive one unlike that of many newcomers who are subjected to ridicule and exclusion. Veteran photographer George Ancona, the son of immigrants, brings both heart and expertise to the sharp black-and-white photographs. Combined with the informative text which includes an unflinching examination of gender roles, this book will provide fascinating reading for youngsters born in the United States and encouragement for those who have recently arrived.

Ages 7–12

Suggestions for the Classroom

1. Carolina has weathered the difficult adjustment period and loves both of her countries. This book provides a contrast to other volumes that reveal the isolation, heartbreak, and confusion experienced by newcomers who are greeted with indifference, suspicion, hostility, and even violence. For additional books, see *Newcomers* in the Subject Index.

2. An excellent resource for educators, librarians, and parents is *The Inner World of the Immigrant Child* by Cristina Igoa. St. Martin's Press, 1995.

- **All Saints Day**
- **All Souls Day**
- **All Hallows Eve**
- **Day of the Dead**

Pablo Remembers: The Fiesta of the Day of the Dead

Bank Street College Children's Book of the Year

During the three-day celebration of the Day of the Dead, a young Mexican boy and his family make elaborate preparations to honor the spirits of loved ones who have died. For Pablo, Shaula, Cristina, and Angelita, this year's celebration is especially important. Their *abuelita* (grandmother) died two years ago and they miss her very much. On October 31, All Hallows Eve, the children make a children's altar, to invite the *angelitos,* spirits of dead children, to come back for a visit. November 1 is All Saints Day, and the adult spirits will come to visit. And November 2 is All Souls Day, when the families go to the cemetery to decorate the graves and tombs of their relatives. The three-day fiesta is filled with marigolds, the flowers of the dead; *muertos,* the bread of the dead; sugar skulls, cardboard skeletons, tissue paper decorations, fruit, nuts, incense, and other traditional foods and decorations. The vivid photographs and the fascinating text will delight and teach readers of all ages and backgrounds. Spanish edition: *Pablo Recuerda.*

Ages 7–Up

Suggestions for the Classroom

1. Creating *Pablo Remembers / Pablo Recuerda* was a very special experience for photojournalist George Ancona. Discuss his statement: "Recently I have been going back to my roots for subjects to photograph and write about" *(Something About the Author Autobiography,* p. 14). Read and discuss his other books that celebrate his heritage.

2. Reread and discuss the words in the glossary and the author's note in which Ancona provides more information about the history of the celebration of the Day of the Dead.

The Piñata Maker / El Piñatero

Parents' Choice Award

- **Bilingual**
- **Fiestas**
- **Piñatas**
- **Mexico**

Told in English and Spanish, this colorful book describes how Don Ricardo, a craftsperson from Ejutla de Crespo, Oaxaca, Mexico makes piñatas for all the village birthday parties and other fiestas. The many steps involved in creating a piñata, from making the paste to cutting and gluing the tissue paper, are documented through photographs and text. For this book, Don Ricardo demonstrates how to make a swan, a carrot, and the traditional *piñata de picos,* or star piñata, but he also makes flowers, animals, and fruits. As he works, he stops to answer the door to visitors who are selecting a piñata for a birthday party. After the piñata is filled with a wonderful assortment of fruits, nuts, sugar cane, small toys, and sweets, the party begins.

Ages 7–12

Suggestions for the Classroom

1. This is a beautiful book about a fascinating art, one that is sure to prompt discussion and enhance appreciation for the skill and hard work that goes into making piñatas.

2. George Ancona provides information about how he and his children made simple piñatas from boxes and balloons. Youngsters will enjoy following these directions to make piñatas of their own.

3. Ancona notes that the setting of this book is in the same area as *Pablo Remembers,* which he had researched a year earlier. Youngsters will enjoy examining both books for recurring characters and scenes.

Powwow

Selected for the New York Public Library Children's Book List of 100 Titles

- **Powwows**
- **Dance**
- **Traditions**

Throughout the year, on reservations and in towns and cities across the United States and Canada, Native People hold powwows, gatherings at which they celebrate their culture and heritage. In this book, veteran photojournalist George Ancona records the events at the annual Crow Fair Powwow held on the Crow Reservation in Montana, the largest one held in the United States. After a parade, the singing, drumming, and dancing begin. There are four main dance categories: Traditional, Grass, Fancy, and Jingle-dress. As Ancona describes each dance, his beautiful full-color photographs capture the variety of the brightly colored costumes. Children of all ages participate, learning an important part of their heritage. Powwows are special times for making new friendships, renewing old ones, celebrating culture, and having fun. Readers will learn about giveaways, the introduction ceremony, the significance of each dance, the materials used to make the dancers' clothes, and much more in this engaging book.

Ages 8–12

Suggestions for the Classroom

1. "Avoid arts and crafts and activities that trivialize Native dress, dance, or ceremony. . . . Don't encourage children to do 'Indian dances' . . . . Don't do or say anything that would embarrass a Native child." From a list of over thirty guidelines in "Teaching Respect for Native Peoples," Oyate Catalog, 2702 Mathews St., Berkeley, CA 94702; (510) 848-6700.

2. George Ancona is the highly regarded photographer and author of over seventy books for young readers. After enjoying the beautiful photographs in *Powwow,* examine the photos in his other books. Inspired by his work, invite youngsters to document an event through photography and writing.

Shonto Begay

Navajo (1954–)

Birthday: February 7
Contact: Michelle Biyuk
Scholastic Publishers
730 Broadway
New York, New York 10003

"I have always had a love for art. From the youngest age I found beauty in almost everything that just cried out to be drawn. I drew from Nature and developed a strong bond with the sights around me. . . . My art is created from my heart and from the earth. It is my truth."
(Unpublished essay by Shonto Begay)

Books by Shonto Begay

WRITTEN AND ILLUSTRATED

***Ma'ii and Cousin Horned Toad.* Scholastic, 1992.**

***Navajo: Visions and Voices Across the Mesa.* Scholastic, 1995.**

***Strawberry Pop and Soda Crackers.* Scott Foresman, 1996.**

ILLUSTRATED

***The Boy Who Dreamed of an Acorn* by Leigh Castler. Putnam, 1994.**

***In My Desert* by Pat Mora. Scott Foresman, 1993.**

***The Magic of Spider Woman* by Lois Duncan. Scholastic, 1996.**

***The Mud Pony* by Caron Lee Cohen. Scholastic, 1988.**

***The Native American Book of Change; The Native American Book of Life; The Native American Book of Knowledge; The Native American Book of Wisdom.* All written by White Deer of Autumn. Beyond Words Publishing, 1992.**

The fifth child of sixteen children, Shonto Begay was born on a cold, snowy night in an earthen home five miles southeast of Shonto, Arizona. His mother wove rugs to help support the family. His father, a traditional Navajo medicine healer, built the hogan that the family lived in. His aunt took care of the children while his parents went to ceremonies which sometimes lasted for days. His grandfather, a respected wheelwright, and his grandmother were also important forces in Shonto's life.

When he was very young, Begay learned to feel, see, hear, and smell the world around him. He learned to savor the beauty of nature and to feel at home among the red mesas and juniper and piñon. "My world was the circular line of the horizon. This was the place that harbors the ancient Gods and animal beings that were so alive in the legends and myths of my people. The teachings of the elders made it clear that this land is sacred and we belong to it; it does not belong to us. I learned that Nature was more than just what I saw—that she is life and therefore gives and maintains life. She commands humility and respect."

From a very early age, Begay loved art; he found excitement in the experience of drawing. As he drew the sights around him, he developed a strong bond with the environment. He found adventure in recreating the natural images of the Arizona landscape. "They became part of my visions and emotions."

When Begay was four years old, he started school; this was his first experience outside his culture. He learned the English language and he learned to read using the "Dick and Jane" books. During these elementary school years, Begay attended federal boarding schools all over the Navajo Reservation. He recalls both grief and joy from those years. He rode the bus thirty miles every day to attend high school in Kayenta, Arizona. His love for art led him to the Institute of American Indian Arts in Santa Fe, New Mexico where he received his Associate of Fine Arts Degree in 1976. He continued his study of art at the California College of Arts and Crafts, where he received his Bachelor of Fine Arts with distinction in 1980.

Begay's art has appeared in over thirty exhibitions. He has been interviewed on television, radio, and for a film documentary. He currently lives in Kayenta, Arizona with his wife Rita, and their children.

- **Folklore**
- **Legends**
- **Tricksters**

Ma'ii and Cousin Horned Toad: A Traditional Navajo Story

Arizona Author Award

Coyote, as the trickster Ma'ii, takes advantage of the generosity of cousin Horned Toad. However, when Ma'ii swallows his small cousin, Horned Toad decides to teach him a lesson he will never forget. First from the belly, and then from the heart of the mischievous coyote, Horned Toad plays a few tricks of his own. From that day on, Ma'ii left cousin Horned Toad alone. Begay's lyrical retelling of this traditional Navajo story is accompanied by magical paintings done in watercolor, gouache and colored pencil on color illustration board. The author explains that the "coyote out walking" stories are teaching tales that show us the proper ways to conduct ourselves, but they are also pure entertainment. A glossary of Navajo words and background information on Coyote and Horned Toad are included.

All Ages

Suggestions for the Classroom

1. Read and discuss the dedication page. Who do you think are some of "those who share in our dreams and struggles"?

2. This story lends itself beautifully to being read aloud. It is also fun to dramatize.

3. Write several journal entries for Ma'ii or Horned Toad. Or write letters back and forth between the two. Share the writings.

4. Begay tells us that this is a teaching tale. What did we learn from this story? It is also pure entertainment. Discuss and share perceptions.

5. Among the Navajo, Coyote has many names. Read the information near the end of the book to find out more about Coyote. Then read other Coyote stories such as *Coyote Tales* by Hettie Jones. Listen to Coyote stories on the cassette tapes "Coyote and the Frost Giant" and "Buffalo and Coyote" from *Indian Wisdom Stories* by Good Mind Records.

6. What is the Navajo tradition when coming across a horned toad? Discuss the fact that Navajo people never harm their "grandfather." What is their philosophy about all living things?

7. For another Toad story, read *Toad is the Uncle of Heaven* by Jeanne M. Lee. See page 141 then pretend that Horned Toad goes to visit Uncle Toad. Dramatize or write about their interactions.

8. What if Ma'ii happens to meet Horned Toad again? Dramatize or write a skit or story.

9. Look closely at Begay's paintings. Notice the small circular lines around Ma'ii and Horned Toad. Read the last page to find out what materials he used to create these paintings. Try some of his techniques in your next painting.

10. This is the first book Begay has written, although he has illustrated several others. Find out more about Begay and his art. What role does art play in his life?

The Mud Pony: A Traditional Skidi Pawnee Tale

A Reading Rainbow Selection

- **Folktales**
- **Hero stories**
- **Horses**

A poor boy, longing for a horse, finally fashions one out of mud. The pony comes alive and leads the boy to great honor. *The Mud Pony* is one of a number of ancient hero stories told among the Skidi group of Pawnee Indians of the American Plains. These stories reflect the belief that no matter how poor one's origin, the path to honor is open through virtues such as humility and constancy. This *Reading Rainbow* book is beautifully illustrated by Shonto Begay. Spanish edition available: *El poni de barro.*

Ages 6 up

Suggestions for the Classroom

1. What did we learn from reading this story? Did poverty keep the boy from achieving his goals?

2. What might have happened to the boy without the pony? Brainstorm other solutions to his problems. Then dramatize or write about one of them.

3. Why did the boy cover the pony with a blanket? (Because she was part of Mother Earth.) What happened when he took the blanket away? (She went back to the Earth.) Discuss.

4. Create a pony out of clay and then pretend the pony came to life. Write and illustrate a story about the pony. Write a note to your pony and then write a response.

5. Read other folktales. Be sure to include folktales from many cultures. Share through book talks, art, and/or drama. (See the Subject Index for the titles of other folktales.)

Navajo: Visions and Voices Across the Mesa

- **Poetry**
- **Art**
- **Environment**
- **Tradition and change**

In this magnificent volume, Shonto Begay juxtaposes twenty of his celebrated paintings with his original poetry. In his poignant introduction, Begay writes, "To those who yearn for a vision into our world, I give this collection of paintings, which are pieces of myself." Throughout the collection, there is a keen awareness of the need for balance and harmony between two cultures, between the natural world and the high-tech world, and between the old and the new. This powerful book provides an excellent opportunity to use literature and art to provide insights into an author's life and thinking.

Ages 8 up

Suggestions for the Classroom

1. Reread and discuss the introduction. Begay's eloquent words will inspire young people to read, write, paint, and most of all, empathize with the joys and sorrows of his life.

2. To fully savor the beauty of these fine poems and paintings, read and discuss one a day. As youngsters examine the relationship between Begay's life and his creative work, they will develop insights into the ways in which he wove his bittersweet memories throughout his canvases and poetry.

3. Many of these poems and paintings address issues of tradition and change. For example, reread and discuss "Storm Pattern." Compare and contrast the images evoked by corporate logos and storm clouds, fax machines and hogans, jet streams and corn pollen.

4. Begay has illustrated several other beautiful books. Study the paintings in all his books. Find out more about Shonto Begay and how he feels about art. Invite youngsters to try some of his techniques in their next painting.

- **Traditions**
- **Origins**
- **Spirituality**
- **Healing**

Native People, Native Ways Series: The Native American Book of Change; The Native American Book of Life; The Native American Book of Knowledge; The Native American Book of Wisdom

The four books in the Native People, Native Ways Series provide information about the origins, history, traditions, and beliefs of several Native tribes. These books help the reader understand many issues from Native perspectives. Wakan-Tanka examines the spirituality of the People from the concept of the Great Mystery to the belief that all life is sacred and interrelated. Medicine Man tells the story of a tribal healer who visits an elementary school. Information about sweat lodges, boarding schools, archaeological findings, childrearing practices, food, and common stereotypes is also included. The black and white illustrations are by Shonto Begay.

Ages 10 up

Suggestions for the Classroom

1. The Circle of Life is an important Native American symbol. What do the colors and directions symbolize? Students might choose to create a large Circle of Life for a bulletin board.

2. Where did the author get the titles of his books? (The powers of the Four Directions: knowledge, life, change, and wisdom.)

3. Invite each student to select a section of one of the books for further study. Then divide the class into eight groups based on these choices; each group works together to present their story to the others through their choices of creative dramatics, visual arts, music, and/or filmstrip. Videotape the presentations. Later the teacher might use the videotape to introduce these books to another group.

4. Reread the quotes at the beginning of each chapter. Each student or group might choose one of these quotes to discuss and respond to in writing.

5. Select key concepts for small group or class discussions such as the environment, tribal healers, the Great Mystery, stereotypes, traditions, boarding schools, children, food growing and gathering practices, etc.

Anilú Bernardo

Cuban American (1949–)

Birthday: December 1
Contact: Arte Público Press
University of Houston
4800 Calhoun
Houston, Texas 77204-2090
713-743-2847

"Young minds are open to learn about others. They're free to see that there are more similarities than differences among the cultures of the world. I want young people to understand that we share the same feelings and values, the same fears and joys, the same aspirations and triumphs. I want readers to identify with my Cuban-American characters, and feel validated and strengthened." (Personal Communication)

Books by Anilú Bernardo

Fitting In. **Arte Público Press, 1996.**

Jumping Off to Freedom. **Arte Público Press, 1996.**

Loves Me, Loves Me Not. **Arte Público Press, 1998.**

Anilú Bernardo has enjoyed writing since she was a young girl. Her earliest writing attempts, poems in Spanish, her native tongue, were left behind and lost when her family left their homeland. Born in Santiago de Cuba, Bernardo found a new life in South Florida, when her family left Cuba in 1961. She grew up in Miami and graduated from Coral Gables High School. She earned a B.A. in Spanish and Education in 1971 and a M.A. in Communications in 1980 from Florida State University. As Director of Public Information for a large organization, she sharpened her writing skills creating media releases and internal communications.

In 1995, Bernardo turned to writing books, determined to use her bicultural perspective to lend a compelling voice to the Cuban exile community. Drawing upon her own experiences and inspired by her maternal grandmother, Bernardo's writing speaks with a lively authenticity about the complexities involved in straddling two cultures. Young Latino/a readers will identify with the experiences of her characters and gain reassurance of their value in society. Her books will also promote an understanding of the commonalities of the human experience among readers from other backgrounds. Bernardo's work has been recognized for the important contribution it makes to intercultural understanding and peace.

An active member of The Book Group in South Florida, Bernardo participates in a critique group of writers. She currently lives in Plantation, Florida with her husband and two daughters.

- **Short stories**
- **Immigrants from Cuba**
- **English as a Second Language**
- **Problem solving**

Ages 11 up

Fitting In

Skipping Stones Award

Patterson Prize for Young Adult Literature

In this delightful collection of stories, Anilú Bernardo gives voice to the experiences of immigrant Cuban girls who are moving from childhood to womanhood while grappling with learning a new language, attending a new school, finding new friends, and adjusting to unfamiliar customs. Faced with tests of moral courage in which the right decision is often not the easiest, these admirable young women learn to solve difficult problems and thus grow in confidence, spirit, and integrity.

Suggestions for the Classroom

1. Topics and themes for discussion and writing include: young people translating for adults; respect for elders; assimilation; identity; the value of learning to solve problems independently; making difficult choices; learning a second language; peer pressure; popularity versus self-respect; the many challenges faced by immigrants; and intergenerational relationships.

2. These stories lend themselves beautifully to creative dramatics, journal writing, and small group discussions.

3. See Immigrants in the Subject Index for related works. An excellent resource for adults is *The Inner World of the Immigrant Child* by Cristina Igoa.

- **Immigrants**
- **Refugees**

Ages 11 up

Jumping Off to Freedom

ALA Recommended Reading for Reluctant Young Adult Readers

New York Library Best Book for the Teen Age

In this riveting story, fifteen-year-old David Leal and his father embark on a treacherous raft trip from Cuba in hopes of starting a new life in the United States. Father and son face fierce weather, seasickness, dangerous sharks, debilitating dehydration and sunburn, and two unpredictable traveling companions. Filled with suspense up to the last page, this survival story also charts the difficult course young people must navigate on their way to adulthood. The protagonist's condescending attitude toward females is somewhat leavened by the changes he undergoes during his dangerous journey into the unknown.

Suggestions for the Classroom

1. Topics and themes for discussion and writing include: the history of Cuba; gender roles; the ways in which David grows and changes; the problems inherent in prejudging people; Brothers to the Rescue; and searching for a better life.

2. Invite youngsters to explore the challenges introduced in the book from the perspective of each character. As they share their perceptions, they will gain insight into the value of multiple perspectives.

3. This novel begs for a sequel. Discuss the challenges the Leals might face in the United States including: language and cultural barriers, prejudice, forced assimilation, rootlessness, alienation, and displacement.

Loves Me, Loves Me Not

- **Career aspirations**
- **Socio-economic class**
- **Intergenerational relationships**
- **Dating**

This entertaining book features Maggie, an intelligent, hardworking, responsible Cuban American teenager who wants to become a doctor. She is given an opportunity to practice her healing skills when she is hired to care for an ailing elderly woman. Meanwhile, Maggie gets involved in the dating game and tries to decide which qualities are the most important in a partner. This interesting novel is as much an exploration of values and perceptions as it is of young love.

Ages 11 up

Suggestions for the Classroom

1. Themes and topics for discussion and writing include: the qualities needed to become a successful doctor; socio-economic class differences and the impact this has on close relationships; internalized classism; parents who struggle to provide for their children; and balancing educational goals with social activities.

2. Invite youngsters to debate the qualities most important to the compatibility between two people, whether they be working together, caregiving, or dating.

Ignatia Broker

Chie Nishio

Ojibway/Chippewa (1919–1987)

Birthday: February 14
Contact: The Minnesota Historical Society Press
345 Kellogg Boulevard West
St. Paul, Minnesota 55102-1906
612-296-2264

"That day thirty years ago when we moved here (Minneapolis), . . . we were the aliens looking for a place to fit in, looking for a chance for a new life, moving in among these people, some of whose 'forefathers' had displaced my ancestors for the same reason: looking for a new life. Their fathers were the aliens then, and now they, the children, are in possession of the land." (Night Flying Woman)

Published Works by Ignatia Broker

- ***Ahmik Nishgahdahzee*** **(Filmstrip and poster story, Indian Elementary Curriculum Project of the Minneapolis Public Schools.)**
- ***Night Flying Woman*****. Minnesota Historical Society Press, 1983; 1988.**
- ***Our People*** **(a series of filmstrips and booklets with teaching guides, Indian Education Program at Cass Lake.)**
- ***Weegwahsimitig*****. Indian Elementary Curriculum Project of the Minneapolis Public Schools.**

In 1941, when Ignatia Broker was twenty-two years old, she left the reservation to live in the Twin Cities in Minnesota. She went to work in a defense plant and took night classes to catch up on the schooling she had missed. She desperately wanted a stable life, but the war years were difficult for everyone, especially people of color.

Although employment was good because of the labor demands of the huge defense plants, Native Americans faced discrimination in restaurants, stores, housing, public offices, and service organizations. Broker lived in a room with six other people. They worked different shifts and slept at different times. They also shared money for food and other expenses. By helping each other, they were able to get a toehold in the city. They started a social group for all Indian people who were trying to start a new life. Isolated in the dominant society, they became an island where supporting each other gave them strength to face adversity.

When the war ended, the labor market tightened and Broker lost her job. She then cleaned the homes of middle-income people. Native Americans dared not approach the relief and welfare office because they knew they would be sent back to the reservation. Later Broker took clerical training and started working in a health clinic.

Broker, a storyteller, elder, and teacher in the Ojibway tradition, was one of the founders of the Minnesota Indian Historical Society. She was an enrolled member of the White Earth Reservation. She was involved with the Upper Midwest American Indian Center in Minneapolis. Her children urged her to recall all the stories and bits of information that she had ever heard her grandparents and other Ojibway people tell. And so Ignatia Broker recorded much of this important information about the history and culture of her People in her books. She died in 1987, having made an important contribution to preserving the heritage of her People.

Night Flying Woman: An Ojibway Narrative

- **Tradition and change**
- **History**
- **Storytelling**
- **Dreams**

In this engrossing book, Broker first writes autobiographically, and then relates the story of her great-great-grandmother Oona, who lived five generations ago in what is now Minnesota. From a young girl/mature woman's perspective, Oona's story relates daily events, losses, changes, and uprootings. Oona and her people made many adjustments during the early 1800s when the strangers became interested in the tall trees in the forests of the Ojibway. After marking treaty papers, groups of Ojibway moved frequently and tried to keep the old ways while absorbing the new. They were finally moved to the White Earth Reservation. A glossary gives phonetic spellings and meanings for sixty-five Ojibway words.

Ages 12 up

Suggestions for the Classroom

1. Reread A-wa-sa-si's statement about the beliefs of the Ojibway people. Discuss and/or write a response.

2. It is the custom of Ojibway people to be guided throughout their lives by their dreams. Reread Oona's dreams. What do you think they mean? Write or tell about a dream you had and illustrate it.

3. What was Oona's special gift? (Her dreams were predictions of the future.) Why was the ability to predict the future so important to Oona's people?

4. What was the Ojibway way of honoring a person who died?

5. What changes did Oona and her people make? What traditions did they keep?

6. What is the Ojibway custom when a girl changes into a woman? Discuss or respond in writing.

7. List the traditional dances. Create a dance for your group or class.

8. How did Oona and her family escape from the soldiers? Discuss.

9. How did the ricing change? Discuss.

10. Read about the First Daughters of America. What did they do?

11. Discuss or respond in writing to quotes you have selected for their wisdom and significance.

12. What did you learn from Broker? Why was it so important that she write this book? (Broker and her relatives felt that it was crucial that the young know their cycle.) What contributions did Broker make to our society?

Joseph Bruchac

Abenaki, English, and Slovak (1942–)

Birthday: October 16
Contact: Greenfield Review Press
2 Middle Grove Road
P.O. Box 308
Greenfield Center, New York 12833

"I try to bring the interior world back into focus, to restore something that has gotten lost from the soul . . ." (Countryside Magazine, *Nov./Dec. 1992)*

"I think that we as human beings will never, never survive unless we recognize and celebrate our differences as well as our similarities."
(Personal Communication)

Books by Joseph Bruchac

Aniyunwiya, Real Human Beings. **Greenfield, 1995.**

The Arrow Over the Door. **Illustrated by James Watling. Dial, 1998.**

Between Earth and Sky: Legends of Native American Sacred Places. **Illustrated by Thomas Locker. Harcourt, 1996.**

Bowman's Store: A Journey to Myself. **(Memoir) Dial, 1997.**

A Boy Called Slow: The True Story of Sitting Bull. **Illustrated by Rocco Baviera. Philomel, 1995; Putnam, 1998.**

The Boy Who Lived with the Bears: And Other Iroquois Stories. **Illustrated by Murv Jacobs. HarperCollins, 1995.**

Children of the Longhouse. **Dial, 1996; Puffin, 1998.**

The Circle of Thanks: Native American Poems and Songs of Thanksgiving. **Illustrated by Murv Jacob. BridgeWater, 1996.**

Dawn Land: A Novel. **Fulcrum, 1995.**

Dog People: Native Dog Stories. **Illustrated by Murv Jacobs. Fulcrum, 1995.**

Eagle Song. **Illustrated by Dan Andreasen. Dial, 1997.**

The Earth Under Sky Bear's Feet: Native American Poems of the Land. **Illustrated by Thomas Locker. Philomel, 1995.**

The Faithful Hunter: Abenaki Stories. **Illustrated by Kahionhes. Greenfield, 1988.**

The First Strawberries: A Cherokee Tale. **Illustrated by Anna Vojtech. Dial, 1993; Puffin, 1998.**

Flying with the Eagle, Racing the Great Bear: Stories from Native North America. **BridgeWater, 1993; 1997.**

Four Ancestors. **BridgeWater, 1997.**

Fox Song. **Illustrated by Paul Morin. Philomel/Putnam, 1993; 1997.**

The Girl Who Married the Moon: Tales from Native North America. **Written with Gayle Ross. BridgeWater Books, 1994; Troll, 1997.**

Gluskabe and the Four Wishes. **Illustrated by Christine N. Shrader. Cobblehill, 1995.**

The Great Ball Game: A Muskogee Story. **Illustrated by Susan Roth. Dial, 1994.**

The Heart of a Chief. Dial, 1998.

Hoop Snakes, Hide Behinds and Side-Hill Winders: Tall Tales from the Adirondacks. Crossing Press, 1991.

Iroquois Stories: Heroes and Heroines, Monsters and Magic. Illustrated by Daniel Burgevin. Crossing, 1985.

Keepers of the Animals: Native American Stories and Wildlife Activities for Children. Written with Michael J. Caduto. Fulcrum, 1997.

Keepers of the Earth: Native American Stories and Environmental Activities for Children. Written with Michael J. Caduto. Illustrated by Carol Word and John Kahionhes Fadden. Fulcrum, 1988.

Keepers of Life: Discovering Plants Through Native American Stories and Earth Activities for Children. Written with Michael J. Caduto. Illustrated by John Kahionhes Fadden and David Kanietakeron Fadden. Fulcrum, 1994.

Keepers of the Night: Native American Stories and Nocturnal Activities for Children. Written with Michael J. Caduto. Illustrated by David Kanietakeron Fadden. Fulcrum, 1994.

Lasting Echoes: An Oral History of Native American People. Illustrated by Paul Morin. Harcourt, 1997.

Long River: A Novel. Fulcrum, 1995.

The Man Who Loved Buffalo. Harcourt, 1998.

Many Nations. BridgeWater, 1997.

Native American Animal Stories. Fulcrum, 1993.

Native American Gardening. Written with Michael J. Caduto. Fulcrum, 1996.

Native American Stories. Fulcrum, 1991.

The Native American Sweat Lodge: History and Legends. Crossing, 1993.

Native American Writers. Cross-Cultural Communications, 1991.

Native Plant Stories. Written with Michael J. Caduto. Fulcrum, 1995.

New Voices from the Long House. Greenfield, 1988.

No Borders. Holy Cow Press, 1999.

Pushing Up the Sky. Dial, 2000.

Raven Tells Stories: An Anthology of Alaskan Native Writing. (Editor) Greenfield, 1991.

Reclaiming the Vision. Greenfield, 1996.

Returning the Gift. University of Arizona Press, 1994.

Return of the Sun: Native American Tales from the Northeast Woodlands. Illustrated by Gary Carpenter. Crossing Press, 1989.

Roots of Survival: Native American Storytelling and the Sacred. Fulcrum, 1996.

Seeing the Circle: Meet the Author. Richard C. Owen Publishers, 1999.

Smoke Rising. Visible Ink, 1995.

Songs from This Earth on Turtle's Back: Contemporary American Indian Poetry (Editor). Greenfield Press, 1983.

Stone Giants and Flying Heads: Adventure Stories from the Iroquois. Crossing Press, 1979.

The Story of the Milky Way: A Cherokee Tale. Written with Gayle Ross. Illustrated by Virginia A. Stroud. Dial, 1995.

Survival This Way: Interviews with American Indian Poets. University of Arizona, 1987; 1990.

Tell Me a Tale: A Book About Storytelling. Harcourt, 1997.

Thirteen Moons on Turtle's Back: A Native American Year of Moons. Illustrated by Thomas Locker. Philomel, 1992; Putnam, 1997.

The Trail of Tears. Random, 1999.

Turkey Brother and Other Tales: Iroquois Folk Stories. Crossing Press, 1975.

Turtle Meat and Other Stories. Holy Cow, 1992.

Wind Eagle and Other Abenaki Stories. Greenfield, 1985.

AUDIOTAPES

Available from Greenfield Review Press, 2 Middle Grove Road, P.O. Box 308, Greenfield Center, New York 12833

Joseph Bruchac is of Abenaki, Slovak, and English ancestry. He most strongly identifies with his Abenaki heritage which came to him from his maternal grandfather. Bruchac and his wife, Carol, now live in the same house in the Adirondack foothills where he was raised by his beloved Abenaki grandfather. As a child, his family did not talk about their roots because his parents and grandparents grew up with a great deal of fear about being Native Americans. Although his grandfather was very Abenaki in manner, behavior, and philosophy, he kept his heritage a secret; the myth of the melting pot was very strong at that time. Later, as a teenager and young adult, Bruchac sought out information about his Native background. He searched for elders who could teach him about his heritage.

As a result, Bruchac is able to share the spirit and heart of his People with his readers and listeners. He has developed his gift for storytelling, a gift he inherited from his grandfather. Now very busy as a writer, storyteller, and conductor of workshops, Bruchac manages to stay relaxed and calm because he lives his life immersed in traditional lore. He tries to live in the moment. He loves to garden; in the spring, he spends more time outside than in.

Bruchac is director and co-founder, with his wife, of the Greenfield Review Press, a small publishing company specializing in Native American poetry and fiction. A prolific writer, his work has been published in over 400 magazines and anthologies. He earned his Ph.D. in Literature from Union Graduate School and has a black belt in Pentjak Silat, the martial art of Indonesia. Bruchac has been honored with numerous awards and fellowships and his work has been translated into Danish, German, French, Italian, Dutch, Polish, Swedish, Czechoslovakian, Macedonian, Russian, and Frisian. He has taught at Skidmore College, SUNY/Albany, and Hamilton College. He travels extensively and is in great demand as a storyteller and lecturer; his schedule is usually booked six months in advance.

For Joseph Bruchac, storytelling is as important today as it was in the past. In villages and cities throughout the United States and Europe, schoolchildren, as well as adults of all ages and backgrounds including prisoners in correctional facilities, are enthralled by his stories. He believes that "storytelling keeps us humane and connects us with past generations." For more information about Joseph Bruchac, read his memoir, *Bowman's Store: A Journey to Myself* (see page 35).

- **Folklore**
- **Environment**

Between Earth and Sky: Legends of Native American Sacred Places

By retelling legends from ten Native Nations, Old Bear teaches his nephew, Little Turtle, respect for everything living and inanimate. Spare text and evocative paintings capture the beauty and grandeur of Mesa Verde, Grand Canyon, Niagara Falls, Great Smoky Mountains, and other inspiring landscapes. Included is an introduction, a pronunciation guide, and a map of North America that shows the locations of many of the original Native Nations as well as the location of each legend. This profound book is especially significant because it tells the story of each majestic place from the perspective of the Native Nation, not as a tourist attraction.

All Ages

Suggestions for the Classroom

1. This inspiring book will provoke introspection as well as discussion, writing, and art.

2. Read and discuss one or two of these legends a day, finding each on the map. Compare and contrast the Native perception of each landscape with the way it is portrayed as a tourist attraction.

3. Joseph Bruchac encourages us to look within, through the eyes of our hearts. Then we will not miss the beauty that is around us and within us. This advice is excellent for use in preparing for field trips and environmental outings, as well as for everyday living.

4. A teaching portfolio of eight 16 × 20 inch full color prints from *Between Earth and Sky* is available from Sky Tree Press, 8700 Riverview St., Stuyvesant, New York 12173.

Bowman's Store: A Journey to Myself

• **Memoir**

In this moving memoir, storyteller and author Joseph Bruchac tells the story of the first twenty-eight years of his life. Weaving Native folklore, dreams, photographs, and memories, he explains how he eventually claimed his Abenaki heritage even though racism forced his beloved grandfather to deny his Native roots. Bruchac writes unflinchingly about family secrets and betrayals, personal fears and embarrassments, and societal racism and discrimination. Readable, fascinating, and lyrical, this is a story of the love between a boy and his grandparents.

Ages 12 to Adult

Suggestions for the Classroom

1. An understanding of the experiences that shaped Bruchac's life and thinking and an examination of the sources of his creativity and imagination will greatly enhance your Author Study. Educators will find this memoir helpful in their preparation for this study.

2. Young people will be inspired by many aspects of Bruchac's memoir: He was bullied and excluded by his peers; he loved books and reading; his father's rejection and his grandparents' overprotective love; the significance of animals and plants; the societal and family forces that kept his grandfather from revealing his heritage; his journey from fearful childhood through awkward adolescence to adulthood as a well-known storyteller and writer; and his search for his cultural heritage.

3. Bruchac was inspired by the autobiography of Theodore Roosevelt who "had been a sick, weak little boy with glasses too. But he had turned himself into an outdoorsman and gotten big and strong." Memoirs and autobiographies *do* have the power to touch the hearts and minds of people of all ages and backgrounds.

The Boy Who Lived with the Bears and Other Iroquois Stories

Boston Globe - Horn Book *Honor Award*

• **Folklore**
• **Storytelling**
• **Iroquois**

This engaging collection of six traditional Iroquois tales is retold in direct, immediate language. Presented as lessons the tribal elders might pass on during winter storytelling gatherings, the tales are accessible to a wide range of ages and interests. The reteller's introduction provides cultural and historical context and sets the mood for these humorous, appealing stories in which animals learn about the dangers of selfishness and pride and the importance of caring and responsibility. Beautifully designed and illustrated, this fine book should be included in the folklore collections of all school and public libraries.

All Ages

Suggestions for the Classroom

1. These tales are ideal for reading and telling aloud. Youngsters will also enjoy dramatizing the tales.

2. Gentle topics for discussion and writing include: don't make fun of others, be satisfied with enough of a good thing, show the love in your heart, and acknowledge your strengths.

3. Reread and discuss the introduction. Like the Iroquois, many youngsters will be concerned about ecological issues as well as finding ways to create peace and harmony. Discuss the connections among these issues and the tales in the book.

4. Inspired by the appealing illustrations and exquisitely designed borders, invite youngsters to adapt some of these techniques when they illustrate their stories.

- **Iroquois**
- **Moving**
- **Schools**
- **Peace**
- **Conflict resolution**

Ages 8–11

Eagle Song

After moving from a Mohawk reservation to Brooklyn, fourth grader Danny Bigtree encounters stereotypes about his Native American heritage. He still doesn't have any friends after two months at his new school where he is subjected to namecalling, pushing, and taunts. When his father visits his class and tells them the legend of the great Iroquois hero Aionwahta and his song of peace, Danny hopes for a breakthrough. But it is after his father is injured at work that Danny puts his father's words into action: "If you believe in peace, then an enemy can become a friend." This contemporary story shows a loving family with a great sense of humor. Illustrations and glossary are included.

Suggestions for the Classroom

1. After the initial discussion of the book, discuss the story within a story. How did Bruchac weave together the traditional and the contemporary to create an important book?

2. Explore ways to incorporate this peaceful book into a conflict resolution program.

3. Other topics for discussion and writing include: the influence of the Great League of Peace on the framing of the U.S. Constitution, adjustment to a new school and culture, gangs, Hollywood stereotypes of Native people, tradition and change, loss of native language, and city life versus reservation life.

- **Folklore**
- **Poetry**
- **Constellations**
- **Sky observations**

All Ages

The Earth Under Sky Bear's Feet: Native American Poems of the Land

In this companion to *Thirteen Moons on Turtle's Back,* twelve lyrical poems and stories celebrate Sky Bear (Big Dipper / Ursa Major). From his place in the sky, the great bear collects many stories about the living earth below. From Lakota to Navajo to Mohawk to Inuit, Sky Bear has much to tell us about this land where we live. Bruchac writes, "There can be as much to see in the living night as in the more familiar light of day." Beautifully illustrated and designed.

Suggestions for the Classroom

1. Although the small girl was afraid of the night, Grandmother encouraged her to listen to "some of the stories our old people tell about what Sky Bear sees and hears through the night." After she heard these tales, how might her feelings about the night have changed?

2. As you read these poems aloud, invite youngsters to think about them from Sky Bear's perspective. As he circles the earth, how might he be prepared to promote understanding and negotiate peace among all people?

3. For more stories and information about the night sky, read *Keepers of the Night: Native American Stories and Nocturnal Activities for Children* (see page 38).

The First Strawberries: A Cherokee Tale

• **Folklore**

The story of how strawberries came into the world is explained in this fascinating Cherokee tale, poetically retold by renowned Abenaki storyteller, Joseph Bruchac, and beautifully illustrated in full color by Anna Vojtech. A quarrel between the first woman and the first man is reconciled when the Sun creates raspberries, then blueberries, next blackberries, and finally, strawberries. To this day, strawberries are a reminder to always be kind to one another, and to remember that respect and friendship are as sweet as the taste of ripe, red berries.

All Ages

Suggestions for the Classroom

1. This tale lends itself nicely to dramatization. Try group pantomime while the story is being read by the teacher or a student.

2. Discuss the following: "Your words hurt me." Is it true that "sticks and stones may break my bones but words will never hurt me"? Discuss the power of words to hurt and to heal. What about the power of "I'm sorry" or "Please forgive me"?

3. Why did the woman walk past the raspberries, blueberries, and blackberries? Find a quote that tells why she didn't notice them: ("... the woman's anger was too great and she did not see them.") What had changed by the time she reached the strawberries? Discuss the importance of a "cooling off" period when one is angry.

4. How did strawberries come into the world? Read "how" stories written by students such as *How the Mouse Got Brown Teeth* and *How the Birch Tree Got Its Stripes* (see page 144). Then work together as a group to write and illustrate a "how" story or stories.

Fox Song

• **Grandmothers**
• **Death**
• **Mixed ancestry**

Inspired by childhood memories, Joseph Bruchac's first picture book is a story about the warm relationship between a girl and her great-grandmother. Jamie, a child of Abenaki and French ancestry, copes with the death of her beloved Grama by remembering the special times they spent together. She recalls the important lessons about the world her Abenaki elder taught her. This moving story about learning to understand and accept death captures the beauty of the natural world through eloquent words and shimmering paintings.

Ages 6–9

Suggestions for the Classroom

1. Grieving is a very private experience. Just as Jamie's parents did not intrude on her mourning, it is important to give youngsters some time to reflect on the book.

2. Just as Grama shared ideas with Jamie, this book provides information about the beauty of the natural world and the lessons it holds for us: how to care for the wild blackberry bushes, respect for the birch tree, caring for the young and old, the tracks of the animals, singing to welcome the new day, and how to find solace in nature.

3. Discuss the words to the song and quotes such as "those who have gone are no further away from us than the leaves that have fallen."

4. Read and discuss the Author's Note. Discuss the many ways in which ideas for stories come to us.

- Environment
- Folklore
- Storytelling

Keepers of Life: Discovering Plants Through Native American Stories and Earth Activities for Children

Keepers of the Animals: Native American Stories and Wildlife Activities for Children

Association of Children's Booksellers Choice Award

Keepers of the Earth: Native American Stories and Environmental Activities for Children

Art and Literary Award from the New York State Outdoor Education Association

Keepers of the Night: Native American Stories and Nocturnal Activities for Children

These highly acclaimed books present Native American stories and related activities designed to inspire children to develop a conservation ethic. Using an interdisciplinary, hands-on approach, the books nurture respect and love for the earth and all her inhabitants. Engaging the whole self through the senses, thoughts, actions, and emotions, these books involve youngsters in science, social studies, math, language arts, creative dramatics, and visual arts. The combination of Native American wisdom with scientific understanding will spark youngsters' imaginations and help them to understand the impact that their behavior has on their surroundings. Glossaries and pronunciation keys to Native American words and names and detailed subject indexes are included. Teacher's Guides are also available.

All Ages

Suggestions for the Classroom

These extraordinary books are filled with excellent interdisciplinary, hands-on activities.

- History
- Oral traditions
- Speeches

Lasting Echoes: An Oral History of Native American People

This powerful history of Native Americans, from their first encounters with the invaders to the present, is must reading for all educators. Skillfully weaving quotations from eloquent Native leaders, Bruchac has created an important resource. Excerpts from speeches by over thirty prominent Native Americans including Black Elk, Chief Joseph, Gertrude Simmons Bonnin, Ada Deer, Geronimo, Linda Hogan, Sitting Bull, Tecumseh, and Sarah Winnemucca speak with wisdom, truth, and vision. An appended list of "Tribal Affiliations and Lifetimes" serves as an index to the quotations. Also included are extensive source notes and suggestions for further reading.

Ages 12 up

Suggestions for the Classroom

1. It is important that educators educate themselves about the issues presented in *Lasting Echoes.* I strongly encourage all teachers, no matter what subject they teach, to read this book.

2. Because many textbooks still contain distortions and inaccuracies, use this book to supplement materials that are a required part of the curriculum. *Lasting Echoes* may be read from beginning to end or used as a reference resource for specific information.

3. Invite individuals or small groups to select one of the thirty-one people listed in the appendix for further research. Encourage creativity in sharing information through interdisciplinary projects combining writing, drama, art, music, and movement.

4. Choose quotes for bulletin boards, newsletters, and display cases. Example: "HOW WILL OUR ACTIONS AFFECT THE LIVES OF THOSE WHO LIVE SEVEN GENERATIONS FROM NOW?"

Roots of Survival: Native American Storytelling and the Sacred

• Storytelling

In this eloquent collection of essays, accomplished storyteller Joseph Bruchac offers his thoughts on the power of stories, how they have influenced his life, and how they provide hope for the future. Stories not only entertain and teach but they also have the potential to heal. He tells us that stories are much more than invented narratives or collections of words—they are living things. He explains the crucial role stories have played in sustaining Native identity and spirit. Weaving stories, poems, and his experiences with Native and non-Native storytellers into his essays, Bruchac passionately addresses many issues of significance to educators, parents, librarians, and anyone committed to cultural understanding. Readable, entertaining, enlightening, I found myself staying up half the night to finish this important book.

Grades 12–Adult

Suggestions for the Classroom

1. Inspired by what Bruchac calls "courageous self-awareness," I encourage educators from all backgrounds to engage in an ongoing process of educating themselves about the complexities of individual and institutionalized racism. This profound reevaluation of basic beliefs, attitudes, and behaviors is crucial to the future of life on our planet. An important part of this process for me is reading books like *Roots of Survival.* Even though I have been involved in the anti-racism movement all my life, I learned something new from this book.

2. Topics, themes, and issues for discussion, writing, and self-reflection include: misappropriation of culture, gender roles, genocide, dispossession, stereotyping, noninterference, humor, assimilation, acculturation, and exploitation.

3. Bruchac offers important suggestions for Native American storytelling such as: treat the story with respect; fully research the story; recognize the origin of the story; acknowledge the Native nation to whom it belongs; and certain stories are to be told at certain times. This section of the book is must reading for non-Native storytellers who are considering telling Native stories.

4. This powerful book is filled with eloquent quotes perfect for discussion, writing, and bulletin boards. Example: "HUMAN BEINGS ARE NEITHER WISER NOR MORE IMPORTANT THAN THE ANIMAL PEOPLE."

- **Poets**
- **Authorship**

Survival This Way: Interviews with American Indian Poets

Paula Gunn Allen, Louise Erdrich, Joy Harjo, Linda Hogan, N. Scott Momaday, Simon Ortiz, Luci Tapahonso, Gerald Vizenor, James Welch . . . twenty-one Native American poets talk about their lives, their struggles to find their own voices, and the forces that shape contemporary Native poetry. Each interview is introduced by a biographical sketch and a poem, followed by a discussion of the writer's craft, personal vision, and connection to the oral traditions of her or his people. Bruchac's sensitive questions bring out the individuality of each poet while speaking to central themes of continuance and renewal. Though these fascinating interviews reflect widely varied backgrounds and a range of poetic styles, they all reveal a love for the People, the earth, and for all living beings.

Grades 12–Adult

Suggestions for the Classroom

1. Bruchac writes in the introduction, "to the American Indian writer, poetry is a language of affirmation." As you read the interviews, watch for the recurring themes of celebration, survival, and hope.

2. As you read the interviews, compile a list of the major issues faced by Native American writers. How have these poets dealt with these issues, individually and collectively?

3. Inspired by the eloquent words in this book, invite individuals or small groups to select a poet for further research, using the materials listed in the bibliography, and share their finding with the large group.

4. Bruchac demonstrated a great deal of skill and preparation in conducting these interviews. Focus on his questions, noticing how he tailored the interviews to the individual poet. Select a local poet, read her/his poetry, create several interview questions suited to that poet, and conduct interviews. Or arrange a conference call with a poet. (Contact addresses for Joseph Bruchac and the other poets featured in *Multicultural Voices* are listed with each chapter.)

- **Storytelling**

Tell Me a Tale: A Book About Storytelling

American Bookseller *Pick of the Lists*

Using a lively autobiographical style, Joseph Bruchac provides a useful guide to storytelling. Incorporating many of his favorite tales from around the world, he discusses the four basic components of this age-old art form: listening, observing, remembering, and sharing. With warmth and wisdom, he shares practical suggestions on where to find stories, how to honor the origins of the stories, and how to share them most effectively with audiences. A "Note to Parents" explores the potential of stories to help youngsters solve problems, form identity, and understand the mysteries of life. Bruchac's love for storytelling and his belief in the power, mystery, magic, and delight of story is apparent throughout this fine resource.

Grade 4–Adult

Suggestions for the Classroom

This excellent book is filled with exciting activities appropriate for the classroom, library, or home. For the beginner as well as the experienced storyteller, Bruchac's suggestions are for people of all ages, fields, and backgrounds.

Thirteen Moons on Turtle's Back: A Native American Year of Moons

- **Legends**
- **Poetry**
- **Seasons**
- **Moon**
- **Environment**

This beautiful book presents one moon legend from each of thirteen tribal nations in different regions of the continent. Each story, powered by the turtle who is believed to hold the mystery of the moon on her back, is lovingly told through poetry and oil paintings. Turtle's back, with the pattern of thirteen scales, represents a kind of calendar for the thirteen moons in each year. This reminds us of the continuing cycle of life and that all things are connected. The reader is left with a deeper respect for the earth and a renewed awareness of the importance of listening to the wonderful world around us. Companion Volume: *The Earth Under Sky Bear's Feet.*

All Ages

Suggestions for the Classroom

1. Divide the class or team into thirteen groups; each group selects a moon. They become the experts on that moon and present it to the others using creative dramatics such as choral readings or storytelling and visual arts.

2. Make a giant turtle with the pattern of thirteen scales for your bulletin board. Individuals or groups illustrate the corresponding moon and place the completed artwork over the appropriate scale on the turtle's back. You might want to add original poems written by the students around the border of the bulletin board, or place the poems on the scales of the turtle's back.

3. For younger students, the teacher might read one poem a day and follow up with discussion or an art activity.

4. Create a list of all the animals in the book. Use these animals and the accompanying poems as the basis for a class or team mural. Add poetry written by the children.

Jeannette Franklin Caines

Black American (1938–)

Contact: HarperCollins
10 East 53rd St.
New York, New York 10022

"I think that it's important that I'm listed as a black writer, that the illustrations in my books are of black children. There aren't many books about black kids, there aren't many black authors going around talking to kids." (Early Years, *March 1983, p. 25)*

Books by Jeannette Caines

Abby. **Illustrated by Steven Kellogg. Harper & Row, 1973; HarperCollins, 1996.**

Chilly Stomach. **Illustrated by Pat Cummings. Harper & Row, 1986.**

I Need a Lunch Box. **Illustrated by Pat Cummings. Scholastic, 1988; HarperCollins, 1993.**

Just Us Women. **Illustrated by Pat Cummings. Harper & Row, 1982; 1984.**

Window Wishing. **Illustrated by Kevin Brooks. Harper & Row, 1980.**

Jeannette Caines was born and raised in Harlem in New York City. When she was in fourth grade, the book bug bit her. She checked out *Call Me Charlie* by Jesse Jackson, a book that turned her into an avid reader; she's never stopped reading since. She always has a book, whether she's at home, at the grocery store, bank, or on the subway.

Caines has been a member of the Coalition of 100 Black Women, the Council on Adoptable Children, and the Negro Business and Professional Women of Nassau County. She also received the National Black Child Development Institute's Certificate of Merit and Appreciation.

Writing comes easily for Caines but sometimes the ideas take time to present themselves. But when the ideas come, she is ready. She wrote *Abby* about her own adopted daughter, Abby.

Caines thinks of herself as a role model for Black kids. Children crowd around her when she visits schools. She thinks that it is important that children find people like themselves in the books they read. But she didn't always want to be a writer. When she was younger, she wanted to be a foot doctor!

Caines is concerned about the hardships others face; she is upset about homeless people. "I saw poor people sleeping in the subway when I came to work this morning and it made me angry inside. They have no place to go, nothing to eat" *(Early*

Years, March 1983). She is similarly upset about the poverty in Mexico which she observed while on vacation there. She encourages others to donate clothing, money, and other things people need.

Caines's books are filled with gentle humor and tell us she has lived what she writes. "Yes, I lived it," she says. "Part of my life is in each of the books."

Abby

• Adoption

Abby, who was adopted when she was eleven months and thirteen days old, seeks reassurance that she belongs and is loved. She looks at her baby book and asks many questions about herself. Her older brother says he doesn't like girls, but later paints a sign that says "Abby is a SUPER girl." Mother is very supportive and reassuring. (This story is based on Caines's own experiences with her adopted daughter, Abby.)

Ages 5–8

Suggestions for the Classroom

1. Why did Abby enjoy looking at her baby book? Do you have a baby book? Why do people make baby books?

2. What did Kevin do that hurt Abby's feelings? What did he do later? Why did Abby need extra reassurance? What advice do you have for Kevin?

3. How did Abby's mother deal with this situation? Why?

4. Write about a time when a relative hurt your feelings. Or when you hurt a relative's feelings.

5. Where did Caines get the idea for this book? (It is based on her own experiences with her adopted daughter, Abby.) She says that part of her life is in each of her books. Discuss. Where might you get ideas for your stories?

6. Create a baby picture bulletin board with a photo or drawing of each person in your class when they were younger. Note: Some children might not have access to photographs of themselves as babies.

7. Check out and read other books about adoption including: *Being Adopted* by Maxine Rosenberg; *The Chosen Baby* by Valentina Wasson; *Families Are Different* by Nina Pellegrini; *Growing Up Adopted* by Maxine Rosenberg; *Horace* by Holly Keller; *We Adopted You, Benjamin Koo* by Linda W. Girard; *Zachary's New Home* by Geraldine Blomquist.

Chilly Stomach

• Child molestation
• Incest
• Sexual abuse
• Body safety

When Uncle Jim comes to visit, Sandy gets a chilly stomach. His tickles, hugs, and kisses don't feel right. Told in a child's words, this book offers a gentle approach to encouraging young readers to share their secret fears and experiences about uncomfortable touching with someone they trust. Perhaps the message to tell someone should have been stronger. This is a good book to use with a unit on sexual abuse or to use with individual students.

All Ages

Note: Preparation and follow-up discussion are strongly encouraged.

Suggestions for the Classroom

1. Read and discuss other books about body safety including: *Hobkin* by Peni R. Griffin; *It's MY Body* by Lory Freeman; *Margaret's Story: Sexual Abuse and Going to Court* by Deborah Anderson; *My Body is Private* by Linda W. Girard; *No More Secrets* by Nina Weistein; *No More Secrets for Me* by Oralee Wachter.

2. Invite guest speakers from rape assistance and awareness programs. Staff development is crucial!

3. View the film (for 5th grade up) *No More Secrets* by Oralee Wachter.

- **Beginning school**
- **School supplies**
- **Jealousy**

Ages 4–7

I Need a Lunch Box

A little boy is envious of his older sister as she gets ready to start first grade. As her family buys her school supplies, he yearns more and more for a lunch box. Caines and Pat Cummings have collaborated to create an appealing story about a little boy's wishes. Especially delightful are Cummings's lunch box designs.

Suggestions for the Classroom

1. Dramatize the story several times, each time emphasizing a different character's perspective.

2. Before you started school, what were your feelings about older siblings or friends who were in school? Discuss and/or write about how you felt.

3. Have you ever felt jealous? Discuss. Write a poem or song about jealousy.

4. Here is a challenge for advanced and older students: How much might one lunch box cost? Calculate the price of two lunch boxes. How much would all the lunch boxes in the little boy's dreams cost?

5. Inspired by Pat Cumming's art, create unique designs for lunch boxes.

6. How does using a lunch box instead of a paper sack help the environment?

- **Travel**
- **Aunts**
- **Vacations**

Ages 4–9

Just Us Women

A young girl and her favorite aunt share the excitement of planning a special car trip to North Carolina in Aunt Martha's new car. With no one to hurry them along, they can take their time and do exactly as they please. Large, warm, cheerful pictures by Pat Cummings and the relaxed rhythm of the text reinforce the feeling of a leisurely, companionable journey.

Suggestions for the Classroom

1. Find North Carolina on a map. Then dramatize the journey to North Carolina.

2. Pretend that you went along with the characters in the book on their trip. Keep a travel journal in which you record your experiences. Share with your classmates.

3. How did the girl and her aunt feel about hurrying? How do you feel about hurrying when you are traveling? Write a poem about your feelings.

4. Read *Talking With Artists* by Pat Cummings to find out more about the way she filled this book with her family. (Cummings's sister Linda and her niece Keija are the main characters in the book. Her mother, husband, grandfather, and other relatives and friends are also in the book.)

5. Plan a trip. Include where, how, who, when, what, etc. Include a map and a budget.

6. Write about a trip you took. Illustrate. Trace it on a map.

7. Would you like to travel with a favorite relative? Who? Why?

Window Wishing

- **Grandmothers**
- **Vacations**
- **Wishes**

A girl and boy spend their vacation with their Grandma Mag who doesn't like to cook. She wears sneakers all the time. When they go window wishing, the girl looks longingly at a book entitled *How To Be a Veterinarian.* This is an excellent book for combating stereotypes; this is not the usual image of the grandmother who is portrayed as having no life of her own.

Ages 5–8

Suggestions for the Classroom

1. Describe Grandma Mag. How is she similar to and different from your grandmother? Discuss the stereotypical grandmother in many children's books and the damage these stereotypes do.

2. What book did the girl want? *(How To Be a Veterinarian).* What book did the boy want? *(How to Fly Airplanes).* Discuss.

3. Write a story about Bootsie's birthday week and illustrate it.

4. Where did they go on Saturdays? (On a picnic at the cemetery where Grandpa Ben was buried.) Dramatize one of their picnics.

5. Write a journal entry one of the children might have written when they got home, telling about their vacation.

6. Predict what might happen the next time the children go to visit their grandmother. Dramatize.

7. Have you ever gone barefooted? Describe how it feels. Write and illustrate a class poem about it.

8. Have you ever stayed at your grandmother's? What did you do? Write a story or poem about your experiences.

9. What is catalog wishing? Try it. What would you wish for? Why?

10. Do you like to go window wishing? Why or why not? If yes, where do you like to go? Describe a typical experience.

Dia Cha

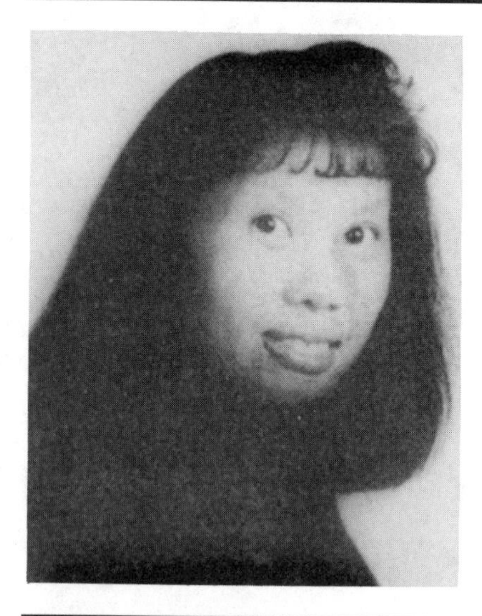

Hmong American (1962–)

Birthday: May 19
Contact: Libraries Unlimited
P.O. Box 3988
Englewood, Colorado 80155

"Like so many ethnic peoples today, the Hmong are facing the rapid erosion of a once-proud and distinctive culture. . . . As has happened before in their long history, the Hmong are being forced to adapt to strange situations, aided only by their resilience, stubbornness, independence, and will to survive. Above all, the Hmong are survivors."
(Folk Stories of the Hmong, *p. 14)*

Books by Dia Cha

Dia's Story Cloth: The Hmong People's Journey of Freedom. **Stitched by Chue and Nhia Thao Cha. Lee & Low, 1996. Published in cooperation with the Denver Museum of Natural History.**

Folk Stories of the Hmong: Peoples of Laos, Thailand and Vietnam. **Written with Norma Livo. Libraries Unlimited, 1991.**

Teaching with Folk Stories of the Hmong: An Activity Book. **Written with Norma Livo. Libraries Unlimited, 2000.**

Dia Cha is a Hmong (pronounced "Mong") immigrant originally from Laos. She currently works as a cultural anthropologist in Boulder, Colorado. Born May 19, 1962 in Laos, Cha fled with her family to Thailand when she was ten years old. They spent over four years in the Ban Vinai refugee camps before gaining entry to the United States. Although she didn't start school until she was fifteen years old, Cha became one of the first Hmong American women to earn an advanced degree. She received her B.A. in anthropology from Metropolitan State College in Denver, Colorado in 1989 and earned a master's in applied anthropology from Northern Arizona University in 1992. She returned to Laos to work with Hmong and Laos women in the refugee camps in 1992.

As a child, Cha learned many traditional Hmong stories while sitting around the home fire of her native village in the highlands of Laos. She enjoyed listening to the stories told by her grandmother, aunts, and uncles. But after the Vietnam War ended and many Hmong people were relocated to the United States, their traditional ways were affected. Traditional art forms including the stories were not being pursued. Cha was concerned that the stories would be forgotten. She began recording the stories and the interpretations of the tales depicted on the *pa ndau* storycloths. These efforts resulted in her first book, coauthored with Norma Livo. Her second book chronicles the lives of the Hmong people in their native Laos and their eventual immigration to the United States.

Dia's Story Cloth: The Hmong People's Journey of Freedom

American Bookseller *Pick of the Lists*
"Choices" Cooperative Children's Book Center
Notable Trade Book in the Field of Social Studies
Bank Street College Children's Books of the Year Selection
Hungry Mind Review Children's Book of Distinction Finalist

- **Autobiographical picture book**
- **Hmong history and culture**
- **Needlework/Embroidery**
- **Art**
- **War**
- **Freedom**
- **Immigration**

"My Aunt Chue and Uncle Nhia Thao Cha sent this story cloth to me and my mother from the Chiang Kham refugee camp in Thailand. . . . This story cloth tells the journey of my people." So begins Dia Cha's beautiful tribute to the lives of her people and their search for freedom. The bedspread-sized embroidered story cloth, shown in its entirety in a double-page spread, is a magnificent labor of love. Enlarged details chronicle the journey of the Hmong people from their native Laos to the United States. Cha weaves autobiographical information into the text of this exquisitely designed book. Bibliography included.

Ages 6 up

Suggestions for the Classroom

1. Set up an Author Center featuring Dia Cha and Hmong culture. Include books, *pa ndau* (story cloth), drawings, etc. Discuss history, art, customs, etc. Invite speakers (call your public library to find Hmong resource people who might be interested in speaking to your class).

2. Find Laos, Thailand, and Vietnam on a map. Use an overhead projector to enlarge the areas. Add details and then trace Dia Cha's journey. Add the map to your bulletin board.

3. Discuss the following quote: "We are called Hmong, which means 'free people'."

4. Study needlework forms from various cultures. Try your hand at stitchery.

Folk Stories of the Hmong: Peoples of Laos, Thailand and Vietnam

- **Folk tales**
- **Hmong history and culture**
- **Tradition and change**
- **History**
- **Art**

This is a beautiful book! It includes information about Hmong history, traditional beliefs and customs, and folk art (jewelry, clothing, story cloths [*pa ndau*]). Lovely color plates of traditional headdresses, necklaces, costumes, etc. are included. The fascinating folk stories are arranged according to themes: in the beginning, how/why, and love/magic/fun. The bibliography includes articles, books, and video productions.

All Ages

Suggestions for the Classroom

1. Inspired by *Dia's Story Cloth,* create a mural based on the folk stories.

2. Each student or group might select a story to present through storytelling, pantomime, skit, illustration, filmstrip or stitchery.

3. Study the beautiful photographs and designs in the book. Then create designs inspired by those in the book. Add these to your Dia Cha bulletin board.

4. Read related books such as: *The Gift: The Hmong New Year* by Ia Xiong; *Fighters, Refugees, Immigrants: A Story of the Hmong* by Mace Goldfarb, and *Nine-in-One GRR! GRR!* by Blia Xiong.

Sook Nyul Choi

Korean American (1935–)

Contact: Houghton Mifflin
222 Berkeley St.
Boston, Massachusetts 02116
617-351-5000

"Having lived through this turbulent period of Korean history (World War II), I wanted to share my experiences. So little is known about my homeland, its rich culture and its sad history. My love for my native country and for my adopted country prompted me to write this book to share some of my experiences and to foster greater understanding."

Books by Sook Nyul Choi

***The Best Older Sister.* Bantam Doubleday Dell, 1997.**

***Echoes of the White Giraffe.* Houghton Mifflin, 1993; Dell, 1995.**

***Gathering of Pearls.* Houghton Mifflin, 1994.**

***Halmoni and the Picnic.* Illustrated by Karen M. Dugan. Houghton Mifflin, 1993.**

***Year of Impossible Goodbyes.* Houghton Mifflin, 1991; Dell, 1992.**

***Yunmi and Halmoni's Trip.* Illustrated by Karen M. Dugan. Houghton Mifflin, 1997.**

Sook Nyul Choi was born in Pyongyang, North Korea in 1935 during the Japanese occupation of Korea. She and her family endured the cruelties of the Japanese military and finally, when World War II ended in 1945, they escaped to South Korea. There she was reunited with some of her family members. However, their happiness and freedom did not last long. In 1950, another war broke out!

Sook Nyul Choi immigrated to the United States where she pursued her college education. After graduating from Manhattanville College and while raising her two daughters, she taught in the New York school system for almost twenty years. She now lives in Cambridge, Massachusetts and devotes most of her time to writing. She is also a speaker and presenter at conferences, libraries, and schools. Her first book, *Year of Impossible Goodbyes,* has been translated into Korean, French, Italian, and Japanese, has won numerous awards, and is on the State Book Awards Master Reading List for many states. Subsequently, Choi has written two more books in this autobiographical series: *Echoes of the White Giraffe* and *Gathering of Pearls.* She has also written several engaging picture books.

Choi writes, "Reading has always been a source of joy and discovery for me. Through writing I try to share my feelings, ideas, and visions with my readers as I would share them with my close friends. Ever since I was young, I wanted to be a writer. In grammar school and high school I wrote short stories, poetry, and newspaper articles in Korean. After immigrating to the United States and teaching in American schools for twenty years, I began to write again, but this time in English. I felt that it was through writing that I could best share my thoughts and experiences" (Houghton Mifflin brochure).

The Best Older Sister

- **Grandmothers**
- **Jealousy**
- **Birthdays**

As the story opens, Sunhi is still struggling with her feelings toward her brother just before his first birthday. When Halmoni realizes that her granddaughter is feeling left out, she wisely asks Sunhi to play a special part in the birthday celebration. Descriptions of Korean traditions are woven throughout this appealing story about a girl adjusting to her role of big sister.

Ages 5–8

Suggestions for the Classroom

1. By examining the text and illustrations, trace the changes in Sunhi's feelings from the beginning of the story to the end.

2. Discuss the Korean traditions incorporated into this story: the importance of the first birthday, the food, and the special clothing sewed by Halmoni.

3. After reading books with similar themes such as *She Come Bringing Me That Little Baby Girl* by Eloise Greenfield and *My Mama Needs Me* by Mildred Pitts Walter, create a handbook for older siblings with advice on how to deal with jealousy. Add a section with advice for parents and grandparents.

Echoes of the White Giraffe

- **Korea**
- **History**
- **Refugees**
- **World War II**
- **Fictionalized autobiography**
- **Tradition and change**

This autobiographical novel is the second in a series that began with *Year of Impossible Goodbyes.* Sookan, now fifteen years old, courageously contends with life as a refugee in Pusan, a city in a southern province of Korea. The Korean War is raging; Sookan, her mother, and brother are separated from her father, three older brothers, and a sister. Sookan longs to return to her happy home in Seoul. During her two-and-a-half years in Pusan, Sookan helps build and then attends a school for refugees, sings in her church choir, and finds that there are precious memories even amidst sadness, uncertainty, and constant change. When the family returns to Seoul to rebuild their lives, and later, when Sookan departs to pursue her college education in the United States, she increasingly challenges the traditions of female behavior. Through the experiences of this freethinking, unconventional young woman, we learn a bit about the role of women in Korean society in the 1950s. In this fictionalized account of her experiences in Pusan, Choi has written another stirring book that reaffirms our faith in the human spirit.

Ages 12 up

Suggestions for the Classroom

1. Compare Sookan's early feelings about being a refugee with how she later perceived her situation.

2. Make a list of the problems Sookan and her family faced. Then discuss the ways they coped with these problems. What advice do you think Sookan might have for other refugees?

3. How did Sookan feel about school? Discuss her aspirations. Why do you think Sookan went to the United States to study?

4. Describe a time in your life when you were faced with uncertainty and constant change. What did you learn from that experience? What advice do you have for others in similar situations?

5. In what ways did Sookan challenge tradition? Read *Gathering of Pearls,* the third book in the trilogy, to find out how she continued to develop her independence.

- **Tradition and change**
- **Fictionalized autobiography**
- **Newcomers**
- **College**
- **Death**

Ages 12 up

Gathering of Pearls

This sensitive novel completes the autobiographical trilogy begun in *Year of Impossible Goodbyes* and continued in *Echoes of the White Giraffe.* It begins in 1954 when nineteen-year-old Sookan Bak is on her way from Korea to attend college in White Plains, New York, where she is the only Korean student at a small Catholic school for women. Her first year of school is filled with the usual problems all students face, plus the added challenges of adapting to a new culture, studying in a new language, working to fulfill her scholarship requirements, and fulfilling expectations to be a goodwill ambassador. Her teachers and schoolmates are remarkably supportive and understanding. The introspective tone of the narrative in this book is very different from the intense drama of the first two novels when Sookan was living as a refugee in war-torn Korea. *Gathering of Pearls* has many strengths including the soul-searching prose; the well-drawn setting; the analysis of the differences between the two cultures; and most of all, the gentle, yet fiercely determined protagonist who follows her heart and makes her own decisions.

Suggestions for the Classroom

1. Themes and topics for discussion and writing include: comparing and contrasting Sookan's two worlds; family expectations; tradition and change; gender roles; perfectionism; communication styles; individualism and collectivism; and the pressure of being different.

2. Choose a character and write a paragraph about Sookan from her/his perspective. Share perceptions.

3. Sookan's siblings constantly reminded her that she was "too expressive, too sensitive, too direct, and too ambitious." Compare this with the feedback she received from her mother and the people at Finch College.

4. Select quotes such as the following for discussion and written response: "I was caught between two very different cultures. Would I be able to balance the two and create my own special world?" 115; "Women are like oysters . . . Create a pearl around the pain" (pp. 115; 145).

Halmoni and the Picnic

Skipping Stones Honor Book

Reading Rainbow *Review Book*

- **Grandmothers**
- **Tradition and change**
- **English as a Second Language**
- **Newcomers**

Yunmi's grandmother, Halmoni, newly arrived in New York City from Korea, faces the challenges of acclimating to a new language and unfamiliar customs. Yunmi is concerned that her grandmother will be overwhelmed with all the changes and decide to return to Korea. When Yunmi's classmates volunteer Halmoni to chaperone their annual picnic in Central Park, Yunmi worries that her classmates will make fun of her grandmother's speech, manners, clothing, and food. But as the story unfolds, we meet a group of unusually caring young people who model acceptance and goodwill. Choi's optimistic approach to a significant problem is an interesting contrast to books that portray youngsters as thoughtless and cruel. The rosy picture presented in *Halmoni and the Picnic* combined with other books such as those listed below will stimulate thought provoking discussions and writing.

Ages 5–8

Suggestions for the Classroom

1. How can youngsters be encouraged to treat newcomers with respect? Dealing with the issues openly has potential for creating an atmosphere of acceptance and kindheartedness. Read and discuss the following books: *Aekyung's Dream* by Min Paek (see page 175), *Molly's Pilgrim* by Barbara Cohen (see page 61), *Angel Child, Dragon Child* by Michele Maria Surat (see page 205), and *The Magic Shell* by Nicholasa Mohr (see page 171). Then as a group, create suggestions for ways to make your school and neighborhood friendly, caring places for everyone.

2. An excellent book to help adults understand the complexities of the immigrant experience is *The Inner World of the Immigrant Child* by Cristina Igoa, St. Martin's Press, 1995.

3. Predict what will happen next. Then read the sequel: *Yunmi and Halmoni's Trip.* See page 52.

Year of Impossible Goodbyes

American Booksellers *Pick of the Lists*

Judy Lopez Children's Book Award

American Library Association Notable Children's Book

American Library Association Best Book for Young Adults

New York Public Library Best Books for the Teen Age

Hungry Mind Book of Distinction

- **Autobiography**
- **World War II**
- **Korea**
- **Refugees**

Ten-year-old Sookan, her mother, aunt, and brother endure the cruelties of the Japanese military occupying Korea during the turbulent period of World War II. (Japanese occupation of Korea lasted for 36 years.) Forced to work for the war effort, Sookan and her family dream of peace and freedom. However, with the end of the war in 1945, their dreams of liberty are dashed as the superpowers divide Korea. Communist Russian troops take control of North Korea, coercing the citizens to embrace the Communist ideology. Sookan's family plans their escape to South Korea. Sook Nyul Choi, in this poignant first person narrative, tells of their ordeal as they struggle to survive and then to escape. This is a novel of historical richness written with grace and clarity. It conveys both the horrors of war and incredible human resiliency in overcoming hardships and keeping hope alive. Don't miss the other books in the series: *Echoes of the White Giraffe* and *Gathering of Pearls.*

Ages 12 up

Suggestions for the Classroom

1. What were the goodbyes that Sookan was forced to make (to Grandfather, Aunt Tiger, Kisa, the sock girls, to her home and belongings, and her city, etc.)? Discuss. Create a poem Sookan might have written for one of them.

2. Discuss Choi's experiences in the Japanese school. Brainstorm recommendations for students regarding their behavior toward newcomers.

3. What did Choi's family do when they were free? What happened to end this freedom? Write a journal entry for one of the characters expressing her/his feelings. Write a poem or song or create a quilt about peace and freedom.

4. Read *So Far From the Bamboo Grove* by Yoko Kawashima Watkins. Discuss the ordeals of both families. Today both Watkins and Choi live in the United States. What might they say to each other now?

5. Predict what might happen next. Then read the sequels, *Echoes of the White Giraffe* and *Gathering of Pearls.*

- **Grandmothers**
- **Korea**
- **Travel**

Yunmi and Halmoni's Trip

In this warmly illustrated sequel to *Halmoni and the Picnic,* Halmoni takes her granddaughter to Korea for a memorial celebration of her late husband's birthday and to meet all their relatives. As the story unfolds, Yunmi becomes increasingly worried that her grandmother will want to stay in Seoul instead of returning to New York with her. After Halmoni affectionately reassures her granddaughter, the two make plans to invite Yunmi's cousins to New York for a visit. This satisfying story provides an introduction to Korean customs and the sights and sounds of Seoul.

Ages 5–8

Suggestions for the Classroom

1. Before reading this book, read the prequel *Halmoni and the Picnic* (see page 51). In this book, it is Yunmi's turn to feel like an outsider. Discuss the ways in which this experience might impact Yunmi and her attitudes toward others.

2. Examine and discuss the illustrations in both books, including the borders. How do they enhance the story? Invite youngsters to experiment with borders in their next art piece.

3. Discuss the ways in which this book crosses generational, cultural, and national boundaries. What did each character learn about these boundaries?

4. Dramatize or write about the time when Yunmi's cousins travel to New York for a visit. What surprises might be in store for them?

Barbara Cohen

Jewish American (1932–1992)

". . . I knew about trying to figure out your place in the world. I knew about trying to establish who you were. I knew about needing your parents and at the same time wanting to be free of them. I knew about being on the outside and hungering to get in. I knew about longing for friendship and love and feeling utterly unworthy of such gifts."

(Something About the Author Autobiography Series, *Volume 2, p. 39)*

Books by Barbara Cohen

Benny. **Lothrop, Lee & Shepard, 1977.**

The Binding of Isaac. **Lothrop, Lee & Shepard, 1978.**

Bitter Herbs and Honey. **Lothrop, Lee & Shepard, 1976.**

Canterbury Tales. **Lothrop, Lee & Shepard, 1988.**

The Carp in the Bathtub. **Illustrated by Joan Halpern. Lothrop, Lee & Shepard, 1972; Kar Ben, 1987.**

The Christmas Revolution. **Lothrop, Lee & Shepard, 1987.**

Coasting. **Lothrop, Lee & Shepard, 1985.**

The Demon Who Would Not Die. **Atheneum, 1982.**

The Donkey's Story. **Lothrop, 1988.**

Even Higher. **Lothrop, Lee & Shepard, 1987.**

Fat Jack. **Atheneum, 1980.**

First Fast. **Union of American Hebrew Congregations, 1987.**

Gooseberries to Oranges. **Illustrated by Beverly Brodsky. Lothrop, Lee & Shepard, 1982.**

Here Come the Purim Players. **Illustrated by Beverly Brodsky. Lothrop, Lee & Shepard, 1984; Illustrated by Shoshona Mekibel. Union of American Hebrew Congregations, 1998.**

I Am Joseph. **Lothrop, Lee & Shepard, 1980.**

The Innkeeper's Daughter. **Lothrop, Lee & Shepard, 1979.**

King of the Seventh Grade. **Lothrop, Lee & Shepard, 1982.**

The Long Way Home. **Lothrop, Lee & Shepard, 1990.**

Lovely Vassilisa. **Atheneum, 1980.**

Lovers' Games. **Atheneum, 1983; Putnam, 1985.**

Make a Wish, Molly. **Illustrated by Jan Naimo Jones. Doubleday, 1994.**

Molly's Pilgrim. **Illustrated by Michael Deraney. Lothrop, Lee & Shepard, 1983.**

The Orphan Game. **Lothrop, Lee & Shepard, 1988.**

People Like Us. **Bantam, 1987.**

Queen for a Day. **Lothrop, Lee & Shepard, 1981.**

Robin Hood and Little John. **Illustrated by David Ray. Philomel Books, 1995.**

R, My Name is Rosie. **Lothrop, Lee & Shepard, 1977; Scholastic, 1979.**

Roses. **Illustrated by John Steptoe. Lothrop, Lee & Shepard, 1984; Scholastic, 1986.**

The Secret Grove. **Union of American Hebrew Congregations, 1985.**

Seven Daughters and Seven Sons. **Atheneum, 1982.**

Tell Us Your Secret. **Bantam Books, 1989.**

Thank You, Jackie Robinson. **Illustrated by Richard Cuffari. Lothrop, Lee & Shepard, 1974.**

213 Valentines. **Illustrated by Wil Clay. Henry Holt, 1991.**

Unicorns in the Rain. **Macmillan, 1992.**

Where's Florrie? **Lothrop, Lee & Shepard, 1976.**

Yussel's Prayer: A Yom Kippur Story. **Illustrated by Michael J. Deraney. Lothrop, Lee & Shepard, 1981.**

Barbara Cohen was born in Asbury Park, New Jersey on March 15, 1932, the oldest of three children of Florence Marshall and Leo Kauder. When she was eight, the family moved to Somerville, New Jersey where they bought the Somerville Inn. A year-and-a-half later, her father died. Her mother, at the age of thirty-three, was left with a pile of debts, a run-down hotel, and three children. But she kept the inn and eventually built it into a successful business. Cohen later based *The Innkeeper's Daughter* on this experience. Cohen loved reading and writing from the beginning. She also loved hearing stories told and read aloud. She read and wrote all the way through grade school, high school, and college. In 1954 she graduated magna cum laude from Barnard College as an English major with a concentration in the area of creative writing. She earned an M.A. from Rutgers University, writing all the while. But then for the next twenty years, she did almost no writing—she was too busy teaching and being a wife and mother.

Encouraged by the success of her first children's book, *The Carp in the Bathtub,* Cohen decided to leave teaching and devote more time to writing. She wrote over thirty books for young people. Everything she wrote grew out of her own experiences and was in some way connected to what happened to her. But she took those experiences and went beyond them in her writing. By writing about her experiences, she was able to reflect on them and arrive at a better understanding of them.

As a child, Cohen felt isolated from other children her age; her family was Jewish in a town where anti-Semitism was still close to the surface. Being a child during the years of the Holocaust left scars; she felt that in some sense every Jew over the age of forty was a survivor.

She elaborated on her feelings of isolation in *The Innkeeper's Daughter,* the most directly autobiographical of her books. She knew first hand about trying to figure out one's place in the world. She wrote about the feelings of being on the outside and hungering to be accepted, of longing for friendship. These are the same issues many children are struggling with. Cohen wrote about them with insight, humor, and clarity.

This insight greatly contributed to the success of Cohen's books. She was a truly remarkable writer, one whose books speak directly to the reader in the voice of an authentic storyteller. She wrote for a wide range of ages as well as about a wide range of topics. Her work won many awards and honors including the Sydney Taylor Body-of-Work Award bestowed by the Association of Jewish Libraries.

Barbara Cohen died on November 29, 1992 at her home in Bridgewater, New Jersey. Some of her books have been published posthumously. The Jewish Book Council has established The Barbara Cohen Memorial Award to honor this outstanding author.

Bitter Herbs and Honey

- **Tradition and change**
- **Jewish holidays**
- **Career aspirations**
- **Immigrants**

During the early 1900s a young Jewish woman's loyalty to family tradition conflicts with her desire to go to college. Though Becky shares her family's devotion to Jewish tradition, she finds herself disagreeing with many of their ideas. Her father believes that no man will marry a woman who is too smart. In 1916 in Winter Hill, New Jersey, is it possible for a young Jewish woman to do something other than what has always been done? The simultaneous constriction and comfort of small town life and the pain caused by a community's anti-Semitism, central issues in the book, were a part of the author's experiences as well as those of the generation that preceded her. This book is based on Cohen's mother's experiences.

Ages 11 up

Suggestions for the Classroom

1. Discuss the title *Bitter Herbs and Honey.* Think of other ways to express mixed feelings.

2. Discuss traditions and how and why changes occur. Give some examples from your own experiences or from other readings.

3. Check your library to see which of Cohen's books are available. Read as many of the books as you can. Which ones are your favorites? Why? Talk to your media specialist about ordering more of her books. Choose one of Cohen's books for your next book talk.

4. Read *Trouble's Child* by Mildred Pitts Walter. See page 221. Martha and Becky were both struggling with family traditions and expectations. They both wanted to pursue their education. What might they have said to each other if they could have confided their feelings? Role-play a meeting between them.

5. Interview women in your family to see what obstacles they have faced because of their gender. Analyze the results. Do you detect any differences in the barriers based on generation? Do you think that attitudes are changing? Discuss.

The Carp in the Bathtub

School Library Journal Best Book of the Year

- **Fish**
- **Animal uniqueness**
- **Pets**
- **Death of an animal companion**

This is the touching story of how two children make a gallant effort to rescue a carp from being made into *gefilte* (stuffed) fish. Leah and Harry befriended the hapless carp just before Passover, just as they have befriended other fish in years past around the times of Rosh Hashanah and Passover. But the year that Leah was nine was the hardest of all. Although most people think that all fish are alike, Leah discovered that wasn't true. This particular carp was unusually playful and intelligent, much livelier and friendlier. So Leah and Harry come up with a scheme to save their new friend. Unfortunately their plan isn't successful.

Ages 7 up

Suggestions for the Classroom

1. What did the children name the carp? (Joe) Why? (after a deceased neighbor) Pretend that the children were able to save Joe's life. Design a new home for him, possibly a backyard pool or a lake.

2. What would you have done if you had been in Leah's or Harry's place? Discuss.

3. Write a letter from one of the characters in the book to another character explaining her/his feelings.

4. Create a cruelty-free recipe (one that does not use animal products).

5. Reread and discuss the last page. Would you tell? Why or why not?

Coasting

- **Friendship**
- **New York City**
- **Career goals**

Ages 12 up

When Metz postpones college for a semester to go from California to New York City for the "experience," his confidence is shaken by the problems he encounters there. Even his friendship with Maddy has changed. Maddy is busy with her own life as a psychology student at Barnard College. As usual, Barbara Cohen skillfully manages to teach the reader about something in addition to the main story, this time about New York City. As Metz explores the city, he begins to mature and learn a lot about himself and about relationships.

Suggestions for the Classroom

1. Write several journal entries that Metz might have written while in New York City. What did he learn? In what ways did he change? What advice might he have for people who are considering postponing college for a year and going to a new place for the experience?

2. Create several ads that Metz might have read while job hunting.

3. Use in a math unit: plan a budget for Metz during his first month at his new job.

4. Write a short sequel, telling what happened to Metz next. Compile these sequels into a class collection. Analyze the sequels, watching for similar themes. Discuss.

5. Write a paragraph from Maddy's perspective.

6. Dramatize an encounter between Maddy and Metz during the most difficult time.

The Christmas Revolution

- **Hanukkah**
- **Christmas**
- **Twins**
- **Drama**

Ages 8 up

Nine-year-old Emily and Sally Berg, nonidentical twins (also featured in *The Orphan Game* and *The Long Way Home*) experience another Christmas as Jewish children. Emily realizes that she doesn't feel right participating in some of the school Christmas activities, such as singing carols and decorating a tree. Sally is selected to sing a solo and thus, doesn't allow herself to question the status quo. Simeon, a new boy who is an Orthodox Jew, bravely refuses to participate in any of the school Christmas celebrations. The peer pressure and general hostility they all experience should help students and teachers alike to be more sensitive after they have read this book. It is about time someone wrote a book on this topic. Christmas can be an extremely oppressive time for people who do not celebrate it. It would have been even more enlightening if the author would have mentioned the fact that there are other groups besides Jewish people who do not celebrate Christmas. The Berg extended family and friends enjoy a Hanukkah play created by Emily and Sally and their group. Excellent information about Jewish holidays is woven into the story.

Suggestions for the Classroom

1. Read other books about Emily and Sally (*The Orphan Game* and *The Long Way Home*). In what ways did each of the twins change as they got older?

2. Christmas can be a very miserable time for some people because of the assumption that everyone celebrates it. How would you feel if you didn't believe in something that almost everyone around you was celebrating? Some non-Christians consider wearing a button that says "How Dare You Assume That I Celebrate Christmas!" Discuss.

3. Write about how Petey treated Emily. What advice do you have for Petey? For

Emily? Write a letter Petey might have written to Emily. Then write a letter Emily might have written back.

4. Have you ever had the courage to openly disagree with the majority? Write about your experiences of being different. Do you think it is important to take a position for your beliefs? Why or why not? Discuss minority and majority rights.

5. Should you accuse someone of doing something if you don't have proof? Discuss why Petey accused Simeon. (prejudice) (anti-Semitism)

6. Make a glossary of Hebrew words from the book. Example: Hanukkah-dedication.

7. Reread Mrs. Glendenning's statement. Even though she tried to be understanding, what do you think about, "I don't want you sitting here like two gloomy lumps on a log while the rest of us are trying to work up some Christmas Spirit"? Discuss.

8. Petey said that Christmas is an American holiday and everybody celebrates it. Is that true? Make a list of groups in the United States who do not celebrate Christmas.

9. Simeon said, "My father says religious symbols don't belong in public schools." Discuss the separation of church and state.

10. Reread and discuss the section about Jewish holidays. Read other books about Jewish holidays.

11. Interview someone who doesn't celebrate Christmas. Are their views more like Sally's, Emily's, or Simeon's? Or maybe they have attitudes that weren't expressed in this book. Discuss the fact that all people are different.

Fat Jack

- **Friendship**
- **Fat oppression**
- **Shakespeare**
- **Mental illness**
- **Drama**

In spite of the insensitive title, this is an excellent novel about not judging a book by its cover. Cohen deals with delicate issues such as fat oppression, eccentricities, school politics, popularity, and honor in this thought-provoking book. The protagonist is bright, active Judith Goldstein, a high school senior who feels different, and has not attempted to have an active social life. Her new friend, Jack Muldoon, a transfer student, is intelligent, funny, considerate, fat, and very talented. An eccentric new teacher directs the senior class play, insisting on Shakespeare's *Henry IV*, Part One. The experience of producing such a challenging and at first unpopular play provides an opportunity for unprecedented growth and change on the parts of all involved. In spite of almost everyone's misgivings, the play is a great success. Cohen skillfully teaches the reader a great deal about Shakespeare as well as about life.

Ages 11 up

Suggestions for the Classroom

1. How did the students' attitudes about the play change? Use quotes to support your answer.

2. Discuss or respond in writing to quotes from the book that you have selected for their profundity.

3. Discuss the roles the prologue and the epilogue play in the novel.

4. Some people who are otherwise aware of treating all people with dignity think it is acceptable to make fun of fat people. What did Jack teach us about being fat? How might his life have been easier if he had had the support of a Fat Pride group? Discuss the oppression of people based on appearance such as height, weight, color, looks, disability, etc.

5. Discuss the concept of not judging a book by its cover. How does this apply to people?

6. Analyze the way fat characters are treated in other books. Did the author present the character with dignity?

- **History**
- **Newcomers**
- **Emigration**
- **Immigration**
- **War**

Ages 7 up

Gooseberries to Oranges

An American Library Association Notable Book

Fanny, a young girl, tells the story of her journey from a cholera-ravaged village in Russia to the United States. She reminisces about the relatives who died before she left, the war, the voyage on the ship, her first impressions of her new country, and her new home with her father. The experiences of thousands of immigrants to the United States during the early decades of the twentieth century are personalized through this fine book.

Suggestions for the Classroom

1. Find Fanny's homeland on a map. Estimate how many miles she traveled to her new home.

2. What were Fanny's first impressions of her new country? Predict how they might change in a few years. Write a short sequel telling about what might happen in five years and illustrate it.

3. Have you ever moved to a new place? If so, tell about your experiences. If not, how do you think you would feel if you were in a similar situation as Fanny?

4. Read other books about newcomers such as *Aekyung's Dream* by Min Paek, *Angel Child, Dragon Child* by Michele Surat and *Molly's Pilgrim* by Barbara Cohen. Write a letter Fanny might have written to Aekyung, Ut, or Molly giving advice on how to adjust to a new country.

5. Why do you think Cohen gave this book the title *Gooseberries to Oranges*? What were some of the other changes Fanny experienced? Think of possible new titles for the book.

- **Drama**
- **Prague**
- **Queen Esther**
- **Purim**
- **Traditions**

Ages 7 up

Here Come the Purim Players

This play tells the story of the origin of Purim, a Jewish holiday now celebrated in February or March. It is in honor of Queen Esther who saved the Jews of Persia from death at the hands of Haman, her husband's (King Ahasuerus) evil advisor. The drama, a celebration of the past, present, and future, transports the audience back to ancient Persia. A lively read-aloud choice.

Suggestions for the Classroom

1. Perform this play for your team or school, or adapt it into short skits to be presented informally.

2. Research Purim. Write a short report to share with your classmates. What are some of the other holidays celebrated by Jews? Find out if any of your classmates celebrate special days that are new to you. Mark these days on your class calendar.

3. In what ways does this drama celebrate past, present, and future?

The Innkeeper's Daughter

- **Hotels**
- **Literature**
- **Mother-Daughter relationships**
- **Authors**
- **Fire**

Sixteen-year-old Rachel Gold helps her widowed mother run a small inn in Waterbridge, New Jersey in 1948. Although Rachel is unsure of herself socially, she is very confident about her academic ability and loves reading great literature. Rachel, at times annoyed with her always perfect mother, is an interesting, strong protagonist who will be enjoyed and admired by readers.

Note: The same characters appear in Cohen's earlier novel, *R, My Name is Rosie.* Rosie is Rachel's younger sister. This is Cohen's most directly autobiographical book. She also grew up in New Jersey in an inn operated by her widowed mother.

Ages 11 up

Suggestions for the Classroom

1. Make a list of authors and/or books Rachel enjoyed. Read one of them.

2. Reread the description of the painting. Then write a description of one of your favorite (or least favorite) paintings.

3. Discuss or write about quotes such as the following: "What can you say to someone who's perfect?"

4. What if everyone decided to ignore the constraints put on them by fashion? Write a short story about someone who decided to wear the "wrong" clothes on purpose. Analyze the fashion industry.

5. Discuss Rachel's relationship with her mother. How do you think it might change in the future? Write about your relationship with someone close to you. How can reading about experiences like Rachel's give you insight into your relationships?

6. This is Cohen's most directly autobiographical book. Read her other books with the same characters.

King of the Seventh Grade

- **Bar Mitzvah**
- **Internalized oppression**

Thirteen-year-old Vic, wanting to fit in, comes up with a plan to rid himself of Hebrew school, bar mitzvah, and other aspects of his Jewishness. But he discovers that getting what one wants is often not at all what one expected.

Ages 10 up

Suggestions for the Classroom

1. Compare Vic's and Jonathan's (*People Like Us*) attitudes about bar mitzvah.

2. Discuss internalized oppression. Sometimes people believe the lies that society tells about their group. Read *The Shimmershine Queens* by Camille Yarbrough. (See page 230.) What did Vic learn about this? How can we as individuals and as a group alleviate this destructive force?

3. Vic wanted to fit in. Discuss peer pressure. How can young people handle peer pressure?

4. Discuss what it feels like to be different. How can we help our society celebrate differences rather than perceiving them as a threat?

5. What advice do you have for Vic? It is important not to trivialize his experiences but to try to think of suggestions that might genuinely help him.

6. Have you ever wanted something and then been surprised or disappointed when you received it? Write about your experience.

7. Check out and read other books about bar and bat mitzvahs: *People Like Us* by Barbara Cohen, *Bar Mitzvah* by Howard Greenfeld, *My Bar Mitzvah* by Richard Rosenblum, *Bar Mitzvah and Bat Mitzvah: How Jewish Girls and Boys Come of Age* by Bert Metter.

- **Cancer**
- **Twins**
- **Shakespeare**
- **Drama**
- **Fat oppression**

The Long Way Home

Sally and Emily Berg, nonidentical twins (also featured in *The Christmas Revolution* and *The Orphan Game*) have always been close, but the summer they are eleven a chasm opens between them. Their mother has breast cancer and is undergoing chemotherapy treatment after surgery. Sally and Emily are sent to camp instead of to the beach where they usually go. Sally is mad at everybody including herself. Communication breaks down because they dare not confront their fears—that their mother might die and, since breast cancer can be hereditary, that they also might die. Sally is helped by Claire, the camp bus driver, a fat, ex-actress in her sixties. She provides wisdom, not just about facing problems, but as their drama coach, she teaches them about Shakespeare and shows them the power of a good story. Barbara Cohen has taken a difficult issue—breast cancer—and sensitively woven it into an honest and at times humorous portrayal of a family who must relearn to talk to one another during a crisis. Note: Barbara Cohen died of cancer in 1992. Concerns: Cohen has improved in her portrayal of fat people (see *Unicorns in the Rain*). *Fat Jack* was much better; however, there are still some oppressive remarks in this book. Also, the powwow at camp might be offensive to some Native Americans.

Ages 9 up

Suggestions for the Classroom

1. Can fat people be actors or actresses? Make a list of fat actors and actresses. (See the activities for *Fat Jack* for more information on fat oppression.) Compare the portrayal of fat people in *Unicorns in the Rain, Fat Jack,* and *The Long Way Home.* Then think about how fat people are portrayed in other books you have read. Write recommendations for how you think writers should present characters who do not fit society's definition of beauty.

2. Have you ever been mad at yourself? Have you ever felt like two people? Write diary entries expressing how you felt.

3. Reread *The Christmas Revolution* and *The Orphan Game.* In *The Christmas Revolution* Emily thought of Sally as Miss Perfect. In what ways have Sally and Emily changed?

4. Barbara Cohen died of cancer two years after this book was published. Check out and read other books about cancer such as *Six Months to Live* by Lurlene McDaniels. Give a book talk and/or write a report on cancer. Do you know someone who has or had cancer? Interview them with sensitivity.

5. Discuss or write about significant quotes such as the following: "The truth chases the monsters out of your head."

6. Why might some Native Americans be concerned about the portrayal of the powwow? Why is it important to be sensitive to the way groups of people feel about their traditions?

- **Birthdays**
- **Passover**
- **Russian Americans**
- **Newcomers**

Make a Wish, Molly

In this companion to the classic *Molly's Pilgrim,* the young Jewish immigrant is elated when her new friend invites her to a birthday party. But when Molly's mother points out that she will not be able to eat the birthday cake because the party falls during Passover, she is faced with a universal dilemma: loyalty to her ideals at the expense of acceptance versus betraying her beliefs in order to fit in. As she reflects on the experience, she muses, "I was as miserable as I had been in the fall. Maybe I was more miserable. Because maybe it's worse to lose a friend than never to have had one at all." However, when Molly's own birthday arrives, she enjoys an impromptu party with fresh-baked rugelach pastries. As her mother helps her share her heritage with her friends while remaining true to herself, Molly realizes that "there is more to being smart than speaking English well," and that her mother is a very special person. This is a thought-provoking story about friendship, prejudice, and self-acceptance.

Ages 6 up

Suggestions for the Classroom

1. Read *Molly's Pilgrim* before reading this book. Then discuss the challenges Molly faced as a newcomer. What lessons did each of the characters learn? Do you think Elizabeth will change? Why or why not?

2. Discuss quotes such as: "At the bottom of my mind, a little question unrolled itself, like a worm."

3. Have you ever been the newcomer? How did you feel? Write about your experiences and feelings.

4. Do you think Molly's class will treat the next newcomer with more kindness? Why or why not? How has your class or school treated newcomers? Read *Angel Child, Dragon Child* by Michele Maria Surat and *Aekyung's Dream* by Min Paek. Do you think that reading these books will help you and your classmates be more sensitive? What advice do you have for others about the treatment of newcomers?

Molly's Pilgrim

An IRA/CBC Children's Choice
Notable Trade Book in the Field of Social Studies
Academy Award for Live Short Film (Movie version)

- **Thanksgiving**
- **Newcomers**
- **Sukkos**
- **Emigration**
- **Immigration**
- **English as a Second Language**
- **Russian Americans**

This is a poignant story based on an incident experienced by a member of Cohen's family. Molly, a Jewish emigrant from Russia to the United States, is excluded by her classmates. They make fun of her appearance and speech. Molly, the only Jewish child in the school, is very unhappy and wants to go back to New York City or to Russia. With the support of her mother and teacher, Molly and her classmates gradually realize that beauty has many forms. Her teacher points out that the Pilgrims got the idea for Thanksgiving from the Jewish harvest holiday of Tabernacles (Sukkos), which is now celebrated in September or October. People of all backgrounds and ages will relate to the pain felt by Molly. This book is available in a Spanish edition: *Molly y los Peregrinos.*

Ages 6 up

Suggestions for the Classroom

1. Write a letter from Elizabeth to Molly. Then write one from Molly to Elizabeth.

2. Rewrite the song Elizabeth sang to Molly so that it shows kindness.

3. This book was made into a movie which won the 1986 Academy Award in the Best Live Action Short Subject category. (Barbara Cohen plays the crossing guard.) View the film and discuss.

4. Why did Barbara Cohen write this book? (It is based on an incident experienced by a member of her family.) Discuss this book within the context of her complete body of work.

5. What might have happened later? Write a sequel, illustrate it, and share it with classmates. Then read *Make a Wish, Molly* which is a companion book to *Molly's Pilgrim.*

- **Twins**
- **Adoption**
- **Beaches**

The Orphan Game

Ten-year-old Sally and Emily Berg, nonidentical twins (featured in *The Christmas Revolution* and *The Long Way Home*), spend their vacation with their family on Long Island Beach. With their two cousins, they have a secret club called the Four Seasons; the four also play a game called the Orphan Game. Another cousin, Miranda (who was adopted), just doesn't seem to fit in at first. As they earn money for a day of fun in Atlantic City, they discover there is more to Miranda than whining, bragging, and tattling. This is an excellent novel with an important message for both insiders and outsiders.

Ages 8 up

Suggestions for the Classroom

1. Compare Miranda's perspective about adoption with her cousins'. What did they learn from her?

2. How did the children's perceptions about Miranda change during the story? Have you ever changed your mind about someone? Write about it.

3. How did Miranda feel as the outsider? Have you ever been in a similar situation? Discuss.

4. How did Sally and Emily feel as the insiders? What do you think of their behavior? What role did peer pressure play in their behavior? Have you ever been in a similar situation? What happened?

5. Analyze the Orphan Game. Were the others sensitive to Miranda's feelings about being adopted? Have you ever participated in a game that you later realized was hurting someone's feelings? Discuss.

6. Write a chapter about the following summer when the "Five" Seasons meet on Long Island Beach again. Illustrate.

- **Friendship**
- **Bar and Bat Mitzvah**
- **Intergroup dating**
- **Intergenerational conflict**

People Like Us

American Library Association Recommended Book for Reluctant Readers

Sixteen-year-old Dinah Adler, a Jewish girl, experiences conflict with her mother and grandparents when she starts dating a Gentile boy. Her family is usually very broadminded and supportive but they oppose intermarriage. They feel that interdating could lead to intermarriage which could lead to the demise of the Jewish people. Dinah struggles with two parts of herself: feeling flattered that the star quarterback and all-around nice guy wants to date her, and the understanding that her values and religious convictions point up major differences between her and Geoff. Cohen provides interesting insights into Jewish family customs and concerns as well as a compelling treatment of intergenerational conflicts.

Ages 13 up

Suggestions for the Classroom

1. Debate the issue of a Jewish person dating a non-Jewish person. For more information about interracial and cross-cultural relationships, see *Different Worlds: Interracial and Cross Cultural Dating* by Janet Bode and *Coping with Cross-Cultural and Interracial Relationships* by Sandra L. Smith.

2. Respond to significant quotes such as: "The Jewish people is made up of individual Jews. The actions of each one affects all. Just because we feel comfortable and secure in this country doesn't mean we can ever forget what happened in Nazi Germany . . ."

3. Research what happened in Nazi Germany. Can anyone who is not Jewish ever truly understand how Dinah's grandparents felt? Cohen wrote that she felt that, as a Jew, she had been scarred for life; that in some sense every Jew who is over forty is a survivor of the Holocaust. Why is it important that non-Jews not trivialize their experience? Why is it important to respect other people's perceptions and feelings even if we don't understand them?

4. Cohen has a talent for helping the reader understand the complexities of situations. Discuss the complexities of the situation in this book.

5. Life isn't simple. There are no easy answers. Write about a situation in your life where you could perceive many sides of an issue. What did you decide? Why?

6. What advice do you have for Dinah? For her mother? For her grandparents? For Geoff?

7. Find the name of the school newspaper. (*The Indian*). Discuss. Do you think the following names would be appropriate for a school newspaper? *The Jew, The Korean, The African American, The Hispanic.* Discuss. Create five names for a school newspaper that would not be oppressive to any group.

Tell Us Your Secret

- **Friendship**
- **Authorship**
- **Holocaust**

This powerful, haunting novel is about humankind's capacity for creativity and decency as well as for evil. Twelve high school students attend a two-week writing conference that results in growth for them as writers and as human beings. Barbara Cohen based this book on her own experiences teaching a two-week writing conference in 1986 in New York. She notes that it was the best teaching experience of her life. In the book, twelve students live and work together with two teachers for two intense weeks. As trust grows, each student gradually reveals more about her or himself. Eve Streitman finds it very difficult to share the horrible stories of her parents' ordeals during the Holocaust. But as she starts opening up to the others, she realizes that she is able to learn more about herself. As she tries to communicate the incomprehensible, the inexplicable, the unbearable, she starts to combat the destructiveness of ignorance and denial. Although Eve feels like an outsider, Sierra is the outcast. Cohen skillfully weaves valuable writing tips into the story.

Ages 13 up

Suggestions for the Classroom

1. Make a list of as many writing tips as you can find in the book and discuss them.

2. "They had coalesced." Write a paragraph responding to this sentence.

3. Write a "revised opinion" for one or more of the characters. Or choose one of the final pieces and develop it further.

4. Reread Eve's description of herself. Then answer her question and share the answers. Reread Eve's poem. Respond with your choice of a poem, painting, song, drawing, or report.

5. Think about Sierra. Does every group have to have an outcast? Develop Sierra's character further in a short story.

6. Discuss the teachers' responses to the prank. What would you have done? Debate various responses.

7. Choose a character. Write a short sequel with that person as the protagonist. Which character did you identify with the most? Why? Discuss your perceptions in small groups, divided according to the characters selected. Share your insights with the large group.

8. Dramatize the discussion between Eve and her parents when they got home.

9. Write a letter from one of the characters to another two weeks after the conference.

10. What did you learn about the Holocaust? Why is it important to educate oneself about the history of humankind? How can we make sure nothing like this happens again?

- **Baseball**
- **Jackie Robinson**
- **Friendship**
- **Death**

Ages 9 up

Thank You, Jackie Robinson

Twelve-year-old Sammy Greene lives with his three sisters and their widowed mother who runs an inn in New Jersey in the 1940s. (Cohen also grew up in New Jersey in an inn operated by her widowed mother. This book is based on her brother's experiences.) Sammy is obsessed with the Brooklyn Dodgers. His best friend, Davy, the 60-year-old African American cook at the inn, shares this enthusiasm for baseball. Davy takes Sammy to his first major league ball game and to many others. The development of their friendship, Sammy's growing willingness to take risks, and the role of Jackie Robinson will interest readers whether they like baseball or not. Davy's illness and death and Sammy's reactions are handled with insight and sensitivity. This book was made into a movie, "Home Run For Love."

Suggestions for the Classroom

1. Discuss the friendship between Davy and Sammy. What did Sammy learn from Davy?

2. Why couldn't Davy and Sammy stop at restaurants to eat? (prejudice against African Americans.) Discuss.

3. Davy was a cook and loved baseball. Give other examples of people whose varied interests do not fit stereotypes.

4. What foods did Sammy like? Did he show a willingness to branch out in this area? Give examples. Discuss risk taking. Give several examples of Sammy's growing willingness to take risks.

5. Another book about prejudice in baseball is *Keystone Kids,* about a rookie catcher who is his team's only Jewish player. (This book was written before Jackie Robinson's breakthrough.)

- **Holidays**
- **Valentine's Day**
- **Gifted/Talented classes**
- **Socioeconomic class**

Ages 7 up

213 Valentines

Wade (who is African American) has problems adjusting when he is transferred to another school to be in a special fourth-grade class for the gifted and talented. Although he excels in academics, he feels that he doesn't belong with these "rich snobs." There are only two other African American students in the class. As the year progresses, Wade continues his friendship with students from his old school. But as Valentine's Day approaches, he comes up with the idea of sending himself 213 Valentines to save himself the embarrassment of not receiving any valentines at the party. By the end of the party, we begin to feel that Wade is being accepted by the class and that he is accepting his new school. Sensitive treatment of issues related to gifted and talented students is included.

Suggestions for the Classroom

1. Discuss how Wade felt at first about his new classmates. What are "rich snobs"? Discuss.

2. The issue of socioeconomic class is often ignored in discussions on human diversity. Why do you think it is important to educate oneself about this issue? Some people feel that classism is as destructive as racism, anti-Semitism, ableism, homophobia, looksism, and gender bias. Discuss.

3. How would you feel if you were transferred to another school? Discuss or write about your feelings. Create a "How to Adjust to a New School Handbook." Interview classmates to get helpful suggestions.

4. Make lists of advantages and disadvantages for Wade at his new school. If you were in Wade's situation, which school would you want to attend?

5. Dramatize a discussion between Darlene and Wade the day after the Valentine party. Or dramatize a discussion among Wade, Marcus, Tony, and Farley in the lunchroom.

6. Interview an adult about how they celebrated Valentine's Day when they were a child. Present your findings to your class.

Yussel's Prayer: A Yom Kippur Story

National Jewish Book Award (Children's Picture Book Category)

U.S.A. Children's Book of International Interest

American Library Association Notable Book

- **Legend**
- **Yom Kippur**
- **Judaism**
- **Socioeconomic class**

This notable children's trade book in the field of social studies is retold by Cohen. This is an ancient rabbinic tale about the importance of feeling with the heart and the unimportance of riches and status.

Ages 6 up

Suggestions for the Classroom

1. Discuss the importance of feeling with the heart and the unimportance of riches and status. Find other books with similar themes.

2. Discuss the issue of socioeconomic class; for more information see the Suggestions for the Classroom for *213 Valentines* by Cohen on page 64–65.

3. What is Yom Kippur? Check out books about Yom Kippur. What are some other Jewish holidays? Choose one and read about it.

4. Make a calendar of holidays that includes the special days celebrated by many cultures. Find out as much as you can about a holiday that is new to you. Why is it important to be aware of days that are special to groups other than your own?

5. Interview someone who celebrates a holiday that is new to you. What did you learn? Share the information with your classmates.

Pat Cummings

African American (1950–)

Birthday: November 9
Contact: c/o HarperCollins
10 East 53rd Street
New York, New York 10022

"Keep doing what you enjoy and don't get discouraged."
(Personal Communication)

"Keep trying new things. Everything you try teaches you something, even if you just find out what doesn't work."
(Talking with Artists: *Volume Two p. 9*)

Books by Pat Cummings

WRITTEN AND ILLUSTRATED

Beauty and the Beast. **Lothrop, Lee & Shepard, 1999.**

The Blue Lake. **Harper/Collins, forthcoming.**

Carousel. **Bradbury, 1994.**

C.L.O.U.D.S. **Lothrop, Lee & Shepard, 1986.**

Clean Your Room, Harvey Moon. **Bradbury Press, 1991; Simon & Schuster, 1994.**

Jimmy Lee Did It. **Lothrop, Lee & Shepard, 1985; 1995.**

My Aunt Came Back. **HarperFestival, 1998.**

Petey Moroni's Camp Runamok Diary. **Bradbury Press, 1992; Simon & Schuster, 1992.**

Talking with Adventurers. **(Compiled and edited) National Geographic Society, 1998.**

Talking with Artists: Volume One. **(Compiled and edited) Bradbury Press, 1992.**

Talking with Artists: Volume Two. **(Compiled and edited) Simon & Schuster, 1995.**

ILLUSTRATED

Beyond Dreamtime **by Trudie MacDougall. Putnam, 1978.**

Chilly Stomach **by Jeannette Caines. HarperCollins, 1996.**

C is for City **by Nikki Grimes. Lothrop, Lee & Shepard, 1995.**

Fred's First Day **by Cathy Warren. Lothrop, Lee & Shepard, 1984.**

Go Fish **by Mary Stolz. HarperCollins, 1991; 1993.**

Good News **by Eloise Greenfield. Putnam, 1977.**

I Need a Lunch Box **by Jeannette Caines. HarperCollins, 1993.**

Just Us Women **by Jeannette Caines. Harper/Collins, 1982; 1984.**

Mariah Keeps Cool **by Mildred Pitts Walter. Simon & Schuster, 1990.**

Mariah Loves Rock **by Mildred Pitts Walter. Simon & Schuster, 1988; Troll, 1996.**

My Mama Needs Me **by Mildred Pitts Walter. Lothrop, Lee & Shepard, 1983.**

Pickin' Peas **by Margaret R. MacDonald. Harper/Collins, 1988.**

Secret of Royal Mounds **by Cynthia Jameson. Coward, McCann & Geoghegan, 1980.**

Springtime Bears **by Cathy Warren. Lothrop, Lee & Shepard, 1987.**

Storm in the Night **by Mary Stolz. Harper & Row, 1988; Harper/Collins, 1990.**

Two and Too Much **by Mildred Pitts Walter. Bradbury, 1990.**

Willie's Not the Hugging Kind **by Joyce Durham Barrett. Harper & Row, 1989; Harper/Collins, 1992.**

For additional reviews of books illustrated by Pat Cummings, please see the Author Units featuring Jeannette Caines and Mildred Pitts Walter.

Pat Cummings grew up in many places; her father was in the army and so her family moved every three years or so. She was always the new kid on the block. This experience exposed her to many different cultures and lifestyles. She learned a great deal from experiencing other cultures from within rather than reading about them in a book or seeing a movie.

Cummings does not remember seeing any picture books with African American characters as a child. She feels that Martin Luther King, Jr. was instrumental in bringing about an awareness of the realities of the diversity of the people in our country. She has since created many outstanding images of African American children in her books. Her earliest memories include her mother reading from a book called *Tales of the Rhine.* Cummings was very fascinated with the dragons and princesses. Although the book wasn't heavily illustrated, she still remembers the scenes as they appeared in her mind.

Cummings's parents encouraged her interest in art; her mother displayed her first scribblings on their refrigerator. Drawing became a constant for Cummings through the years; a form of entertainment, an enjoyment, and an ice-breaker in new school situations. Now she gets her ideas for her art and writing from family experiences, from her travels, from her dreams, and from "the ether." For example, *C.L.O.U.D.S.* was inspired by a sunset. She writes when inspired, when a story presents itself. By contrast, she does her art work on a schedule.

When she graduated from Pratt Institute in the 1970s, Cummings had a portfolio filled with story ideas and the dream of illustrating children's books. She currently lives in a big loft in Brooklyn, New York with her husband, Chuku Lee. Her interests include swimming, photography, painting, yoga, piano, and collecting children's books. She spends most of her time doing what she likes best—illustrating. Artist Tom Feelings provided generous guidance on the first book she illustrated, *Good News* by Eloise Greenfield. His assistance inspired her to help others who are getting started in the field of illustrating children's books.

Cummings likes to put surprises in her pictures, such as patterns and objects that draw children into the story and personalize it for them. Readers of all ages will enjoy her intriguing illustrations.

For more information about Pat Cummings, see *Talking With Artists: Volume One,* a beautiful book which she compiled and edited.

Carousel

- **Birthdays**
- **Merry-go-round**

Disappointed that her father didn't get home in time for her birthday party, Alex storms off to her room clutching the carousel her father left for her. When she falls asleep, the merry-go-round animals come to life. Her dream world is filled with captivating zebras, giraffes, flamingoes, and frogs cavorting in the moonlight. Entertaining and magical, this playful tale affirms that disappointments don't last forever.

Ages 5 up

Suggestions for the Classroom

1. Alex's birthday had some good news and some bad news. What might she have written in her journal about the real and the fantastical aspects of this special day?

2. Alex's mother and aunts did their best to make her birthday special. Dramatize a conversation between Alex and her Aunt Lea the next day.

3. Write and illustrate another dreamscape with Alex and the carousel animals. What if they could talk? Perhaps the zebra has a birthday party. Or maybe the frog has a sore throat.

- **Alphabet books**
- **Cities**
- **Poetry**

Ages 5 up

C is for City

Irresistible sights, sounds, smells, and tastes abound in this rhyming alphabet book set in New York City. Each page is brimming with playful images reflecting the diversity of urban life. Pat Cummings is up to her old tricks of mischievously hiding items amidst her illustrations. Alphabet books will never be the same after this rollicking adventure!

Suggestions for the Classroom

1. People of all ages enjoy searching for the cleverly hidden items. There is a key at the back of the book so readers can check that they found them all.

2. This is no ordinary alphabet book. Children of all ages and backgrounds will be charmed by the dancing images. It is also perfect for older children who are engaged in a study of Cities.

3. The wide range of topics, neighborhoods, animals, and people is sure to inspire creativity. Provide numerous options for response: writing, art, drama, music, dance.

- **Cleaning**
- **Poetry**

Ages 5 up

Clean Your Room, Harvey Moon

Harvey spends a Saturday working on a long avoided chore, cleaning his room. What a mess! Long-lost items are hiding under his bed and in his closet. Cummings tells this humorous tale of Harvey's cleaning spree in lively verse. Bright, detailed illustrations add to the action.

Suggestions for the Classroom

1. Study Cummings's illustrations of Harvey's room. Then draw a picture of your room. Put in lots of details! Display these pictures in your classroom.

2. Where did Harvey put everything? What do you think will happen next? Dramatize.

3. What do you think the warm, gray lump was? Discuss. Dramatize.

4. Rewrite the story from Mother's perspective. From the cat's perspective. From the warm, gray lump's perspective. Illustrate the stories.

C.L.O.U.D.S.

Coretta Scott King Honor Book for Illustration

- **Weather**
- **Clouds**
- **Art**
- **Sky observations**
- **New York City**
- **Science fiction**

Chuku has just started working at the department of Creative Lights, Opticals, and Unusual Designs in the Sky. He is disappointed at first when he is assigned to design skies for New York City. However, he grows to love his job when a little human girl inspires him to create splendrous cloud formations, rainbows, and sunsets. His supervisor praises his ingenuity, "That's a particularly uninspiring area, but you've made advantages out of your disadvantages." Cummings's brilliantly inspired paintings in watercolor, airbrush, and pencil will delight readers of all ages. Chuku and his coworkers are portrayed with blue skin tones which gives them an other-worldly appearance.

Ages 7 up

Suggestions for the Classroom

1. ". . . you've made advantages out of your disadvantages." What does this mean? Discuss. Think of ways you can make advantages out of your disadvantages. The next time you need to make a decision, use Chuku's Advantages/Disadvantages plan.

2. Rewrite or tell the story from Chrissy's perspective. What do you think Chrissy will do when she grows up?

3. What if Chuku met Chrissy? Dramatize what they would say to each other.

4. Design some special clouds using cotton. Glue the cotton onto blue paper. Write a poem or song to go with your cloud formations.

5. Design a sky for your city. Be creative!

6. Create some interesting names for colors such as Sea Mist Green and Oh So Turquoise.

7. Write a story about what Chuku did next—did he stay in New York City? Or did he get transferred to a new job? Describe how he made the best of each situation. Dramatize. What if Chuku had gone to the tropics? Design a sky for the tropics. Write about how he felt about his new assignment.

Jimmy Lee Did It

- **Siblings**
- **Poetry**
- **Practical jokes**

Angel tells about the messes that her brother Artie claims were caused by Jimmy Lee. Since brother Artie is the only one who has ever seen Jimmy Lee, Angel decides to play detective and try to catch the culprit. Delightful verse and illustrations.

Ages 5 up

Suggestions for the Classroom

1. Who was Jimmy Lee? Does everyone agree? If not, debate.

2. Do you think Angel really knew what was going on? Why or why not? Dramatize what might have happened if she had been able to catch the culprit.

3. Rewrite the story from Artie's perspective. From Jimmy Lee's perspective. Share.

4. Have you ever blamed someone else for something you did? Or has someone else blamed you for something they did? Write a story or poem telling what happened. Use humor. How does humor make the story more interesting?

- **Board book for toddlers**
- **Aunts**
- **Travel**

Ages 2 up

My Aunt Came Back

This exuberant little book features a loving aunt who returns from travels around the world with gifts for her niece.

Suggestions for the Classroom and Parents

1. For toddlers just discovering the joy of mimicking words and sounds, this playful chant is perfect to read aloud.

2. HarperFestival has a number of quality books to share with babies and toddlers at each stage of development. Six age groups are included, from newborn to age three.

- **Camps**
- **Raccoons**
- **Vacations**
- **Mystery**

Ages 5 up

Petey Moroni's Camp Runamok Diary

This book takes us on a humorous romp through fourteen days at Camp Runamok, as recorded in Petey Moroni's diary. The campers can't figure out what's happening to all their carefully hidden snacks. The reader catches a glimpse of a paw here, a tail there, and some suspicious chocolate footprints; but the campers, try as they might, cannot outwit that tricky raccoon. This playful book is filled with delightful illustrations.

Suggestions for the Classroom

1. Pretend you are a detective. What clues can you find? Keep a detective log for each day. Share your log with your group or class.

2. Dramatize the camp meeting when everybody tried to solve the mystery. Improvise.

3. Brainstorm a plan to outwit the raccoon next summer.

4. Write a paragraph from the raccoon's perspective. Or dramatize a meeting the raccoon might have had with her raccoon friends after the campers were gone.

5. Cummings likes to hide surprises in her illustrations. Study the pictures and discuss the surprises. Try hiding some surprises in your next art piece.

- **Weather**
- **Sounds**
- **Grandfathers**
- **Fear**
- **Cats**

Ages 5 up

Storm in the Night

Coretta Scott King Honor Book for Illustrations
ALA Booklist Children's Editors' Choice
Notable Children's Trade Book in Social Studies
International Reading Association Teacher's Choices

Thomas, his grandfather, and his cat Ringo sit out a thunderstorm together. Grandfather tells a story about his childhood when he was frightened by a thunderstorm. As they rediscover the half-forgotten sounds and smells around them, Grandfather subtly convinces Thomas that fear is a perfectly natural feeling. Mary Stolz and Pat Cummings have created a beautiful, captivating book.

Suggestions for the Classroom

1. Why do you think Grandfather didn't come right out and say he knew Thomas was afraid? What did Grandfather do instead? Discuss. Have you ever handled a delicate situation in a similar manner?

2. How do you feel about lightning and/or thunder? Write a poem about your feelings. What advice do you have for someone who is afraid of storms? Create a class "How to Survive Storms" booklet.

3. What responsibilities do humans have to their animal companions? Do you agree with the man when he said, "If you don't take better care of him, you shouldn't have him at all."?

4. Read *Go Fish,* another book about Thomas, his Grandfather, and Ringo by the same author and illustrator.

Talking with Artists: Volume One

School Library Journal *Best Book of the Year*

ALA Notable Book

ALA Booklist Editor's Choice

Boston Globe/Horn Book *Award for Nonfiction*

Talking with Artists: Volume Two

- **Art**
- **Artists**
- **Biography**
- **Illustrators**

These exciting books contain fascinating conversations with artists who illustrate children's books. Volume One includes: Victoria Chess, Pat Cummings, Diane Dillon, Leo Dillon, Richard Egielski, Lois Ehlert, Lisa Campbell Ernst, Tom Feelings, Steven Kellogg, Jerry Pinkney, Amy Schwartz, Lane Smith, Chris Van Allsburg, and David Wiesner. Volume Two includes: Thomas B. Allen, Mary Jane Begin, Floyd Cooper, Julie Downing, Denise Fleming, Sheila Hamanaka, Kevin Henkes, William Joyce, Maira Kalman, Deborah Nourse Lattimore, Brian Pinkney, Vera B. Williams, and David Wisniewski. These distinguished artists answer questions most frequently asked by children such as: "Where do you get your ideas?"; "What is a normal day like for you?"; "Where do you work?"; "What do you enjoy drawing the most?"; "What do you use to make your pictures?"; and "How did you get to do your first book?".

Ages 5 up

Suggestions for the Classroom

1. Divide the class or team into groups, one group for each artist. (Let the children choose their group.) Then work together to present information to the other students about each artist through reports, drama, book talks, murals, displays, etc. One artist might be featured each day or week.

2. Following the pattern created by Cummings, individuals or groups might select additional artists, and then research and write chapters about them.

3. Create Artist Centers. Set up a display of the books illustrated by each artist. One artist might be featured each week or month. Student art inspired by the artist could be added to the bulletin board. Use quotes from some of the artists to decorate the center.

4. How are the artists alike? How are they different? Is there only one way to create art?

5. Share this exciting book with your art teacher! Work with her or him to invite one of the artists to your school!

6. Read the introductions. Why did Cummings compile these books? What advice does she have for young artists?

7. Study the piece of artwork done by each artist when she or he was a child. Then look at the sample they did as an adult. Why did Cummings include the early work of the artists?

8. Write letters to the artists. Include student art work. If you want a response, send a self-addressed, stamped envelope.

9. Try some of the art techniques described in the glossaries. Display your work on a bulletin board above your Artist Center.

- **Hugging**
- **Friendship**
- **Self-confidence**
- **Peer pressure**

Ages 5–8

Willie's Not the Hugging Kind

Willie stops hugging his family because his friend Jo-Jo thinks hugging is silly. But Willie misses hugging and being hugged more than he realized. His family continues to hug each other but not Willie because, "You're just not the hugging kind." As Willie craves hugging more and more, he tries hugging trees, stop signs, and even an old towel. But he realizes he needs to hug someone who will hug him back.

Suggestions for the Classroom

1. Discuss possible explanations for Jo-Jo's reaction to hugging.

2. Why do people like hugs? How do some animal companions feel about hugs? Discuss.

3. Create three journal entries that Willie might have written: one each for the beginning, middle, and end of the story. How did Willie change? What advice might he have for his friends?

4. Write a letter from Jo-Jo to Willie. Then write one from Willie to Jo-Jo.

5. Discuss peer pressure. Have you ever given in to what your friends think, even if it doesn't seem right to you? How can people avoid peer pressure? Write a poem or create a "How to" booklet and illustrate it.

Vivian Sheldon Epstein

Humanist (1941–)

Birthday: June 21
Contact: VSE Publisher
212 South Dexter Street
Denver, Colorado 80222

"Each man, woman and child is important. We each have the power within us to make our world a better place. If we are all able to bring out the best that is within us, with no one telling us what we can or cannot do simply because we are male or female, our world will grow to be a much better one and we as individuals will grow to our fullest potentials."

Books by Vivian Sheldon Epstein

The ABCs of What a Girl Can Be. **VSE Publisher, 1980.**

History of Colorado for Children. **A. B. Hirschfield Press, 1975.**

History of Colorado's Women for Young People. **VSE Publisher, 1998.**

History of Women Artists for Children. **VSE Publisher, 1987.**

History of Women for Children. **VSE Publisher, 1984.**

History of Women in Science for Young People. **VSE Publisher, 1994.**

Vivian Sheldon Epstein was born on the first day of summer, June 21, 1941. She had a happy and secure childhood growing up in a small community on Long Island, New York, four blocks from the ocean. She spent many happy days playing at the seashore. Epstein was a shy, quiet child who loved to listen to soap operas on the radio. From these programs, she learned a great deal about people and their problems. While listening to the radio, she painted, drew, and made cutout dolls. She savored quiet time alone and this ability to enjoy her own company exists even today. She loved reading and read over twenty books in the *Pollyanna* series. This series changed her life; from it, Epstein learned that if there is a problem, there is usually a solution. There is a creative way of taking that problem and changing one's perspective about it. Epstein enjoyed books so much, she spent her allowance on *Nancy Drew* books, reading them beneath two trees in her garden hammock. Epstein also enjoyed writing, quietly going to her room and putting all her thoughts on paper. She kept a daily diary. One of her writings about her much loved father was read aloud to the parents at Back to School Night.

At age thirteen, Epstein moved with her family to Denver. She attended the University of Colorado, the University of Michigan, and graduated from the University of

Denver, where she majored in History and Elementary Education and minored in Art History. She taught elementary school in the Denver public school system. Epstein initiated a parent volunteer art history project for students in grades K–8 in a Denver private school. She was a PTA president, editor of a historical society newsletter, and did a research project for Historic Denver. She is on the Board of the National Museum of Women in the Arts, Colorado Chapter. Epstein's husband is an attorney, ultra-endurance athlete, and sculptor. They have one daughter. The worst experience of Epstein's life was the death of her son, Teddy, at age 23.

Epstein writes for her own pleasure as well as professionally. When she travels, she always writes down her impressions. She has written, illustrated, published, and marketed a number of books for young readers. Each of these excellent books is on a topic that has not been attempted before for young children. She thoroughly researches each topic for one to three years and then sifts through the information collected to get to the essence. Each word of the text is carefully selected to be clear, to paint a visual image, and to be age appropriate. Her writing style is therefore crisp, bright, and to the point.

Each of Epstein's inspiring books is unique in the field of literature for young children. By taking complex subjects and skillfully simplifying them for the young reader, she has made a significant contribution to children's literature. In tackling the issue of women's empowerment, she has beautifully demonstrated her commitment to human liberation. Her books leave the reader, both child and adult, with a feeling of hope for the present and the future. Epstein continues to affirm the outstanding accomplishments of women of all societies and the importance to our world of nurturing the talents of us all, female and male.

- **Careers**
- **ABCs**
- **Women**
- **Gender roles**

The ABCs of What a Girl Can Be

In this inspiring career opportunity book, Epstein has created rhyming text and attractive color drawings that describe job options that are now open to women. The jobs described and illustrated include archaeologist, astronaut, carpenter, doctor, inventor, lawyer, ophthalmologist, president, plumber, sculptor, scientist, veterinarian, and many more. If this book had been available in the 1950s, I might have found a way to follow my dream of being a veterinarian!

Ages 4 up

Suggestions for the Classroom

1. Read *The History of Women for Children* by Epstein. Then discuss why job options for women have been limited until recently.

2. Check out and read other books on careers. Analyze the text and illustrations to see which jobs are presented as open to women. Analyze your textbooks to see which jobs are represented for women and men. Tally the results on a chart and discuss them.

3. What are your career goals? Write a statement expressing how you would feel if your career goals were limited. How can we as a society improve career options for everyone? What can school counselors do? What can you do?

4. Read biographies of women in your chosen field. What characteristics enabled them to do well in that field?

5. Choose a nontraditional career. Interview a woman who is working in that field. Ask her about any obstacles she may have encountered. Report back to the class.

6. Discuss gender bias or sexism. How might books like those written by Epstein combat this bias? What can you do to help?

History of Colorado for Children

- Colorado
- States

Epstein has taken a complex topic—Colorado history—and simplified it for the young reader. In this much needed book, she tells the story of Colorado in clear, concise language and includes charming illustrations. The book chronicles the main events in Colorado history from the dinosaurs to the present. It ends with suggestions for ways people can keep Colorado healthy and beautiful.

Ages 4–12

Suggestions for the Classroom

1. Where did Colorado get its name? (In Spanish, Colorado means red). Make a list of places with Spanish names.

2. Plan a trip to Dinosaur National Monument or a place of interest in your state. Include a map, budget, itinerary, etc.

3. Plan a celebration that people might have had when your state became a state.

4. Make a list of problems facing your state today. Then make a list of things people can do to keep your state healthy and beautiful. Write a play based on these lists. Videotape your play and share it with other classes and schools.

History of Colorado's Women for Young People

- Colorado
- Women

The important contributions of women in the founding and development of Colorado are documented in this carefully researched book. Full-page profiles of twenty-seven fascinating women from diverse backgrounds and fields provide inspiration for young readers. Brief sketches of hundreds of additional women listed by field augment this extraordinary book. Bibliography included. A must for every Colorado school and library as well as people outside the state who are interested in women's history.

Ages 7 Up

Suggestions for the Classroom

1. Inspired by this remarkable book, invite students to research the history of women in the development of your state. Analyze textbooks and library books to find out what information is available. Have similar books been written about other states? Discuss.

2. Invite students to write letters to newspapers in the state of their choice requesting information about the availability of similar books. Compile the results and discuss.

History of Women Artists for Children

"Choices" One of Best Books of 1987

- Art
- Artists
- Women
- Biography
- Gender roles

This outstanding book is the first and only children's book that traces women's stories as artists from the 1500s to the present. This vibrant book presents large, clear reproductions in color and black-and-white of women's art from the Middle Ages to the late 20th century. The text tells the story of thirty women artists in clear, simple language. Included are: Artemisia Gentileschi, Rachel Ruysch, Rosa Bonheur, Edmonia Lewis, Harriet Hosmer, Mary Cassatt, Georgia O'Keeffe, Augusta Savage, Marisol, Maria Martinez, Judy Chicago, and others. The last page lists over 100 additional women artists. A rare, much needed book! Inspiring!

Ages 5 up

Suggestions for the Classroom

1. Reread the first few pages of the book. Why has it been difficult for women to be artists? Why were women's names excluded from art history books? Discuss.

2. Invite each student or group to choose an artist from the book to research further and present to the class.

3. What happened to Augusta Savage's sculpture? Why? "Lift Every Voice and Sing" is the African American national anthem. Learn the song and discuss the words.

4. Check out and view films about Maria Martinez. Then make or sketch pottery.

5. Study Georgia O'Keeffe's paintings. Then create Georgia O'Keeffe-style paintings of your state flower or of your favorite flowers. See *Inspirations* by Leslie Sills for more information about Georgia O'Keeffe.

6. Examine the art books in your library. How many books are there about women artists? Men artists? Evaluate and make recommendations to your media specialist for additional books that might be included.

7. Call or visit your local art museum. Make a list of women artists exhibited there. Discuss. Is there a gender balance? If not, talk to the director of the museum.

- **Women**
- **History**
- **Gender roles**

History of Women for Children

Highlighted as one of five of the best 600 children's books in ten years in **A Guide to Non-Sexist Children's Books.**

This extraordinary book represents the first time anyone has written a book on women's history for the younger child. Easy-to-read, the book chronicles the history of women from prehistoric times when women were valued for their mystical ability to produce babies, through their transition as the property of men, to the present day when they are making progress toward shaping their own lives. This is an interesting, brightly illustrated book with appeal for people of both genders and of all ages. An added bonus is the listing of women as rulers, painters, sculptors, writers, musicians, mathematicians, scientists, in medicine, in law, in education, and in women's rights and civil rights. A great deal of research went into these lists; the book is priceless for this information alone. Older students will especially enjoy this section of the book.

All Ages

Suggestions for the Classroom

1. Read and discuss the dedication/acknowledgment page. What is human liberation? What can you do to make our world a better place?

2. Read one to two pages a day and discuss. Or invite each student or group to choose a page to research further and share with the class.

3. Analyze your textbooks and library books to see how many include the history of women. Discuss.

4. Choose one woman to research. Use poetry, music, art, filmstrip, drama, and/or report to tell about her life.

5. Examine the biographies in your library. How many are about women? Make a list of women about whom you would like to read biographies. Make a copy of this list for your media director along with a written request explaining why you think these biographies should be added to the library collection.

6. Create a speech, song, poem, play, quilt, etc. based on this book.

7. Contact The National Women's History Project, 7738 Bell Road, Windsor, CA 95492-8518, 707-838-6000 for a catalog of additional materials celebrating the contributions of women.

History of Women in Science for Young People

- **Scientists**
- **Women**
- **Biography**
- **Careers**
- **Gender roles**

Epstein traces the history of women as scientists from pre-civilization to the present, describing their exclusion and then acceptance in a field dominated by men. The exciting lives of twenty-nine women scientists in diverse scientific areas will inspire young women to become involved in science and hopefully, to consider it as a career. To dispel the myth that there were no women scientists until recently, or that Marie Curie was the only female scientist, the author used the last six pages of her book to list by century hundreds of women scientists and their contributions. At a time when we need the talents of all our young people more than ever, this inspiring book affirms that girls can be anything they want to be! It is an excellent resource for helping girls build confidence in their capacities to pursue a full range of interests and careers in any field they might choose.

Ages 9–15

Suggestions for the Classroom

1. This is an excellent book to use with the study of careers, scientists and/or women, or to infuse with science units.

2. Read aloud and discuss the information about one woman scientist each day. Or each student or group might select one of the scientists in the book for further research and then present their findings to the class.

3. Examine the biographies in your library. How many are about women scientists? Make a list of women scientists about whom you would like to read biographies. Make a copy of this list for your media director along with a written request explaining why you think these books should be purchased.

4. Check out and read other books on careers. Analyze the text and illustrations to see which jobs are presented as open to women. Tally the results on a chart and discuss.

5. Read Epstein's other books. Discuss gender bias. What can we each do to insure that all people have equal opportunities? Why is this important?

6. Read *Taking a Stand Against Racism and Racial Discrimination* by Patricia McKissack. In what ways are racism and sexism alike? How might we use some of Patricia McKissack's recommendations for fighting racism to combat gender bias?

7. Use this book with materials such as the photo display "Outstanding Women in Mathematics and Science," the video "You Can Be a Scientist, Too," and/or the biography series, "American Women in Science" available through the National Women's History Project, 7738 Bell Road, Windsor, CA 95492-8518, 707-838-6000.

Nancy Garden

Tim Morse 1982

German Italian American (1938–)

Birthday: May 15
Contact: Dorothy Markinko, Agent
McIntosh and Otis, Inc.
310 Madison Avenue
New York, New York 10017

"One of the things I try to say in my books is 'You have a right to be whoever you are. Be true to yourself, whoever that self is, and follow your own dreams, whatever they are. If those dreams include writing, read all you can, and try to write regularly. The more you read, the more you'll learn about writing, and the more you work at your writing, the better your chances will be of learning to write well.'"
(Personal Communication)

Books by Nancy Garden

Annie On My Mind. **Farrar, Straus and Giroux, 1982; 1992.**

The Door Between. **Farrar, Straus and Giroux, 1987.**

Dove and Sword: A Novel of Joan of Arc. **Farrar, Straus and Giroux, 1995; Scholastic, 1997.**

Fours Crossing. **Farrar, Straus and Giroux, 1981.**

Good Moon Rising. **Farrar, Straus & Giroux, 1996.**

Holly's Secret. **Farrar, Straus & Giroux, 2000.**

The Kids' Code and Cipher Book, **Holt, 1981; Shoe String, 1991.**

Lark in the Morning. **Farrar, Straus & Giroux, 1991.**

Monster Hunters Case. **Pocket, 1994.**

My Brother, the Werewolf. **Random, 1995.**

My Sister, the Vampire. **Knopf, 1992.**

Mystery of the Midnight Menace. **Farrar, Straus and Giroux, 1988; Pocket, 1991.**

Mystery of the Night Raiders. **Farrar, Straus and Giroux, 1987; Pocket, 1991.**

Mystery of the Secret Marks. **Farrar, Straus and Giroux, 1989; Pocket, 1992.**

Peace, O River. **Farrar, Straus and Giroux, 1986.**

Prisoner of Vampires. **Farrar, Straus and Giroux, 1993.**

Watersmeet. **Farrar, Straus and Giroux, 1983.**

Werewolves. **HarperCollins, 1973.**

Witches. **HarperCollins, 1975.**

The Year They Burned the Books. **Farrar, Straus and Giroux, 1999.**

Nancy Garden was born May 15, 1938, in Boston, Massachusetts. Her parents often read aloud to her, and when she was older they sometimes all read aloud to each other. She started writing when she was eight. She wrote poems, mostly. She writes, "One reason, I think, why books and writing were always so important to me is that they were important to my family. . . . I was shy, and I think I took refuge in books, in writing and in telling long stories to myself and sometimes acting them out" (*Something About the Author*, Volume 12, p. 86).

When she was twelve, she wrote a long adventure story for school, which prompted her English teacher to suggest that she might someday become a writer. She liked the idea but was interested in many other fields, such as veterinary medicine. She wrote a book called *Dogs I Have Known*, a collection of biographies of every dog she'd ever met. "That was no small number because I was always seeking dogs out."

In high school, Garden became interested in theatre: first in acting and then in lighting design and directing. Some of her written pieces were published in the school literary magazine. She later earned her B.F.A. and M.A. at Columbia University, worked at odd jobs, and in theatre, and taught. But she always went on writing. She is best known for her groundbreaking book, *Annie On My Mind*, which features two young women who fall in love. She notes, "I wrote it to give solace to young gay people, to let them know they were not alone, that they could be happy and well adjusted and also to let heterosexual kids know that we gay people aren't monsters" (*Booklist*, April 15, 1996). Garden has given her young readers a rare and much needed gift by writing *Annie On My Mind* and later *Lark in the Morning* and *Good Moon Rising*. The field of young adult literature needs more books with positive images of lesbians and gays. It is important that all young people be able to find themselves in the books they read.

Annie On My Mind

American Library Association Best Book For Young Adults
Booklist Reviewers' Choice
American Library Association Best of the Best Books for Young Adults

- **Lesbianism**
- **Teachers**
- **Student Council**

During her first semester at MIT, 18-year-old Liza Winthrop reminisces about her senior year in high school when she met and fell in love with Annie Kenyon. She thinks about their beautiful love for each other and the bigotry that threatened to keep them apart. Liza attended a snobby private high school where, even though she was the student council president, she never felt like she belonged. Annie, from an Italian American working class family, attended a public high school where she was able to develop her gifts in music. This compelling book about two real and likable young women provides much needed information about lesbianism and the prevalent bigotry that typifies our so-called democratic society. The firing of two excellent teachers demonstrates the distance we still have to travel. This outstanding book should be made available to all young students in support of those who are struggling with figuring out their sexual orientation, as well as heterosexual students who, hopefully, will become more aware and supportive. Also recommended for adults, especially those who work with young people.

Ages 12 up

Suggestions for the Classroom

1. *Annie On My Mind* has been recognized as a landmark book and has won several important awards. However, it has also been banned from some school libraries. One of the controversies took place in Kansas City, MO, where conservatives burned the book and students successfully filed suit to have it returned to the library shelves. For more information about this important case, see "Annie On My Mind: How It Feels to be the Author of a Challenged Book," by Nancy Garden in *Voice of Youth Advocate Journal,* June, 1996. Invite youngsters to research other censorship attempts of this book and others.

2. Topics and themes for discussion and written response include: the School Charter and the Reporting Rule; Plato's description of true love; the poem "Invictus"; the board of trustees' decision; socioeconomic class differences; coming out to parents and friends; and the many faces of bigotry.

3. Write a chapter from Ms. Stevenson's or Ms. Widmer's perspective. Then read and discuss *The Last Closet: The Real Lives of Lesbian and Gay Teachers* by Rita M. Kissen, Heinemann, 1996.

4. Discuss or respond in writing to the following quotes: "Even when I was little, I'd always felt as if I didn't quite fit in with most of the people around me; I'd felt isolated in some way that I didn't understand." ". . . I don't want to hide the best part of my life, of myself."

5. Nancy Garden is currently working on the stage version of *Annie On My Mind.*

6. Related resources for young adults and educators are listed on page 82.

- **Lesbians**
- **Theatre**

Ages 12 up

Good Moon Rising

Lambda Young Adult Book Award

A lesbian love story takes center stage as a high school in New Hampshire prepares a production of *The Crucible* by Arthur Miller. Janna Montcrief, an accomplished actor just back from a rewarding experience at summer stock, is stung when a new student, Kerry Socrides, wins the leading role in the play. Mrs. Nicholson, the drama teacher, assigns Jan a new challenge: Stage Manager and Assistant Director. Her disappointment and resentment evaporate quickly as she and Kerry work together, become close friends, and fall in love. When Mrs. Nicholson is forced by a grave illness to take a leave of absence, Jan realizes that her beloved mentor has been preparing her to step in as Director. Kent, the male lead, spurred by his growing resentment of Jan's new position and his suspicion that the two young women are lesbians, launches a campaign of harassment against them. Like Liza and Annie who were the targets of homophobia in Garden's landmark book, *Annie on My Mind,* Jan and Kerry must decide whether or not to remain silent about their love for each other. Garden skillfully draws parallels between the hysteria of the Salem Witch trials in *The Crucible* and the homophobic attacks on the two young lesbians. She takes the reader inside the dynamics of homophobia, exposing its foundation of ignorance, intolerance, and cruelty. This is Garden at her finest: strong writing, powerful characterization, and most of all, a message of hope for young lesbian and gay readers who may be facing erasure, hostility, and violence. It will also help heterosexual students understand and support their lesbian and gay classmates.

Suggestions for the Classroom

1. In places where *Good Moon Rising* might be considered controversial, educators should first check their district's policy on controversial materials and should always inform their supervisors in advance about their plans to use these materials. However, do not avoid using this fine book because a few parents might object. It is essential that educators provide a safe and supportive learning environment for *all* students.

2. As Arthur Miller used the Salem Witch trials to comment on McCarthyism, Nancy Garden used them to comment on homophobia. Kent appropriated the anti-witch rhetoric of the play in his attack on Jan and Kerry. This analysis provides a number of thought-provoking topics for discussion, writing, and further research.

3. Examine the impact Jan's experience as assistant director and then director had on her and the ways in which this growth paralleled the other changes in her life.

4. Try the suggestion for giving depth to a characterization on page 10: Write an autobiography of a character, starting with her/his earliest memory and going up to the time of the play.

5. Related resources for young adults and educators are listed on page 82.

Lark in the Morning

- **Lesbianism**
- **Runaways**
- **Child abuse**

Seventeen-year-old Gillian Harrison spends a summer with her family at their vacation home in Rhode Island. She is feeling clear about her love for her best friend, Suzanne, and their lesbianism although she hasn't told her parents yet. She stumbles across the thieves who broke into their vacation home but they turn out to be young runaways who have fled an abusive father. When she learns their story, especially about fourteen-year-old Lark's suicide attempt, she decides she must help them, secretly. Garden has given us a likable, admirable lesbian protagonist who follows her own ethics in making important decisions. Gillian is an important role model for young lesbians searching for positive images in books. This book should be read by lesbian, gay, and straight youth and adults.

Ages 12 up

Suggestions for the Classroom

1. Would you have helped Lark and Jackie? Why or why not?

2. Write a coming out letter that Gillian might have written to her parents. Write a response. For sample coming out letters, see *Coming Out: An Act of Love* by Rob Eichberg Dutton, 1990.

3. The oppression of lesbian and gay people has taken many forms. Research the persecution of lesbians and gays by the Nazis during World War II. Read *The Pink Triangle: The Nazi War Against Homosexuals* by Richard Plant. Holt, 1986.

4. Approximately 10 percent of the population is lesbian or gay. Make a list of well-known lesbian and gay people.

5. Some people who are against other forms of bigotry think it is okay to discriminate against lesbians and gays. How does this attitude reflect the principles of a democratic society?

6. Does your school district have a policy that forbids discrimination? If so, see if it includes sexual orientation. If not, find out why this group has been left out. What can you do about this?

Additional Resources

YOUNG ADULT BOOKS

Am I Blue? Coming Out from the Silence, edited by Marion Dane Bauer. HarperCollins, 1994.

Created Equal: Why Gay Rights Matter to America by Michael Nava. St. Martin's Press, 1994.

Happy Endings Are All Alike by Sandra Scoppettone (see page 184).

Tommy Stands Alone by Gloria Velásquez. Arte Público Press, 1995.

Two Teenagers in Twenty: Writings by Gay and Lesbian Youth, edited by Ann Heron. Alyson Publications, 1993.

Young, Gay and Proud! edited by Sasha Alyson. Alyson Publications, 1991.

FOR ADULTS

Bridges of Respect: Creating Support for Lesbian and Gay Youth: A Resource Guide by Katherine Whitlick. American Friends Service Committee, 1989.

Death by Denial: Studies of Suicide in Gay and Lesbian Teenagers edited by Gary Remafedi. Alyson Publications, 1994.

The Last Closet: The Real Lives of Lesbian and Gay Teachers by Rita M. Kissen. Heinemann, 1996.

Lesbian and Gay Voices: An Annotated Bibliography and Guide to Literature for Children and Young Adults by Frances Ann Day. Greenwood, 2000.

One Teacher in Ten edited by Kevin Jennings. Alyson Publications, 1995.

Carmen Lomas Garza

Chicana (1948–)

Birthday: September 12
Address: c/o Children's Book Press
246 First Street, Suite 101
San Francisco, California 94105

"From the time I was a young girl, I always dreamed of being an artist. I practiced drawing every day." (Family Pictures)

"If you see my heart and humanity through my art then hopefully you will not exclude me from rightfully participating in this society." (A Piece of My Heart, *p. 13)*

Books by Carmen Lomas Garza

Family Pictures/Cuadros de Familia. **Children's Book Press, 1990.**

In My Family/En mi familia. **Children's Book Press, 1996.**

Magic Windows: Papel Picado Ventanas mágicas. **Children's Book Press, 1999.**

Making Magic Windows: Creating Papel Picado/Cut-Paper Art. **Children's Book Press, 1999.**

Papel Picado: Paper Cutout Techniques. **Xicanindio Arts Coalition, 1984.**

A Piece of My Heart/Pedacito de mi Corazón: The Art of Carmen Lomas Garza. **Laguna Gloria Art Museum, 1991; New Press, 1994.**

VIDEOTAPES

"Aqui y Ahora/Female Creators: A Profile of Carmen Lomas Garza"

"Homenaje A Tenochtitlan: An Installation for Day of the Dead." Call (512) 467-7306

Carmen Lomas Garza was born September 12, 1948 in Kingsville, Texas, near the border with Mexico. From the time she was a young girl she dreamed of becoming an artist. Her mother inspired her to follow her heart and helped her plan her future. Garza taught herself how to draw by practicing every day. She earned her BS at the Texas Arts and Industry University in Kingsville, Texas; her MA in Education at Juarez-Lincoln/Antioch Graduate School in Austin, Texas; and her MA in Art at San Francisco State University in California.

Garza has won many awards, grants, and fellowships for her art. She has had numerous solo exhibitions as well as group exhibitions. Her work is displayed in museums, libraries, and schools including the Smithsonian Institution in Washington, D. C. She works in a wide variety of media including oil on canvas, acrylic on canvas, gouache on arches paper, papel picado (paper cutouts), lithographs, and metal cutouts.

Garza presently lives in California. She is considered one of the major Mexican American painters in the United States. She is also an art instructor and curator. Some of her posters, videos, and cards are available through: A Medio Dia Productions, P.O. Box 140304, Austin, TX 78714; 512-467-7306.

- Art
- Artists
- Bilingual (Spanish)
- Autobiography
- Traditions

Family Pictures/Cuadros de Familia

American Library Association Notable Book
Texas Bluebonnet Award
Pura Belpré Honor Award
Parents' Choice Approved Book
Library of Congress "Best Books of the Year" Selection
School Library Journal "Best Books of the Year" Selection

In My Family/En mi familia

Américas Picture Book Award
Hungry Mind Review Children's Books of Distinction Award
Skipping Stones Book Award
International Reading Association Notable Book
Pura Belpré Honor Award for Illustration

All Ages

Carmen Lomas Garza's memories of her childhood in a rural Mexican American community in Kingsville, Texas, near the Mexico border, inspired her to create these two magnificent books. Her engaging, detailed pictures and accompanying bilingual text portray the day-to-day experiences of her early years. She elaborates on her great dream of becoming an artist and how her mother inspired and supported this aspiration. *In My Family* includes a fascinating section: "Carmen Lomas Garza Answers Questions From Children." *Family Pictures* is also available in Big Book format.

Suggestions for the Classroom

1. Study Garza's paintings. Notice how much detail she includes. She writes that it takes from two to nine months to complete a painting. Inspired by her example, encourage young artists to include details in their artwork.

2. Research papel picado (paper cutouts). This is a traditional Mexican folk art technique. Study the black paper cutouts Garza created to portray intricate images. Invite youngsters to try the technique.

3. Garza based these books on her childhood experiences. Discuss her childhood and her dream of becoming an artist. What did she do to make her dream come true? How did her mother help?

4. Using the information in these books, invite youngsters to write a chapter about Garza following the pattern Pat Cummings established in her books, *Talking With Artists: Volumes I and II*. See page 71.

A Piece of My Heart/Pedacito de mi Corazón: The Art of Carmen Lomas Garza

- **Art**
- **Artists**
- **Autobiography**

All Ages

This beautiful book gathers together thirty-seven vivid full-color and black-and-white reproductions of Carmen Lomas Garza's art. It includes a poignant autobiographical piece by the author, an interpretative essay about her art, and an extensive bibliography.

Suggestions for the Classroom

1. Read and discuss Garza's autobiographical essay and the way she turned to art to heal the wounds inflicted by years of exclusion and humiliation. What can we each do to end the discrimination and suffering of all people?

2. Examine Garza's paintings closely. Discuss the intricate details and the empowerment of the familiar.

3. Discuss the title of her book: *A Piece of My Heart*, the early criticism of her art, and her comparison of her art with the aloe vera plant.

4. The interpretative essay is divided into themes. Invite older students to choose a theme for further exploration through writing, art, drama, or dance.

Nikki Yolanda Giovanni

Black American (1943–)

Birthday: June 7
Address: Virginia Polytechnic Institute & State University
215 Williams Building
Blacksburg, Virginia 24060

"We (teachers and writers) are the dream makers."
(Virginia Tech Brochure)

"We must include as many writers of as diverse backgrounds as possible. Just as we identify with white males, so must we identify with Black men, Black women, Chinese-Americans, etc."
(Personal Communication)

Books by Nikki Giovanni

Appalachian Elders: A Warm Hearth Sampler. **(Editor) Pocahontas Press, 1992.**

Black Feeling, Black Talk/Black Judgment. **Morrow, 1971.**

Cotton Candy on a Rainy Day. **Morrow, 1980.**

Ego-tripping & Other Poems. **Lawrence Hill Books, 1973; Lawrence Hill Books, 1993.**

Deer in the Headlights. **Morrow, forthcoming.**

Gemini: An Extended Autobiographical Statement on My First Twenty-Five Years of Being a Black Poet. **Viking, 1976.**

The Genie in the Jar. **Illustrated by Chris Raschka. Holt, 1996.**

Grand Mothers: Poems. Reminiscences, and Short Stories about the Keepers of Our Traditions. **(Editor) Holt, 1994; 1996.**

Knoxville, Tennessee. **Scholastic, 1994.**

Life: Through Black Eyes. **Rom Publications, 1996.**

Love Poems. **Morrow, 1997.**

My House. **Morrow, 1974.**

A Poetic Equation: Conversations Between Nikki Giovanni and Margaret Walker. **Howard University Press, 1974.**

Racism 101. **Morrow, 1995.**

Sacred Cows . . . And Other Edibles. **Morrow, 1988; 1989.**

The Selected Poems of Nikki Giovanni. **Morrow, 1996.**

Shimmy Shimmy Shimmy Like My Sister Kate: Looking at the Harlem Renaissance through Poems. **Holt, 1996.**

Spin a Soft Black Song. **Illustrated by George Martin. Farrar, Straus & Giroux, 1971, 1985; 1987.**

The Sun Is So Quiet. **Holt, 1996.**

Those Who Ride the Night Winds. **Morrow, 1983; 1984.**

Vacation Time: Poems for Children. **Illustrated by Marisabina Russo. Morrow, 1980.**

The Women and the Men. **Morrow, 1979.**

Nikki Giovanni was born June 7, 1943 in Knoxville, Tennessee. Her family moved to Cincinnati, Ohio when she was two months old. As a child, she loved to read and to be read to. She loved heroic stories such as folk tales and family tales. She enjoyed poetry and can still recite poems her mother and sister taught her. Her family encouraged her creativity by admiring the stories she created. They played creative games at dinner such as "What are you eating and where are you?"

After earning her B.A. in History at Fisk University in 1967, she attended the University of Pennsylvania School of Social Work and Columbia University. She has won many awards and has honorary doctorates from eight universities. Numerous honors such as a citation from *Ebony Magazine* in 1969 as one of the ten most admired Black women and selection as the 1985 Outstanding Woman of Tennessee have resulted in her being in demand on the lecture circuit. People have called her "The Princess of Black Poetry" and "Black America's Most Celebrated Word Magician."

Today Giovanni is a world renowned poet. She never does any thing half-way, whether it is writing, teaching, lecturing, or volunteering. She is a professor of English at Virginia Tech in Blacksburg, Virginia. She agrees that her years in New York gave her that "Let's-get-it-done" attitude. She urges writers and students alike to jump in and *do,* to make mistakes in order to achieve creativity.

Giovanni writes about Black Soul, Black Experiences, and Black Awareness. Many of her poems and stories are about her childhood. Her poems exalt "common" people and their daily lives to a place where they can understand and appreciate themselves more clearly. A significant role model for young African American writers, she gives voice to their experience and, in so doing, becomes a catalyst for generations of writers to speak up and speak out. Through her voice, writers and readers alike perceive a world ripe with potential. Her life and work serve as an inspiration to all.

Ego-tripping and Other Poems for Young People

• Poetry

Fly like a bird in the sky with these poems. "The filings from my fingernails are precious jewels." Ego-tripping is empowering with poems by word magician, Nikki Giovanni.

Ages 9 up

Suggestions for the Classroom

1. Do some ego-tripping. Inspired by Giovanni's poetry, write a class poem, print it in large letters and use it as the basis for a bulletin board. Invite interested youngsters to add illustrations.
2. Set up a Poetry Center in your classroom. Be sure to include poetry from many different cultures.
3. Read poetry by other African Americans such as Eloise Greenfield, Paul Laurence Dunbar, Langston Hughes, Alice Walker, and Gwendolyn Brooks.

The Genie in the Jar

• Poetry

Profound and lyrical, this joyous book is a tribute to the power of love and community. As Giovanni weaves her words into inspiring images of trust, hope, and independence, a little African American girl dances, floats, and spins. A celebration of learning to risk, create, and believe in oneself.

Ages 4 up

Suggestions for the Classroom

1. Read and reread this book together, letting the words and images soar. Encourage spontaneous responses through words, art, music, and dance.

2. Nikki Giovanni originally dedicated this poem to the singer, Nina Simone. It is appropriate for older children if it is thought of as a cautionary, reassuring, and universal message for anyone trying their wings.

• Poetry

Ages 7 up

Spin a Soft Black Song: Poems for Children

A New York Times Outstanding Book of the Year

These thirty-five poems are enchanting presentations of life as experienced by African American children. No condescension here, the poems observe, lament, and celebrate daily life. Giovanni, with her unique combination of casual energy and sudden wit, "waltzes with the children to the mountains of their dreams." Empowering!

Suggestions for the Classroom

1. The teacher or a student reads "The Tunnels of Rumpelstiltskin" to the group. Discuss. Each student or group chooses a line to write about and/or illustrate. Compile and display.

2. Discuss lines such as "to see not only those aspects unseen but those unseeable."

3. Invite each student to choose a poem to print up and illustrate on a poster. Use for a Nikki Giovanni bulletin board.

4. Read "A Heavy Rap." Then write a Tall Tale or Tall Poem about your accomplishments.

• Poetry

Ages 6 up

Vacation Time: Poems for Children

Children's Reading Roundtable of Chicago Award

A carefree, fanciful collection of twenty-two poems for children by one of America's favorite African American poets. With imaginative ventures into ordinary daily events—playing hide-and-seek, taking a bath, watching sunsets, saying goodnight to family members; and into fantasy—stars dancing, boats made of rainbows, a cat who reads and writes—Nikki Giovanni "wraps up her mind in her heart and makes Vacation Time."

Suggestions for the Classroom

1. Read "Houses." Discuss questions such as these: Do all Eskimos live in igloos? Do all Indians live in tents? What is a rat hole?

2. Each student may choose a poem to print up and illustrate on a poster. Use for a Nikki Giovanni bulletin board.

3. Paula the Cat can read and write. Write a story or poem about her adventures or the adventures of one of your animal friends and illustrate it.

4. Choose a poem to memorize and recite for your class. (This should be optional. Do not require all students to do this.)

5. Choose a poem. Make a booklet out of it with a line or stanza on each page. Illustrate it and add to your library.

Eloise Greenfield

African American (1929–)

Birthday: May 17
Contact: HarperCollins
10 East 53rd Street
New York, New York 10022

"There's a desperate need for more Black literature for children, for a large body of literature in which Black children can see themselves and their lives and history reflected. I want to do my share in building it."
(Something About the Author, *Volume 61, p. 98)*

Books by Eloise Greenfield

Aaron and Gayla's Alphabet Book. **Illustrated by Jan Spivey Gilchrist. Writers and Readers, 1993; 1994.**

Aaron and Gayla's Counting Book. **Illustrated by Jan Spivey Gilchrist. Writers and Readers, 1993.**

Africa Dream. **Illustrated by Carole Byard. John Day, 1977; 1981; HarperCollins, 1989; 1992.**

Alesia **(with Alesia Revis). Putnam, 1981.**

Big Friend, Little Friend. **Writers and Readers, 1991.**

Childtimes: A Three-Generation Memoir **(with Lessie Jones Little). Crowell, 1979; HarperCollins, 1993.**

Daddy and I. **Writers and Readers, 1991.**

Darlene. **Routledge, 1980.**

Daydreamers. **Illustrated by Tom Feelings. Dial Books, 1981; 1985.**

Easter Parade. **Illustrated by Jan Spivey Gilchrist. Hyperion, 1998.**

First Pink Light. **Illustrated by Jan Spivey Gilchrist. Black Butterfly Children's Books, 1991; 1993.**

For the Love of the Game. **Illustrated by Jan Spivey Gilchrist. HarperCollins, 1997.**

Good News. **Putnam, 1977.**

Grandmama's Joy. **Illustrated by Carole Byard. Philomel Books, 1980.**

Grandpa's Face. **Illustrated by Floyd Cooper. Philomel Books, 1988; Putnam, 1996.**

Honey, I Love. **Illustrated by Jan Spivey Gilchrist. HarperFestival, 1995.**

Honey, I Love and Other Love Poems. **Illustrated by Diane and Leo Dillon. HarperCollins, 1978; 1996.**

I Can Do It By Myself **(with Lessie Jones Little). HarperCollins, 1978.**

I Make Music. **Writers and Readers, 1991.**

Kia Tanisha. **Illustrated by Jan Spivey Gilchrist. HarperCollins, 1997.**

Kia Tanisha Drives Her Car. **Illustrated by Jan Spivey Gilchrist. HarperCollins, 1997.**

Koya DeLaney and the Good Girl Blues. **Scholastic, 1992; 1995.**

Lisa's Daddy and Daughter Day. **Illustrated by Jan Spivey Gilchrist. Sundance, 1993.**

Mary McLeod Bethune. **Illustrated by Jerry Pinkney. Crowell, 1977; HarperCollins, 1994.**

Me and Neesie. **Illustrated by Moneta Barnett. Crowell, 1975; HarperCollins, 1984.**

My Doll, Keshia. **Writers and Readers, 1991.**

Nathaniel Talking. **Illustrated by Jan Spivey Gilchrist. Black Butterfly Children's Books, 1988.**

Night on Neighborhood Street. **Illustrated by Jan Spivey Gilchrist. Dial Books, 1991; Puffin, 1996.**

On My Horse. **Illustrated by Jan Spivey Gilchrist. HarperCollins, 1995.**

Paul Robeson. **Illustrated by George Ford. HarperCollins, 1975.**

Rosa Parks. **Illustrated by Eric Marlow. Crowell, 1973; HarperCollins, 1996.**

She Come Bringing Me That Little Baby Girl. **Illustrated by John Steptoe. Lippincott, 1974; HarperCollins, 1990; 1993.**

Sister. **Crowell, 1974; HarperCollins, 1987; 1992.**

Sweet Baby Coming. **Illustrated by Jan Spivey Gilchrist. HarperCollins, 1994.**

Talk About a Family. **Illustrated by James Calvin. Lippincott, 1978; Scholastic, 1978; HarperCollins, 1991; 1993.**

Under the Sunday Tree. **Illustrated by Amos Ferguson. HarperCollins, 1988; 1991.**

William and the Good Old Days. **Illustrated by Jan Spivey Gilchrist. HarperCollins, 1993.**

Eloise Greenfield was born May 17, 1929 in Parmele, North Carolina. Her family soon moved to Washington, D. C. where Greenfield has made her home ever since. As a child and teenager, Greenfield studied piano. Music has always been an important part of her life. She also loved movies and books. She enjoyed reading words but writing them was the farthest thing from her mind at that time.

Her first publication was a poem for adults which was published in 1962 in the *Hartford Times.* Throughout the 60s and early 70s, she had short stories and articles published in periodicals. In 1972 her first book, *Bubbles,* was published. Throughout the seventies, she wrote one or two books a year. She has written over thirty outstanding books for young readers. Recently, she has written a number of engaging board books for toddlers.

Greenfield's writing has an important purpose. "I want to give children a true knowledge of Black heritage.... The distortions of Black history have been manifold and ceaseless.... It is necessary for Black children to have a true knowledge of their past and present, in order that they may develop an informed sense of direction for their future" (*Something About the Author,* Volume 61, p. 100).

In addition to numerous awards for individual books, Eloise Greenfield has been honored many times for her entire body of work; these awards include: Citation from the Council on Interracial Books for Children, 1975; National Black Child Development Institute Award, 1981; National Council of Teachers of English Award for Excellence in Poetry for Children, 1997; and Hope Dean Award sponsored by the Foundation for Children's Books, 1998.

For more information about Eloise Greenfield, see *Something About the Author,* Volume 61 and *Something About the Author Autobiography Series,* Volume 16.

- **Africa**
- **Travel**
- **Dreams**

All Ages

Africa Dream

Coretta Scott King Award

In words and images, a child fulfills longings and imaginings of the faraway land of her ancestors. "I went all the way to Africa in a dream one night," she begins. In long ago Africa, she reads old books, visits cities and villages, meets ancestors, dances, and sings. Greenfield dedicated this book "With love, to all children of African descent, May they find in their past the strength to shape their future."

Suggestions for the Classroom

1. Reread and discuss the dedication page. How might our past shape our future?

2. What if the girl in the book had stayed in Africa for another week? What other experiences might she have had? Write several journal entries she might have recorded during that week.

3. Write a letter home to a classmate from the girl in the book. What might she have said about her trip into the past?

4. Pretend you are returning to the home of your ancestors. Write and illustrate a story or poem describing your journey. Or make up a song or play about your journey. Combine all the stories, poems, songs, and plays into a booklet.

Childtimes: A Three-Generation Memoir

1979 Notable Children's Trade Book in Social Studies

- **Autobiography**
- **Washington, D.C.**
- **Family trees**
- **History**

Three African American women—grandmother, mother and daughter—recall significant aspects of their respective childhoods and their family history from the 1880s through the 1950s. These memoirs and the accompanying photographs give us poignant images of the history of one African American family.

Ages 9 up

Suggestions for the Classroom

1. How did life change for each generation? Discussion could include education, travel, home, beliefs, traditions, racism, etc. What changes did Parmele, North Carolina go through?

2. Discuss the following topics: ironing, laundry, ice box, vendors, hunger, snakebite, candy, farm work, and swimming pools.

3. Greenfield worked with her mother to write this history of their family. What insights does this book give us into her motivation for writing?

4. Invite interested youngsters to research their family trees or write their autobiographies. (Make sure these projects are optional because some children may not have access to this information.)

Daydreamers

A* Reading Rainbow *Book

An American Library Association Notable Book

- **Daydreaming**

Beautifully illustrated by Tom Feelings. African American children are shown thinking, dreaming, watching "... their memories with spirit eyes seeing more than they saw before." The significance of reflection is captured in a few words.

All Ages

Suggestions for the Classroom

1. What does the author mean by "This dreaming has made them new."? How can dreams hopscotch? Dance? Crisscross? Discuss Greenfield's gift for spinning words.

2. Choose one of the children in the book. Make up a story about what s/he is thinking about.

3. Do you ever daydream? What do you think about? Does daydreaming help you? How? Write a poem about the way your thoughts go when you are daydreaming.

4. Read "About the Art" on the last page. Try the techniques described.

First Pink Light

Ages 5–8

A little boy tries to wait up all night to surprise his father when he comes home. Beautiful illustrations by Jan Spivey Gilchrist in gouache and pastels.

Suggestions for the Classroom

1. Many of Greenfield's books were illustrated by Jan Spivey Gilchrist. Examine and discuss these illustrations. Discuss the way the author and illustrator work together as a team.

2. Read *A Little House of Your Own* by Beatrice de Regniers, *I'm Hiding* by Myra Cohn Livingstone, and *Hiding* by Dorothy Aldis.

3. Have you ever tried to stay awake all night? What happened? Write and illustrate a story about your experience.

4. Have you ever made a hiding place out of boxes or blankets? Design a new hiding place. Create a song or poem about it.

For the Love of the Game: Michael Jordan and Me

- **Poetry**
- **Basketball**
- **Self-realization**

Ages 5–8

This inspirational book celebrates the human spirit through eloquent poetry and vibrant watercolors. Young people are encouraged to believe in themselves, to follow their dreams, and to spread their wings and fly. This poetic message of hope and determination is designed to help youngsters overcome obstacles and cope with an all too often confusing and hostile world.

Suggestions for the Classroom

1. Reread and discuss the stirring dedication. This eloquent message is a beautiful summary of Eloise Greenfield's life work.

2. Examine and discuss the eagle motif incorporated into this book. Analyze the connections among the images of Michael Jordan and the eagle.

3. "I choose to choose . . . ." Roleplay making positive, self-loving choices.

4. Share this book with parents as a fine example of the potential of literature to touch the hearts and minds of young people. Discuss the importance of self-esteem and the role books like this play in building confidence.

Grandmama's Joy

A Reading Rainbow *Selection*

- **Grandmothers**
- **Moving**

Ages 7 up

Rhondy tries to cheer her Grandmama up but this time it doesn't work. Grandmama is very upset; she and Rhondy will have to move because she can't afford the rent anymore. As the story unfolds, we learn that Rhondy's parents were killed in a car accident. Rhondy has lived with her Grandmama ever since. So Rhondy reminds Grandmama that they still have each other, they are still each other's joy.

Suggestions for the Classroom

1. Write and illustrate a story about Rhondy and her Grandmama after they are settled in their new home.

2. Create a "show" that Rhondy might have used to cheer up her Grandmama. How would you cheer up a sad friend or relative?

3. Brainstorm ways that Grandmama and Rhondy could stay in their home.

4. What if you had to move from your apartment or house? How would you feel? Write and illustrate a story, poem, or song.

Grandpa's Face

An American Library Association Notable Book
Notable Children's Trade Book in Social Studies

- **Grandfathers**
- **Drama**

One day Tamika sees her beloved Grandfather make a mean face while he rehearses for one of his plays. Tamika becomes afraid that some day he will look at her with that mean face, a face that could never love her or anyone.

Ages 7 up

Suggestions for the Classroom

1. Imagine the part Grandpa was playing when he used that mean face. Write a short play or story.

2. Write a poem expressing the way Tamika felt when she saw her Grandpa's mean face.

3. Look in the mirror and practice showing a variety of emotions.

Honey, I Love and Other Love Poems

An American Library Association Notable Children's Book
A* Reading Rainbow *Book

- **Poetry**
- **Harriet Tubman**

This book consists of sixteen fine poems that are excellent for reading aloud. It includes an outstanding poem about Harriet Tubman. Greenfield has given children "words to love, to grow on."

Ages 7–11

Suggestions for the Classroom

1. Read aloud and discuss one poem a day.

2. Use the Harriet Tubman poem for your African American history assembly.

3. Read "Honey, I Love." Then write a poem about all the things you love. Use for a group booklet or bulletin board.

4. Read poems by other African American poets (see Nikki Giovanni's chapter). Also read Greenfield's other books of poetry featured in this chapter.

Kia Tanisha Drives Her Car

- **Board book for toddlers**

The belief that education should start early is enhanced by a number of engaging board books by Eloise Greenfield and Jan Spivey Gilchrist. In this exuberant title, Kia Tanisha drives her little car up the street to visit her friend, Angie.

Ages 1–4

Suggestions for the Classroom and Parents

1. This book is designed to help build positive attitudes toward reading. Enjoy the book in a relaxed atmosphere time and time again. Encourage youngsters to chime in on their favorite lines.

2. For more adventures with the main character, read *Kia Tanisha.*

3. After enjoying this book with young children, check the subject index for other board books.

- **Anger**
- **Humor**
- **Music**

Ages 8–12

Koya DeLaney and the Good Girl Blues

Sixth-grader Koya DeLaney has a great sense of humor. However, her denial of her anger creates problems especially when her best friend betrays Koya's sister. When rude fans threaten to ruin her cousin Del's concert, Koya learns to acknowledge and express her anger. A well-crafted and enjoyable story.

Suggestions for the Classroom

1. Discuss the many emotions Koya experienced. "Koya felt limp, weary, as if her emotions had been tumbling over one another all day . . ." (p. 99). Why was it important that she learn to experience and express anger?

2. Koya had an active imagination which often led to her giggling episodes. How did her classmates and teachers respond? Why?

3. Reread and discuss Koya's dream (pp. 109–110). What role did this dream play in Koya's acceptance of her anger?

4. Reread and discuss Del's comments about music (p. 102). Music has been an important part of Eloise Greenfield's life. Discuss the ways she incorporated a love of music into this story.

- **Biography**
- **Teachers**

Ages 8 up

Mary McLeod Bethune

Classroom Choice Book

This is an inspiring biography of Mary McLeod Bethune (1875–1955), who was a highly notable educator of African American youth. In her will Bethune left a message for African American people about believing in themselves, always trying to build a better world, and about the importance of education. There is a statue of Mary McLeod Bethune in a park in Washington, D.C.

Suggestions for the Classroom

1. What was Bethune's dream? What did she do to make it come true? What is your dream?

2. Write a talk Bethune might have given to raise funds for her school. Why did she think education was important?

3. What might she have written in her journal after she started her first school?

4. What if Bethune could visit your school? What do you think she would say to your class? What questions would you ask her?

Me and Neesie

An American Library Association Notable Children's Book

A Reading Rainbow Selection

- **Friends**
- **Starting school**

Neesie and Janell are best friends. But no one else will believe that Neesie is real because they can't see her. Janell enjoys her invisible friend who does all kinds of mischievous things that Janell can't do. When Janell starts school she makes new friends and then she can't find Neesie anymore.

Ages 4–8

Suggestions for the Classroom

1. Who was Neesie? Have you ever had an invisible friend?

2. What if Neesie had gone to school with Janell? Tell or write a story about what might have happened.

4. Dramatize Mama and Aunt Bea discussing Neesie.

5. Do you think Neesie will come back? Why or why not? Write a letter Janell might have written to Neesie.

Nathaniel Talking

An American Library Association Notable Book

Coretta Scott King Award for Illustrations

- **Poetry**

Eighteen splendid poems make up this book. Topics include rap, knowledge, being nine years old, death, making friends, misbehaving, and the future.

Ages 7 up

Suggestions for the Classroom

1. Read and discuss Greenfield's other books of poetry featured in this chapter. Then read poetry by other African Americans (see Nikki Giovanni's chapter).

2. Read "A Note to My Friends" at the back of the book. Then read the information on a twelve-bar blues poem. Write a class poem and then individual poems. Print on large pieces of construction paper, illustrate, and make into a class booklet or display on a bulletin board.

3. Write individual or group raps on topics related to your science or social studies units.

4. Reread "Grandma's Bones." Then create dances to go with the poems you have written.

Night on Neighborhood Street

National Council of Teachers of English Notable Trade Book

Sequoyah Award Nominee

Horn Book Fanfare Book

Coretta Scott King Honor Book for both author and illustrator

- **Poetry**

Greenfield dedicated this book of sixteen excellent poems "To Marie Dutton Brown for her steadfast commitment to spread the true story of African American people." Topics include bedtime, the blues, new baby, drugs, friends, empty houses, fears, dreams, jokes, and much more.

Ages 7 up

Suggestions for the Classroom

1. Reread and discuss the dedication. Greenfield often writes about the importance of African American children having accurate information about their past and present in order to develop an informed sense of direction for the future.

2. Choose a poem to respond to in writing—a story, poem, play, or song.

3. Pantomime one of the poems and invite classmates to try to guess which poem.

4. Read Greenfield's other books of poetry featured in this chapter. Then read poems by other African Americans such as Nikki Giovanni.

- **Biography**
- **Music**
- **Singers**
- **Drama**

Paul Robeson

Runner-up 1976 Coretta Scott King Award
A Notable Children's Trade Book in Social Studies
Jane Addams Children's Book Award

Biography of Paul Robeson (1898–1976) who became a famous singer, actor, and spokesperson for human rights all over the world. Paul Robeson spoke out for the rights of African American people. He started a newspaper called "Freedom." He also wrote his autobiography called *Here I Stand.* He was punished for talking and fighting for freedom but he didn't give up. This is an inspiring book about a dynamic, creative person.

Ages 8 up

Suggestions for the Classroom

1. Read other books about Robeson. (Virginia Hamilton has written a biography of Robeson for older children.) Make a list of his strengths. Discuss.

2. What if Robeson had pursued a law career? What do you think he might have done?

3. Make a sign that Paul Robeson might have carried in front of a theater where African American people had to sit in an assigned area.

4. If Paul Robeson could come to your classroom, what do you think he would say? Write or give a talk that he might give.

- **Biography**
- **Civil Rights**

Rosa Parks

Carter G. Woodson Award for Social Education 1974
A Notable Children's Trade Book in Social Studies

Biography of Rosa McCauley Parks (1913–). In December, 1955 Parks refused to give up her seat on the bus to a white man. She was arrested and put in jail. This was the beginning of the Montgomery Bus Boycott. Parks became known as "the Mother of the Civil Rights Movement." After almost a year, the United States Supreme Court said that the bus company had to change its rules. It was a great victory for African American people and for all people who believe in freedom for everyone.

Ages 6–12

Suggestions for the Classroom

1. Write a play or readers' theatre about Parks. Perform it for your team or school.

2. What if you had been in Parks' situation on the bus? What would you have done? Write a story.

3. Make a list of the racist rules that African American people had to live by. Then research which ones have changed. What work remains to be done?

4. What if Parks could visit your school? What might she say to your class? What questions would you ask her?

5. Read *Dear Mrs. Parks: A Dialogue with Today's Youth.* Then invite interested youngsters to write to Rosa Parks, c/o The Parks Legacy, 1201 Bagley, Detroit, Michigan 48226.

She Come Bringing Me That Little Baby Girl

American Library Association Notable Children's Book
Irma Simonton Black Award
IRA/CBC Children's Choices
Boston Globe–Horn Book *Award Honor Book*

- **Siblings**
- **Jealousy**

A little boy's jealousy diminishes after his baby sister has been home for a while. "I looked at her again and she wasn't all that ugly any more. She was a little bit cute, even with the wrinkles."

Ages 5 up

Suggestions for the Classroom

1. Do you have a younger sibling? Write about your feelings when the baby first arrived. If not, how do you think you might feel? Do you have older siblings? Ask them how they felt when you first arrived.

2. Make a list of ways Kevin could help his family.

3. Create a "Handbook for Older Sisters and Brothers" with advice on how to deal with jealousy.

4. Read *My Mama Needs Me* by Mildred Pitts Walter. Compare the way the two boys felt about their new baby sisters.

Sister

New York Times *Outstanding Book of the Year*

- **Alienation**
- **Death**
- **Grief**
- **Sisters**

Doretha looks back through her "Doretha Book—Memories" and reminisces about her 9th, 10th, 11th, and 12th years. Now she is thirteen and she realizes that these reflections are what have given her the insight and courage to be herself. She has dealt with her father's death, her sister's alienation, and her mother's grief. She has learned about her ex-slave ancestor, a freedom lover. She joins a school called Ndugu Na Ndada (The Brothers and The Sisters) to learn more about her heritage.

Ages 9 up

Suggestions for the Classroom

1. Of what value was Doretha's journal? Do you keep a journal? What does it mean to you?

2. Make a list of all the problems Doretha faced. How did she deal with each of them?

3. Doretha decided to show Alberta "what she had seen." Dramatize these interactions between the two sisters.

4. Write a paragraph from Alberta's point of view.

• Families
• Divorce

Ages 8 up

Talk About a Family

Junior Literary Guild Selection

Genny has been upset lately because her parents have been arguing. She's counting on her older brother, Larry, to fix everything when he comes home from the Army. But when he gets home, there is nothing he or any of the children can do to get their parents back together. Genny realizes that families come in all different shapes and sizes.

Suggestions for the Classroom

1. Make a list of all the emotions Genny experienced during the story. How did she deal with her feelings? What can you do when you are upset?

2. Choose another character. Tell the story from her or his perspective.

3. Genny went to Mr. Parker for advice. Where do you go for advice? Why? Does anyone ask you for advice? What qualities make a person a good advisor?

4. What might have happened next? Write a new chapter.

• Poetry
• Bahamas
• Traditions

Ages 7 up

Under The Sunday Tree

Coretta Scott King Honor Book for Illustrations
American Library Association Notable Children's Book

This book has twenty poems and paintings about the Bahamas. Topics include weather, water lilies, fire fighters, trees, tourists, sailboat races, traditions, birds, donkeys, and friendship.

Suggestions for the Classroom

1. The leader or a child might read one or two poems a day to the large group. Then encourage everyone to participate in a discussion.

2. Find the Bahamas on a map. Try to calculate the distance from where you live to the Bahamas.

3. Read Greenfield's other books of poetry featured in this chapter. Create a poetry bulletin board. Each student chooses one of her poems to print in large letters on colorful construction paper.

4. Read poems by other African Americans such as Nikki Giovanni.

Virginia Hamilton

Carlo Ontal

African American (1936–)

Birthday: March 12
Contact: The Book Group
Scholastic, Inc.
555 Broadway
New York, New York 10003

"I believe that knowing about all manners of people and events out of the historical past is vital to our living intelligently in the present" (From the Inside Out—The Author Speaks, *Alfred A. Knopf Brochure).*

"There is a common bond among us, writer and reader, that we are not without the other. Writers connect with and in. We cannot do without. Ours is a multicultural, polycentric, pluralistic nation of the world village where we must enter into the bond of learning and understanding together, in community." (Many Faces, Many Voices, *p. 7)*

Books by Virginia Hamilton

The All Jahdu Storybook. **Harcourt, 1991.**

Anthony Burns: The Defeat and Triumph of a Fugitive Slave. **Knopf, 1988; 1993.**

Arilla Sun Down. **Knopf, 1988; Scholastic, 1995; 1997.**

THe Bells of Christmas. **Harcourt, 1989; 1997.**

Cousins. **Philomel, 1990; Scholastic, 1997. (Also in Spanish: *Primos.* Santillana, forthcoming.)**

The Dark Way: Stories From the Spirit World. **Harcourt, 1990.**

Drylongso. **Illustrated by Jerry Pinkney. Harcourt, 1992; 1997.**

Dustland **(Book Two in the Justice Cycle). Greenwillow, 1980; Harcourt, 1989.**

The Gathering **(Book Three in the Justice Cycle). Harcourt, 1989; Scholastic, 1998.**

Her Stories: African American Folktales, Fairy Tales, and True Tales. **Illustrated by Diane and Leo Dillon. Scholastic, 1995; African American Images, 1996.**

The House of Dies Drear **(Book One in the Dies Drear Chronicles). Macmillan, 1984.**

In the Beginning: Creation Stories from Around the World. **Illustrated by Barry Moser. Harcourt Brace, 1988; 1991.**

Jaguarundi. **Illustrated by Floyd Cooper. Scholastic, 1995; 1997.**

Jahdu. **Greenwillow, 1980.**

Junius Over Far. **HarperCollins, 1985.**

Justice and Her Brothers **(Book One in the Justice Cycle). Harcourt, 1989; Scholastic, 1998.**

A Little Love. **Philomel, 1990.**

The Magical Adventures of Pretty Pearl. **HarperCollins, 1986; 1991.**

Many Thousand Gone: African Americans from Slavery to Freedom. **Illustrated by Leo and Diane Dillon. Knopf, 1993; Random, 1995.**

M. C. Higgins, the Great. **Macmillan, 1974; 1988; Simon & Schuster, 1993.**

The Mystery of Drear House **(Book Two in the Dies Drear Chronicles). Greenwillow, 1987; Scholastic, 1997.**

Paul Robeson: The Life and Times of a Free Black Man. **HarperCollins, 1974; Dell, 1979.**

The People Could Fly: American Black Folktales. **Illustrated by Diane and Leo Dillon. Knopf, 1985; 1994.**

Plain City. **Blue Sky Press, 1993; Scholastic, 1993; 1995.**

The Planet of Junior Brown. **Macmillan, 1971; 1986; Simon & Schuster, 1993.**

A Ring of Tricksters. **Scholastic, 1997.**

Second Cousins. **Scholastic, 1998.**

Sweet Whispers, Brother Rush. **Putnam, 1982; Avon, 1983.**

Virginia Hamilton. **Scholastic, 1995.**

W. E. B. Du Bois: A Biography. **HarperCollins, 1987; 1992.**

When Birds Could Talk and Bats Could Sing. **Illustrated by Barry Moser. Scholastic, 1996.**

White Romance, A. **Putnam, 1987; Harcourt, 1989; Scholastic, 1998.**

Willie Bea and the Time the Martians Landed. **Greenwillow, 1983; Macmillan, 1989.**

The Writings of W. E. B. Du Bois. **Crowell, 1975.**

Zeely. **Illustrated by Symeon Shimin. Macmillan, 1967; Simon & Schuster, 1993.**

The youngest of five children, Virginia Hamilton was born March 12, 1936 in Yellow Springs, Ohio, a station on the Underground Railroad. Five generations of her family have lived in the sweeping landscape of southern Ohio. Her mother, Etta Belle (Perry) Hamilton, was the oldest daughter of Levi Perry, a fugitive slave from Virginia. Grandfather Perry escaped slavery, crossed the Ohio River to the abolitionist John Rankin's house in Ripling, Ohio, following the Underground Railroad system to Jamestown, Ohio, and later settled in Yellow Springs, Ohio. He was one of the 100,000 slaves who fled from the South in the first half of the nineteenth century. Grandfather Perry became a farmer; as a fugitive from injustice, land and a home gave him a sense of place, of freedom. Later, he often gathered his ten children around him and told them the story of slavery and why he ran away so it would never happen to them.

The Perry clan had a strong influence on Hamilton's life. Her mother's family was warm-hearted, generous, and frugal. They were great storytellers, spinning tall tales combining mystery, myth, and folklore as well as family history and gossip. In fact, both of Hamilton's parents were fine storytellers. Her father was politically committed; during the Depression he helped unemployed people by giving them work and food. The family grew their own food, and even though they were dollar poor, they always had food to share. Kenneth Hamilton graduated from Iowa State Business College in the early 1890s, a time when many African Americans did not complete high school. As a former newspaper person, he subscribed to *The New Yorker, Collier's, Life,* and *The Crisis Magazine* (from the National Association for the Advancement of Colored People). Hamilton was greatly influenced by her father's love of reading.

Hamilton did not talk much as a young child; she preferred to listen. Her four older siblings were there ahead of her, full of intelligence and competitive spirit. But Hamilton, the baby of the family, bright and sensitive, loved to sing; she often sang at church socials. She had a high, sweet voice that would sail out over the smiling, upturned faces of the congregation. She memorized many songs; her performances made her parents very proud of their young daughter. (This experience, no doubt, provided inspiration for Hamilton's portrayal of Pesty in *The House of Dies Drear.*) Later, Hamilton entered public speaking contests; she traveled around the country with the family pastor, winning prizes for her speaking ability.

As her ancestors before her, Hamilton loved the land. She recalls her childhood as a happy time, spent freely exploring the countryside. Her mother's brothers all had farms adjacent to the Hamilton farm; Hamilton and her cousins spent summers together from sunup to sundown. Although she sometimes helped with the farm chores, she was not expected to do any housework. However, her mother did demand that she stay on the Honor Roll at school.

She was the only African American girl in her class until the seventh grade; she attended a small country school with a very limited curriculum. The history that was taught ignored African American history except to emphasize that they had been slaves. It was not until many years later that Hamilton felt reasonably well educated. As her father before her, she especially loved reading. She has fond memories of winning awards for having read the most books in school reading contests. The prizes were perfect: glorious new books! Hamilton read anything and everything. She enjoyed the Nancy Drew books but it was adult books that she loved the most, such as the works of Poe and de Maupassant. When Hamilton was fourteen, she discovered *There Was Once a Slave: The Heroic Story of Frederick Douglass* by Shirley Graham. It was written in a way that brought the book alive and Hamilton remembered it later when she was writing her biographies. She was an attentive student and her school years were marked by high achievement. She excelled at basketball, track, choir, and cheerleading and graduated from high school with honors.

Hamilton wrote a play during her senior year in high school that was performed for the senior presentation assembly. She had started writing in second or third grade but it was later when she started college that writing became more important than the other subjects. She remembers keeping a notebook at an early age in which she would jot down words, phrases, and euphemisms that she didn't understand, determined to figure out the meanings of these new terms.

Even though Hamilton enjoyed her childhood and was very involved in school, she desperately wanted to leave the small town of Yellow Springs, Ohio and go to New York City. She felt trapped until one of her teachers arranged for a five-year scholarship to college. Hamilton enrolled at Antioch College in Yellow Springs with a major in writing. She spent summers in New York City working as a bookkeeper. In a few years, she moved to New York City where she spent mornings working as a cost accountant for an engineering firm, afternoons writing, and evenings reading or going out. She read voraciously, enrolled in a writing course at The New School, and enjoyed the camaraderie of other New York writers and artists. She attended Ohio State University and studied literature and the novel at The New School for Social Research. By this time she thought of herself as a writer and was seriously trying to be a published author. In 1967 her first book, *Zeely,* was published. After fifteen years in New York City, Virginia returned to Yellow Springs, Ohio, to the land that she loves. She feels that we carry our past with us wherever we go. This time motif is woven into many of her books. She is deeply attached to the land and to the very air of the countryside. She is both bound and freed by the fine Ohio soil where she finds the warmth of clan and race.

Hamilton is one of the most highly acclaimed writers of our time. She has won every major award honoring United States children's book writers. She was the first African American to win the Newbery Medal, in recognition of *M. C. Higgins, the Great.* In 1992, she won the prestigious Hans Christian Anderson Award, an award given for the entire body of work of an author or illustrator. She was awarded the 1995 Laura Ingalls Wilder Medal for lifetime achievement and in 1995 she was the first writer for children to receive the MacArthur Foundation Genius Award. With her brilliant, distinguished body of work, she has heightened the standards for children's literature.

Known for her innovative approaches to language, style, form, and story, Virginia is a wordkeeper, a lover of language. She is free from a set view of writing; she is very daring in her work, breaking out of traditional forms. With a remarkable combination of imagination, research, insight, and poignancy, she blends genres, weaving African American folklore and history, and her own family's story into many of the books she writes. She writes the stories no one else has ever written in a unique style that has seldom been equaled. Also remarkable is the fact that each of her books is very different from the others. Her body of work includes fiction, mythology, folklore, mystery, fantasy, biography, adventure, and even a ghost story.

Equally extraordinary are Hamilton's unforgettable characters. Each one, entirely different from the others, is an intriguing, admirable, sometimes almost eccentric person.

Hamilton says that she begins with a fairly clear concept of a story, only to have the characters who must live it take over. Her characters become individuals who shape the plot according to their own personalities. Memorable characters such as Zeely, Pluto, M. C. Higgins, Cammy, Pretty Pearl, Willie Bea, and Brother Rush evoke our love, respect, and compassion. Virginia succeeds in creating for her readers original and startling images of themselves; these characters provide unique and positive role models who celebrate being African American.

Hamilton's books beautifully portray a universal theme: the growth and maturation of a young person toward an understanding of self and others. Her books also enhance an awareness of African American heritage, history, and experience. Hamilton, first and foremost a writer, has an image in the back of her mind of crusading sociologists such as Shirley Graham, Jacob Riis, Lincoln Steffens, and W. E. B. Du Bois. Visions of these social reformers inspire her to write liberation literature such as *Anthony Burns* and *Many Thousand Gone.* She feels that such literature creates an awareness of those who lived before us who worked so hard for their freedom that we best take care and keep watch over our own freedom. As we read about the struggles and victories of past heroines and heroes, we, too, feel a sense of liberation.

Hamilton is married to Arnold Adoff, an accomplished poet and anthologist. Their two grown children, Leigh and Jaime, are both musicians. Hamilton travels frequently, speaking at conferences across the country. She is Distinguished Visiting Professor at Queens College in New York City and Ohio State University in Columbus, Ohio.

As she writes at her desk in her study, Hamilton looks through the sliding glass doors at a hundred-year-old sage orange hedgerow. As she gazes out at the beloved Ohio land, the trees, and the farmhouses, she sees not only through her own eyes, but through her mother's and her grandmother's eyes as well. Hamilton, distinguished storyteller, novelist, biographer, and lecturer, describes herself as a woman working, a writer learning.

A video or sound filmstrip "Meet the Newbery Author: Virginia Hamilton" is available through American School Publishers, 800-843-8855.

- **Biography**
- **Fugitive Slave Act**
- **U.S. history**
- **Slavery**
- **Abolitionists**

Anthony Burns: The Defeat and Triumph of a Fugitive Slave

American Library Association Best Book for Young Adults
American Library Association Notable Book
Boston Globe–Horn Book *Award for Nonfiction*
Coretta Scott King Honor Book
The Horn Book *Fanfare Honor Book*
International Reading Association Teacher's Choice
Jane Addams Children's Book Award
Notable Children's Trade Book in the Field of Social Studies
School Library Journal *Best Book of the Year*
South Carolina Young Adult Book of the Year

Hamilton combines her extraordinary gifts for writing with her love for African American history in this riveting account of the escape, capture, and controversial trial in 1854 of Anthony Burns, a fugitive slave. She alternates two kinds of historical reconstruction: the segments of the book that deal with Burns's imprisonment and trial are documented from primary sources;

these are interspersed with invented fictional segments portraying his childhood as a slave in Virginia. She illuminates the atrocities of slavocracy and the ways enslaved people found to cope with this horrific institution.

A list of characters, selections from The Fugitive Slave Act of 1850, a bibliography, an index, and the author's comments add to the usefulness of this excellent biography. It takes the reader directly into the life of Anthony Burns and helps us understand what his life was like.

Ages 10 up

Suggestions for the Classroom

1. Read the dedication page and "The Abolitionist Hymn." What tone is set for the book? Discuss.

2. The author uses a writing technique called a flashback to portray Anthony's life as a child. Discuss the use of this technique; how did the author provide for a smooth transition from chapter to chapter? Students might want to try using flashbacks in their next written piece.

3. How did Anthony Burns cope with intolerable situations? Find passages that describe the way he closed his eyes and went far inside himself to escape the cruelty.

4. Anthony's mother and sister were forced to be breeders. What does this mean? Why was this a common practice during slavery? Discuss.

5. Choose a month in Anthony Burns's life. Write a journal entry for each week of that month. Compile into a booklet and use for further discussion.

6. Read and discuss the Epilogue. What was the Personal Liberty Law of 1855? Why was it passed?

7. Write an article about the trial for an abolitionist newspaper.

8. How do you think Anthony Burns would have felt about Hamilton's story of his life? Write a letter he might have written to her. Then write a response.

Cousins

American Library Association Best Book for Young Adults
American Library Association Notable Book
Booklist *Editors' Choice*
Child Study: Bank Street Book Committee
New York Public Library 100 Best Titles for Reading and Sharing
Notable Children's Trade Book in the Field of Social Studies

- **Death**
- **Cousins**
- **Grandmothers**
- **Grief**
- **Socioeconomic class**

Eleven-year-old Cammy knew how she felt about people; in fact, her mother said she was different from most children by the way she cared about other people's feelings. But she often wished she could be as hard as nails like her too pretty, too smart, too perfect cousin, Patricia Ann. Now Gram Tut, Cammy was just full of love for her. Why was Cammy the only one who took the time to visit Grandmother in the nursing home? Couldn't everyone understand that she would soon be gone? But it is Patty Ann who dies. Cammy, who witnesses the accidental drowning, experiences a myriad of feelings: shock, denial, guilt, fear, anger, and confusion. When she sinks into a deep depression, it is her beloved Gram Tut who helps her sort out her feelings and finally accept the tragedy. Hamilton, in another stirring novel, has written about childhood rivalries, family entanglements, bulimia, alcoholism, divorce, poverty, unemployment, aging, death, and grief. (Sequel: *Second Cousins.*)

Ages 8 up

Suggestions for the Classroom

1. Cammy prided herself on her sensitivity to people's feelings. And yet, think about how she treated Elodie and Esther. Analyze the ways Cammy treated each person in the book. How did she justify her behavior toward those less fortunate than herself?

2. Hamilton does an excellent job of portraying ambivalence. Discuss Cammy's mixed feelings about Patty Ann. Then write about a person you feel ambivalent about. Do Cammy's experiences help you better understand your own feelings?

3. Hamilton writes about the complexities of life. What did you learn from reading *Cousins* about bulimia, alcoholism, unemployment, adoption, nursing homes, disabilities, aging, poverty, death, and/or grief? Choose one of these topics for further research. Share your insights with your classmates.

4. The last section of the book is entitled "I Get It." What did Cammy get? How did she get it? Do you think this will help her cope with her grandmother's death? Why or why not?

5. Gram brought out the best in Cammy, and Patty Ann brought out the worst. Who brings out your best? Your worst? Why?

- **Droughts**
- **Dust storms**
- **Erosion**
- **Farm life**
- **Environment**

All Ages

Drylongso

Lindy and her father are busy planting tomato plants in the dry soil of their garden when a great wall of dust moves across their drought-stricken farm. Drylongso, a boy who knows about finding water, blows into their lives along with the dust storm, bringing hope to Lindy's family. The Author's Note at the end of the book provides background information on droughts and on the word *drylongso.*

Suggestions for the Classroom

1. As you read the book, keep a list of the terms that are used creatively in word play, such as gravy, Mamalou, and garden-a-chance. Discuss. Try playing with words in your next written piece.

2. Lindy enjoyed turning things around. How did her sense of humor add to the story? Compile a list of things she turned around. Discuss.

3. Who was Drylongso? What special talents did he have? How did he bring hope to Lindy and her parents?

4. What do you think happened to Drylongso after he left Lindy's family? Write a letter from Drylongso to Lindy telling about his new adventures. Or write and illustrate a sequel about the eighties when Drylongso returned to Lindy's farm.

5. Hamilton often finds a way to include a story within a story. Read aloud the Tall Tales. Then write and illustrate a Tall Tale of your own about a dust storm.

- **Folklore**
- **Tricksters**
- **Women**

Her Stories: African American Folktales, Fairy Tales, and True Tales

Coretta Scott King Award for Text

Coretta Scott King Honor Book for Illustration

American Library Association Notable Children's Book

American Library Association Best Book for Young Adults

Booklist *Editors' Choice*

School Library Journal *Best Book of the Year*

Hungry Mind Review *Book of Distinction*

Parenting Magazine *Best Book of the Year*

Book Links *Best Book*

Blackboard African American Bestsellers *Book of the Year*

Notable Children's Trade Book in the Field of Social Studies

Dedicated to "our mothers and grandmothers, aunts and great-aunts," the nineteen tales in this captivating book feature mermaids, vampires, fairies, witches, shape-shifters, animals, and real women. Humorous, scary, sad, magical, touching, and inspiring, the characters are as varied as the narratives. (Be prepared for suicide and violence.) Each story is accompanied by an author's note that explains its origin and language, what it means, and how it traveled and changed. Striking illustrations! Bibliography included.

All Ages

Suggestions for the Classroom

1. Reread and discuss the dedication. Then follow the author's advice: "*Her Stories* are meant for you to enjoy. Read them to yourself, or read them out loud. By all means, share them with one another."

2. Motifs for discussion, writing, art, and drama include: transformation, pourquoi, cautionary, shape-shifter, false message, and substitution of one for the other.

3. As Hamilton points out, most tales of this sort are about males. Celebrate the beauty of these African American females, including the three real women featured in the last section of the book. Discuss the fact that John Henry is well-known but until now, Annie Christmas has been ignored in literature for young readers.

4. Use the information about the author in "More About *Her Stories*" with your Author Study of Virginia Hamilton; it includes important insights into her early sources of imagination and creativity.

The House of Dies Drear

American Library Association Notable Book
The Ohioan Award for Best Juvenile Fiction by an Ohioan
Edgar Allen Poe Award ("The Edgar"), Mystery Writers of America, Inc.
***Best of Best Books,* School Library Journal**

- **Mystery**
- **African American history**
- **Underground Railroad**

This book is Part One of the Dies Drear Chronicle. When thirteen-year-old Thomas Small moves with his family from North Carolina to a house that had once been a station on the Underground Railroad, he becomes fascinated by the secrets held by the old house. Its century-old legend of how the abolitionist, Dies Drear, and two fugitive slaves were murdered, and how their ghosts were said to wander its passageways, leads Thomas and his family on a spellbinding search to unravel the mysteries of the past. Thomas's journey leads him not only to the extraordinary answers about the house but to a deeper understanding of his own heritage. This is a suspenseful and immensely satisfying story about a present day African American family bravely embarking on a new life. Don't miss the sequel, *The Mystery of Drear House.*

Ages 10 up

Suggestions for the Classroom

1. Trace the route the Small family took when they moved from North Carolina to Ohio via the Blue Ridge Mountain Highway through Pisgah National Forest into Virginia, and through West Virginia over the Ohio River at Huntington into Ohio.

2. Sketch or create a model for the Dies Drear house, following the descriptions in the book. Sketch the maze of tunnels and secret passageways.

3. Of the 100,000 slaves who escaped from the South to Canada between 1810 and 1850, 40,000 passed through Ohio. Because Ohio is just across the river from the slave states of Kentucky and Virginia, it had the most active Underground Railroad routes. Research and discuss this part of United States history. (See *Many Thousand Gone* by Virginia Hamilton.)

4. This story lends itself beautifully to dramatizations. Try dramatizing Chapter 18. Then try to find the movie based on this book.

5. Reread the descriptions of the triangles and sketch them. Discuss the significance of the triangles.

- **Creation**
- **Mythology**
- **Folklore**

In the Beginning: Creation Stories from Around the World

AIGA Award

American Bookseller "Pick of the Lists"

American Library Association Best Books for Young Adults

American Library Association Notable Book

The Horn Book *Fanfare Selection*

Learning Magazine *"Winners Across the Curriculum" One of the fifteen best books of the year*

National Science Teachers' Association Outstanding Science Trade Book for Children

Newbery Honor Book

Notable Children's Trade Book in the Field of Social Studies

Parents' Magazine *Best Books of Year Listing*

Time Magazine *One of Twelve Best Books for Young Readers*

This stunning book is a collection of twenty-five creation myth stories from cultures around the world. Researched extensively by both the author and the illustrator, each story retains its cultural specificity; together the stories reflect the remarkable range of human imagination. Each story is followed by comments from the author that tell about its origin. Also included are opening and closing notes and a list of sources.

Ages 9 up

Suggestions for the Classroom

1. These stories lend themselves beautifully to being read aloud. The leader or a child might read one story each day followed by discussion, drama, writing, or an art activity.

2. Create a class mural that includes all the stories, letting the borders of one story blend into the next.

3. Groups of youngsters might select stories to present to their class or to another class through storytelling, art, and/or music.

4. As each story is read, find the corresponding location on a map.

- **Endangered animals**
- **Rainforest**

Jaguarundi

This engaging picture book introduces young readers to a variety of rainforest animals who must struggle to find a way to survive the destruction of their habitat. Told through the voices of the animals, it is a compelling plea to save the rainforest and its dwellers. Jaguarundi and Coati embark on a perilous journey north in search of a safe place to live. But wherever they go, they find more fences, houses, people, dogs, and stripped land. Hamilton notes, "The story parallels humans who escape from their homelands in search of better, safer lives. I was astounded to discover the added bonus, with the animals, of a classic symbolism of fleeing North—crossing the Great River into the Promised Land."

All Ages

Suggestions for the Classroom

1. Children of all ages often have very strong feelings about the plight of endangered animals. So even though this is a picture book, it will appeal to older children as well as the usual picture book set.

2. Youngsters and adults alike will appreciate the appended information about the 17 species featured in the story. The pictures and factual paragraphs will motivate many readers to search for more information.

3. Some youngsters may feel so moved by this story that they will be inspired to join Save the Rainforest groups. One successful school program involves fundraising efforts such as Walk-a-thons to earn money to support habitat preservation. Contact Rainforest Action Network (415) 398-4404.

The Magical Adventures of Pretty Pearl

Coretta Scott King Honor Book
Notable Children's Trade Book in the Field of Language Arts
American Library Association Best Book for Young Adults
American Library Association Notable Children's Book
Notable Children's Trade Book in the Field of Social Studies
School Library Journal *Best Book*

- **Historical fantasy**
- **Myth**
- **Folklore**
- **Magic**

Pretty Pearl, a young African woman/goddess child travels from Kenya to the New World to live among a group of free Black people who have created their own separate world deep inside a vast forest. The Inside Folks, as they call themselves, are linked to the outside world only through their connections with Cherokee and Shawnee Amerinds. Pretty Pearl finds herself drawn to the winning ways of the humans and forgets the godly rules of her past. Finding herself in serious trouble, she must choose between her immortal power and her emerging identity within a mortal world. Based on Black legend, myth, and history, this story is filled with magic, beauty, and mystery. The African English spoken by the characters, the integral role played by the Native Americans, and the importance of nature to the plot add to the power of this novel. The blending of imagination, historical fact, and folklore demonstrates the author's willingness to experiment with new forms and to challenge herself. Once again, Hamilton has told a story only she can tell.

Ages 11 up

Suggestions for the Classroom

1. Since this book is over 300 pages, the teacher might introduce it by reading selections—possibly the first chapter and some of the songs. Try dipping into different places in the book. This might be a good introduction even for students as old as thirteen so that they may more easily get caught up in the story and hear the auditory effects of the language.

2. In "A Conversation With Virginia Hamilton" by Marilyn Apseloff in *Children's Literature in Education* (Winter 1983, page 210), Hamilton says that *Pretty Pearl* is a culmination of all the work she has done and all the things she has tried to do in her books. In *Pretty Pearl* her love for mythology and the folklore of Black culture and Black history and her love for creating characters and plots seemed to come together. She feels that she had lived the book in a very special way, especially the forest sections of the story. She feels very close to the book and is very satisfied with it. Discuss Hamilton's motivation for writing the book and her creativity in blending genres in the book.

3. How is *Pretty Pearl* different from any book you have read? Try experimenting with the next piece you write. Then reflect upon your experiment. Share your perceptions.

4. Choose a song from the book and add verses. Share with your classmates.

5. Discuss Pretty Pearl's journey. Create a class mural or collage based on the book. Try combining media as Hamilton combined genres, possibly using both words and pictures.

- **Underground Railroad**
- **Fugitive slaves**
- **Juneteenth**
- **U.S. history**

Many Thousand Gone: African Americans From Slavery to Freedom

Here is the much needed history of the slavery and liberty of Black people in the United States. A powerful book that begins with the earliest slave trading and ends with the Emancipation Proclamation, this groundbreaking work is an extraordinary contribution to children's literature. Told in the voices and individual profiles of the people who lived it, we meet familiar heroines and heroes such as Harriet Tubman, Anthony Burns, Frederick Douglass, and Sojourner Truth. Also recounted are the stories of lesser known people such as Eliza, later immortalized in *Uncle Tom's Cabin*, who raced across the icy Ohio River seeking liberty; Henry Box Brown, who cleverly built a crate and shipped himself North to freedom; as well as Crispus Attucks, Nat Turner, Elizabeth Freeman, Dred Scott, and many others.

Daring escapes, desperate rebellions, ingenious tales of the Underground Railroad, steadfast abolitionists, and fascinating accounts of court cases bring history alive for readers of all ages. This carefully researched book is a tribute to those who helped pave the way to freedom as well as to those who continue to protect it. An introduction, afterword, bibliography, and index are included.

Ages 8 up

Suggestions for the Classroom

1. Use this excellent book to supplement United States history textbooks. Analyze your text for the information presented in *Many Thousand Gone*. What information about African Americans is included? Evaluate.

2. Discuss the significance of June 19 (Juneteenth). Find out if special events are planned in your area.

3. Reread and then sing the anthem of freedom. Then find other freedom songs such as "We Shall Overcome." Write individual or small group songs of freedom.

4. Start a Freedom Club. Plan activities that will help protect the freedom of all oppressed people.

5. After students have read this book once, individuals or small groups might choose topics from the index for further research. Findings might be presented through drama, art, music, poetry, and/or multimedia projects.

6. The National Women's History Project has created a Harriet Tubman Board Game and Study Set that may be ordered from NWHP, 7738 Bell Road, Windsor, CA 95492-8518. Or create your own board games based on the information presented in *Many Thousand Gone.*

7. Hamilton has done extensive research in African American heritage and culture. Discuss her motivation for writing liberation literature. Read her other books. What contribution has she made to the field of children's literature?

- **Environment**
- **Strip mining**
- **Appalachian Mountains**

M. C. Higgins, The Great

Newbery Medal Book

American Library Association Notable Book

Lewis Carroll Shelf Award

National Book Award

New York Times Outstanding Children's Book of the Year

U.S. Honor Book, International Hans Christian Andersen Award

Boston Globe–Horn Book *Award for Fiction*

M. C. Higgins, the Great is regarded as one of the great works of juvenile fiction in the United States. It has been translated into many languages including Japanese and German. Considered a landmark in literature for young readers, this novel received the John Newbery Medal as well as the *Boston Globe–Horn Book* Award and the National Book Award, making it the only book ever to receive all three major awards. Hamilton was the first African American to receive the Newbery Medal.

Thirteen-year-old Mayo Cornelius "M. C." Higgins hopes to escape the danger of a spoil heap precariously hovering above his Appalachian mountain home. Strip mining has left the summits of the mountains shredded away into ruin; an enormous boil of trees, rocks, and earth plastered together by rain is hanging suspended far above the house where M. C. lives with his family. M. C. ponders the family's fate while sitting atop his forty-foot pole of glistening, cold steel. There on a bicycle seat he surveys the hills and valleys of Sarah's Mountain, keeps watch over his brothers and sister, and dreams of escape for himself and his family. He hopes that a stranger who has been recording mountain music will record his mother's wondrous voice, that she will become a singing star, and they will all move to a safe place.

Hamilton has again created an unforgettable protagonist whose search for survival, though complicated and painful, leads him through dreams and reality, past and present, to a dramatic solution. This powerful novel provides insight into significant issues such as family conflict, poverty, prejudice, cultural heritage, community, survival, love of the land, and destruction of the environment.

Ages 9 up

Suggestions for the Classroom

1. Trace the journey that M. C. Higgins embarked upon to save his family. Consider the responsibilities he had as the oldest child in the family. What did he learn? How did he change? What characteristics make him one of Hamilton's unforgettable characters?

2. Examine the prejudice that the Higgins family felt toward the Killburns. How did Lurhetta's attitude influence the way M. C. felt about Ben's family? Compare Jones's attitude toward M. C.'s "second sight" with the way he felt about the Killburns. Discuss prejudice as portrayed by Jones and M. C.

3. What happened to M. C.'s dream that his mother would become a singing star? (James K. Lewis was a preserver—not a promoter—of rural music. He realized that making Banina Higgins a performing star would destroy her ingenuousness.) Discuss. What might have happened if she had become a star?

4. Discuss or write about the possible meanings of the following symbols: M. C.'s pole, the Killburn's net, Lurhetta's knife, M. C.'s cave bedroom, the spoil heap, Sarah's tombstone, the green grass snake, and the wall M. C. begins building. Add other symbols. Discuss the role of symbolism in writing. Try using symbolism in your writing.

5. Discuss nonschool intelligence. How might schools change to recognize and nurture the genius of students like M. C.?

6. What is it about this book that makes it a landmark in juvenile literature? Hamilton won many awards for this book including the Newbery Medal. Make a list of other African American authors who have won the Newbery Medal. Discuss.

7. The most obvious problem created by mining was the spoil heap. What were some of the other problems? Research strip mining and other assaults on the earth. Write an analysis and include recommendations for ways these problems might be solved.

- Mystery
- Underground Railroad
- U.S. history

The Mystery of Drear House: The Conclusion (Book Two) of the Dies Drear Chronicle

This book is the sequel to *House of Dies Drear.* Hamilton continues the gripping chronicle of the Drear house, once the home of abolitionist Dies Eddington Drear, and a station on the Underground Railroad. Thomas Small and his father, having discovered the magnificent treasure hidden in a nearby cavern, must decide on the best way to keep it safe. Professor Small, who teaches at a nearby college, spends his weekends cataloguing the priceless antiques that have been hidden for a hundred years. Does the treasure belong to the foundation that owns the property; to Mr. Pluto, the caretaker who has faithfully guarded its secrets in memory of Dies Drear, or to the community? What is the best way to protect the antiques from thieving neighbors as well as from collapsing walls? This suspenseful story introduces two more intriguing characters: Thomas's great grandmother Rhetty Lalette Jeffers and a neighbor, Mrs. Mattie Darrow. This conclusion to the Dies Drear chronicle is an engaging book filled with history, legend, and excitement.

Ages 10 up

Suggestions for the Classroom

1. After reading *The House of Dies Drear* and before reading *The Mystery of Drear House,* predict what might happen in the sequel. Later, reflect on your predictions and discuss them.

2. Make a list of the discoveries the Smalls made about their new home. Add these discoveries to your earlier sketches of the tunnels and secret passageways.

3. Reread the descriptions of the treasure. Then draw sketches of it and add to your Virginia Hamilton bulletin board.

4. Select one of the main characters. (Notice how each of the characters in Hamilton's books is a unique individual.) How did this character change during the book? What special qualities distinguish this character from the others? Compile your perceptions and make character charts for each of the main characters in the Drear Chronicle.

5. Great grandmother Jeffers believed chicory had special powers. What are some other ways people try to ward off calamity? Discuss.

6. Read *Many Thousand Gone* by Virginia Hamilton. Discuss the advantages of reading both fiction and nonfiction when studying history. What did you learn from each of these books that wasn't in your textbooks?

- Biography
- Musicians
- U.S. history

Paul Robeson: The Life and Times of a Free Black Man

American Library Association Notable Children's Book

This is a carefully researched and lovingly written biography of Paul Robeson (1898–1976), athlete, lawyer, scholar, singer, actor, and political activist. Hamilton's skillful writing takes the reader into the life and times of Paul Robeson and helps us understand who he was and what motivated him. In the 1930s and 1940s, he was loved and respected throughout the world. But his own country later rejected him because of his political beliefs. This book also provides insight into the history of African American people. Don't miss Hamilton's introduction "The Knowledge"; it gives the reader a glimpse into her childhood and her motivation for writing. Black and white photographs show Robeson from age 19 to age 65. A bibliography and an index are included.

Ages 12 up

Suggestions for the Classroom

1. Paul Robeson was a highly gifted person. Make a list of his talents and accomplishments. Robeson was ahead of his time. What if he had been born fifty years later? Would his ideas have been so controversial? How might his life have been different?

2. This book could be subtitled "Achievement Against the Odds." What obstacles did Robeson face? How did he cope with these barriers? Imagine what he might have achieved if he had had equal opportunities.

3. Why was information about Robeson kept from a generation of Americans? How can we be sure that parts of our history will not be suppressed again?

4. Read Paul Robeson's autobiography *Here I Stand.* Do you think you have or will some day have the courage to take a position for your beliefs? Discuss other people who have taken a stand. Read *Taking a Stand Against Racism and Racial Discrimination* by Patricia McKissack.

5. Read "The Knowledge" in the introduction. What is the knowledge? What did you learn about Virginia Hamilton and her motivation for writing this biography?

6. Research the Committee on Un-American Activities. What other individuals did they target?

The People Could Fly: American Black Folktales

• **African American folktales**

American Library Association Notable Book

Booklist *Editor's Choice*

Coretta Scott King Award

The Horn Book *Fanfare Honor Book*

National Council of Teachers of English Choice

New York Times *Best Illustrated Book*

Notable Children's Trade Book in the Field of Social Studies

Parents' Choice Award Recording

Read-Aloud Handbook *Selection*

School Library Journal *Best Book of the Year*

This beautifully readable collection of twenty-four folktales celebrates the indomitability of the human spirit. Echoing the voices of African American slaves and fugitives, this is a treasury of spirited trickster tales, spine-chilling ghost stories, tall tales, and stirring tales of freedom, including the poignant title story, "The People Could Fly." Following each tale is information on its origin and its relationship to other versions of the tale. An introduction, an extensive bibliography, and a glossary of *gullah* words are included. A cassette tape of the stories narrated by Virginia Hamilton and James Earl Jones is available.

All Ages

Suggestions for the Classroom

1. Read and discuss the introduction. Discuss Hamilton's reasons for writing this book.

2. These stories lend themselves beautifully to read-aloud, storytelling, and dramatizations. Youngsters might work individually or in small groups to present the tales to the class or to another class. This activity works well for cross-age groupings.

3. Create a class or team mural based on the book. Let the illustrations for each tale blend into those for the next.

4. Gather folktales from many cultures for a classroom center. Add student created tales and illustrations.

5. Write a poem or song based on your favorite tale. Illustrate and add to your Virginia Hamilton Center or your Folktale Center.

- **Folklore**
- **Tricksters**
- **Storytelling**

A Ring of Tricksters: Animal Tales from the Americas, the West Indies, and Africa

Eleven amusing trickster tales follow the migration of African folklore to America via the West Indies. Each features a resourceful animal who uses wit and cunning to take advantage of bigger and stronger animals. Here Bruh Rabby, Bruh Gator, Bruh Wolf, and Anansi and a tangle of others take part in lively contests, deceptions, magic, trickery, and wrestling matches. Hamilton's distinctive language is memorable: "Now's a now, and it's an it." "Guess is guess, and who is who."

All Ages

Suggestions for the Classroom

1. These tales beg to be read aloud. Hamilton noted, "You can be as dramatic as you want to be when you read them, but at the same time you need to be very conversational. . . . Story is a very natural thing; it's call and response."

2. Reread and discuss the introduction. How is this ring of tales like a circle? Read and discuss the notes at the end of the book for further information about each tale. Provide options for extensions: art, drama, writing, music.

3. Invite youngsters to choose a trickster and compare and contrast her/his exploits in this book with those in other books. See Tricksters in the Subject Index.

4. Each book that Hamilton has written is very different from the others. Create a list of her books and the genres they represent. Make a chart with this information for your Virginia Hamilton bulletin board. What type of book do you think Hamilton will write next?

- **Folklore**
- **Birds**

When Birds Could Talk and Bats Could Sing: The Adventures of Bruh Sparrow, Sis Wren, and Their Friends

An* American Bookseller *Pick of the Lists

This collection of eight humorous tales specializes in down-home morals delivered in an easy-going, sassy style. Unlike the characters in most folktales, some of these lively protagonists are female! In the afterword, Hamilton attributes these tales to Alabama folklorist Martha Young who collected them from African descent people before and after the Civil War. Hamilton's lyrical prose imbues the tales with new life: "For true!" "Don't you know?"

All Ages

Suggestions for the Classroom

1. Hamilton noted that she wrote these tales "especially for children, to make them smile. They are meant to be read aloud, too." So have fun first before engaging in extended activities such as writing, illustrating, dramatizing, and analyzing.

2. Compile a list of words and phrases used playfully such as "nary, "swish-swash," and "For true!" Discuss. Invite youngsters to play with words in their next written piece.

3. These tales are written in a prose style called *cante fable*, stories that include verse or song and end with a moral for people to live by. Encourage youngsters to find and discuss lessons such as "Pick on your own size" and "Mind your own business."

Willie Bea and the Time the Martians Landed

American Library Association Notable Book

- **Halloween**
- **Farm life**
- **Extraterrestrial beings**

It is late October, 1938 in rural Ohio and Willie Bea Mills can hardly wait to go trick-or-treating. As she spends the day with her extended family, she shivers with anticipation. But when Orson Wells's "War of the Worlds" broadcast creates pandemonium, it is Willie Bea who takes off on homemade stilts to negotiate with the extraterrestrial beings. It is a Halloween Willie Bea will never forget. Adventuresome Willie Bea is another of Hamilton's many unique characters. She has a mind of her own and is a great risk taker. She is a strong role model for girls and African Americans. Written with humor and insight, this is one of my favorite books by Virginia Hamilton.

Ages 9 up

Suggestions for the Classroom

1. Hamilton is known for creating unique characters. Describe Willie Bea. How do her personality traits make her an intriguing, admirable person?

2. Willie loved scary thoughts. How did her personality prepare her for the strange encounter on the Kelly place? How might you have felt if you had been there that night?

3. Dramatize parts of the book. Willie Bea's encounter with the combines would be great fun to dramatize. Or you might want to try the scene at the farmhouse right after the radio broadcast.

4. Compare Willie Bea with Geeder in *Zeely.* (They both love fantasy.) Analyze fantasy and reality as experienced by Geeder and Willie Bea. Write a letter from Willie Bea to Geeder telling her about her Halloween experiences. Dramatize a time when they got together to share stories.

5. Discuss Willie Bea's responsibilities and accomplishments such as the creation of the Halloween costumes. If you couldn't afford to buy a costume, what might you create to wear? Illustrate it. Compare commercial costumes with homemade ones.

6. Research and discuss what happened around the country as a result of Orson Wells' radio broadcast. Do you think people would believe the "War of the Worlds" today? Discuss the changes that have taken place since 1938.

Zeely

American Library Association Notable Book
Nancy Block Memorial Award

- **Heroines**
- **Farm life**

Zeely, Hamilton's first book, was published in 1967. I enjoyed it as much in 1993 as I did over twenty-five years ago. Eleven-year-old Elizabeth "Geeder" Perry and Zeely are the first of a long line of unforgettable, truly unique characters who grace Hamilton's books.

Geeder and her younger brother are spending the summer with their uncle on his farm. Geeder, determined to make this summer special, idealizes Zeely, a beautiful, six-foot-tall Black woman who raises razorback hogs. Geeder finds a photograph in an old magazine of a Watutsi queen who looks just like Zeely. Geeder, caught up in her fanciful imaginings, tells the neighbor children that Zeely is a queen. When word reaches Zeely, she decides to have a talk with Geeder to help her understand that reality is sometimes as special as fantasy. Her wise stories leave Geeder with much to ponder. Geeder and Zeely are fine role models who inspire the reader to continue the search for a better world.

Ages 8 up

Suggestions for the Classroom

1. What did Geeder learn from Zeely? Why is Zeely such an important character in children's literature? Read *Women of Hope* (see page 120) for more strong African American female characters.

2. Rewrite the part about the hog drive from Zeely's perspective. Discuss the rights of all animals to be treated with kindness.

3. Read *In the Beginning: Creation Stories from Around the World* by Virginia Hamilton. Does it include a story similar to Zeely's? Create a class mural or individual paintings based on Zeely's story about the beginning of the world.

4. Reread the descriptions of the rooms in Uncle Ross's house. Have you ever been in a pantry, pump room, or parlor? Make a sketch of your favorite room in the farmhouse and write a paragraph about it.

5. Choose parts of the book to dramatize. Zeely's story about her home in Canada lends itself nicely to dramatization.

6. Geeder and Willie Bea in *Willie Bea and the Time the Martians Landed* have a lot in common. How are they alike? Different? Write a story about the two of them at Uncle Ross's farm.

7. This is Virginia Hamilton's first book and it is still in print. What other books has she written? Set up a center in your classroom with all of her books.

Joyce Hansen

Austin Hansen

African American (1942–)

Birthday: October 18
Address: P.O. Box 3462
West Columbia, South Carolina 29171

"Encourage your students to write from their hearts—to look at what is right before them and to use that as material for stories and poems." (Personal Communication)

"The more we learn about each other, the less we will be afraid of each other. Underneath our differences there is a common ground where we all connect as humans." (Personal Communication)

Books by Joyce Hansen

Between Two Fires: Black Soldiers in the Civil War. **Franklin Watts, Inc., 1993.**

Breaking Ground, Breaking Silence: The Story of New York's African Burial Ground. **Written with Gary McGowan. Holt, 1998.**

The Captive. **Scholastic, 1994.**

The Gift-Giver. **Houghton Mifflin, 1980.**

Home Boy. **Houghton Mifflin, 1982.**

I Thought My Soul Would Rise and Fly: The Diary of Patsy, a Freed Girl. **Scholastic, 1997.**

Out From This Place **(sequel to *Which Way Freedom?*). Walker & Company, 1988.**

Which Way Freedom? **Walker & Company, 1986.**

Women of Hope: African Americans Who Made a Difference. **Scholastic, 1998.**

Yellow Bird and Me **(sequel to *The Gift-Giver*). Clarion, 1986.**

Joyce Hansen was born October 18, 1942 in New York City. From an early age, she loved books; she remembers her mother reading to her and wishing she knew how to read. When she went to school, the children were not encouraged to create their own stories or poems so she did not think of herself as a writer until later. She did well in school and was an avid reader.

Hansen's love of books and writing came from her mother who wanted to be a journalist, but did not get to finish high school because of the Depression. She learned the art of storytelling from her father.

Hansen earned her B.A. from Pace University and her M.A. in English from New York University. She taught creative writing in a New York City intermediate school as well as literature and writing at Empire State College. She has written a number of significant books for young people. "I hope to be able to continue writing as long as I can hold a pen" (personal communication). Her books have been highly praised, and in 1989 the Bronx Historical Society presented her with its Edgar Allan Poe Award.

Hansen's ideas for her books come

from everyday life and events and people in her past. The people who lived in her old Bronx neighborhood and her extended family have provided her with enough characters to populate many books. Her ideas for the historical novels came from her own reading of history. She usually becomes fascinated by a little known historical event and uses that as the basis for a story.

One of Hansen's motivations for writing is to entice readers into the world of books. She writes what she knows to be true of young people, in fact, rather than in theory. Her characters function and feel like real people. They are young people who, through circumstances of birth and economic marginality, feel excluded. She hopes to nurture a sturdy pragmatism in young readers.

Hansen recently retired after teaching in the New York City public schools for twenty-two years. She presently lives in South Carolina where she is a full-time writer.

- **Civil War**
- **U.S. history**

Between Two Fires: Black Soldiers in the Civil War

This carefully researched book documents the neglected history of the 180,000 African Americans who fought in the Civil War. The recruitment, training, and struggles of the Black soldiers who made up ten percent of the Union Army is dramatically chronicled through their personal stories drawn from accounts by journalists and other observers, officers' reports, the soldier's own letters and diaries, and other historical sources. Hansen has written a much needed book detailing the experiences of the un-celebrated, often unnamed African Americans who braved two fires—enemy fire and the fire of racism—in a courageous attempt to prove their loyalty and worth and to gain liberty and justice. Photographs, a bibliography including primary sources, and an index are included.

Ages 10 up

Suggestions for the Classroom

1. This is an excellent book to supplement the information provided by history textbooks. Analyze your textbook(s) to see if information about the African American soldiers who fought in the Civil War is included. Information about the contributions of people of African descent as well as other diverse groups is often left out of teaching materials. Why? Discuss the impact that omission and exclusion has on everyone. How do you feel about being told only part of the story of your country's history? Brainstorm a list of recommendations for the way history textbooks should be researched and written.

2. Read and discuss the Author's Note. Discuss the ways in which racism ultimately weakens a nation and makes victims of us all.

3. What were the two fires? (enemy fire and the fire of prejudice) What was The Other Enemy? (racism) What forms did racism take? (Unequal pay, improper health care and medical attention, restrictions on promotion, recruitment restrictions, extreme punishment, unfair expectations, etc.) Discuss.

4. Notice that Hansen included the contributions of women during the Civil War. Who were these women? Does your history books mention them? Evaluate.

Breaking Ground, Breaking Silence: The Story of New York's African Burial Ground

- **Archaeology**
- **Cemeteries**
- **New York City**

In another important effort to reclaim lost history, Joyce Hansen describes the rediscovery and study of the African burial site found in Manhattan in 1991 and what it reveals about the lives of Black people in Colonial times. This well-researched book traces the history of African descent people in New York City from the first slaves to 1827 when slavery was finally abolished in the state.

Ages 10 up

Suggestions for the Classroom

1. Reread and discuss the Foreword and the Epilogue. Discuss quotes such as "A people who had no voice when they were living, and left no written records, would at last have their story told." (p. 13).

2. ". . . the ground opened up like a giant history book." (p.12). Hansen hopes to encourage young people to consider archaeological work as a career. Discuss how what we learn from the past helps us understand who we are now.

The Captive

Coretta Scott King Honor Book
African Studies Association Children's Book Award
Notable Children's Trade Book in the Field of Social Studies

- **Historical fiction**
- **Slavery**

Inspired by the slave narrative "The Life of Olaudah Equiano, or Gustavus Vassa, the African," this riveting first-person story covers twenty-three years in the life of a young Ashanti aristocrat. Vivid details recount the horror of Kofi's experiences from his 1788 kidnapping in West Africa to his agonizing voyage on a slave ship to his cruel enslavement on a Massachusetts farm. Deprived of his freedom, language, and rights, Kofi never forgot his family and heritage. Finally, he escaped and met Paul Cuffe, the sea captain and abolitionist, who helped him gain his freedom. This thoughtfully researched and well-crafted novel perceptively contrasts two cultures and reveals the inhumanity and injustices of an abhorrent era in history. It is especially significant because it is one of the few books for young readers available that addresses the slave trade in Africa.

Ages 10 up

Suggestions for the Classroom

1. How did Kofi's flute sustain him through the grief and hardship he faced? What did the flute symbolize for him? Discuss other events, beliefs, memories, and individuals that helped him endure the twenty-three year nightmare.

2. Find and analyze the descriptions of Kofi's feelings about learning to speak, read, and write in a new language such as: "Words grew on my tongue like the green leaves on the trees." (p. 133).

3. Hansen perceptively contrasts Kofi's two worlds. Discuss passages about the differences in climate, customs, beliefs, and behavior such as the following: "Again, I wondered why people in this strange place didn't carry baskets on their heads as any sensible person would do." (p. 118).

4. Reread and discuss Kofi's realization about his father's slave: "Oppong was wrong to betray Kwame, but one human being could never own another." (p. 127). Discuss Kofi, Ama, and Joseph's decision to dedicate their lives to helping fugitives who escaped from slavery.

- **Peer pressure**
- **Friendship**
- **The Bronx**

The Gift-Giver

This is a beautiful story of friendship set in the Bronx in New York City. The neighborhood and the individual children (especially Doris and Amir) are portrayed with sensitivity and insight. Doris, who has been struggling with peer pressure and her parents' strict rules, is amazed that Amir, a gentle loner and the new boy on the block, doesn't seem to care what the other kids think. As they become friends, they help each other grow in self-confidence and understanding of others. This well written, perceptive portrayal of a young girl's coming of age presents the inner city as a place where people struggle, dream, and grow. Modified Africanized English is used in both narrative and dialogue. Don't miss the sequel, *Yellow Bird and Me.*

Ages 9 up

Suggestions for the Classroom

1. How did Doris change during the story? Include the relationship with her mother. Predict what she will be like in sixth grade. Read *Yellow Bird and Me* to see if your predictions are accurate.

2. What did Doris learn from Sherman's grandmother and the Nit Nowns? (not to prejudge people) Find examples of how she put this learning into practice.

3. Joyce Hansen wrote about being strong enough not to follow the crowd. Which characters resisted peer pressure? Discuss the nature of peer pressure. Write advice for students who are struggling with peer pressure.

4. What was the name of the school the children attended? (Paul Laurence Dunbar) Explain. [Paul Laurence Dunbar (1872–1906) was a gifted African American poet and novelist. See *Paul Laurence Dunbar* by Patricia McKissack. (See page 163.)] Discuss the significance of naming schools after people of color. Research the names of schools in your city. Are any named after people of color and/or women? If not, find out why these groups have been left out. What can you do to make sure they are included in the future?

- **Diary**
- **Historical fiction**
- **Reconstruction Era**
- **South Carolina**

I Thought My Soul Would Rise and Fly: The Diary of Patsy, a Freed Girl

Coretta Scott King Honor Book Award

This inspiring book traces the growth of an orphaned recently freed slave in South Carolina in 1865, right after the end of the Civil War. Through diary format that captures the drama of the times, Joyce Hansen tells the compelling story of Patsy, who secretly taught herself to read and write. As her confidence increases, she overcomes her stutter, and follows her dream of becoming a teacher.

Ages 9 up

Suggestions for the Classroom

1. Before reading this book, discuss perceptions of the quality of life of newly freed slaves after the Civil War. (Many people assume that life suddenly improved.) After reading this book, discuss the obstacles that remained.

2. Reread and discuss the epilogue, historical note, and the additional material appended. As with many of Joyce Hansen's books, this is an excellent resource to supplement the information provided by history textbooks.

3. Document Patsy's journey toward personal and intellectual freedom through quotes such as "My heart and head hold so many thoughts, but my mouth is like a jailer that won't release them" (p. 84). Discuss the significance of Patsy's chosen name, Phillis Frederick.

4. The title of this book comes from the song "Free at Last" (see pages 192–193). After learning the words and music for this song, research and sing other freedom songs.

Out From This Place

- Historical fiction
- Civil War
- Slavery
- Fugitive slaves

This is the sequel to *Which Way Freedom?* In *Which Way Freedom?*, readers met Easter and Obi, slaves who heard that freedom was possible and who made a daring escape to find it. Now this book is Easter's story. Based on events that happened during the Civil War, this absorbing book tells about the newly freed people that were settled on tracts of land on the islands off the Carolina coast. Forty thousand people were relocated in this region and were given temporary title to the abandoned lands formerly held by the Confederates. But in May of 1865, President Andrew Jackson changed this policy and the land was returned to the former owners. Some African Americans, refusing to give back their acreage, armed themselves and fought to keep the land until they were forcibly removed by the army. However, there were cases where freed people were able to purchase land. New Canaan, in *Out From This Place,* is based on an all-African American community in South Carolina, developed after the Civil War.

Ages 10 up

Suggestions for the Classroom

1. Before reading the book, discuss perceptions about the quality of life of the former slaves after the Civil War. Do students think life was suddenly greatly improved? Then revisit these perceptions after reading the book.

2. Read about the Reconstruction period in your textbooks. Do the textbooks mention the events that Joyce Hansen includes in her books? Discuss the perspectives presented in your textbook and evaluate them.

3. Find and discuss or respond in writing to quotes such as the following: "The whole world opened to me when I learned to read." (Mary McLeod Bethune).

Which Way Freedom?

Coretta Scott King Honor Book
American Library Association Notable Book
CCBC Choices
NCSS–CBC Notable Children's Trade Book in the Field of Social Studies

- Historical fiction
- Civil War
- Slavery
- Fugitive slaves
- Death

1861–1864 South Carolina. This dramatic historical fiction novel is based on the story of the Twenty-fifth Corps, which was the first army corps composed entirely of African American regiments. Some 200,000 African Americans fought in the Civil War. Historically, their contributions have been neglected. Obi escapes slavery, joins an African American Union regiment and survives the bloody massacre at Fort Pillow, Tennessee. His dream is to find his mother from whom he had been sold away when he was younger, and to be reunited with his slavemates, Easter and Jason, and for them all to go together in freedom to Mexico. His plans are changed by the war but as the book ends, there is hope that he might go North with a new friend. Don't miss the sequel, *Out From This Place.*

Ages 10 up

Suggestions for the Classroom

1. Read and discuss the quotes from original sources that introduce each chapter.

2. Research the Civil War. Do the books you checked out include information about the contributions of the 200,000 African Americans who fought in the war? Analyze the historical neglect of information about the contributions of African Americans. Discuss Hansen's motivations for writing this book.

3. Make a list of the losses Obi experienced including the deaths of Buka and Daniel, separation from Easter, Jason, and his mother, etc. Discuss and/or write about each.

4. How did Obi feel about his name (Obi Jennings), wearing boots, and learning to read? Put yourself in Obi's place during the beating. Write about your feelings.

- **Biography**
- **Women**

Women of Hope: African Americans Who Made a Difference

Inspirational biographies of thirteen African American women accompanied by striking full page black-and-white photographs. Includes a list of thirty-five additional women and an annotated bibliography. These beautiful images of strong, courageous, and creative women will nourish the hearts and minds of people of all ages and backgrounds.

All Ages

Suggestions for the Classroom

1. This exquisitely designed book is a very special treasure. Read and discuss one biography a day. Invite youngsters to select women from the appended list for further research and to share their findings with the class.

2. This book is based on a series of posters entitled Women of Hope, available through Bread and Roses Cultural Project, Inc., 330 West 42nd Street, Floor 7, New York, NY 10036. 212-631-4565. Order the posters and display them in your school or library. There is a very strong connection between images and identity!

- **Dyslexia**
- **Friendship**
- **Peer pressure**
- **Drama**
- **The Bronx**
- **Teachers**

Yellow Bird and Me

In this sequel to *The Gift-Giver,* Doris adjusts to the loss of Amir, her best friend, who had to move away to a group home. Doris gets better acquainted with Yellow Bird, the class cut-up and sixth grade basketball star. Although she had always regarded him as annoying, she begins to realize that despite his silly ways, he is shy underneath. As she begins to help him with his studies, a strong, new friendship develops. Hansen again has done an excellent job with the characterization. This plus the lively dialogue and the strong city setting within a busy, thriving neighborhood add up to a warm, satisfying book. The book incorporates sensitive information about dyslexia.

Ages 9 up

Suggestions for the Classroom

1. In what ways did Doris's perceptions of Yellow Bird change? Make two lists: one of her early perceptions, and one of her later perceptions. Have you ever misjudged someone? Discuss what happened.

2. Did Doris follow through on her resolutions at the end of *The Gift-Giver*? She experienced many changes in the two books. Discuss these changes and what prompted them. Be sure to include her growing assertiveness in talking to Mrs. Barker, standing up to Russell, and going out on a limb to help friends.

3. Amir encouraged Doris to try to see inside Yellow Bird. Did Doris try to see inside Mrs. Barker? Did Mrs. Barker try to see inside her students? Have you tried to see inside someone? How did that change your perceptions? Discuss.

4. Examine the chapter titles. Why are they written this way? (People with dyslexia sometimes see mirror images. Joyce Hansen wants us to understand the problems this presents with reading.) What is dyslexia? What did Joyce Hansen teach us about dyslexia? Why? (She is a retired educator who works to sensitize her readers to problems with learning.)

Minfong Ho

Dewey Neild

Overseas Chinese (1951–)

Birthday: January 7
Contact: Dorothy Markinko
McIntosh and Otis, Inc.
310 Madison Avenue
New York, New York 10017

"I feel lucky to have lived in such diverse cultures, and to have learnt to love each one. Writing, for me, is a bit like weaving together threads of different colors to make a sarong with intricate patterns."
(Personal Communication)

Books by Minfong Ho

Brother Rabbit: A Cambodian Tale. **Written with Saphan Ros. Illustrated by Jennifer Hewitson. Lothrop, Lee & Shepard, 1997.**

The Clay Marble. **Farrar, Straus, & Giroux 1991; 1993; Singapore Times, 1991; Silver Burdett, 1996.**

Hush! A Thai Lullaby. **Illustrated by Holly Meade. Orchard, 1996.**

Maples in the Mist: Children's Poems from the Tang Dynasty. **(Translator) Lothrop, Lee & Shepard, 1996.**

Rice Without Rain. **Andre Deutch London, 1986; Heinemann UK, 1989; Singapore Times; Lothrop, Lee & Shepard, 1990.**

Sing to the Dawn. **Illustrated by Kwoncjan Ho. Lothrop, Lee & Shepard, 1975; Singapore Times, 1978.**

The Two Brothers. **Written with Saphan Ros. Illustrated by Jean & Mou-sien Tseng. Lothrop, Lee & Shepard, 1995.**

Minfong Ho was born January 7, 1951 in Rangoon, Burma and grew up on the outskirts of Bangkok, Thailand in an airy house next to a fishpond, large garden, and rice fields where water buffalo wallowed in mudholes. Her parents, who are from China, recited poetry and told her bedtime stories in Chinese. So she thinks of Chinese as the language of her heart. She gradually absorbed Thai from interacting with people in the marketplaces, streets, and temple fairs of Bangkok. For her, Thai is a functional language and she thinks of it as the language of her hands. Much later, she learned English at school, so she thinks of English as the language of her head. Today she is fluent in Chinese, Thai, and English, and also speaks basic French.

After completing her initial schooling in Thailand, Ho studied Chinese literature at Tunghai University in Taiwan. She earned a B.A. in Economics and History and an M.F.A. in Creative Writing at Cornell University in Ithaca, New York. She started to write only after she left home as a way to combat homesickness. Her first book, *Sing to the Dawn,* grew out of those early words she wrote about her homeland. Since then she has written a number of other excellent award winning books for young readers. She is one of the few authors in the United States who is writing children's and young adult books set in Cambodia and Thailand. Rooted in her personal experiences, her work is distinguished by its authenticity, historical analysis, and social commentary.

In addition to writing books for young readers, Ho has worked as a journalist in Singapore, taught at a university in Thailand, and volunteered as a relief worker on the Thai-Cambodian border. Having lived in six countries, Ho notes, "Writing is my way of gluing it, the bits of my roles, together." (*The Nation,* no date available). She identifies as Overseas Chinese, which "encompasses all ethnic Chinese living outside of China, and I DO feel a sense of kindred spirit with them, whether they are say, American-Chinese or Thai-Chinese, Peruvian-Chinese or Indonesian Chinese." (personal communication).

- **Folklore: Cambodia**
- **Rabbits**
- **Tricksters**

Brother Rabbit: A Cambodian Tale

New York Library's Children's Book List
International Reading Association Storytelling World Award Honor Title
Prints *Regional Award of Excellence for Design*

Ages 4–8

A recurring theme in Cambodian folktales (as with trickster tales from other cultures) involves a small but clever animal or person outwitting someone stronger but not as intelligent. In this captivating tale, Brother Rabbit outsmarts a sharp-fanged crocodile, two elephants, and a human. With exuberant mischief, funny, unexpected turns, and saucy illustrations, this tale is sure to provoke laughter and discussion in young audiences.

Suggestions for the Classroom

1. After rereading the author's note, discuss the reasons oppressed and less powerful people have a special affinity for trickster tales. Older students will be interested in discussing the history of Cambodia and the connection between this tale and Cambodian resiliency and perseverance.

2. The rabbit has a reputation in folklore for being quick-witted and mischievous. See the subject index for more trickster tales. After comparing and contrasting rabbit with other tricksters, youngsters might want to write and illustrate some trickster tales of their own.

- **Cambodia**
- **Refugees**
- **Historical fiction**
- **Death**
- **War**

The Clay Marble

American Bookseller Pick of the Lists
Notable Children's Trade Book in the Language Arts
Hungry Mind Review *Children's Book of Distinction*
NCSS-CBC Notable Children's Book in the Field of Social Studies
Parents Magazine's *List of Best Books*

Twelve-year-old Dara and her family are among the thousands of people who are forced to flee from their village in war-torn Cambodia in 1980. They travel in an oxcart to Nong Chan, a refugee camp on the border of

Cambodia and Thailand. When Dara and her new friend Jantu are separated from their families during a shelling, Jantu gives Dara a clay marble, saying, "It will make you strong and brave and patient." (p. 70). Believing in the magic of the marble, Dara reunites her family. Later, when she faces the death of Jantu and the warlike behavior of her brother, Dara realizes that the strength is in herself and not the marble. This moving story, written with passion and clarity, has many strengths: the portrayal of a strong female protagonist; the tangible details of life as a refugee; the dramatic grounding of the story in historical events outlined in the preface; the special friendship between the two young women; and the powerful indictment of a cruel and senseless war.

Ages 10–14

Suggestions for the Classroom

1. Minfong Ho worked as a nutritionist with an international relief organization on the Thai-Cambodian border in 1980. She dedicated this book to "the little girl who gave me a clay marble my first day at the Border." She provides powerful insights into the writing of this book in "The Shaping of the Clay Marble," *Battling Dragons: Issues and Controversy in Children's Literature* edited by Susan Lehr (Heinemann, 1995).

2. Discuss the symbolism of the clay marble, the toy village, and the rice seed.

3. Discuss the special friendship between Dara and Jantu. How did Jantu help Dara discover and develop her confidence and courage? How did this growth impact her life?

4. This book provides an excellent forum for a discussion about war and peace. Analyze the changes in Sarun and the implications for his family. Find quotes for discussion such as, "There are far more guns than farm tools being distributed, far more bullets than rice seed." (p. 142).

Hush! A Thai Lullaby

Caldecott Honor Book

American Library Association Notable Book

Horn Book *Fanfare*

Hungry Mind Review *Book of Distinction*

- **Poetry**
- **Thailand**
- **Babies**

Lilting verse and whimsical illustrations tell the story of a mother's efforts to quiet various animals so her baby can sleep. While mother hushes a succession of noisy animals from a small mosquito to a great gray elephant, the playful antics of baby provide an amusing parallel story.

Ages 2–5

Suggestions for the Classroom

1. This gentle tale is designed to be enjoyed time and time again, providing a warm experience of sharing between adult and child. Youngsters will enjoy chiming in on the rich animal voices and adding a few from their own time and place.

2. Reread and discuss the dedication. Bedtime stories sometimes leave youngsters "more wide-eyed than sleepy." Experiment with various interpretations of the animal sounds comparing those that stimulate with those that sooth.

- **Poetry**
- **Bilingual**
- **China**

Maples in the Mist: Children's Poems from the Tang Dynasty

International Reading Association Notable Book for a Global Society
American Library Association Notable Book
Children's Book Committee Book of the Year (Outstanding Merit)
Hungry Mind Review *Book of Distinction*
New York Public Library Children's Books "100 Titles for Reading and Sharing"

Sixteen ancient and timeless poems from the Tang Dynasty (618–907 A.D.) celebrate the precious wonders of life, from white egrets to spring blossoms to harvest moons. Writer Minfong Ho's inspiration for translating the poems from Chinese to English was "to bridge the linguistic gap between my mother's language and my children's. My mother had recited these poems when she was a child, as had her parents and grandparents before her for more than a thousand years."

Ages 5 up

Suggestions for the Classroom

1. Reread and discuss the note from the translator. Minfong Ho tells us that Chinese children have always learned to read by reading poetry. Discuss this innovative approach with children and colleagues.

2. Minfong Ho's mother made her memorize these poems. Discuss Ho's hope for "one long unbroken chain." What contribution might this book make toward that goal? Invite interested youngsters to memorize their favorite poem.

3. The Tang Dynasty is often referred to as the Golden Age of China, when the country was generally at peace and the people were prosperous. How might a peaceful atmosphere nurture creative work such as the poetry in this book?

4. Read and discuss "About the Poets." Many of these poets were famous during their lifetime. Invite youngsters to search for more poems by their favorite poet(s).

- **Historical fiction**
- **Class struggle**
- **Tradition and change**
- **Thailand**
- **Drought**

Rice Without Rain

American Library Association Best Book for Young Adults
Booklist *Editors' Choice*
New York Public Library Books for the Teen Age Award
Parents *Choice Award*
First Prize: National Book Development Council of Singapore
Second Place, Prose Section: Commonwealth Book Council of London

Based on student protests and peasant rebellions in Thailand in the 1970s, this compelling novel is important reading for anyone interested in understanding the issues surrounding civil rights movements around the world. As the dramatic story unfolds, seventeen-year-old Jinda Boonrueng gradually understands some of the complex factors impacting her family, village, and country during the political movement to combat inequities, poverty, and corruption. Two years of drought have brought deprivations to her village the summer four young intellectuals from Bangkok arrive. At first the farmers are suspicious of the social rebels but they finally decide to participate in the rent resistance movement. Jinda goes to Bangkok to speak at a political rally, which ends in a bloody massacre. This remarkable novel combines a survival theme and intense political story with a romantic subplot. *Rice Without Rain,* Minfong Ho's second novel, has been hailed as a valuable, memorable book, and has been popular with readers in the United States, especially with high school students.

Ages 12 up

Suggestions for the Classroom

1. Minfong Ho dedicated this book "To those who were killed at Thammasart University on October 6, 1976." Read and discuss the foreword and the role historical fiction plays in bringing alive important events from the past.

2. The title, adapted from a Thai folk ballad, symbolizes the importance of agriculture in the lives of people everywhere. Ho wrote that she used rice as a symbol for farmers. Discuss the symbolism in the book and Jinda's decision to stay with the soil.

3. Themes and topics for discussion and writing include: feudalism and democracy; traditional healing and modern medicine; taking charge of one's destiny and fighting those who get in the way; gender issues, idealism and realism; paradoxical issues in and strategies for creating a better world; people as symbols of feudal oppression; uneven distribution of wealth; "Thai in Thailand means free" (p. xii); rural and urban differences; family dynamics; exploitation of the masses; and change through peaceful or violent means.

4. "There are many roads to the same shrine." (p. 162). Compare and contrast the roads chosen by the farmers and the activists, the decisions made by Jinda and Ned, and the worlds represented by Sri and Jinda.

Sing to the Dawn

First Prize: Council on Interracial Books for Children

- **Gender bias**
- **Career goals**
- **Grandmothers**
- **Buddhism**
- **Thailand**

When she wins a scholarship competition, fourteen-year-old Dawan faces the hostility of her brother who places second and her father who says, "She's only a girl!" As she seeks support from family and community members, she faces her own ambivalence about leaving her beloved home and going to the big city. In her first book for young people, Minfong Ho has created a passionate cry for freedom and equality. It is one of the best books I have read in a long time! The compelling plot, admirable protagonist, respect for the natural world, and eloquent tribute to determination are sure to touch the hearts of readers of all backgrounds. Proceeds from the sale of the book were used to help set up a scholarship for young Thai women from the countryside. *Sing to the Dawn* was adapted as a musical in 1996 for the Singapore Arts Festival.

Ages 10 up

Suggestions for the Classroom

1. Themes and topics that are sure to stimulate discussion include: favoritism toward male children, socioeconomic class struggle, contrasts between city and country life, family dynamics, tradition and change, and the responsibility that accompanies opportunity.

2. Discuss the symbolism of the sparrows and the lotus bud. Then find quotes for discussion such as "Must one person's joy be based on another's sorrow?" (p. 138). Explore the roots of and solutions to scarcity.

3. Compare and contrast the responses of relatives and community members to Dawan's request for support. Discuss the tangled webs of sexism and brainstorm strategies for eradicating it.

4. Dawan had many admirable goals. Find passages that describe her hopes for building a better world and her thirst for knowledge such as "the pride, the power, and the promise of newly-learned knowledge" (p. 61).

5. For other dramatic stories about young women's struggles to get an education, read *Trouble's Child* by Mildred Pitts Walter, page 221 and *Bitter Herbs and Honey* by Barbara Cohen, page 55.

- Cambodia
- Folklore
- Buddhism

The Two Brothers

An American Bookseller Pick of the Lists

Raised in a Buddhist monastery, two brothers go out into the world to very different fates. Armed with the advice of a wise abbot, Kem becomes a merchant and prospers. But Sem ignores the words of wisdom and falls upon hard times. When he finally follows the abbot's guidelines, his life improves and he eventually becomes the king of Cambodia. This engaging tale reflects the rich texture of Cambodian life, including an introduction to village life, a Buddhist monastery, the royal court, and even a mythological creature.

Ages 5–9

Suggestions for the Classroom

1. The author's note provides an introduction to Cambodia's long and rich history. This is important reading for adults and older children. Parts of it may be adapted for discussion with young children.

2. Discuss the age-old conflict between free will and predestination and the way in which the authors reconciled it in this tale.

3. Adapting Minfong Ho's description of the folk plays in the author's note, try pantomiming the action while a narrator reads or tells the story. Invite everyone to participate in this captivating approach to creative dramatics.

Johanna Hurwitz

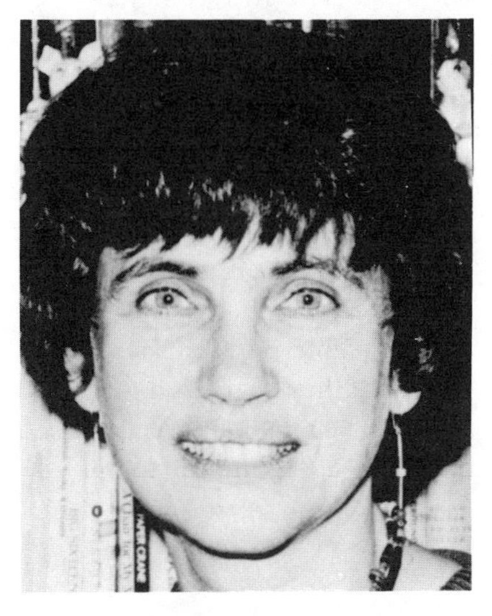

Jewish American (1937–)

Birthday: October 9
Contact: Morrow Junior Books
1350 Avenue of the Americas
New York, New York 10019

"I loved the library so much that I made the firm decision by age ten that someday I would become a librarian. And I also planned that I would write books, too." (Something About the Author, *Volume 20, p. 88)*

"I couldn't think of a single person in a book who was Jewish like me." *(*Once I Was a Plum Tree*)*

Books by Johanna Hurwitz

The Adventures of Ali Baba Bernstein. Morrow, 1985; 1995.

Aldo Applesauce. Morrow, 1979; 1989.

Aldo Ice Cream. Morrow, 1981; 1989.

Aldo Peanut Butter. Morrow, 1990; 1992.

Ali Baba Bernstein: Lost and Found. Morrow, 1992; 1995.

Anne Frank: Life in Hiding. The Jewish Publication Society, 1988; 1993.

Baseball Fever. Morrow, 1983; 1991.

Class President. Scholastic, 1990.

Class Clown. Morrow, 1987.

The Cold and Hot Winter. Morrow, 1988.

Dede Takes Charge. Morrow, 1984.

The Down and Up Fall. Morrow, 1988.

A Dream Come True: Meet the Author. Richard C. Owen, 1998.

"E" is for Elisa. Morrow, 1991.

Elisa in the Middle. Morrow, 1995.

Even Steven. Morrow, 1996.

Faraway Summer. Morrow, 1998.

Hot and Cold Summer. Morrow, 1989; 1995.

Hurray for Ali Baba Bernstein. Morrow, 1989.

Hurricane Elaine. Morrow, 1986.

Law of Gravity. Morrow, 1991.

Leonard Bernstein: A Passion for Music. Jewish Publication Society, 1993.

A Llama in the Family. Morrow, 1994; 1996.

Make Room for Elisa. Morrow, 1993; 1995.

Much Ado About Aldo. Morrow, 1978; 1989.

New Neighbors for Nora. Morrow, 1979; 1991.

New Shoes for Silvia. Morrow, 1993.

Nora and Mrs. Mind-Your-Own-Business. Morrow, 1982; 1991.

Once I Was a Plum Tree. Morrow, 1980; 1992.

Ozzie on His Own. Morrow, 1995.

Rip-Roaring Russell. Morrow, 1983; 1989.

Roz and Ozzie. Morrow, 1992; 1995.

Russell and Elisa. Morrow, 1990.

Russell Rides Again. Morrow, 1985.

***School's Out.* Morrow, 1991.**

***School Spirit.* Morrow, 1994.**

***Spring Break.* Morrow, 1997.**

***Superduper Teddy.* Morrow, 1990.**

***Teacher's Pet.* Scholastic, 1988.**

***Tough-Luck Karen.* Morrow, 1982; 1991.**

***The Up and Down Spring.* Morrow, 1993.**

***Yellow Blue Jay.* Morrow, 1993.**

Johanna Hurwitz was born October 9, 1937 in New York City. Her mother was a librarian and her father was a bookseller and journalist. Hurwitz's parents read to her often. "My parents met in a bookstore and there has never been a moment when books were not important in my life. . . . The walls of our apartment were lined with books." (*Something About the Author*, Volume 20, p. 88).

As soon as Hurwitz was old enough, she excitedly got her library card so she could have access to even more books. She knew at age ten that she wanted to become a librarian. She started working for the New York Public Library when she was still in high school and became a full fledged librarian in 1959. Having earned her B.A. at Queens College in 1958, she went right on to earn her M.A. in Library Science in 1959.

In 1976 Hurwitz's first book for children, *Busybody Nora*, was published. Since then she has written many more books for young people. A natural storyteller, she has a special skill in describing commonplace situations with humor. She has also addressed significant issues with sensitivity and warmth. She writes not only about Jewish children but children of other ethnic groups as well, such as Aldo, the Italian vegetarian boy in the Aldo series, and Julio Sanchez, the Latino boy featured in *Class President* and *Class Clown*.

Johanna Hurwitz gets her ideas for writing from her memories and her observations of the children with whom she works. She can remember her childhood in great detail. She also gets ideas from the experiences of her daughter and son. Her friends know that they might find themselves or their animal companions in one of her engaging books.

Aldo Applesauce

An IRA/CBC Children's Choice

- **Moving**
- **Vegetarianism**
- **Friendship**

This is the second book in the Aldo series. Fourth-grader Aldo Sossi moves with his family from New York City to Woodside, New Jersey. This is the story of Aldo's adjustment to his new house, school, neighborhood, and city. His classmates start calling him Applesauce when he accidentally spills the applesauce from his vegetarian lunch. DeDe, a girl who wears a fake moustache, is the only friendly classmate. Aldo's latest misadventures will be greeted with smiles and sympathetic recognition. Hurwitz has written another excellent book about what causes children pleasure and embarrassment and how they respond to changes. Aldo is an important character in children's literature because he is a nonconformist who is true to himself. This is one of the few books for children about vegetarianism.

Ages 8 up

Suggestions for the Classroom

1. Read the other books in the Aldo series. Make a character board featuring all the characters in the books.

2. How does Aldo resist peer pressure? In what ways does he remain true to his beliefs? What are Aldo's reasons for not eating tuna? Discuss.

3. Discuss Aldo's best friends, Peabody and Poughkeepsie, the cats. Did you know that animals can be best friends with humans? Each animal is an individual, as unique as each human.

4. Make a list of the changes Aldo faced because of moving. Have you ever moved? What changes did you face? Make a "How to Adjust to Moving" booklet giving advice to other students.

Aldo Ice Cream

An IRA/CBC Children's Choice

- **Elderly people**
- **Vegetarianism**
- **Birthdays**

This is the third book in the Aldo series. Nine-year-old Aldo Sossi discovers the satisfaction of doing volunteer work for Meals On Wheels to help the older and housebound people of his community. He also decides to try to earn the money needed to buy his sister the ice cream freezer she wants for her birthday. Aldo's love for animals, his ingenuity, and his divergent thinking make him fascinating company for readers of all ages.

Ages 8 up

Suggestions for the Classroom

1. Predict how Aldo will spend his ninth summer. Aldo is a curious person and likes to try new things. Write about something new you tried or learned recently. Do you think it is important to take risks? Why or why not?

2. What is ichthyology? How did Aldo make friends with Mr. Puccini? What did they have in common?

3. Mrs. Thomas's and Karen's birthdays were on the same day. How much older was Mrs. Thomas? (Eighty years) Predict what Aldo will give Mrs. Thomas for her birthday.

4. "Sometimes, when his sisters teased him, Aldo thought he liked animals even better than people." Discuss why Aldo felt that way.

Aldo Peanut Butter

- **Dogs**
- **Vegetarianism**

This is the fourth book in the Aldo series. Aldo is now eleven years old and holding strong to his resourceful, divergent ways of thinking. In this book, he tries to train his two new puppy friends. When his parents have to leave for two weeks in July, Aldo and his sisters learn that running a household is harder than it looks. Aldo and DeDe solve the mystery of the visitor who tears up the neighbor's lawn. And Aldo comes up with the idea of his grandparents renting the house next door for a few months while his grandfather recuperates from a serious illness.

Ages 8 up

Suggestions for the Classroom

1. Predict who the villain is before finishing the book. Were you right?

2. What is a humane exterminator? What happened to the raccoon? Read Petey Moroni's *Camp Runamok Diary* by Pat Cummings for another encounter between a raccoon and humans.

3. Stop before reading Chapter 10. Predict to whom Mrs. Crosby will rent her house. Were you right? Why did Mrs. Crosby tell Aldo he would make a fine real estate agent?

4. How did Aldo feel about the lobster? How did he solve the problem? Discuss vegetarianism. (See Suggestions for the Classroom for *Much Ado About Aldo* for more information on vegetarianism.)

5. Discuss statements such as "He liked his family, but he sometimes felt he liked animals even more."

- **Biography**
- **World War II**
- **Holocaust**
- **History**
- **Death**

Anne Frank: Life in Hiding

A Notable 1988 Children's Trade Book in the Field of Social Studies
Nominated for the Texas Blue Bonnet Award

This excellent biography tells about Anne Frank and her family, their lives before World War II, the Nazi persecution of Jews, the Franks' two years in hiding, and the tragic ending of Anne's life. Anne kept a diary and wrote about those two years of hiding. After the war ended, her father found her diary and arranged to have it published. Her account of the horrors of war was widely read; it still touches readers all over the world. Hurwitz has written an outstanding biography, enabling younger readers to learn about Anne Frank. Includes a map, a list of important dates, and an excellent index.

Ages 8 up

Suggestions for the Classroom

1. Study the map in the front of the book. Find Frankfurt, Amsterdam, Westerbork, Auschwitz, and Bergen-Belsen.

2. How did Anne feel about her diary? What are the rewards of journal writing?

3. An optional activity for older students: If Anne had been able to continue writing in her diary after she was sent to the concentration camps, what might she have written? Choose one of the following: Westerbork, Auschwitz, or Bergen-Belsen.

4. Anne planned to be a journalist. Write an article she might have written after the war was over if she had survived.

5. Write a poem about any or all of the following: Anne's early childhood, Anne and her family in hiding, and/or the concentration camps. Read *I Never Saw Another Butterfly.*

6. Anne's diary was made into a movie, a play, and a ballet. Make a list of places and things named after Anne Frank including stamps, roses, schools, clubs, homes, youth hostels, forests, tulip, etc.

7. Reread the Author's Note. Discuss Hurwitz' reasons for writing this book.

8. What can we each do to prevent such atrocities from ever happening again?

9. Read other books about the Holocaust. (See *The Upstairs Room* and *Journey Back* by Johanna Reiss on pages 177–178. See the Suggestions for the Classroom for each of these books.)

- **Puerto Rico**
- **Leadership**
- **Teachers**

Class President

This is the sequel to *Teacher's Pet.* Julio (pronounced Hulio) Sanchez is surprised to find that his new fifth-grade teacher is also Latino. When Mr. Ernesto Flores announces that they will have an election for class president, the students begin learning about the skills it takes to be a good leader. Julio learns more about his heritage and his own specialness as the campaign progresses. Hurwitz has a knack for getting inside kids' heads as well as for portraying classroom dynamics. See *Teacher's Pet* for the story of these same students' fourth-grade experiences.

Ages 8–12

Suggestions for the Classroom

1. Make a list of qualities necessary to be a good leader. Compare your list with the list Julio's class created. For whom would you have voted? Why? Debate with classmates.

2. Role play the meeting with the principal. Write about a similar experience that you had.

3. Find Puerto Rico on a map. What did Julio teach his classmates about Puerto Rico? (That Puerto Ricans are American citizens.) Discuss Julio's feelings about this.

4. Julio thought he wasn't good with words. Do you agree? (Think about the meeting with the principal.) Discuss self-esteem. Make a list of things Julio learned about himself. Discuss.

5. How would you spend a million dollars? Devise a plan and present it to your class. (Good for cooperative group work.)

A Dream Come True: Meet the Author

- **Autobiography**
- **Authorship**

In this delightful autobiography, Johanna Hurwitz shares early memories, introduces the members of her family, and describes how she turns ideas into books. "I had a secret dream. Ever since I was young, I wanted to be a writer." Fascinating text and photographs.

Ages 6–10

Suggestions for the Classroom

1. This autobiography is perfect for introducing an Author Study of Johanna Hurwitz. When youngsters identify closely with an author, they are more motivated to read her books. By nurturing the bond between reader and writer, we help youngsters understand the creative process and learn to read as writers.

2. Wherever Hurwitz goes, she jots down ideas for future books. Discuss her sources of inspiration, her creative process, her daily activities, and how they are all intertwined.

3. How did Hurwitz make her dream come true? Examine her complete body of work and discuss her contributions to the field of children's literature.

Faraway Summer

- **Diaries/Journals**
- **Farm life**
- **Vermont**

Under the auspices of The Fresh Air Fund, Hadassah Rabinowitz, a poor Jewish orphan from New York City, spends two weeks at a farm in Vermont during the summer of 1910. With her journal as her closest companion, twelve-year-old Dossi reflects on her interactions with her Christian host family and her new experiences. She not only learns about gardening and canning, fireflies and stars, snowflakes and milking cows, but about friendships and forgiveness. Engaging historical details are woven into this richly textured novel about expectations, understanding, and growth.

Ages 8–12

Suggestions for the Classroom

1. When Dossi arrived at the farm, she wasn't sure she wanted to stay. At the end of the two weeks, she was anxious to return the following summer. What happened during those fourteen days to change her mind? Discuss first impressions and the wisdom of giving new ideas and experiences time to percolate.

2. Discuss the role Dossi's journal played in helping her analyze situations, cope with challenges, and solve problems.

3. Additional discussion and writing topics include: city and country life; cross-cultural experiences and friendships, the Fresh Air Fund; the Triangle Shirtwaist Factory; poverty; the snowflake photographs; and the varied sources and inspirations authors use to create books like this one.

4. Discuss quotes such as "You can't keep trouble from coming, but you don't have to give it a chair to sit in." (p. 106).

- **Vegetarianism**
- **Animal rights**
- **Science**

Much Ado About Aldo

This is the first book in the Aldo series. Eight-year-old Aldo Sossi, an animal lover, is interested in everything! When his teacher introduces a new unit on the relationships of animals and humans, Aldo is intrigued. He loves the new crickets that arrive to live in the classroom. But when the chameleons arrive, Aldo realizes that the relationship they are studying is between consumer and consumed. Deeply shocked, he gives up eating meat and embarks on an attempt to rescue his friends, the crickets. A tender story about confronting a conflict of principles and making significant personal decisions. Engaging, earnest, humorous. Be sure to read the other books in the Aldo series.

Ages 8 up

Suggestions for the Classroom

1. World Vegetarian Day is October 1. Create a menu for a celebration.

2. Aldo is one of the few vegetarians in books for young readers. Why did he decide to become a vegetarian? Some very famous people were vegetarians. See how many of these famous historical names you recognize: Plato, Diogenes, Pythagoras, Buddha, Seneca, Virgil, Ovid, Horace, St. Paul, Plutarch, Shakespeare, Leonardo da Vinci, Newton, Rousseau, Voltaire, Benjamin Franklin, Darwin, Emerson, General William Booth, Thoreau, Shelley, Alexander Pope, Tagore, Tolstoy, H. G. Wells, Edison, Einstein, George Bernard Shaw, Schweitzer, General George Montgomery, Gandhi. More recent vegetarians include: Linda and Paul McCartney, k. d. lang, Cassandra Elvira Peterson, E. B. White, Frances Ann Day, Alex Pacheco, Geoffrey Giuliano (formerly Ronald McDonald), Carl Sagan, Jane Goodall, and Peter Singer.

3. What is a cruelty free diet? (a diet that does not cause the suffering or death of any animal)

4. Did you know that meat production and livestock agriculture use hundreds of billions of gallons of water every day for crop irrigation? Produce serious soil erosion? Use more energy per capita than the less developed countries spend per capita on energy for *all* purposes? Are the major contributors to deforestation in the U.S. and in the tropical forests of Central and South America, where forests are being chopped down at the rate of 25–100 acres per minute?

5. Valuable resources on vegetarianism include the following books: *Good for Me* by Marilyn Burns, *Diet and Nutrition* by Brian Ward, *Charlotte's Web* by E. B. White, *The Complete Guide and Cookbook for Raising Your Child as a Vegetarian* by Nina and Michael Shandler, and *Vegetarian Children* by Sharon Yntema. For further information contact the North American Vegetarian Society, P.O. Box 72, Dolgeville, NY 11329. Read the magazine *PETA Kids* (People for the Ethical Treatment of Animals), P.O. Box 42516, Washington, D.C. 20015 (subscription with tax deductible donation).

- **Seder**
- **Bronx**
- **World War II**
- **Passover**
- **Jewish identity**

Once I Was a Plum Tree

This is the warm and humorous yet serious story of ten-year-old Geraldine Flam's search in 1947 for her Jewish identity. Her parents are nonobservant Jews and say, "We are assimilated. We fit into American life like everyone else." Gerry's ancestors came to the United States in the 1850s. During World War I, her grandfather changed his German-sounding name from Pflaumenbaum, which means plum tree, to Flam to show that he was truly American. Gerry often feels rootless: She doesn't fit in with her Catholic friends or her Jewish classmates. But through her persistence and her new friendships with refugees from Nazi Germany, she finally begins to learn what being Jewish means. In this first person narrative, the reader gains insight into Gerry's thoughts and feelings and identifies with her quest as she deals with the contradictions, questions, and exclusions in her life.

Ages 9 up

Suggestions for the Classroom

1. What were some of the contradictions in Gerry's life? Are there any contradictions in your life? Write about them.

2. What were some of the anti-Semitic things that happened to Gerry and her family? Include examples such as the swastika on the mailbox, the incident when Paul stopped Gerry and Edgar on the street and accused them of killing Jesus, etc. Discuss. Have you experienced or witnessed such bigotry? Respond in writing.

3. What philosophy did Gerry's parents have about their Jewishness? Did Gerry understand their thinking? Do you think she ever will?

4. In what ways was Gerry different from her schoolmates?

5. What did Gerry learn from the Wulfs? What are some of the possible directions she might go with her quest to establish her identity?

6. Discuss Gerry's thoughts and feelings about piano lessons, Girl Scouts, the Star of David, the Bronx, kosher kitchens, the Wulfs, and her family.

7. Discuss and/or respond in writing to quotes such as: "I am glad that I am me. And for once I really meant it."

8. Gerry had the courage to be herself. How was she different from her parents? From her grandparents? Are all Jewish people alike? Do all people of any group agree with each other about everything?

Teacher's Pet

- **School**
- **Teachers**
- **Competition**

Cricket Kaufman doesn't have many friends because she has always been too busy competing for the teachers' attentions. But now that she is in fourth grade, she finds that her new teacher has a different philosophy about her students. Cricket also gradually realizes that Zoe Mitchell, a new student who is also a high achiever, has something to teach her. Cricket re-evaluates her competitive style and begins learning how to be a good friend. See *Class President* for the story of Cricket's and her classmates' experiences in fifth grade.

Ages 8–12

Suggestions for the Classroom

1. Make a list of things that went wrong for Cricket. How was fourth grade different from K–3? Predict how she will handle these changes.

2. Discuss Zoe's observation, "That's very sexist of her. Girls are strong enough to carry their own books, too." Make a list of sexist incidents that you have noticed. What can you do to create an awareness of gender bias? Write an editorial.

3. Compare Zoe's ideas about teachers' pets with Cricket's.

4. In what ways did Cricket change? Write about some changes that you have made. Interview an adult about changes they have made. Discuss.

5. Choose a related activity such as researching birthstones, writing an article for a newspaper, or writing about the double meaning of the title of the book.

6. Predict what will happen in the sequel, *Class President.*

Joy Nozomi Kogawa

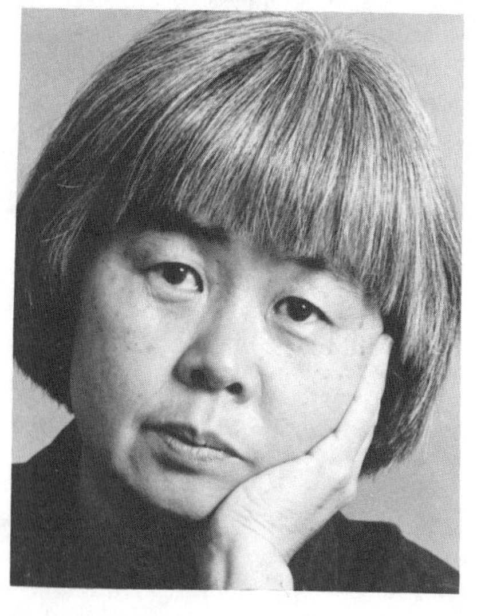

Japanese Canadian (1935–)

Birthday: June 6
Contact: Writers' Union of Canada
24 Ryerson Avenue
Toronto, Ontario, Canada, M5T 2P3

"It is hard to understand, but Japanese Canadians were treated as enemies at home, even though we were good Canadians. Not one Japanese Canadian was ever found to be a traitor to our country."
(Naomi's Road)

"We come from Canada, this land that is like every land, filled with the wise, the fearful, the compassionate, the corrupt." (Obasan)

Books by Joy Kogawa

FOR CHILDREN

Naomi's Road. **Oxford University, 1988; Stoddart Canada, 1994.**

FOR YOUNG ADULTS

Naomi no Michi. **Shogakkan, Japan.**

Obasan. **Lester & Orpen Dennys Canada, 1981; David Godine, 1982; Penguin Canada, 1983; Anchor Books, 1994.**

FOR ADULTS

A Choice of Dreams. **(Poetry) McClelland & Stewart, 1974.**

Itsuka. **(Novel) Viking, 1992; Penguin, 1993, Doubleday, 1994.**

Jericho Road. **(Poetry) McClelland & Stewart, 1977.**

The Rain Ascends. **(Novel) Knopf Canada, 1995; Vintage Canada, 1996.**

The Splintered Moon. **(Poetry) University of New Brunswick, 1967.**

Woman in the Woods. **(Poetry) Borgo Press, 1995; Mosaic Press, 1996.**

Joy Kogawa was born June 6, 1935 in Vancouver, British Columbia, Canada. She is a Nisei, the child of Japanese immigrant parents. Her mother was a kindergarten teacher and her father was a minister. Kogawa's books for young people are fictionalized accounts of her experiences as a Japanese Canadian during World War II. Her family was torn apart by Canadian government officials and exiled into the Canadian wilderness. Canada and Japan were enemies and Japanese Canadians were treated with hatred and cruelty by their government and by some other Canadians. They were evacuated from their homes and relocated. Their property was liquidated. Not one Japanese Canadian was ever found to be a traitor to Canada. (See the Author Unit on Yoshiko Uchida for information on the way Japanese Americans were treated during this time.)

Kogawa attended the University of Alberta in 1954, the Anglican Women's Training College in 1956, the Conservatory of Music in 1956, and the University of Saskatchewan in 1968. She has been a freelance writer and a writer-in-residence at the University of Ottawa.

Joy Kogawa is a superbly gifted poet and writer. Her first novel, *Obasan,* won many awards. Her second book, *Naomi's Road,* is written for younger children. Both books are based on her experiences during World War II. And both are beautifully written and very powerful books. *Naomi's Road* is the first Canadian novel for young readers to deal with this ugly chapter in Canadian history. Kogawa has received numerous honors and awards including the Grace MacInnis Visiting Scholar Award, the Urban Alliance Race Relations Award, and Doctor of Laws or Letters, Honoris Causa from three universities.

Naomi's Road

- **Fictionalized autobiography**
- **History**
- **Canada**
- **World War II**
- **Relocation of Japanese Canadians**
- **Aunts**

Naomi's Road is Kogawa's first book for young children and the first Canadian novel for young readers to deal with a tragic and painful part of Canadian history. The story is told by Naomi Nakane about her childhood experiences during World War II. We follow Naomi from her home in Vancouver to an internment camp in the interior of British Columbia, and then to a farm in Alberta, feeling the impact of war through the voice of a child growing up with prejudice and hardship. Even though the book deals with racism and persecution, Naomi's strength of spirit enables her to also experience hope and understanding. This is an important book written with the skill of a poet. Do not avoid it because of the tragic subject matter. Joy Kogawa has a gift for balancing the horrific with a sense of hope.

Kogawa writes, ""It is hard to understand, but Japanese Canadians were treated as enemies at home, even though we were good Canadians. Not one Japanese Canadian was ever found to be a traitor to our country. Yet our cameras and our cars, radios and fishing boats were taken away. After that our homes and businesses were also taken and we were sent to live in camps in the mountains."

Ages 8 up

Suggestions for the Classroom

1. Read "A letter from the author" in the front of the book. Discuss and respond in writing.

2. What does the title mean? What is Naomi's road? Discuss a variety of interpretations.

3. Read Daddy's definition of war. Write your own definition of war.

4. Where did Naomi's mother go and why didn't she return? (She went to Japan to take care of her ill mother and then couldn't return because of the war.) Discuss.

5. "The world is beautiful as long as there is music." Compose a song that Stephen might have played to cheer up the family. How can music heal?

6. Reread and discuss Naomi's dream. How did it relate to her experiences with racism, separation, and relocation?

7. Discuss and/or respond in writing to quotes such as: "There is a time for crying . . . Someday the time for laughing will come."

8. Even though this book is about a very sad time, Joy Kogawa is able to leave the reader with a sense of hope. How does she do this? Find words, phrases, and sentences that have a hopeful feeling.

9. Read books about the evacuation and relocation of Japanese Americans. See Yoshiko Uchida's chapter starting on page 191.

10. *Naomi's Road* and other books about this period in history are available through Asian American Books for All Ages Catalog, P.O. Box 1587, San Mateo, CA 94401; 650-343-9408.

- **Fictionalized autobiography**
- **History**
- **World War II**
- **Canada**
- **Relocation of Japanese Canadians**
- **Aunts**

Obasan

Before Columbus Foundation American Book Award
American Library Association Notable Book Citation
Canadian Authors Association Book of the Year Award
Periodical Distributors Best Paperback Award
First Novel Award—Books in Canada

This is Joy Kogawa's powerful fictionalized account of her experiences as a Japanese Canadian child during World War II and its aftermath. This intense, deeply-felt novel is brilliantly poetic in exposing the racist horrors of war. Obasan's narrator, Naomi Nakane, searches for the truth about what happened to her, to her family, and to her people. Her quest to understand the incomprehensible is unforgettably poignant. The losses of home, property, relatives, community, nationality, and all rights, cause her to respond wearily, "the sadness and the absence are like a long winter storm . . . burying me beneath a monochromatic weight." Evacuation, relocations, living in a chicken coop, working in beet fields, her father's illness and death, her mother's disappearance, the silence, abuse, nightmares, and more are all here in this portrayal of lives shattered by war. Note: Issei—first generation; Nisei—second generation; Sansei—third generation.

Ages 14 up

Suggestions for the Classroom

1. This is a significant book about a tragic time that all young people should know about so that it never happens again. Important questions include: How could this have happened? Could it happen again? What can we do to prevent such atrocities?

2. Select quotes such as the following for discussion and written response: "How well they both hid the cacophony life wrote in their bones." "To a people for whom community was the essence of life, destruction of community was the destruction of life."

3. *Obasan* is such a powerful book that some readers will want to synthesize their thoughts and feelings in another form. Options include poetry, drama, music, art, dance, journal writing, etc.

4. Why did "speech hide like an animal in a storm"? When the incomprehensible happens, people often find it difficult to express their thoughts and feelings.

5. Research the evacuation and relocation of Japanese Americans. See Yoshiko Uchida's chapter on pages 191–203.

6. Kogawa wrote *Itsuka* in which she explores important questions such as: When would the incarceration of the Japanese Canadians be recognized as a wrong doing? When would the government compensate them for the lost property that was never returned?

Jeanne M. Lee

Chinese American (1943–)

Birthday: May 17
Contact: Farrar, Straus & Giroux
19 Union Square West
New York, New York 10003

"Read as much as you can afford the time; live, taste the world, then write about it." (Personal Communication)

Books by Jeanne Lee

WRITTEN AND ILLUSTRATED

***Ba-Nam.* Holt, 1987.**

***I Once Was a Monkey.* Farrar, Straus & Giroux, 1999.**

***Legend of the Li River: An Ancient Chinese Tale.* Holt, 1983.**

***Legend of the Milky Way.* Holt, 1982; 1990.**

***Silent Lotus.* Farrar, Straus & Giroux, 1991; 1994.**

***The Song of Mu Lan.* Front Street, 1995.**

***Toad is the Uncle of Heaven: A Vietnamese Folktale.* Holt, 1985; 1989.**

ILLUSTRATED

Butterfly Boy *by Laurence Yep. Putnam, 1994.* ***See page 238.***

***The Ch'i-lin Purse: A Collection of Ancient Chinese Stories* retold by Linda Fang. Farrar, Straus & Giroux, 1995; 1997.**

Jeanne M. Lee spent her childhood in Vietnam. She has traveled extensively in Southeast Asia, Europe, and the United States. She received her B.A. in Fine Arts from Newton College of the Sacred Heart in Massachusetts.

Lee currently lives in Brookline, Massachusetts. She is a freelance artist, graphic illustrator, and author. Her illustrations and writing are characterized by simplicity and tranquility. Critics have praised her art for its restraint, elegance, and grace.

She writes, "When I was a child in South Asia, I was reading most of the time, imagining about far away places and drawing, drawing things that surrounded me. Now that I am older, I write about my young experiences yet still reading and imagining about far away places, and drawing the present, but also the past" (personal communication).

- **Elderly people**
- **Cemeteries**
- **Thanh-Minh Day**
- **Weather**

Ages 6 up

Ba-Nam

This story is based on the author's childhood experiences in South Vietnam. In Vietnam there is a special day of the year reserved for honoring ancestors. The day is Thanh-Minh (tan-min), meaning "pure and bright." On Thanh-Minh Day, families visit the graves of their ancestors and present them with offerings such as flowers, cakes, incense, and paper money.

At first, Nan is afraid of the old woman, Ba-Nam, who is the keeper of the graves. But when a severe storm comes up, Ba-Nam rescues Nan. Nan learns that Ba-Nam was injured by a falling tree during a storm long ago. By the time the family leaves the cemetery, Nan and Ba-Nam have become friends.

Suggestions for the Classroom

1. Why was Nan afraid of Ba-Nam at first? How did her feelings change? Why? What did Nan learn about judging people by their appearance? Have you ever wrongly prejudged someone? Write or tell about what happened.

2. Write a paragraph from Ba-Nam's perspective.

3. Write and illustrate a story about what might happen the following year when Nan and her family return to the cemetery.

4. Does your family honor ancestors? When? What traditions does your family have regarding Memorial Day, Thanh-Minh Day, Feast of Pure Brightness, Ching Ming, Days of the Dead, etc.

- **Folklore (Chinese)**

Ages 8 up

The Ch'i-lin Purse: A Collection of Ancient Chinese Stories

(Ch'i-lin is pronounced chee-lin.) Extensively researched, these nine entertaining tales were adapted from Chinese opera, legends, and early novels. More sophisticated than most folktales, the stories have elaborate plots with unexpected reversals of fortune and twists of fate. Jeanne M. Lee painstakingly rendered period details in her graceful black-and-white illustrations. Includes a pronunciation guide, glossary, source notes, and author's note.

Suggestions for the Classroom

1. These tales are vivid, lively, and read aloud well. They are also excellent for independent reading. The operatic roots of several of the tales are apparent. Transformations and disguises will inspire lively dramatizations.

2. Invite students to respond to quotes such as "If you have a chance to do something good, be sure to do it. Happiness will come back to you." (p. 14). Other discussion and writing themes/topics include: charity rewarded, wit triumphant, supernatural spirits, reformed thieves, and resolving differences.

3. For more folktales from China, see *The Rainbow People* and *Tongues of Jade* by Laurence Yep. For folklore from many cultures, see the Subject Index.

4. "The Two Miss Peonys" has also appeared in its Sino-Vietnamese version in *The Golden Carp and Other Tales from Vietnam* by Lynette Dyer Vuong. Compare the two versions of this tale.

Legend of the Li River: An Ancient Chinese Tale

- **Folklore (China)**
- **Great Wall of China**

This ancient Chinese tale is beautifully retold and illustrated by Jeanne Lee. The story tells how the beauty of the Li River came into being. A sea princess, who wishes to lessen the hardships on the poor laborers forced to build the Great Wall of China, seeks help from the Goddess of Mercy. In her efforts to help the laborers, the princess creates beauty where it is least expected.

All Ages

Suggestions for the Classroom

1. Do you think the sea princess would have the courage to speak to Chin Shih Huang Ti, the Emperor of China during the building of the Great Wall? If so, what might she say? Dramatize a meeting where she speaks on behalf of the laborers.

2. Find the Li River and the Great Wall on a map. Estimate the length of the Great Wall (approximately 1500 miles). Study pictures of the Great Wall. Then create a class mural of the Great Wall. Include the Li River.

3. Read books about the Great Wall such as *The Great Wall of China* by Leonard Everett Fisher. Discuss the cruelties involved in building the wall including regulations against rest and runaways, the burying of dissidents alive in the rocks of the wall, and general terrorizing of the workers. Why do you think the legend of the Li River was created? (When people are forced to live under horrific conditions, they sometimes survive through their creativity.)

Legend of the Milky Way

A Reading Rainbow Book

- **Folklore (Chinese)**
- **Legend**
- **Milky Way**
- **Stars**
- **Origin tale**
- **Constellations**
- **Space**

This ancient Chinese legend is elegantly retold and illustrated by Jeanne M. Lee. This is her version of the sky-maiden origin tale or how the Milky Way was formed. A heavenly weaver princess is drawn to earth by the music of a young shepherd playing his flute. She marries the earthly young man and is happy in her new home. But the Queen Mother has her brought home and then separates the two by turning them into stars separated by the Milky Way. Constellation information is included on the last page.

All Ages

Suggestions for the Classroom

1. Compare this book with other versions of the origin of the Milky Way (see Subject Index). Then read nonfiction books about the Milky Way.

2. Reread the last page. Then, on a clear night, look for the bridge of birds across the "Silver River."

3. Invent a way to travel through the Milky Way.

4. Read other origin and creation stories. See *In the Beginning: Creation Stories from Around the World* by Virginia Hamilton on page 106.

- **Deafness**
- **Dance**
- **Cambodian court ballet**
- **Aspirations**

Ages 5 up

Silent Lotus

Reading Rainbow *Selection*

Lotus, a young Cambodian girl who cannot hear or speak, loves to walk among the cranes, egrets, and herons, joining them in their graceful steps. When she travels to the palace in the city, she is enchanted by the temple dancers and is accepted as a dance student. As she studies, she begins to speak with her hands, body, and feet; she learns to tell the tales of the gods and kings through dance. She becomes the most famous dancer in the Kmer kingdom, dancing in the court and in the temple of the gods. Jeanne M. Lee, inspired by the beauty of the twelfth-century temple at Angkor Wat, beautifully combines vivid watercolors with the touching story of an eloquent dancer to bring to life the thousand-year-old tradition of the Cambodian court ballet.

Suggestions for the Classroom

1. How did Lotus deal with being deaf? How did her parents, playmates, the queen and king, and the other dancers treat her? Find other books with deaf characters such as *The Secret in the Dorm Attic* by Jean F. Andrews. Discuss the many faces of prejudice, including against deaf people.

2. Read other books about dance. What qualities did Lotus possess that helped her become such an accomplished dancer? Create a dance inspired by the movements of birds such as cranes, herons, and egrets.

3. The Cambodian court ballet has a thousand-year-old tradition. Discuss traditions. What might be the significance of the dances Lotus learned? Then discuss tradition and change. Do you think the dances may have changed through the years? Why or why not?

4. Read books about Cambodia such as *Cambodian Folk Stories from the Gatiloke*, retold by Muriel Carrison, which includes an extensive introduction, lengthy appendix, and a glossary, providing historical, geographical and cultural background information.

- **Bilingual (English and Chinese)**
- **Poetry**
- **Folklore**
- **Gender roles**
- **War**
- **China**

All Ages

The Song of Mu Lan

Originating during the Northern and Southern Dynasties (386–534 A.D.), this attractively presented folk poem celebrates the bravery of a young woman. When the emperor calls her ailing father to war, Mu Lan volunteers to take his place. Disguised as a male soldier, she shows remarkable skill as a warrior and becomes a famous general. After twelve hard years, she is honored with twelve medals of honor and a thousand strings of gold. Jeanne M. Lee's elegantly illustrated bilingual version of this 1500-year-old ballad is closely translated, with pleasing crisp stanzas. It is accompanied by the Chinese text reproduced in original calligraphy by Lee's father, Chan Bo Wan. The Sung and Ming versions of the poem are attractively reproduced on the end papers.

Suggestions for the Classroom

1. Fifteen centuries later, Mu Lan continues to be an inspiration to girls and women. Her story will prompt interesting discussions about gender roles and women in the military among readers of all ages.

2. Mu Lan's story has inspired numerous Chinese poems, essays, paintings, operas, and even comic books. Recently, Disney produced a movie based on her life. Compare and contrast these interpretations and the authenticity of each. Encourage readers to explore a variety of forms for presenting Mu Lan's story.

3. Readers of all ages will be interested in exploring the similarities and differences in the experiences of Mu Lan, Deborah Sampson, Emma Edmonds, Joan of Arc and other women. Invite students to dramatize, illustrate, or write about their findings.

4. Jeanne M. Lee carefully composed each scene, reminding the reader that this ballad has entered the repertoire of Chinese opera. How did she use her skills as an artist to achieve a balance between war and nature? Examine and discuss the illustrations in her other books.

Toad Is the Uncle of Heaven: A Vietnamese Folktale

Parents' Choice Honor Award for Illustration

- **Folktales**
- **Drought**
- **Rain**

Toad leads a rooster, a tiger, and some bees to ask the King of Heaven to send rain to the drought stricken earth. After several skirmishes, the King grants their wish and adds, "Uncle Toad, next time, when you need rain, you do not have to come all the way to these heavenly courts. Just croak, and I will know to send you rain." The book has elegant drawings in rich colors.

All Ages

Suggestions for the Classroom

1. In Vietnam, what does it mean if you call someone "Uncle"?

2. Like many folktales, this story lends itself nicely to dramatization. While the leader or an older child reads the story, everyone pantomimes the actions.

3. What does toad symbolize in Vietnam? (rain) Why? Write and illustrate a story about what might have happened the next time Toad needed rain.

4. What is a drought? What if we had a drought here? Make a list of ways we could save water. Then read *Drylongso* by Virginia Hamilton, which is also about droughts (see page 104). Dramatize a meeting between Toad and Drylongso.

George Littlechild

Photo: Matthew Jacob

Plains Cree Canadian (1958–)

Birthday: August 16
Contact: c/o Children's Book Press
246 First Street, Suite 101
San Francisco, California 94105
415-995-2200

"Working as an artist is my way of healing the pain of the past and helping the next generation of Indian people. My goal is to heighten awareness of the history and experiences of Native Peoples of the Americas and to promote understanding among all people."

Books by George Littlechild

WRITTEN AND ILLUSTRATED

***This Land Is My Land.* Children's Book Press, 1993.**

ILLUSTRATED

***How the Birch Tree Got Its Stripes.* Freda Ahenakew, translator and editor. Fifth House (Canada), 1989.**

***How the Mouse Got Brown Teeth.* Freda Ahenakew, translator. Fifth House (Canada), 1988.**

***In Honour of Our Grandmothers.* Poetry by Reisa Smiley Schneider and Garry Gottfriedson. Paintings by George Littlechild and Linda Spaner Dayan Frimer. Theytus Books (Canada), 1994.**

***A Man Called Raven* by Richard Van Camp. Children's Book Press, 1997.**

***What's the Most Beautiful Thing You Know about Horses?* by Richard Van Camp. Children's Book Press, 1998.**

FOREWORD AND DEDICATION

***We Are All Related: A Celebration of Our Cultural Heritage* by students at George T. Cunningham Elementary School, 2330 East 37th Avenue, Vancouver, BC, Canada V5R 2T3, 1996.**

George James Littlechild was born August 16, 1958 in Edmonton, Alberta, Canada. His mother, Rachel Littlechild, was Plains Cree Indian. His father, James E. Price, was Scottish, French, English, MicMac Indian, Welsh, and Dutch. After World War II, many Native people were forced to leave the reservations to try to find jobs in the cities. Unprepared for city life and white culture, many became involved with drugs, alcohol, and prostitution. George's grandparents, mother, and her sisters and brothers went to boarding schools where they grew up without their families and didn't learn how to raise children of their own. They were torn away from their culture, their language, their traditional ways, and their loved ones. Many boarding school survivors died on skid row of alcoholism, including George's mother. His father also died a violent death in the inner city.

Littlechild was taken in by a white family and he attended an all white school. The white students called him a "fat, ugly, stupid Indian." At that time, Littlechild didn't know what an Indian was. He heard these hateful words every day and eventually he started to believe them. Living among people who found him different and who didn't understand him, he learned that he was always wrong and that the white people were always right. His teachers graded the students by using stars; the gold stars were for the best students and the red stars meant failure. Littlechild remembers getting mostly red stars. He was taught the song "This land is your land, this land is my land." When he got older, he thought it was very strange to be singing about the ownership of the land. He learned that the first people to live on the land were Indians and that they prefer to be called First Nations or First Peoples because all the land was their homeland first. Littlechild also remembers his teachers saying that Columbus was a great man because he had discovered America. Even then, Littlechild wondered how Columbus could have discovered America when his people were already there.

Years later, Littlechild included figures and symbols of these hurtful experiences in his paintings to assuage the pain and to heighten awareness of the history of his people. The words he uses to describe his brother Raymond could also be used to describe him: "My brother Raymond overcame all the hardships. He succeeded against tremendous odds. He stayed in school. He went on to the University and earned a degree. . . . He is proud of being an Indian and he is helping to give the next generation the opportunities he never had."

Today, Littlechild is an artist of international renown. His paintings combine texture and vivid color with a spiritual quality and an awareness of both Native and non-Indian worlds. He thinks of his art as a means of expressing his feelings about both cultures, using a contemporary style to communicate the Native traditions that are the focus of his work. He maintains his native identity while drawing from the best of all cultures.

Writing is often incorporated into his drawings. Littlechild believes it is another natural form of expression that adds to the impact of his work. He frequently uses geometrical shapes such as circles and triangles that have symbolic meanings. He is inspired to paint at night; as he stares at the night sky, he begins to dream. "The sky is like a doorway into the other world, the spirit world."

Littlechild is also a highly accomplished printmaker. He is a graduate from the Art and Design program at Red Deer College; he completed his Bachelor of Fine Arts Degree at the Nova Scotia College of Art and Design; and he completed an Independent Study Program at the Banff Centre in Alberta. In the meantime, he has been adding to an already substantial list of group exhibition credits and has had many solo exhibitions. He is represented in several public collections, including the Native Secretariat, Trent University, Red Deer College, the Alberta Art Foundation, and Alberta Indian Arts and Crafts Society. Littlechild's unique style won him a Second Runner-up Award in the Alberta Indian Arts and Crafts Society's 1986 ASUM MENA Festival. He has won a number of other scholarships, grants, and awards and has illustrated several children's books.

Littlechild's work is celebrated for its themes from his Plains Cree background, its exciting use of color, and its spirit of playfulness. His paintings have been exhibited in galleries in Canada, the United States, Japan, and Europe. For more information about George Littlechild, see *This Land Is My Land* on page 145.

- **Canada**
- **Myth**
- **Trees**
- **Cree**
- **Art**

Ages 5 up

How the Birch Tree Got Its Stripes: A Cree Story for Children

This is a student story that was written in a Cree course at Saskatoon, Canada. A boy catches some ducks and while they are cooking, he asks two birch trees to hold him fast and not let him get away so he can see if he can go for a long time without eating. Later the birch trees will not let him go and the animals eat all the ducks. When the birch trees finally release him, he is so angry that he breaks off some willow branches and gives the birches a real whipping. And that's why, to this day, birch trees are striped. Full page illustrations.

Suggestions for the Classroom

1. What if the birch trees still would not let go? Encourage many responses—maybe someone would rescue the boy, etc.

2. What advice do you have for the boy? Brainstorm and compile a class list.

3. This book was written by a group of students. Write a group story about another way that the birch might have gotten its stripes, and illustrate it.

4. Go outside and look at trees. Then choose a tree and write and illustrate a story about how that tree got the way it is.

- **Canada**
- **Myth**
- **Mice**
- **Cree**

Ages 5 up

How the Mouse Got Brown Teeth: A Cree Story for Children

This is a student story that was written in a Cree course at Saskatoon, Canada. When a boy catches the sun in his snare, he asks the animals to bite through the snare. Finally the mouse frees the sun but burns her teeth in the effort. And that's why, even to this day, the mouse has brown teeth. Full page illustrations.

Suggestions for the Classroom

1. What if the sun had remained in the snare?

2. What if the boy had obeyed his grandmother? How could he get his arrow back? What advice do you have for the boy? How else might he have solved the problem?

3. Why did the animals try to help? What other animals might have been able to help?

4. This is a student story. After discussing ways to create a student story, publish one of your own.

- **Art**
- **Poetry**
- **Cultural survival**

Ages 14 up

In Honour of Our Grandmothers

The poets and artists who created this magnificent book—two Native, two Jewish, two women, two men—embarked upon a healing journey of remembrance, commemoration, and transformation. This is a powerful book filled with compelling poetry and luminous art that cry out in sorrow and pain, resolution and hope. The paintings and poetry by these gifted Native and Jewish artists and poets are linked by the similarities of their childhood experiences, their strong connection with their ancestors, their acute awareness of the oppression of their peoples, and their dedication to cultural survival.

Suggestions for the Classroom

1. This profound book should be part of the library collection in every high school and college!

2. Themes and topics for discussion, writing, and art include: cultural survival, genocide, forced assimilation, historic inheritance, the Holocaust, harmony between humanity and nature, history through art and poetry, remembrance or silence, and similarities between the histories of Native and Jewish people.

3. Reread and discuss the preface. Respond in writing to quotes such as, "They tried to kill the spirit of both of our people." "When we remember, our culture survives."

A Man Called Raven

- **Ravens**
- **Kindness to animals**
- **Respect for nature**

Based on Dogrib folklore, this intriguing book is a tribute to the wisdom of the raven and respect for all living beings. When two boys try to hurt a raven, a mysterious man enters their lives to teach them the story of the raven and the meaning of respect for nature. Well-written, brilliantly illustrated, with an important message, this is a wonderful book. As part of the transformation ritual, Raven Man was using tobacco, which is a sacred plant when used properly. With the growing awareness of the dangers of smoking and the impressionability of young people, information about this spiritual custom should have been provided.

Ages 6 up

Suggestions for the Classroom

1. Chris and Toby learned an important lesson. How will this experience change their behavior? Discuss what they will do the next time they see a raven. What might they tell children when they become elders?

2. Every once in a while, the raven became a human again to teach people that if they hurt any living being, they hurt themselves. Youngsters will realize that this man *was* the Raven Man, coming back to remind people that all life is connected. Discuss the significance of his lesson and how he gained this wisdom.

3. Encourage youngsters to think critically about the smoking issue. Smoking was not allowed in Toby and Chris's house. How was Raven Man's use of tobacco different? Because of the dangers of smoking, should have the author and publisher provided information about the spiritual custom of using tobacco as a sacred plant?

4. As a child, no one ever told me that animals deserve to be treated with respect and kindness. Do not assume that children already know this. Provide explicit messages about the importance of the ethical treatment of all animals, great and small.

This Land Is My Land

Jane Addams Picture Book Award
National Parenting Publication Award
Horn Book *Fanfare List*
Hungry Mind Review *"Children's Books of Distinction" Finalist*
Parent's Choice Book

- **Autobiographical short stories**
- **Plains Cree history**
- **Artists**

This is the first book George Littlechild has written, although he has illustrated several others. *This Land Is My Land* is an eloquent collection of autobiographical short stories accompanied by dramatic, vivid paintings. Beginning with the first meeting between his Plains Cree ancestors and the Europeans, he takes the reader on a powerful personal and historical journey of memories, insights, healing, and humor. Giving thanks to Wahkomkanak, his ancestors, he honors their wisdom and courage as he tells of their struggles and triumphs. After World War II, many Native people were forced to leave the reservations; unprepared for city life, some became caught up in drugs, alcohol, and prostitution. George Littlechild and his sisters and brothers were raised on welfare after both of their parents died violent deaths on skid row. "Life in the cities for us was just as much a prison as life on the reserves had been. . . . For me, working as an artist is my way of healing the pain of the past and helping the next generation of Indian people." George Littlechild dedicated this beautiful book to his ancestors and included rare photographs of eleven of them on the dedication page.

Ages 6 up

Suggestions for the Classroom

1. This book is an excellent historical resource as well as a poignant personal story and an artistic delight. With younger students, read and discuss one or two pages a day. For older students, teachers might use it with their literature and/or language arts classes, North American history units, and/or art classes.

2. Read and discuss the dedication page. Who are Wahkomkanak? (ancestors) Read the book to find out more about Littlechild's ancestors. Discuss the importance of his ancestors to him.

3. Find out more about Littlechild's childhood. What were some of the challenges he faced? How does he face hardships? (through his art) Discuss.

4. When Littlechild was a boy, he was taught the song "This land is your land, this land is my land." How did he feel about this song when he got older? Why?

5. Littlechild is an artist of international renown. Study his paintings in his books. How would you describe his painting style? Try some of his techniques in your next painting.

6. Art is very important to Littlechild. How does it help him? How do his paintings help others understand him and his people?

7. Choose a painting. Read the accompanying story to find out more about the meaning of the figures, shapes, and colors in the painting. Share your findings with your classmates.

8. How did Littlechild's trip to New York City influence his art? Discuss the fact that artists and writers are constantly learning and changing. Read *Talking With Artists* by Pat Cummings to find out more about the changes other artists have made.

9. Littlechild is known for his art, which celebrates a spirit of playfulness and humor as well as its exciting use of color and Plains Cree themes. In what ways did he balance the sad parts of his book with humor? How does humor help people deal with hardships?

10. Examine your history books to see if they include information from Native People's perspectives. Why is it important that we have information from multiple perspectives?

11. Children's Book Press published *This Land Is My Land.* Find out more about Children's Book Press, which is a nonprofit educational organization. What is their philosophy? What other books have they published? (See Author Units on Carmen Lomas Garza, page 83 and Min Paek, page 174.)

- **Art**
- **Bilingual**
- **Mixed ancestry**

We Are All Related: A Celebration of Our Cultural Heritage

This extraordinary book features art and writing by twenty-eight children, ranging in age from eight to twelve years old. For eight months these students were engaged in an intergenerational and intercultural project that eventually led to the publication of this unique book. Inspired by the art of George Littlechild, they each created a Heritage Collage and then wrote a piece to accompany it. The students' ancestors came from Canada, China, Fiji, Germany, Hong Kong, India, Ireland, Italy, Mexico, Philippines, Portugal, Ukraine, United Kingdom, and Vietnam. First Nations ancestry includes: Kwakiutl, Northern Tutchone, and Ojibway.

All Ages

Suggestions for the Classroom

1. Inspired by this remarkable book, enlist the support of colleagues, parents, and community members and initiate a similar project. Whether the project be large or small, do what you can to follow the example of the educators who implemented this exemplary project. For more information, write to: G. T. Cunningham School, 2330 East 37th Avenue, Vancouver, BC, Canada V5R 2T3.

2. After reading and discussing the book as a group, brainstorm related activities. Many youngsters will enjoy interviewing their elders, creating Heritage Collages, and writing pieces to accompany it. Note: Some youngsters might not have access to information about their ancestors. If they are adopted, they may be interested in rereading pages 36–38.

What's the Most Beautiful Thing You Know About Horses?

- **Horses**
- **Questions and answers**
- **Mixed ancestry**

On January's coldest day of the year in a small community in the Northwest Territories in Canada, a stranger to horses searches among family and friends for answers to the question: "What is the most beautiful thing you know about horses?" The answers he gets range from zany to profound: "They always know their way home." "They can run sideways." "Sometimes they like to compete with the wind." This humorous, one-of-a kind book follows no formula for story structure, yet it is a great success. Fascinated readers, both horse lovers and horse strangers, will find themselves responding to the interactive style of the text and paintings with their own brand of zaniness or profundity.

All Ages

Suggestions for the Classroom

1. Richard Van Camp and George Littlechild worked together to create this unique book. What is it that makes it so special? Explore the value of being innovative in approaching any task, including writing and painting.

2. Read and discuss the author's note on the last page. Richard Van Camp found that his curiosity was contagious. His humor, creativity, and inquisitiveness will spread to readers as they respond through writing, art, and discussion.

3. As with many of the books published by Children's Book Press, this title will appeal to readers of all ages. Invite children and adults alike to respond to the questions posed in the book. And even if they are strangers to horses, as was Richard Van Camp before embarking on this project, they will learn to appreciate the beauty of these magnificent animals.

Bette Bao Lord

Bachrach

Chinese American (1938–)

Birthday: November 3
Contact: HarperCollins Publishers
10 East 53rd Street
New York, New York 10022

"Look for the universal in all characters regardless of race, background and country." (Personal Communication)

"Writing is rewriting again and again until each word is the appropriate one, until each sentence flows into the next, until each paragraph achieves its purpose and reveals a voice." (Personal Communication)

Books by Bette Bao Lord

FOR CHILDREN

***In the Year of the Boar and Jackie Robinson.* Illustrated by Marc Simont. HarperCollins, 1984; 1986.**

FOR ADULTS

***Eighth Moon.* Knopf, 1990.**

***Legacies, a Chinese Mosaic.* Knopf, 1990; Macmillan, 1991.**

***The Middle Heart.* Knopf, 1996; Fawcett, 1997.**

***Spring Moon.* Avon, 1982; HarperCollins, 1990.**

Bette Bao Lord was born November 3, 1938 in Shanghai, China and came to the United States when she was eight years old. She tells about her first year in the United States in her fictionalized autobiographical novel for children, *In the Year of the Boar and Jackie Robinson.* She arrived in Brooklyn one day and the very next day enrolled in school. Because Chinese people consider a child to be one-year-old when born and two upon the new year, eight-year-old Bette was placed in the fifth grade. She didn't speak a word of English but rapidly learned the new language.

In college, she studied chemistry and earned an M.A. at the Fletcher School of Law and Diplomacy. She taught and performed modern dance in Geneva and Washington, DC. She has six honorary doctorates and was named to the International Women's Hall of Fame in 1989. She has won many other awards.

Lord has written several books for adults in addition to the one for children. Two of her books were bestsellers. One of her most recent novels, *The Middle Heart,* is the story of three childhood friends. The novel takes place in China from the 1930s to the 1990s. Lord has also written numerous articles for newspapers and magazines.

Lord served as a consultant to CBS News during the pro-democracy demonstrations in China in 1989. She and her husband, Ambassador

Winston Lord, were posted in Beijing from November 1985 through mid-April 1989.

For more information about Bette Bao Lord see *Something About the Author,* Volume 58.

In the Year of the Boar and Jackie Robinson

An American Library Association Notable Children's Book

- **Immigrants**
- **English as a Second Language**
- **Baseball**
- **China**

This touching, humorous story details the problems and triumphs ten-year-old Shirley Temple Wong experiences when she moves from China to the United States. Struggling with the new language, new classmates, and new customs, Shirley discovers baseball and Jackie Robinson. In realizing that an African American person, the grandson of a slave, can make a difference in America, Shirley discovers her own personal potential for growth and success. The story takes place over twelve months, January through December, 1947, The Year of the Boar, 4646. Marc Simont's adorable illustrations capture the amusing mood of the story.

"Here S. T. Wong was somebody. She felt as if she had the power of ten tigers, as if she had grown as tall as the Statue of Liberty."

Ages 8 up

Suggestions for the Classroom

1. Shirley Temple Wong left behind in China an ancestral home filled with relatives whose traditions reach back for thirty-nine generations. Discuss. Then make a list of problems she faced as a newcomer.

2. What were Shirley's names in China? (Bandit, Sixth Cousin) What might your name be?

3. How did Shirley get her new name? What name would you choose if you were moving to China? Why?

4. What was in the letter? (Father sent for Shirley and her mother to join him in the U.S.) How did each respond? Mother? (smile) Grandmother? (cry) Grandfather? (angry)

5. Describe Grandmother's feet. Research footbinding. Read *The Serpent's Children* by Laurence Yep for a description of an attempted footbinding. Discuss.

6. What were the two white boxes in the kitchen? (stove and icebox) Draw them as they are described in the book.

7. Reread Shirley's version of the Pledge to the Flag. Tell or write about a time when you got confused about some words.

8. Reread the tale of Wispy Whiskers. Discuss. Respond by writing and illustrating a related poem.

9. Reread Mrs. Rappaport's talk on Jackie Robinson and baseball. Read books about Jackie Robinson. (See *Thank You, Jackie Robinson* by Barbara Cohen.)

10. Find a Chinese or U.S. custom that led to confusion for Shirley and/or her family. Compile a class list. Discuss.

11. Reread Shirley's speech for Jackie Robinson. Then write a speech that you would like to give for Jackie Robinson.

12. Shirley and her mother traveled from Chungking, China to San Francisco to Brooklyn, New York. Trace their journey on a map.

13. Respond in writing or with a class discussion of the following quotes. Then find additional interesting quotes to discuss. "Upon your shoulders rests the reputation of all Chinese." "Things are not what they seem. Good can be bad. Bad can be good. Sadness can be happiness. Joy, sorrow."

14. This book tells about Bette Bao Lord's first year in the United States. Find out what she has done since then.

15. Research the Chinese zodiac. Read *The Rat, The Ox and the Zodiac: A Chinese Legend* by Dorothy Van Woerkom and *Chinese New Year* by Tricia Brown. Find your animal sign. Read about your traits. Make a poster showing your animal and your characteristics and illustrate it.

Sharon Bell Mathis

African American (1937–)

Birthday: February 26
Contact: Viking Penguin, Inc.
40 West 23rd Street
New York, New York 10010

"All I knew was that the more I wrote, the more I wanted to write."
(Something About the Author, *Volume 58, p. 130)*

"Writing allows me an opportunity to reenter childhood, to explore it anew, and to be enchanted."
(Autobiographical Sketches by Notable Authors of Books for Young Adults, *p. 135)*

Books by Sharon Bell Mathis

Brooklyn Story. **Illustrated by Charles Bible. Hill & Wang, 1970.**

Cartwheels. **Scholastic, 1977.**

The Hundred Penny Box. **Illustrated by Diane and Leo Dillon. Viking, 1975; Houghton Mifflin, 1995.**

Listen for the Fig Tree. **Puffin, 1974; 1990.**

Ray Charles. **HarperCollins, 1973.**

Red Dog, Blue Fly. **Illustrated by Jan Spivey Gilchrist. Viking, 1991; Puffin, 1995.**

Running Girl: The Diary of Ebonee Rose. **Harcourt Brace, 1997.**

Sidewalk Story. **Illustrated by Leo Carty. Viking, 1971; Puffin, 1986.**

Teacup Full of Roses. **Puffin, 1972; 1987.**

Sharon Bell Mathis was born February 26, 1937 in Atlantic City, New Jersey and grew up in Bedford Stuyvesant, Brooklyn, New York. As a child, she wrote poems and stories that made her mother very proud. Her mother also wrote poetry and sketched pictures. Mathis enjoyed reading and often read sitting on the fire escape outside their apartment. She felt that anything was possible as she sat and imagined on that fire escape. She read every chance she got; her mother also read constantly.

Mathis's mother was often sick. When Mathis grew into adolescence, her mother began to suffer heart attacks. Mathis, already an introverted teenager, grew more inward. She kept her circle extremely small. At school, she concentrated on writing.

After graduating from Morgan State College in Baltimore, Mathis taught Special Education in a junior high school in Washington. In 1974, she took a sabbatical leave to attend Catholic University where she earned an M.S. in Library Science. She continued to write while raising her three daughters and teaching. She also wrote a monthly column for *Ebony Jr.* She has won many awards and honors for her books. A retired school librarian, she now lives and writes in Fort Washington, Maryland.

For more information about Sharon Bell Mathis, see *Something About the Author,* Volume 58.

The Hundred Penny Box

Newbery Honor Book
New York Times *Outstanding Book*
Boston Globe–Horn Book *Honor Book for Text*
Child Study Association of America Children's Book of the Year
Notable Children's Trade Book in the Field of Social Studies
An American Library Association Notable Book

- **Aunts**
- **Keepsakes**
- **Elderly people**

Michael's great-great-aunt Dew is a hundred years old; she has an old box filled with pennies, one for each year of her life. Michael loves to count out the pennies while Aunt Dew recounts the story of each one, the story of her life. Michael's mother doesn't understand the significance of the box; she plans to throw it out and replace it with a new one. Michael knows the importance of saving the box that represents Aunt Dew's life. This touching book is uniquely illustrated with watercolors applied with cotton; the shadowy watercolors combine with the text to provide a fascinating study of childhood and advanced age.

Ages 6 up

Suggestions for the Classroom

1. Why do you think Michael was able to understand Aunt Dew when his mother couldn't?

2. Dramatize Michael trying to explain the importance of the hundred penny box to his mother.

3. Do you or does anyone in your family have a special keepsake? Write a story about that keepsake and why it is special. What if someone tried to take it away?

4. Make a list of possible keepsakes. Illustrate.

5. Read other books about elderly people (see Subject Index). Are they presented in a complete way or as stereotypes? Discuss. Write a short story about one of your elderly relatives.

6. Use in a math unit. If each person in your family saved a penny for each year of their life, how many pennies would there be altogether?

7. Write about something that happened each year of your life. Ask your parents to help you. Print on large charts and display around the room.

Listen for the Fig Tree

- **Blindness**
- **Grief**
- **Kwanzaa**
- **Poverty**
- **Death**

Sixteen-year-old Muffin deals with her mother's grief over the death of her father, in addition to poverty and her own blindness. Her first celebration of Kwanzaa gives her a sense of the past and the strength to deal with her problems.

Ages 12 up

Suggestions for the Classroom

1. Make a list of the challenges Muffin faced. Discuss each. Choose one and write about how you would cope if you were in a similar situation.

2. What advice do you think Muffin might have for someone who is facing some of the same problems she faced?

3. Research Kwanzaa. How did Kwanzaa help Muffin?

4. Read *Cousins* by Virginia Hamilton. (See page 103.) What did these two books teach you about the grieving process?

Red Dog, Blue Fly: Football Poems

- **Poetry**
- **Football**

Ages 7–10

Poetry and paintings combine to capture the excitement of football season. Football enthusiasts will enjoy this book from the first kickoff to the victory banquet. Colorful illustrations by Jan Spivey Gilchrist.

Suggestions for the Classroom

1. Discuss the significance of the title of the book.

2. Reread and discuss the poem "Football." Then write a poem to a basketball, softball, or volleyball.

3. Reread and discuss "Ebonee" and "Cheerleaders." Discuss gender bias in sports.

4. Reread and discuss "Leg Broken." Have you ever had a broken bone? Write a poem or story telling about it and illustrate it.

5. Use in a math unit. Make a class graph showing how many classmates have broken an arm, wrist, finger, leg, etc.

6. Reread and discuss "Cousins." Write a story or poem about one of your cousins.

7. Reread and discuss "Playoff Pizza" and "Victory Banquet." Dramatize a victory celebration your team might have.

8. Write a poem about your favorite sport and illustrate it. Combine these into a booklet or use for a bulletin board.

Running Girl: The Diary of Ebonee Rose

- **Diaries**
- **Running**
- **Track and field**

Ages 7–12

In her diary eleven-year-old Ebonee Rose records her passion for running, the inspiration she receives from the great African American women athletes who have come before her, and her preparation for the All-City Track Meet. Ebonee's thoughts, dreams, and fears are juxtaposed with colorful photographs of and inspiring quotes from extraordinary runners like Wilma Rudolph, Jackie Joyner-Kersee, and Gail Devers. *Running Girl* is a delightful tribute to the sport of running and to the great tradition of African American women champions.

Suggestions for the Classroom

1. Ebonee Rose was inspired by women runners who have broken color barriers and gender-based stereotypes. Invite youngsters to choose one of the women profiled in this book for further research. What kept them going "when the walls were closing in" (p. 40)?

2. Ebonee's doctor nicknamed her Little Encyclopedia. Her diary is filled with Olympic anecdotes and facts. What purpose did all this information serve for her? How might it help others who are facing similar challenges?

3. The sports/poetry connection is a natural extension just as it was for Mathis's earlier book, *Red Dog, Blue Fly: Football Poems*. Invite interested youngsters to print their poems on large sheets of colorful paper and display around the classroom or library.

4. In addition to the inspiration Ebonee received from women champions, relatives and friends supported her passion for running. What did each person do to help her succeed?

5. Discuss Queenie's friendship with Ebonee. Invite interested youngsters to create several diary entries Queenie might have written during the twenty days before the track meet.

6. The author's note lists contact organizations for youngsters interested in track club involvement. If there is no group in your area, she encourages young people to lobby adults to start one.

Sidewalk Story

Council on Interracial Books for Children Award Winner
Child Study Association of America's Children's Books of the Year

- **Eviction**
- **Friendship**
- **Poverty**

When her best friend's family is evicted from their apartment, nine-year-old Lilly Etta decides to try to do something to help. This sensitive, heart-warming story shows that one child *can* make a difference. "It didn't matter if nobody in the city cared; Lilly Etta did. She knew what friendship was and she wasn't going to let her friend be thrown out without a fight."

Ages 7–11

Suggestions for the Classroom

1. Do you think one child can make a difference? What did Lilly Etta do that made a difference? Discuss. Then write about something you have done or would like to do to make a difference.

2. Dramatize Lilly Etta's telephone call to Mr. Frazier.

3. What does eviction mean? Have you ever known anyone who was evicted? Write about what happened. Is eviction ever justified?

4. Write one sentence about the eviction from each person's perspective: Lilly Etta, Tanya, Mrs. Allen, Mrs. Brown, the landlord, the marshall, the movers, Mr. Frazier, and a person reading the newspaper. Discuss perceiving events and issues from different perspectives.

5. Write a letter from Tanya to Lilly Etta a few weeks later.

Teacup Full of Roses

An American Library Association Notable Book
A* New York Times *Outstanding Book of the Year

- **Death**
- **Drugs**
- **Aspirations**

This is the sensitive and beautifully written story of an African American urban family. The tragedy of one of the brother's drug addiction haunts the family. Joe has a plan to hold the family together and to achieve his own dreams at the same time.

Ages 12 up

Suggestions for the Classroom

1. How did Paul's drug addiction impact each of the members of his family?

2. Choose a character. Write a paragraph from her or his perspective. Compile into a classroom collection and share.

3. What do you think will happen next? Write a short sequel to this book.

4. Read and discuss other books by Sharon Bell Mathis.

5. Use this book with your program on drugs and alcohol.

Patricia C. McKissack

African American (1944–)

Birthday: August 9

Contact: All-Writing Services
P. O. Box 967
Chesterfield, Missouri 63006-0967

"Somewhere around age seven, I discovered reading. And so began my lifelong love affair with the printed word. To me, reading is like breathing, both are essential to life. . . . I write because there is a clear need for books written about the minority experience in America—fiction and nonfiction. I also write for the love of it!"

(The Inside Out—The Author Speaks: *Random House Brochure)*

Books by Patricia McKissack

African American Inventors. **Millbrook, 1994.**

African American Scientists. **Millbrook, 1994.**

Big Bug Book of the Alphabet. **Milliken, 1987.**

Big Bug Book of Counting. **Milliken, 1987.**

Big Bug Book of Opposites. **Milliken, 1987.**

Big Bug Book of Exercise. **Milliken, 1987.**

Big Bug Book of Places to Go. **Milliken, 1987.**

Big Bug Book of Things to Do. **Milliken, 1987.**

Bugs! **Children's, 1987; 1988.**

Can You Imagine? **Richard C. Owen, 1997.**

The Civil Rights Movement in America: 1865 to the Present. **Written with Fredrick McKissack. Regensteiner, 1987; Children's, 1991.**

Constance Stumbles. **Written with Fredrick McKissack. Children's, 1988.**

Country Mouse and City Mouse. **Children's, 1985.**

Dark-Thirty: Southern Tales of the Supernatural, The. **Illustrated by Brian Pinkney. Knopf, 1992; 1996; Random, 1998.**

Flossie and the Fox. **Illustrated by Rachel Isadora. Dial Books, 1986.**

Frederick Douglass: The Black Lion. **Written with Fredrick McKissack. Children's, 1987.**

Great African American Series **(18 biographies). Written with Fredrick McKissack. Enslow, 1992.**

History of Haiti. **Holt, 1996.**

It's the Truth, Christopher. **Augsburg Fortress, 1984.**

James Weldon Johnson: Lift Every Voice and Sing. **Children's, 1990.**

Jesse Jackson. **Scholastic, 1990.**

A Long Hard Journey: The Story of the Pullman Porter. **Written with Fredrick McKissack. Walker, 1989; 1995.**

Ma Dear's Aprons. **Illustrated by Floyd Cooper. Atheneum, 1997.**

Martin Luther King, Jr.: A Man to Remember. **Children's, 1984.**

Mary McLeod Bethune. **Children's, 1985; 1993.**

Messy Bessey. **Written with Fredrick McKissack. Children's, 1987.**

Messy Bessey's Birthday Sleepover. **Children's, 1998.**

Messy Bessey's Closet. **Written with Fredrick McKissack. Children's, 1989.**

Messey Bessey's Garden. **Written with Fredrick McKissack. Children's, 1991.**

Messy Bessey's School Desk. **Written with Fredrick McKissack. Children's, 1998.**

Million Fish . . . More or Less, A. **Illustrated by Dena Schutzer. Knopf, 1992; Random, 1996.**

Mirandy and Brother Wind. **Illustrated by Jerry Pinkney. Knopf, 1988.**

Monkey-Monkey's Trick. **Random, 1988.**

Nettie Jo's Friends. **Illustrated by Scott Cook. Alfred A. Knopf, 1989.**

Our Martin Luther King Book. **Child's World, 1986.**

Paul Laurence Dunbar: A Poet to Remember. **Children's, 1984.**

A Picture of Freedom: The Diary of Clotee, a Slave Girl. **Scholastic, 1997.**

Rebels Against Slavery: American Slave Revolts. **Written with Frederick McKissack. Scholastic, 1996.**

Red-Tail Angels: The Story of the Tuskegee Airmen of World War II. **Written with Fredrick McKissack. Walker, 1995.**

The Royal Kingdoms of Ghana, Mali, and Songhay: Life in Medieval Africa. **Written with Fredrick McKissack. Holt, 1995.**

Run Away Home. **Scholastic, 1997.**

Sojourner Truth: Ain't I a Woman? **Scholastic, 1992.**

Taking a Stand Against Racism and Racial Discrimination. **Written with Fredrick McKissack. Franklin Watts, 1990.**

Tennessee Trailblazers. **Written with Frederick McKissack. March, 1993.**

Who Is Coming? **Children's, 1989; 1990. (Available in Big Book format.)**

Who is Who? **Children's, 1983.**

Young, Black, and Determined: A Biography of Lorraine Hansberry. **Holiday, 1998.**

Patricia C. McKissack was born and raised in a small town outside Nashville, Tennessee. Long before she became a writer, she was a listener and an observer. Her relatives were dynamic and skilled storytellers. On hot summer evenings the family would gather on the porch and listen to Patricia's mother, grandmother, and grandfather tell stories.

When she was a child, Patricia had no idea that her heritage would one day be the springboard for her career. She loved reading and majored in English literature in college. She received her B.A. from Tennessee A. & I. University and her M.A. in early childhood education and children's literature from Webster University. She taught junior and senior high school English for nine years and then became a children's book editor. Six years later, she became a freelance writer. A year later, her husband gave up his career as an engineer to help her research and write stories about African American leaders.

Shocked when she discovered that her students had no concept of who Frederick Douglass and Mary McLeod Bethune were, McKissack was even more appalled when she realized that many of the other teachers had never heard of these heroines and heroes either. So she decided that she had to do something to preserve the stories of our country's great African American leaders. Subsequently, she has written over sixty books for young readers, winning many awards and honors.

McKissack believes that African American writers bring a deeper understanding, often based on personal experiences, to stories about their own history. Her mother inspired her to follow her dreams, the way Mary McLeod Bethune did. As Bethune-Cook College was built on $1.50 and a dream, so could McKissack accomplish her goals. This determination has resulted in a body of work that is a beautiful tribute to those who helped pave the way to freedom and dignity and to those who continue to strive to preserve it.

A special collection of children's books, primarily by African American authors, has been set up at Lindenwood College in St. Charles. The collection is called the McKissack Center for Black Children's Literature and contains all of the McKissacks' working papers and several reference books. The funds for the Center were donated by the owners of Book Lures, Inc., a publishing company in O'Fallon, Missouri.

- **Biography**
- **Inventors**

African American Inventors

In this commendable addition to the Proud American series, the McKissacks document the lives and achievements of African American inventors throughout the 19th and 20th centuries. They consider the inventors and their inventions within the context of American history and the sociological and technological state of the times. They provide an excellent description of patent law, explaining the five different types available. The life stories of individual inventors is fascinating, providing inspiration for young inventors. A bibliography and index are included.

Ages 9 up

Suggestions for the Classroom

1. This excellent book belongs in every library. If your library doesn't have it, write a rationale for why it should be included and present it to your librarian or principal.

2. Young people love to invent! Infuse the information in this fine book with a school-wide unit on Inventors and Inventions. Encourage youngsters to solve problems, design, create, invent, and try new ideas. Culminate with an Invention Convention, similar to a Science Fair. Invite parents, grandparents, and community members.

3. In the introduction, the McKissacks quote a Maryland politician who said that "not one black person [has] ever yet reached the dignity of an inventor." This is similar to a statement a professor made when I was in graduate school: "There were no women inventors." How might erroneous statements like these impact young people? How did the McKissacks respond?

- **Biography**
- **Scientists**

African American Scientists

This excellent book documents the lives and achievements of African American scientists from colonial days to the present, including Benjamin Banneker, George Washington Carver, Dr. Charles Drew, Shirley Ann Jackson, and Dr. Mae Carol Jemison. Their scientific contributions are placed within the larger context of United States history. Includes photographs, drawings, a bibliography, and an index.

Ages 9 up

Suggestions for the Classroom

1. Read and discuss the introduction. How will this book (and others by the McKissacks) help overcome several centuries of discrimination? How did each of the scientists profiled overcome hardships and follow their dreams?

2. People from each state will have local scientists to add to the roster. For example, Denverites are proud of the contributions of Dr. Justina Ford who was the first African American woman doctor in Colorado. Encourage youngsters to research African American scientists from their town or city. For more information about Justina Ford and other Colorado women scientists, see page 75.

3. After discussing the importance of role models, invite youngsters to examine the biographies in your library. How many are about African American scientists? Ask your school to include biographies about the scientists introduced in this book.

Can You Imagine?

- **Autobiography**
- **Authorship**

In this delightful autobiography, Patricia McKissack shares early memories, introduces the members of her family, shares early sources of inspiration, and describes how she turns ideas into books. She describes listening as a child to storytellers in her family and later telling her own stories to school children. Youngsters will especially enjoy the photographs of her when she was a child.

Ages 6–10

Suggestions for the Classroom

1. This autobiography is perfect for introducing an Author Study of Patricia McKissack. When youngsters identify closely with an author, they are more motivated to read her books. By nurturing the bond between reader and writer, we help youngsters learn to understand the creative process and learn to read as writers.

2. McKissack has written over sixty books and she still finds time to keep a journal. Inspired by her example, invite youngsters to keep a journal about their literary experiences.

3. McKissack wrote her first book about her favorite American poet, Paul Laurence Dunbar. See page 163. Examine her complete body of work and discuss her contributions to the field of children's literature.

4. Examine the sources of McKissack's imagination and creativity. She remembers a teacher saying, "You have a wonderful imagination." What a difference a comment like that can make to a child! This example serves as an inspiration to teachers everywhere.

The Civil Rights Movement in America: From 1865 to the Present

- **Civil Rights movement**
- **U.S. history**
- **U.S. Constitution**

From the beginning of Reconstruction to the present, this carefully researched book traces the struggle of African Americans to gain their civil rights. It includes an overview of the problems of some other groups: American Indian civil rights, Mexican American civil rights, rights of people with disabilities; and the women's movement. This large 320-page volume could be used as a textbook and/or reference book. The 120-year-struggle for freedom and justice is divided into three parts: "One Step Forward: Two Steps Back," "Separate As the Fingers On the Hand," and "Climbing to the Mountaintop." Highlights key people, places, and events. Excellent index and photos.

Ages 9 up

Suggestions for the Classroom

1. Use as a textbook and/or reference for U.S. history. Analyze textbooks to see what information about African Americans is included. Discuss omission as a form of bias and the damage it does.

2. Study the time lines. Compare them with the time lines in a traditional U.S. history textbook. Discuss.

3. After creating a list of the African American people included in the index, individuals or small groups might select one person for further research and share the results with the large group.

4. Read and discuss the poems "Booker T. & W. E. B." and "Sympathy." Why *does* the caged bird sing?

5. Analyze the origins of racism. After reading *Taking a Stand Against Racism and Racial Discrimination* by the same authors, discuss what you, your class, and your school can do to eradicate racism.

- **Bicycles**
- **Perseverance**

Ages 4–7

Constance Stumbles

A Rookie Reader. In spite of many setbacks, Constance doesn't give up. She keeps trying and finally learns to ride a bicycle. This charming book includes a word list.

Suggestions for the Classroom

1. Did Constance give up? If she had given up, would she have learned to ride the bicycle? What advice might she have for a younger person trying to learn something new? Roleplay.

2. Tell or write about learning to do something new such as riding a bicycle.

3. Older students might enjoy reading this book to younger children.

- **Ghost stories**
- **Horror stories**
- **African American history**
- **Slavery**

Ages 10 up

The Dark-Thirty: Southern Tales of the Supernatural

Newbery Honor Book

This is a collection of ten original, suspenseful tales rooted in African American history and the oral storytelling tradition. When Patricia McKissack was growing up in the South, the children called that eerie half hour just before nightfall the dark-thirty; they had exactly thirty minutes to get home before the monsters came out. The author provides an introduction for each mesmerizing tale. The sources for the stories range from the time of slavery to the civil rights era: fugitive slaves, the Ku Klux Klan, the Brotherhood of Sleeping Car Porters, and the Montgomery bus boycott are included. Brian Pinkney's scratchboard art adds to the spine-tingling quality of the book. Following the tradition of her grandmother who told hair-raising tales while shelling peas or picking greens, McKissack has created a unique book that combines strange and often tragic stories with the enchantment of the dark-thirty. Even youngsters who resist history textbooks will learn a great deal about African American history, as well as the art of storymaking, while reading or listening to these stories.

Suggestions for the Classroom

1. These stories lend themselves to being read aloud, to storytelling, and to dramatizations. The teacher or a student might read one story each day followed by discussion, dramatization, an art activity, and/or a writing activity. (It is important to provide several choices.)

2. Individual students or small groups might select stories to present in a variety of ways: possibly combine storytelling, visual arts, filmstrip, pantomime, and/or choral readings.

3. As you read the book, keep a list of interesting words, phrases, and proverbs such as "bitter as quinine," "meaner than a swamp snake," and "Truth crushed to earth will rise again." Youngsters might want to try some of these sayings or make up some of their own to use in their stories.

4. After reading and discussing "The Chicken-Coop Monster" based on McKissack's own experience, invite youngsters to write a ghost story based on their own experiences; try sprinkling it with creative wordplay. Illustrate the stories and collect them into a booklet to be added to your class library.

Flossie and the Fox

School Library Journal *Best Book*

- **Foxes**
- **Tricksters**

Flossie Finley sets off through the woods to deliver eggs to a neighbor who has been troubled by a fox. When Flossie meets the wily fox, she outsmarts him by insisting on proof that he is a fox before she will be frightened. Intriguing illustrations complement this humorous story told in the rich dialect of the rural South. This tale was told to McKissack by her grandfather who was an expert storyteller. Excellent for reading aloud and dramatization.

All Ages

Suggestions for the Classroom

1. How did the fox try to prove he was a fox? Make a list of fox attributes and illustrate each.

2. Study the illustrations. Discuss the expressions on everyone's faces including the animals. What do the expressions convey? Which illustration is your favorite? Why?

3. What if the fox had not fallen for the trick? How might Flossie have protected the eggs?

4. Retell or rewrite the story from the fox's perspective.

5. Reread and discuss the author's note. What makes a good storyteller? Check out books on the art of storytelling. (See *Tell Me a Tale* on page 40.) Practice telling stories at home and then try them on your class.

Frederick Douglass: The Black Lion

- **Biography**
- **Abolitionist**
- **Slavery**
- **Orator**

This inspiring biography of Frederick Douglass (1817?–1895) chronicles the life of the man who escaped slavery to become an orator, writer, and leader in the antislavery movement of the nineteenth century. Carefully researched, the book includes photographs, a time line, and an index.

Ages 10 up

Suggestions for the Classroom

1. See the activities listed for The Great African American Series by Patricia McKissack.

2. For more information about Frederick Douglass, see *The Civil Rights Movement in America* by Patricia McKissack.

Great African American Series

- **Biography**
- **African Americans**

This is an excellent series of eighteen biographies written for young children: Marian Anderson: A Great Singer; Jesse Owens: Olympic Star; Louis Armstrong: Jazz Musician; Satchel Paige: The Best Arm in Baseball; Mary McLeod Bethune: A Great Teacher; Paul Robeson: A Voice to Remember; Ralph J. Bunche: Peacemaker; Mary Church Terrell: Leader for Equality; George Washington Carver: The Peanut Scientist; Sojourner Truth: A Voice for Freedom; Frederick Douglass: Leader Against Slavery; Madam C. J. Walker: Self-Made Millionaire; Langston Hughes: Great American Poet Booker T. Washington: Leader and Educator; Zora Neale Hurston: Writer and Storyteller; Ida B. Wells-Barnett: A Voice Against Violence; Martin Luther King, Jr.: Man of Peace; Carter G. Woodson: The Father of Black History.

Ages 5 up

Suggestions for the Classroom

1. Set up a Biography Center or a Patricia McKissack Author Center. Display the books and use book jackets, posters, and/or illustrations for a bulletin board to accompany the center. Add student work as the unit progresses.

2. Create a time line that shows the times when all these great heroines and heroes lived. This will provide a visual picture of when their lives overlapped and where they fit into history.

3. Find two people who lived at the same time. Write letters back and forth between these people, telling about their feelings about the events in their lives.

4. Prepare skits or plays based on the lives of the people in the series.

5. Use these biographies to supplement history textbooks and integrate these books into the curriculum. For example, use the book on George Washington Carver with a unit on inventions and inventors.

6. As a group, prepare several interview questions for each of the heroines and heroes. Then ask these questions and call on anyone who wants to answer in the voice of the person being portrayed.

- **Porters**
- **Railroads**
- **Trains**
- **Careers**

Ages 8 up

A Long Hard Journey: The Story of the Pullman Porter

Coretta Scott King Award

Jane Addams Children's Book Award

This award winning book tells the inspiring story of the first African American controlled union called the Brotherhood of Sleeping Car Porters. These Pullman porters, after years of unfair labor practices, staged a battle against a corporate giant resulting in a "David and Goliath" ending. A tribute to the legacy of courage that helped trigger the modern civil rights movement, this inspiring book includes poetry, photographs, a bibliography, and an index.

Suggestions for the Classroom

1. Read the list of demands. How many eight-hour days would they have to work for a basic 240-hour work month? (30) Discuss. How would you feel about working 30 days a month? How would you feel about less than four hours of sleep a day?

2. Make a list of other unfair and inhumane things that happened to the porters such as being accountable for the items passengers stole as "souvenirs."

3. Discuss the philosophy "The customer is always right." Then read and discuss Milton Webster's story.

4. Read and discuss the poems in the book, including "The Sleeping Car Porter". Invite youngsters to write and illustrate related poems.

- **Domestic workers**
- **Mother-Son relationship**
- **Keepsakes**

Ages 5–8

Ma Dear's Aprons

Charlotte Zolotow Honor Award

This is Patricia McKissack's loving tribute to her great-grandmother and countless other domestic workers who washed, ironed, cleaned, and cooked for other people. Ma Dear wears a series of six aprons, one for each day of the work week. On laundry day Mondays, she wears her blue apron with the long pocket across the front for clothespins. Accompanied by her son, she works hard all week but finds time for small treats, games, and picnics. Heartfelt text and warm illustrations capture the dignity one widowed African American woman brought to her exhausting work in the rural South at the turn of the century.

Suggestions for the Classroom

1. Patricia McKissack recently inherited a very special keepsake that prompted this story. Reread and discuss the author's note and the way that a seemingly ordinary item can symbolize so much and provide the inspiration for writing.

2. Discuss the working conditions Ma Dear endured: backbreaking work, low pay, long hours, and condescending employers. How did she manage to weave joy into her strenuous schedule?

3. Discuss the inspiration David Earl might have gotten from both his mother's and his father's lives. How might this legacy impact the lives of descendents like Patricia McKissack?

Mary McLeod Bethune: A Great American Educator

- **Biography**
- **Teachers**
- **Slavery**

This inspiring biography of Mary McLeod Bethune (1875–1955) is an excellent chronicle of her life from her childhood in the cotton fields of South Carolina to her success as a teacher, crusader, and presidential advisor. The book includes a thorough time line, index, and rare photographs.

Ages 10 up

Suggestions for the Classroom

1. See the activities for *Mary McLeod Bethune* by Eloise Greenfield on page 94.

2. Also see the activities for The Great African American Series by Patricia McKissack.

3. For additional information on Mary McLeod Bethune see *The Civil Rights Movement in America* by Patricia & Fredrick McKissack.

Messy Bessey
Messy Bessey's Birthday Sleepover
Messy Bessey's Closet
Messy Bessey's Garden
Messy Bessey's School Desk

A series of charming books featuring Bessey, an energetic little girl who sometimes makes a mess but always finds a way to accomplish her goals. Rhyming text, appealing illustrations, and interesting adventures make these books fun to read.

Ages 4–7

Suggestions for the Classroom

1. For each book, find a way to infuse the ideas with the curriculum. For example, after reading and discussing Messy Bessey's closet, have a class "garage" sale (incorporate with a math lesson) and use the money to buy a special book.

2. M*essy Bessie's Garden* correlates nicely with a science unit on plants and planting.

3. Even though Bessey makes mistakes, she doesn't give up. Discuss the ways in which she corrected her mistakes and accomplished her goals.

- **Tall tales**
- **Fishing**

A Million Fish . . . More or Less

Hugh Thomas learns that the truth is often stretched from Papa-Daddy and Elder Abbajon. He gets a chance to create his own tall tale during a day of fishing on the Bayou Clapateaux in southern Louisiana. The illustrations by Dena Schutzer are exuberant. This is a great book to read aloud and share.

All Ages

Suggestions for the Classroom

1. As the teacher or a student reads the story, youngsters might pantomime or dramatize selected parts. Encourage improvisations.

2. Make a list of animals Hugh Thomas encountered. Then add another animal of your choice and tell how this animal challenged Hugh Thomas. Illustrate the list.

3. Write a letter from Hugh Thomas to one of the animals in the book. Then write a response and share with classmates.

4. Use in a math unit. By how many jumps did Hugh Thomas win the rope skipping contest? (5553 – 5552 = 1)

5. Create a Tall Tales Center for your classroom. Include books and add student produced stories and illustrations as the unit progresses. Inspired by *A Million Fish*, write your own tall tales.

- **Cakewalk**
- **Dance**
- **Wind**
- **Traditions**

Mirandy and Brother Wind

A Caldecott Honor Book

Mirandy sets out to catch the Wind and get him to be her partner in the cakewalk. First introduced in America by slaves, the cakewalk is a dance rooted in African American culture. It is performed by couples who strut and prance around a large square, keeping time with fiddle and banjo music. McKissack was inspired to write this book by a rare photograph of her grandparents dated 1906. They were teenagers at the time and had just won a cakewalk. This charming story, beautifully illustrated by Jerry Pinkney, is full of life's joy. It truly captures the Wind!

All Ages

Suggestions for the Classroom

1. Mirandy wanted to dance with the Wind. What happened to her plan? Why? How do you think she felt about the change of plans?

2. How did Mirandy try to catch the Wind? Brainstorm new ideas for catching the Wind.

3. This story is perfect for dramatization. Try pantomime, skits, or acting it out while the teacher or a student reads the story.

4. Read other books about cakewalks. See *Family Pictures* by Carmen Lomas Garza on page 84. Discuss the similarities and differences in the cakewalks.

5. Organize a cakewalk for your class or team. Create special dance steps for your cakewalk.

6. Read other stories where Wind has magical powers. See *Brother to the Wind* by Mildred Pitts Walter, on page 215. Discuss the similarities and differences in Wind.

- **Monkeys**
- **Animals**
- **Hyenas**
- **Practical jokes**
- **Folktales**

Ages 4–8

Monkey-Monkey's Trick

Greedy Hyena's tricks on Monkey-Monkey eventually backfire when Monkey-Monkey realizes what is happening. Monkey-Monkey thinks of a clever plan to get Hyena to fulfill his promise to help build a house. Based on an African folktale, this humorous story lends itself well to dramatization.

Suggestions for the Classroom

1. Why did Monkey-Monkey need a new house? (The rainy season was coming.) Design a new house for Monkey-Monkey.

2. Rewrite this story in the Good News/ Bad News style.

3. Create a list of "Watch Out For's" for Monkey-Monkey.

4. What did Hyena learn? Write a letter from Hyena to Monkey-Monkey apologizing for the mean tricks.

5. Read "Monkey and Crab" in *Tales From the Bamboo Grove* by Yoko Kawashima Watkins (see page 226). Then compare the two monkeys. Dramatize a meeting between the two monkeys in which they tell each other their problems. What advice might they have for each other?

Nettie Jo's Friends

- **Sewing**
- **Dolls**
- **Animals**
- **Friendships**

Nettie Jo sets out on a search for a needle so she can sew a new dress for her beloved doll. Along the way she helps Miz Rabbit, Fox, and Panther with their problems but they don't seem inclined to help her with hers. However, eventually her good deeds pay off and she gets her needle. This satisfying tale of friendship and generosity is accompanied by beautiful oil paintings.

Ages 7 up

Suggestions for the Classroom

1. What did Nettie Jo do to help each of the animals? How did they help her? How can you help your friends? Write and illustrate a story about friends helping friends.

2. Nettie Jo was a problem solver. Notice how she solved each problem. Compile a list of suggestions for solving problems.

3. Retell or rewrite the story from Annie Mae's perspective.

4. What if Nettie Jo couldn't find a needle? Write a new ending telling what happened.

5. Nettie Jo was good at finding new uses for old items. Make a list of all the things she found. Then brainstorm creative uses for each.

Paul Laurence Dunbar: A Poet to Remember

- **Biography**
- **Poets**

This is a biography of Paul Laurence Dunbar (1872–1906), the turn of the century African American poet and novelist whose works were among the first to give an honest presentation of African American experiences. Dunbar is best remembered for his whimsical dialect poetry, but his serious poetry is also stirring and beautiful. This is Patricia McKissack's first book. Includes photographs, time line, and an index.

Ages 10 up

Suggestions for the Classroom

1. Dunbar is Patricia McKissack's favorite American poet. Her mother recited his poetry when Patricia was a child. Read some of Dunbar's poetry aloud to your class. Discuss.

2. As a child, Patricia McKissack jumped rope to the rhythm of Dunbar's poetry. Try "Jump Back, Honey, Jump Back" and other poems while jumping rope.

3. Dunbar wrote a poem entitled "Sympathy" in which he talks about a caged bird. Why do you think the caged bird sings? (The poem is available in another book by Patricia McKissack, *The Civil Rights Movement in America.*)

4. Maya Angelou named her autobiography *I Know Why the Caged Bird Sings.* Where did she get this title? Why do you think she chose it?

- **Diaries/Journals**
- **Slavery**
- **Abolitionists**

A Picture of Freedom: The Diary of Clotee, a Slave Girl

Twelve-year-old Clotee records in her diary her hopes and dreams as well as her fears and struggles as a slave in Virginia in 1859. She secretly learned to read and write, a "crime" for which she could be beaten and sold to the Deep South. After long, hard days, she hides away to record the daily events: the humiliations, threats, harassment, and violence inflicted by cruel slaveholders along with the joys of storytelling, quilting, and friendships. As the story unfolds, Clotee's "picture of freedom" becomes increasingly clear and compelling. In her first full-length work of fiction, Patricia McKissack has given her readers a vibrant, lovable protagonist whose belief in herself and her people led to her important work as a conductor on the Underground Railroad. McKissack based this inspiring story on the life of her great-great-great grandmother, Lizzie Passmore.

Ages 8–12

Suggestions for the Classroom

1. Issues and topics for discussion and writing include: Clotee's thirst for knowledge, the Underground Railroad, abolitionists, and the many abhorrent practices of slavocracy such as separation of families, forced marriages, imposed motherhood, disinheritance of mixed-race children, denial of literacy, overwork, food deprivation, humiliations, threats, harassment, violence, and in Clotee's words, "Never havin' a say in what happens to yourself."

2. Patricia McKissack wrote, "Finding Clotee's voice was the most difficult problem I had to overcome. Once I heard, in my head, how she would say things, then the story was easy to tell. She told it to me." Discuss the use of voice in this book, the unique way that Clotee had of expressing herself, and her determination to thrive in spite of cruel circumstances.

3. Discuss quotes such as "Nobody should have to live as a slave," and "When we abolitionists end slavery, everybody will have a bed to sleep in."

4. Invite youngsters to choose a character and write or dramatize a part of the story from her/his perspective.

- **Abolitionists**
- **Slavery**
- **Underground Railroad**

Rebels Against Slavery: American Slave Revolts

Coretta Scott King Honor Book

"The movement to end slavery started the moment it started." Weaving facts, quotes, photographs, and drawings, the McKissacks bring new insights to the story of the struggle for emancipation. Spanning more than 250 years of African American history, this informative book pays tribute to people who fought and often died for their inalienable rights. Among those profiled are Toussaint Louverture, Gabriel Prosser, Denmark Vesey, Nat Turner, Joseph Cinque, Harriet Tubman, John Brown and other heroes who fought in the war against slavery. This is an important resource to use in the ongoing effort to provide accurate historical information about African Americans for young people.

Ages 10 up

Suggestions for the Classroom

1. After the first reading of the book, invite youngsters to divide into groups according to chapter or topic and present the information to the large group through storytelling, readers theatre, or skits combined with art and music.

2. Compare and contrast the information about Joseph Cinque in this book and in the movie "Amistad."

3. Discuss or write about the relationship between African Americans and Native Americans.

4. Discuss or respond in writing to quotes such as: "Others may be our allies, but the battle is ours." (p. 97).

5. The McKissacks end their book with this question: "Could the rebels rest in peace at last?" For information about the period following the Civil War, see Reconstruction Era in the Subject Index of this book *(Multicultural Voices)*.

Run Away Home

- **Historical fiction**
- **Runaways**
- **Alabama**
- **Apaches**

Rooted in the author's family history, this is the compelling story of an eleven-year-old African American girl and her family who give refuge to a runaway Apache boy in Alabama in 1888. The narrator is Sarah Jane Crossman who befriends Sky after he escapes from the train transporting Geronimo and his people-in-exile from Florida to Alabama. Well-developed characters, a suspenseful plot, and details of late nineteenth century life combined with vital themes result in a moving, thought-provoking story.

Ages 10 up

Suggestions for the Classroom

1. Discussion and writing themes and topics include: persecution of African Americans and Native people, family dynamics, interpersonal relationships, economic survival, solidarity among oppressed peoples, and the many dimensions of freedom.

2. Examine the conflicting attitudes toward the conciliatory approach urged by Booker T. Washington. Debate which is more important for the survival of an oppressed people: political rights, economic progress, or a combination of the two. Research the positions taken by Washington and W. E. B. Du Bois. Read the poem "Booker T. and W. E .B." by Dudley Randall in *The Civil Rights Movement in America*. See page 157.

3. Reread and discuss the author's note. Then examine the role Patricia McKissack has played in reclaiming the past. See the Subject Index for more historical fiction.

Taking a Stand Against Racism and Racial Discrimination

- **Civil Rights**
- **Discrimination**
- **U.S. history**
- **Constitution**

This excellent book examines the different forms of racism. In this rare, much needed book, the McKissacks outline the history of racism and the movements that have combatted it. They present ideas for getting involved in the struggle against racism in your school and community. Here also are stirring profiles of well known civil rights activists such as Rosa Parks and W. E. B. Du Bois as well as unsung heroines and heroes. Information about civil rights organizations is included. This is a very readable book—take a position against racism by using this book to help re-examine personal beliefs. Help us find a cure for the virus of hatred! The book includes important photographs and a thorough index that will facilitate research.

Ages 9 up

Suggestions for the Classroom

1. Use this book to help implement James Banks's Social Action Approach to Multicultural Curriculum Reform—reform in which students make decisions on important social issues and take action to help solve them.

2. Write a rationale for including this book in every school library.

3. Describe the different forms racism can take, from snobbish social exclusion to state sponsored genocide.

4. Stereotyping is perpetuated by name calling, racial slurs, and jokes. Find examples in the media and discuss them. How can a joke hurt someone? Examine cartoons for stereotyping.

5. Play the "what if" game outlined in Chapter Two. Write a response and discuss.

6. Discuss positive anger. Write about examples of positive anger.

7. Read and discuss "Incident by Countee Cullen." Find other poems about racism. Write poems, print on large posters, and display on your bulletin board. (See "Sympathy" by Paul Laurence Dunbar in *The Civil Rights Movement.*)

8. Discuss the origins of racial slurs. Recommend ways to eliminate them.

9. Start a chapter of Partners in Achievement or your own social action group. Or join one or more of the organizations mentioned in the book.

10. Reread the problem attitudes. Use for role play, discussion, and/or written responses.

11. How could government sponsored racism and discrimination exist within a democracy?

12. Examine the wording of the Emancipation Proclamation. Rewrite it adding typical Lincoln eloquence such as is found in the Gettysburg Address.

13. Give the above rewritten version of the Emancipation Proclamation as a speech to your class and/or team.

14. Roleplay or debate the positions taken by Booker T. Washington and W. E. B. Du Bois. Which style is most like yours? (See the poem "Booker T. and W. E. B." by Dudley Randall in *The Civil Rights Movement in America* by the McKissacks.)

15. Read the examples of people who have taken a stand and choose one for further research. (See Yoshiko Uchida's books for information on the World War II concentration camps where Japanese Americans were unjustly imprisoned.)

16. Examine the origin and goals of the Ku Klux Klan. Compile a list of recommendations for eradicating the violence of hate groups such as the KKK.

17. Essay theme: "How do you think education should change to help people from different cultures understand each other and live together peacefully?"

18. Choose some of the activities from "Becoming an Activist." Add some ideas of your own. Keep a log of your experiences.

19. Try Jesse Jackson's call, "Repeat after me: I am somebody!" How do affirmations help people? Write several affirmations.

20. Select quotes such as the following to discuss or respond to in writing: "Taking a stand against racism and racial discrimination, internally and externally, is a personal investment in your own mental health and development and in the place where you live."

21. Theatre is a very effective way to get your message across. (See Portland Birchfield's story.) Write and produce a play inspired by the ideas in this book.

- **Twins**
- **Individuality**
- **Antonyms**

Ages 4–7

Who is Who?

This is a book of opposites. Even though Johnny and Bobby are twins, they like different things. The book includes a word list.

Suggestions for the Classroom

1. What if Johnny and Bobby had both wanted to sit in the front seat? What if they had both wanted the top bunk bed? How could they compromise? Roleplay.

2. Make and illustrate a list of antonyms.

3. Encourage older students to read this book to younger children.

Young, Black, and Determined: A Biography of Lorraine Hansberry

ALA Best Book for Young Adults

- **Biography**
- **Playwrights**
- **Activism**

In this carefully researched and moving biography, the McKissacks explore the life and times of gifted playwright Lorraine Hansberry (1930–1964). In her short thirty-four years, she was not only one of the most successful playwrights of a generation but a brilliant essayist, a spirited activist, and social critic. Through engaging prose, black-and-white photographs, excerpts from Hansberry's journals, and interviews with her sister, the authors have created a significant tribute to this gifted writer who is best known for her play, *A Raisin in the Sun.* This noteworthy biography is made even more special by the way it is framed within the context of the events, people, and literature of the times.

Ages 12 up

Suggestions for the Classroom

1. Analyze the literary, social, political, and artistic influences that shaped Hansberry's life, thinking, and writing.

2. Use the time line, bibliography, and index as sources for discussion, writing, drama, and further research.

3. Read, discuss and respond in writing to Hansberry's work including *A Raisin in the Sun.*

4. To read Hansberry's letters printed in the *Ladder,* a Lesbian publication, see *Gay American History: Lesbians and Gay Men in the U.S.A.* by Jonathan Katz.

Nicholasa Mohr

Puerto Rican American (1938–)

Birthday: November 1

"Because of who I am, I feel blessed by the work I do, for it permits me to use my talents and continue to 'make magic'. I can recreate those deepest of personal memories as well as validate and celebrate my heritage and my future." (Bantam Brochure)

Books by Nicholasa Mohr

All For the Better: A Story of El Barrio. **(Stories of America Series) Illustrated by Rudy Gutierrez. Raintree Steck-Vaughn, 1992.**

El Bronx Remembered. **HarperCollins, 1993.**

Felita. **Illustrated by Ray Cruz. Dial, 1979; Bantam, 1990; 1995.**

Going Home. **Dial, 1986; Bantam 1989; 1997.**

Growing Up Inside the Sanctuary of My Imagination: A Memoir. **Messner, 1994.**

In Nueva York. **Arte Público Press, 1988.**

The Magic Shell. **Illustrated by Rudy Gutierrez. Scholastic, 1995. Spanish edition:** ***El regalo magico.***

A Matter of Pride and Other Stories. **Arte Público Press, 1997.**

Nilda. **Harper & Row, 1973; Arte Público Press, 1986.**

Old Letivia and the Mountain of Sorrows. **Viking, 1996. Spanish edition:** ***La Vieja Letivia y el monte de los pesares.***

Rituals of Survival: A Woman's Portfolio. **Arte Público Press, 1985.**

The Song of el Coquí and Other Tales of Puerto Rico. **Illustrated by Antonio Martorell. Viking, 1995. Spanish edition:** ***La canción del coquí y otros cuentos de Puerto Rico.***

Nicholasa Mohr was born November 1, 1938 in New York City in the oldest Spanish-speaking community known as El Barrio (the neighborhood), or Spanish Harlem. When she started school, she moved with her family—mother, father, and six older brothers—to the Bronx where she spent most of her growing-up years. "Growing up in a household of six older brothers, and being part of a family who still held old-fashioned Puerto Rican concepts about the male and female roles, was often a struggle for me" (Bantam brochure). Mohr eloquently elaborates on these struggles in her books.

From the beginning, Mohr found magic in creating pictures and writing letters. Her art provided adventure, freedom, and space in the small crowded apartment where she lived with her extended family. Her mother lovingly provided support and encouragement for Mohr's achievements. (Her father died when she was eight years old.)

Drawing and painting sustained Mohr through otherwise depressing conditions in both her home and school life. By using her imagination, she was able to create something pleasing and interesting. She used her skills and imagination to further develop her creativity, first in visual arts, and later in her writing.

Mohr wanted to attend a college preparatory high school, but due to the intervention of a bigoted guidance counselor, she attended a trade school instead. She majored in fashion illustration. After she graduated, she attended the Art Students' League in New York City where she studied drawing and painting. Her love for books led her to discover the works of Mexican artists; she later studied art and printmaking in Mexico. She has taught art in colleges in New York and New Jersey.

As Mohr's art developed, her feelings and experiences as a Puerto Rican woman born in the United States came through. This led to a publisher asking her to write about her life. Mohr was aware of the lack of Puerto Rican-American literature so she eventually agreed to the suggestion. "I was well aware that there were no books published about Puerto Rican girls or boys . . . I was also reminded that when I was growing up, I'd enjoyed reading about the adventures of many boys and girls, but I had never really seen myself, my brothers or my family in those books. We just were not there" (Bantam brochure).

Writing was difficult at first but she worked hard at it; by applying some of the techniques she had developed as a visual artist to her new challenge as a writer, she has become a successful author. She writes about the ongoing struggles of Puerto Rican people on the mainland to gain their basic human rights. Her work, often incorporating a strong social statement, reflects the perspectives of the Puerto Rican people in all their complexity and variety. She has written numerous books for young people in addition to plays, screenplays, articles, and essays. She has won many awards and honors, including an honorary doctorate from State University of New York and a Lifetime Achievement Award from the National Congress of Puerto Rican Women.

For more information about Nicholasa Mohr, see *Something About the Author,* Volume 8; *Authors and Artists for Young Adults,* Volume 8; *¡Latinas! Women of Achievement* edited by D. Telgen and J. Kamp; and *Growing Up Inside the Sanctuary of My Imagination: A Menoir.*

All For the Better: A Story of El Barrio

- **Biography**
- **Boycotts**
- **Depression Era**
- **Moving**

In this easy-to-read biography of Evalina Lopez (Antonetty) (1922–1984), Nicholasa Mohr pays tribute to an inspiring woman whose leadership, determination, and ingenuity made a significant difference in the lives of the people in her community. When the Great Depression brought hard times, Lopez became an activist on behalf of her community. She founded the United Bronx Parents Group, worked with Head Start, and organized adult literacy programs.

Ages 7–10

Suggestions for the Classroom

1. In 1933, eleven-year-old Evalina was forced by economic hardship to leave Puerto Rico and live in New York City. How did this difficult uprooting impact her life and influence her decisions?

2. Evalina was a problem solver. Discuss the problems she tackled and the solutions she implemented.

3. Reread and discuss the introduction. What qualities enabled Evalina to make a difference? How does her example inspire others to care enough to make a difference?

- **Moving**
- **Grandmothers**
- **Death**
- **Nonviolence**
- **Newcomers**

Felita

Notable Children's Book in the Field of Social Studies

Eight-year-old Felita loves her neighborhood in New York City. To her disappointment, her parents decide to move. "We're off to a better future," her father announces. Only her wise and loving grandmother, Abuelita, who moved to New York from Puerto Rico, understands how much Felita will miss her old neighborhood and Gigi, her best friend. The people in the new neighborhood taunt and tease Felita because she is different from them. Faced with unrelenting prejudice in their new location, Papi, Mami, Felita, and her two brothers finally decide to return to their old neighborhood. Felita finds that many things have changed while she was gone and some of the most significant changes are within herself. She has learned much about her heritage and about how to deal with the prejudice the family has faced. When her beloved grandmother dies, Felita vows to visit Puerto Rico—a trip she had long hoped to take with her grandmother. Don't miss the sequel, *Going Home.*

Ages 8 up

Suggestions for the Classroom

1. Write letters from Felita to Gigi at the beginning, middle, and end of the book. How had Felita changed by the time she returned to her old neighborhood?

2. Dramatize one of the discussions between Felita and her grandmother.

3. Discuss the incidents that caused Felita's family to move back to their old neighborhood. As newcomers, they were treated very badly. See Newcomers in the Subject Index for additional books about newcomers. How do the people in your neighborhood treat newcomers? What can be done to improve the way families like Felita's are treated?

4. Invite youngsters to research the concept of nonviolence and the proponents of this philosophy.

- **Travel**
- **Puerto Rico**

Going Home

A Parents' Choice Remarkable Book for Literature
Notable Trade Book in the Field of Social Studies

This book is the sequel to *Felita.* At the end of *Felita,* when her beloved grandmother dies, Felita vows to visit Puerto Rico. Now the twelve-year-old protagonist takes this journey, the one she had long hoped to enjoy with her grandmother. However, her trip is different from what she expected. At first, none of the other girls wants to be friends with a "Nuyorican." As Felita becomes involved with a community play, she is met with both admiration and jealousy. By summer's end, she has made a close friend, used her creativity and talent, and learned about her heritage. She goes home with a richer understanding of herself and her homeland. Felita's first person narrative is lively and honest.

Ages 10 up

Suggestions for the Classroom

1. Invite interested youngsters to create journal entries Felita might have written, noting the changes she undergoes as her journey progresses.

2. Use quotes to document the changes in Felita's life after she turned twelve. Discuss gender restrictions and how they impacted her life.

3. How might Felita's trip to Puerto Rico have been different if she had gone there with her grandmother? If Felita could tell her grandmother about her trip, what might she say?

4. When Felita was on her way home, she realized she was both happy and sad. Invite youngsters to discuss or write about a time when they had mixed feelings.

The Magic Shell

- **Dominican Republic**
- **Emigration and immigration**
- **Newcomers**

When his family moves from the Dominican Republic to New York City, Jaime uses his great-uncle's magic shell to transport himself back to his beloved homeland where he was free to play in the warm out-of-doors with his friends. This poignant story captures the pain and frustration often felt by the newcomer, the outsider. Spanish edition available.

Ages 7–10

Suggestions for the Classroom

1. The problems in Jaime's new environment seemed endless. What were these problems and how did he gradually overcome them?

2. When Jaime returned to his homeland and visited with his uncle, he made an important discovery about the magic shell. How might this realization help him overcome future obstacles?

3. For additional books about newcomers, see the Subject Index. An excellent book for adults is *The Inner World of the Immigrant Child* by Cristina Ioga.

In Nueva York

Notable Trade Book in the Field of Social Studies

American Library Association Best Books of the Year

New York Times *Outstanding Book of the Year*

- **Puerto Rican American**
- **Lower East Side: New York**
- **Short stories**

This is a collection of short, interrelated stories that depict life in one of New York City's Puerto Rican communities. Written candidly, sympathetically, and with wry humor, Mohr portrays her characters with warmth and sophistication. *In Nueva York* is Mohr's third book; it is a significant contribution of humor and pathos to the usual bleak depiction of life in the Lower East Side.

Ages 12 up

Suggestions for the Classroom

1. Invite individuals or small groups to select one of the stories to present to the class through drama, poetry, music, art, and/or filmstrip.

2. Write a letter from a character in one of the stories to a character in another story. How does putting ourselves in the character's place help us understand them?

3. Puerto Rican people on the mainland are constantly struggling to receive their basic human rights. How have authors like Mohr created an awareness of the complexities of her people?

4. When Nicholasa Mohr was a child, she did not find any Puerto Ricans in the books she read. How much has this situation improved? Make a list of books for young people with Puerto Rican main characters.

- **Mother-Daughter relationship**
- **Death**
- **Barrio**

Nilda

***Best Books* School Library Journal**
New York Times *An Outstanding Book of the Year*
American Library Association A Best Book of the Year
Jane Addams Children's Book Award of U.S. Women's International League for Peace and Freedom

Mohr dedicated *Nilda,* her first novel, with love to the children of El Barrio—and of all the many barrios all over the world. This is the candid story of three years in Nilda's life—from age 10 to 13—and takes place in the barrio in New York City from 1941 to 1945. It chronicles the day-to-day experiences of a poor Puerto Rican family. Nilda tells about going to the welfare office with her mother and then later having their apartment inspected by the social worker. Her head is inspected for lice at the health office. She tells about police brutality, racist teachers, and her mother's death. This is an exceptional story of hardship, family ties, and neighborhood interactions. Humorous and sad, the book is rich in detail, full of a child's thoughts and feelings. Note: Contains strong language.

Ages 12 up

Suggestions for the Classroom

1. Reread and discuss Mohr's dedication of this book.

2. Select quotes such as the following to discuss and/or respond to in writing: "For some time now, Nilda had experienced a feeling of helplessness gnawing at her insides."

3. Make a list of the hardships that Nilda faced. Write journal entries for Nilda at the beginning, middle, and end of the book. Compile these journal entries into a class booklet. How do these journal entries enhance understanding of how Nilda might have felt?

- **Folklore**
- ***Curanderas***

Old Letivia and the Mountain of Sorrows

To end the fierce winds that threaten a Puerto Rican village, Letivia and her friends set out on a dangerous odyssey to break an ominous spell cast by the Mountain of Sorrows. Letivia is granted four wishes but she learns that "one cannot get everything and give nothing in return." This captivating original tale is rich in Puerto Rican language, culture, and symbolism. Spanish edition available.

Ages 5-9

Suggestions for the Classroom

1. Discussion and writing topics include: courage, friendship, change, healing, prejudice, and respect for and appreciation of nature. The magical illustrations will inspire whimsical paintings and drawings.

2. Mohr's portrayal of Letivia as a wise, heroic healer contrasts with the negative images of witches found in European folklore. Encourage older children to explore these differences further. Examine the attitudes of the townspeople toward Letivia. Then read two books by Gloria Anzaldúa that feature *curanderas*: *Friends From the Other Side* and *Prietita and the Ghost Woman.*

3. Cervantes, the whistling turtle magician, was transformed into a wandering star. Some reviewers interpreted this as self-sacrifice and death. Yet, he continues to travel the solar system. Discuss these and other interpretations.

The Song of el Coquí and Other Tales from Puerto Rico

- **Folklore**
- **Frogs**
- **Slavery**
- **History**

This engaging collection of three folktales features animals that represent three groups of people in Puerto Rico. El coquí (frog) represents the indigenous Tainos, the guinea hen symbolizes the African people who were brought to the island as captive slaves, and the story about the mule is a parable about the Spaniards who conquered the island. Together the tales form a composite of a culture comprised of very different and special strands. Spanish edition available.

All Ages

Suggestions for the Classroom

1. This is an excellent example of a picture book that is appropriate for all ages. People of all ages and backgrounds will enjoy the vibrant tales and exquisite paintings.

2. Reread and discuss the dedication and afterword. Then invite youngsters to respond to this captivating book through art, music, drama, dance, or writing.

3. Mohr was an artist before she became an author. Find out more about her art. How did being an artist help her with her writing? Why did she decide to try writing?

Min Paek

Korean American (1950–)

Birthday: June 28
Contact: Children's Book Press
246 First Street, Suite 101
San Francisco, California 94105
415-995-2200

"We are all in one place called earth; it is important that we survive together. There is no such thing as 'me only' 'us only'. Prejudice is most unmodern. Diversity is here and we need to accept it, otherwise we'll become victims and will perish." (Personal Communication)

Books by Min Paek

Aekyung's Dream. **Children's Book Press, 1978; 88; 92.**

Min Paek was born June 28, 1950 in Seoul, Korea. Her mother taught her to read and write when she was five years old. Then her father started buying her books every month on payday. "I was very anxious to wait for father's payday." She loved to read and write and was encouraged by her family. She was pleased to find out that her sisters, brothers, and cousins liked her stories. She also was encouraged to draw and paint at an early age.

She says, "I write usually at night. It's quiet and nice. Sometimes I really feel like I must write and then I have to write before I lose my thoughts." She writes about her life experiences. "I love to observe people and things in detail like why they look the way they look and why they act the way they act. It's fascinating to me. Also I am greatly fascinated by myself" (personal communication).

"Most of the time I know exactly what I want to write. My problem is rather I come up with several ideas and stories and I don't know which one I should choose to use." Paek's future writing plans include more books about Korean American experiences and immigrant experiences. She advises young writers, "Do not get hung up on ideas of writing. Go out and fully experience life and be observant. Make a commitment to the role of being a writer."

Paek advises teachers of young writers as follows: "Instead of asking them to write something, ask them to go out and observe and experience something and then have them come back to write. Encouragement is very important, even to the bad writers. Do not push to write" (personal communication).

Min Paek immigrated to the United States in 1973. She has worked as a professional artist both in Korea and in the United States. She has also been a family counselor at the Korean Community Service Center in San Francisco.

Aekyung's Dream

- **Newcomers**
- **Immigrants**
- **English as a Second Language**
- **Bilingual (Korean and English)**
- **Language**

This book was written, illustrated, and translated into Korean by Min Paek. Since the repeal of restrictive immigration laws in 1965, there has been a large influx of Koreans into the United States. Aekyung, a recently arrived young Korean girl, experiences the same problems of adjustment all immigrants share—that of adjusting to an unfamiliar, sometimes hostile, often bewildering culture. Aekyung struggles for an ethnic identity in the mainstream society. Her classmates exclude her and tease her about her appearance. One night she has a marvelous dream about the fifteenth century palace of King Sejung in the Yi Dynasty. This dream inspires her to be strong like a tree with deep roots. Gradually, her talents and individuality are recognized and affirmed by her classmates and she once again becomes the happy, confident person she had been before leaving her homeland.

All Ages

Suggestions for the Classroom

1. Compare how Aekyung felt at the beginning and end of the story. What changes occurred that changed the way she felt about her new country? Write journal entries for Aekyung at the beginning and end of the story and share them.

2. How did Aekyung's dream help her? Read more about the history of Korea. What can knowing the history of your people do for you?

3. Make a "How to Welcome Newcomers" booklet giving advice to schoolmates on how to help new students feel welcome at your school.

4. Create a "Buddy System" so that new students have helpers. Discuss what the buddy should do to help the newcomer.

5. Have you ever moved to a new school, city, or country? How did you feel? Write about your experiences.

6. Pretend that your family has moved to Korea. If the Korean language is new to you, try to read the Korean words in the story. How would you want to be treated? Write about your feelings.

7. What are Kiwa houses? (traditional Korean houses) Discuss the changes in Seoul and illustrate them.

8. Set up a center in your classroom on Korea. Check out books, make a bulletin board, and make task cards.

9. What might have happened next? Write a new chapter telling about another new student who came to Aekyung's school.

10. Read other books about newcomers and discuss their experiences. Recommended books include:

Angel Child, Dragon Child by Michele Maria Surat (see page 205)

In the Year of the Boar and Jackie Robinson by Bette Bao Lord (see page 148)

Molly's Pilgrim by Barbara Cohen (see page 61)

My Name is María Isabel by Alma Flor Ada

The Magic Shell by Nicholasa Mohr (see page 171)

11. An excellent book for adults is *The Inner World of the Immigrant Child* by Cristina Igoa.

Johanna Reiss

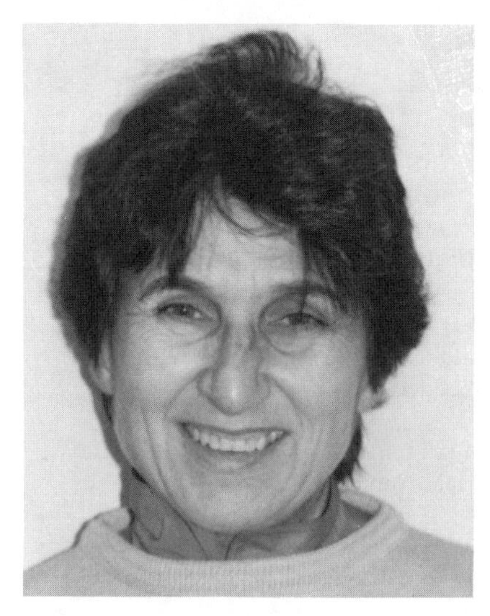

Jewish American (1932–)

Contact: Catherine Balkin
HarperCollins Publishers
10 East 53rd Street
New York, New York 10022
212-207-7450

"People are fragile. They are strong, too, but wars leave emotional scars that take a long time to heal, generations perhaps."
(Something About the Author, *Volume 18, p. 253)*

Books by Johanna Reiss

***The Upstairs Room.* Crowell (now HarperCollins), 1972; 1990.**

***The Journey Back* (sequel). Crowell (now HarperCollins), 1976; 1987.**

***Die Fatale Nacht (That Fateful Night).* Holland, 1988.**

Johanna Reiss *nee* deLeeuw was born in 1932 in Winterswijk, Holland. She was the youngest of three sisters. Her sisters, Sini and Rachel, were ten and fifteen years old when she was born. Her father was a cattle dealer. Her mother died when Reiss was ten years old.

In 1942, Jewish people in Holland were increasingly persecuted by the Nazis who occupied Winterswijk. Reiss's family scattered into Gentile homes for protection. Reiss (Annie) and Sini were hidden in a farm house with Johan, Dientje and Opoe (Johan's mother) Oosterveld. Reiss later wrote about these years in hiding in *The Upstairs Room.* She started writing the account especially for her two daughters. She says, "I didn't think it would take me more than a week. Not until I started to write did I find out how much I remembered, things I had never talked about with anyone because they were too painful. I was looking at myself and revisiting a part of my life that was very painful, so thinking and writing about it . . . was exhausting. It took me three years to write, because I had never written a book before and also because I was writing in English, which is not my native language."

The sequel, *The Journey Back,* is Reiss's account of her readjustment after World War II. From a political view, the war was over ". . . but wars leave emotional scars that take a long time to heal, generations perhaps." Both of these books have been translated into numerous languages. Her third book, *Die Fatale Nacht (That Fateful Night),* is about a flood that took place in Holland in the 1950s. She is currently working on another autobiographical book.

Reiss taught elementary school in Holland several years after she graduated from college. Then she went to the United States, at the age of 23, intending to stay for just one year. Now, over thirty years later, she is still in the United States, living in New York City. She and her two daughters have made many trips to Holland to visit her sisters and, while they were still alive, the Oostervelds.

Reiss says, "I absolutely adore music. I sing in a choir, and go to concerts often. I have written a column in Dutch called 'Johanna Reiss, New York, New York' for a Dutch magazine. I teach Dutch too, to anyone who wants to learn to speak it. Also since I grew up in the country, I love to garden. I am growing some odds and ends on the terrace of my apartment. I planted them in kegs, so my acreage is very small—I plow with a fork and I weed with tweezers!"

In response to the question: "Do you think today's kids can understand the terrible things that happened during the Holocaust?" Johanna says, as noted in a Scholastic Book Club author profile, "Well, even my own children have had a hard time understanding it. When they were younger, they went with me to Holland and I took them to the house where I was hidden. They met the people who hid me, and saw the tiny 'hiding place' in the closet, which is still intact. Yet even as they stood with me right on that spot, they couldn't quite believe it really happened. I myself almost can't believe it, but it did happen. Let's hope it never will again."

The Journey Back

- **Holocaust**
- **World War II**
- **Holland**
- **Netherlands**
- **Autobiographical novel**
- **Step-family**

This book is the sequel to *The Upstairs Room,* Johanna Reiss's moving account of her experiences as a Jewish child during the German occupation of Holland during World War II. Annie and her sister Sini had spent over two years hiding in a tiny room with a farm family. In the spring of 1945, when Annie was thirteen, the horrible war was finally over. Unlike millions of Jews and others, Annie, Sini, and their father and sister survived the war. (Their mother had died of a long-term illness in 1942.) This sequel describes Annie's reunion with her much-changed family. During the first years of peace Holland was faced with the enormous task of rebuilding itself, and Annie's family was faced with picking up the pieces and fitting them together in meaningful ways. "From a political point of view, the war is over but in another sense it has not really ended. People are fragile. They are strong, too, but wars leave emotional scars that take a long time to heal, generations perhaps."

Ages 10 up

Suggestions for the Classroom

1. Johanna Reiss writes about how people behave in times of disaster and how those who survive pick up the pieces of their lives. How did Annie's family go about picking up the pieces? Discuss.

2. The war not only left emotional scars but physical illness too. Tell what illness each had. Annie? (deformed legs) Sini? (jaundice) Rachel? (tuberculosis)

3. Pretend you are Annie's doctor. Write a report explaining what happened to Annie's legs and your recommendations for treatment.

4. Discuss the problems Holland faced after the war. How did the country rebuild itself?

5. Examine the relationship between Annie and the Oostervelds. Write a poem or song about the Oosterveld family and/or farm and illustrate it.

6. Make a list of the other groups the Nazis targeted for persecution and death. Discuss.

7. Dramatize the relationship between Annie and her stepmother.

8. What happened during the following year? Write a short sequel to *The Journey Back.*

9. Make a list of other books for young people about the Holocaust. Select one to read and present to the group.

- **Holocaust**
- **World War II**
- **Holland**
- **Netherlands**
- **Autobiographical novel**

The Upstairs Room

Newbery Honor Book
An American Library Association Notable Children's Book
Jane Addams Peace Association Honor Book
Jewish Book Council's Charles & Bertie G. Schwartz Juvenile Award
Buxtehuder Bulle–German Children's Book Award for a Children's Book Promoting Peace

This is the powerful story of Johanna Reiss's experiences as a child in Holland during the German occupation of World War II. The youngest child in a Jewish family, ten-year-old Annie and her sister were hidden in a farm home for over two years. Written from the perspective of a child, the writing captures with forthrightness and sincerity "Annie's" daily life, fears, and hopes. Annie candidly describes her relationships with her father, mother, two sisters, and the three members of the sheltering Gentile family. With her, we await D-Day and liberation, sharing the monotony, anxiety, and ups-and-downs of life in a cramped refuge. Don't miss the sequel, *The Journey Back.*

Ages 10 up

Suggestions for the Classroom

1. Create several journal entries one of the characters might have written. Or create a letter Annie might have written to another character. Use these letters to stimulate discussion.

2. Annie spent untold hours cooped up in a cramped space. Create quiet activities to assuage the anxiety and monotony while waiting for liberation.

3. As an optional activity, invite youngsters to write a letter from one of the characters or from themselves to the Nazis.

4. Research all the symbols the Nazis used including stars and triangles to target various groups. Who were these groups and why were they persecuted by the Nazis?

5. Read the sequel, *The Journey Back,* in which Johanna Reiss describes what it was like to be free again.

6. The Holocaust is an atrocity too immense and horrifying for children to fully grasp, yet too important for them not to know about. To keep silent is to lie. An excellent resource for educators is "Bearing Witness to the Holocaust" by Hazel Rochman, *Book Links Journal* (January, 1998).

7. One of the best ways to encourage young people to think about the Holocaust is for them to ask themselves, "What would I have done?" An excellent book for older students and adults is *Conscience and Courage: Rescuers of Jews During the Holocaust* by Eva Fogelman.

8. "Facing History and Ourselves" is a national training organization whose mission is to engage educators in an examination of anti-Semitism, racism, and prejudice in order to promote the development of a more humane and informed citizenry. Contact Facing History and Ourselves, 16 Hurd Rd., Brookline, MA 02146; 617-232-1595.

Faith Ringgold

African American (1930–)

Birthday: October 8
Address: 127 Jones Road
Englewood, New Jersey 07631
Web address: www.art in context.com/artist/ringgold

"I am inspired by people who rise above their adversity. And also I'm inspired by the fact that if I really, really want to, I think I can do anything.... Nothing is going to stop me in my life and I'm going to pursue anything that turns me on. I'm not going to hear "No." If I want to achieve something, if it excites me—I can do it."
(from Talking to Faith Ringgold, *pp. 3, 44)*

Books by Faith Ringgold

Aunt Harriet's Underground Railroad in the Sky. **Crown Publishers, 1992; 1996.**

Bonjour, Lonnie. **Hyperion, 1996.**

Colors. **Crown, 1999.**

Crown Heights Children's History. **Crown, 1998.**

Dancing at the Louvre: Faith Ringgold's French Collection and Other Story Quilts. **University of California Press, 1998.**

Dinner at Aunt Connie's House. **Hyperion, 1993; 1996.**

If a Bus Could Talk: The Story of Rosa Parks. **Simon & Schuster, 1999.**

The Invisible Princess. **Crown, 1998.**

My Dream of Martin Luther King. **Crown, 1996.**

My Grandma's Story Quilt. **Crown, 1999.**

Numbers. **Crown, 1999.**

Talking to Faith Ringgold **by Faith Ringgold, Linda Freeman, & Nancy Roucher. Crown, 1996.**

Tar Beach. **Crown Publishing, 1991; 1994.**

We Flew Over the Bridge: The Memoirs of Faith Ringgold. **Bulfinch Press, Little Brown, 1995.**

BOOKS ABOUT FAITH RINGGOLD

Inspirations: Stories About Women Artists **by Leslie Sills. Whitman, 1989.**

Who's Who in American Art, **1984.**

Who's Who Among Black Americans, **1981.**

Who's Who in America, **1992.**

Women, Art and Society, **1990.**

VIDEOTAPES FEATURING FAITH RINGGOLD

"Tar Beach"

"Faith Ringgold"

Faith Ringgold was born at Harlem Hospital in New York City on October 8, 1930. Asthma frequently kept her home from school so her mother helped her keep up with her lessons. When Ringgold's studies were completed, her mother gave her fabric, thread, needles, crayon and paper. Because Ringgold's mother was a fashion designer and dress maker, she showed her daughter many ways of working with cloth. They also went to museums and concerts. These experiences contributed to Ringgold's feeling different from other children, yet special. Her sense of being different plus the confidence she gained from the love and encouragement provided by her parents influenced her artistic development.

When Ringgold graduated from high school in 1948, she wanted to be an artist. But City College in New York would not allow women to be liberal arts students at that time. So she enrolled in the School of Education and taught kindergarten through college for almost twenty years. Meanwhile, she experimented with various art forms. Her art gradually became more political, and in the 1970s she began using cloth again. With fabric, she could combine many interests—African art, politics, and her experiences growing up as an African American female in New York City's Harlem. When she left teaching, she began sewing masks, sculpture, and quilts. She sometimes combined these with storytelling, singing, dancing, chanting, and audience participation.

Now an artist of international renown, she divides her time between Englewood, New Jersey and La Jolla, California, where she is a professor of fine arts at the University of California at San Diego. She has received many awards and honors for her art and writing, including seven honorary doctorates. As a woman and as an African American, Ringgold has encountered some resistance to her work. With the love of her family, the community support of Harlem, and her own unconquerable confidence, she has persevered and is achieving her goals. Her innovative art and writing continue to grow and change.

- **Harriet Tubman**
- **Underground Railroad**
- **Runaway slaves**
- **Flight**
- **African American history**

All Ages

Aunt Harriet's Underground Railroad in the Sky

Cassie Louise Lightfoot of *Tar Beach* fame returns to the skies where she and her brother, Be Be, discover Harriet Tubman flying an old ramshackle train. Be Be jumps on board along with hundreds of bedraggled women, men, and children but Cassie misses the train. With Harriet Tubman as her guide, Cassie embarks on a harrowing journey, one that retraces the route escaping slaves took on the real Underground Railroad. Finally, reunited with Be Be, they join the other passengers on the Underground Railroad for a joyous celebration in the sky. This fine tribute to an inspiring woman includes a map of the Underground Railroad, additional information about Harriet Tubman, and a bibliography.

Suggestions for the Classroom

1. Read *Tar Beach* first before reading this book. Then discuss Cassie's growth from the beginning of *Tar Beach* to the end of this book. What has she learned? How has she changed? What did Cassie learn about the history of her people and of her country?

2. Use this book to supplement your United States history textbook. It provides an excellent summary of slavery and the Underground Railroad.

3. Look for the flying motif in other African American literature such as *The People Could Fly: Black American Folktales* by Virginia Hamilton. Why do you think slaves dreamed of being able to fly? Discuss.

4. Ringgold is known for her story quilts. Find the star quilt in this book. What did the quilt mean? Reread the background information on Harriet Tubman to discover more about the use of quilts. Read more books about quilts.

Bonjour, Lonnie

- **Orphans**
- **People of mixed ancestry**
- **Paris**
- **World Wars I and II**
- **Harlem Renaissance**

Ages 7–10

Lonnie, an African American Jewish boy, traces his ancestry with the help of the Love Bird of Paris. He finds the spirits of his deceased grandparents and parents who explain his mixed racial heritage and African Americans' contributions to the arts and the role they played in the two World Wars. This fantastical, complex book invites repeated examination; it is one of the few children's books that deals with biracial experiences.

Suggestions for the Classroom

1. Because this book tackles numerous issues and historical references it may provoke many questions, providing a great opportunity for stimulating discussions, further research, and creative work.

2. Lonnie, introduced in *Dinner at Aunt Connie's House,* makes some profound discoveries during his search for his roots. Reflect upon and discuss the many changes in his life prompted by his journey to Paris.

3. Discuss the role the Love Bird plays in bridging the realism and fantasy elements of the story. Examine and discuss the magical elements in Ringgold's other books. Invite young writers to incorporate some magic into their next story.

4. Reread and discuss Ringgold's stirring dedication. Then invite youngsters to find out more about the people and events introduced in the book.

Dinner at Aunt Connie's House

NCSS - CBC Notable Children's Trade Book in the Field of Social Studies

- **Art**
- **Biography**
- **History**
- **Women**

Ages 5–9

When Aunt Connie invites her relatives to her annual dinner and unveiling of her artwork, Melody and her cousin Lonnie discover twelve beautiful portraits in the attic. The portraits are of famous African American women including Rosa Parks, Mary McLeod Bethune, Zora Neale Hurston, Harriet Tubman, and Sojourner Truth. When the portraits speak to them in the voices of the women they depict, the children learn a great deal about their heritage.

Suggestions for the Classroom

1. Melody and Lonnie were inspired by Aunt Connie's artwork. Discuss the ways in which their aspirations were heightened by the gallery of famous African American women. Evaluate the impact of role models in our lives.

2. Faith Ringgold often adds an element of magic to her books. Analyze and discuss the magic in each of her books. How does this enhance each book?

3. Reread and discuss the afterword. Discuss the transformation of Ringgold's quilt into a book for young readers. Then analyze her other books for their origins.

4. Analyze your history textbooks to see if they include information about these women. Then find out if your school and local libraries have books about them. If not, request that they be added to the collections.

- **Biography**
- **Civil Rights**
- **Dreams**

My Dream of Martin Luther King

Narrating this inspiring book in her own voice, Faith Ringgold describes a dream she had about Martin Luther King, Jr. In this innovative approach to biography, she blends the story of his life with her powerful, full page paintings. Framing her dream is her soul-stirring visualization of the people of the world gathering in King's memory to trade in their prejudice, hate, ignorance, and violence for the slain hero's dream. This captivating book ends with a time line, bibliography, and author profile.

All Ages

Suggestions for the Classroom

1. Faith Ringgold is known for her innovative approach to art and writing. Read and compare other biographies about Martin Luther King, Jr. How did Ringgold use her unique artistic sensibilities to create a one-of-a kind book?

2. Examine the ways in which Ringgold incorporates the Dream concept into her books. "Every good thing starts with a dream." This is a great theme to inspire creative thinking and projects.

3. Imagine a world in which people traded in their prejudice, hate, ignorance, violence, and fear for hope, freedom, peace, and love. Express your feelings about this image through art, writing, music, drama, or dance.

4. Ringgold is an artist of international renown. Study her illustrations closely. Find out more about her life. Set up a Faith Ringgold Center in your classroom or library. Add student work as the unit progresses.

- **Art**
- **Bridges**
- **Quilts**
- **Dreams**
- **Autobiographical fiction**
- **Flying**
- **Harlem**

Tar Beach

Caldecott Honor Book

Coretta Scott King Award for Illustrations

New York Times *Best Illustrated Book*

Ringgold based this beautiful book on her 1988 story quilt painting which is now displayed in the Guggenheim Museum in New York City. The quilt exquisitely combines painting, quilt making, autobiography, and fictional narrative in one art form. Set in Harlem in 1939, the first-person narrative tells Cassie Louise Lightfoot's story of how her family goes to the tar paper roof of their tenement—Tar Beach—to picnic, laugh, and tell stories. While her parents play cards, eight-year-old Cassie dreams of power and freedom. Flying is how Cassie will achieve her dream, echoing a significant motif in African American folktale literature. This is a lovely, innovative book, a celebration of the indomitability of the human spirit.

All Ages

Suggestions for the Classroom

1. How did dreaming help Cassie? (It helped her cope with the everyday realities of her life.) How do you think dreaming will help Cassie find solutions to the problems she encounters?

2. Flying is a classic image of our longing for freedom. Dreaming about flying was also one of the ways slaves coped with the horrific institution of slavocracy. Discuss flying, a significant motif in African American folktale literature. Read *The People Could Fly: American Black Folktales* by Virginia Hamilton. See page 111.

3. Ringgold is an artist of international renown who is best known for her story quilts. Try combining fabric with paint in your next project. Then check out and read books about quilts. Read *Sweet Clara and the Freedom Quilt* by Deborah Hopkinson. Then design a quilt. Does your quilt tell a story?

4. Study the pictures of Ringgold's art in her autobiography *We Flew Over the Bridge*. Discuss her use of flight, bridges, and other motifs in her art and writing.

Sandra Scoppettone

Linda Crawford

Italian American (1936–)

Birthday: June 1
Address: c/o Ballantine Books
400 Hahn Rd.
Westminster, Maryland 21157

". . . I don't want to spend the rest of my life being what other people want me to be." (Happy Endings Are All Alike, *p. 201)*

". . . we're all afraid of things we don't understand. Homosexuality—and that includes lesbianism—has been part of life as long as there have been people and it always will be." (Trying Hard to Hear You, *p. 189)*

Books by Sandra Scoppettone

FOR CHILDREN

Bang Bang, You're Dead. **HarperCollins, 1969; 1986.**

Playing Murder. **HarperCollins, 1985; 1987.**

FOR YOUNG ADULTS

Happy Endings Are All Alike. **Harper and Row, 1978; Dell, 1988; Alyson, 1991.**

The Late Great Me. **Bantam, 1976; 1984; 1993.**

Long Time Between Kisses. **HarperCollins, 1982; Bantam, 1984;**

Trying Hard to Hear You. **Alyson Publications, 1974; 1991; 1996.**

FOR ADULTS

Donato and Daughter. **Carroll & Graf, 1995.**

Innocent Bystanders. **NAL/Dutton, 1982; 1984.**

Razzamatazz. **Carroll & Graf, 1995.**

Some Unknown Person. **Putnam, 1977; Carroll & Graf, 1995.**

Such Nice People. **Putnam, 1980; Fawcett, 1981.**

A Creative Kind of Killer. **Carroll & Graf, 1995.**

LAUREN LAURANO MYSTERY SERIES FOR ADULTS

Everything You Have Is Mine. **Little, Brown, 1991; Ballantine, 1992.**

Gonna Take a Homicidal Journey. **Little, Brown, 1998.**

I'll Be Leaving You Always. **Little, Brown, 1993; Ballantine, 1994.**

Let's Face the Music and Die. **Little, Brown, 1996; Ballantine, 1997.**

My Sweet Untraceable You. **Little, Brown, 1994; Ballantine, 1995.**

Sandra Scoppettone was born June 1, 1936 in Morristown, New Jersey; she grew up in South Orange, New Jersey. She started out at age twenty as a novelist and then switched to writing for the theatre. Her work has been produced for television and film as well as on the stage. In 1972 she received a Eugene O'Neill Memorial Theatre Award. A year later she was selected to receive a grant from the Ludwig Vogelstein Foundation.

She has had much success with her novels, but as a playwright she has run into obstacles based on gender bias and has concluded that there is little room at this time for women playwrights. She has directed plays; in the summer of 1973, she directed a production of "Anything Goes" with about sixty teenagers. "The kids and an incident and the fact that I'm a lesbian led me to write this book (*Trying Hard to Hear You*), that deals with homosexuality" (*Something About the Author,* Volume 9, p. 162).

Her book *The Late Great Me* is about a sixteen-year-old alcoholic. Because alcoholism among teenagers is a very serious problem and because she is a recovered alcoholic, she decided to write this book. Scoppettone later wrote an excellent book with lesbian characters, *Happy Endings Are All Alike.* Her books are especially important because, unfortunately, there are still very few books for young people about homosexuality. (See Nancy Garden's chapter on page 78 for additional books with lesbian protagonists.)

In addition to writing, Scoppettone's interests include antiques, going to auctions and yard sales, old movies, and suspense novels. Her interest in suspense is apparent in her books, especially in her mystery series. She writes with humor, dignity, perception, and depth. Her sensitive novels should serve as models for new authors attempting to write about realistic issues. For more information about Sandra Scoppettone, see *Something About the Author,* Volume 9.

- **Lesbianism**
- **Rape**

Happy Endings Are All Alike

An American Library Association Best Book for Young Adults

Eighteen-year-old Jaret Tyler feels very happy and clear about her lesbian relationship with Peggy Danziger but she knows there are plenty of people in this world who would put it down. Even though they feel right about their love, society (represented by various relatives, "friends," and community members) constantly tries to undermine their relationship. A friend of Jaret's brother sees Jaret and Peggy in the woods together. He realizes he now knows a secret he can use for his own brutal purposes. He savagely rapes and beats Jaret, assuming she won't report the crime in order to protect her "secret." The resulting "scandal" puts pressure on Jaret and Peggy's relationship. But Jaret is very clear and strong about who she is. Scoppettone explores an array of prejudices and fears about lesbianism, about rape, and about women. She has written a touching love story with interesting characters. Many of the "issues" about a lesbian relationship are woven skillfully throughout the story so that page after page increases the awareness of the reader. Most of the characterizations are excellent. However, I am concerned about the portrayal of Claire, Peggy's sister. I hope all authors will re-examine their characterizations of so-called unattractive people (by society's standards) and treat them with more dignity and complexity. Another concern is with the portrayal of the rapist as disturbed. Research shows that most rapes are committed by ordinary men. In spite of these reservations, I recommend this book for the positive way it deals with lesbianism and for the excellent writing. It is especially important because, unfortunately, there are still very few good books for young people about lesbianism. Educators and librarians have a responsibility to search out such rare books and make them available to young people in an effort to combat the inexcusable prejudice against lesbians and gays that is rampant in our society.

Ages 12 up

Suggestions for the Classroom

1. Jaret's mother read the letters from Peggy. Analyze this invasion of privacy. Write a policy statement for parents regarding privacy.

2. Mid thought his crime against Jaret would go unreported because of her sexual orientation. Examine his thinking and write an editorial stating your analysis.

3. If you were serving on the jury in the rape trial, what would your verdict be? Write a statement defending your position.

4. Analyze the way Claire's character is portrayed. Is this another stereotype, this time based on appearance? Rewrite her character so that she has more complexity and dignity.

5. Analyze the character of Police Chief Foster. Did you know that his prejudices toward lesbians are representative of many people in the law enforcement, judicial, and medical fields? Is this changing? Write a skit or play based on a related incident.

6. Write a sequel to the book telling about the rape trial, Jaret and Peggy's relationship, and what happened to the other characters.

7. Does your community have an equal protection ordinance that protects lesbians and gays from discrimination in housing, employment, education, health care, public accommodations, and welfare services? Research which other cities have similar ordinances. (Call your public library or the Gay and Lesbian Community Center in your area.)

8. Sometimes people who have been working for the civil rights of lesbians and gays and other disenfranchised groups become discouraged with our bigoted society. Create a slogan, write a song or poem, or design a poster to encourage them to continue this important work.

9. Write a rationale for why excellent books about lesbians and gays should be included in the library collections at all middle and high schools.

10. Does your school district have a policy that protects lesbians and gays from discrimination? If so, find the policy and read it. If not, what can you do to initiate a policy?

11. Read other books with lesbian protagonists. For a list, see page 279.

12. For a list of related resources, see page 82.

The Late Great Me

- **Teenage Alcoholism**
- **Mother/Daughter relationship**
- **Mental illness**

Geri Peters is an alcoholic. She tells her story beginning with her introduction to liquor on the first day of her junior year in high school and continuing with her descent into a horrible nightmare. Geri refuses to acknowledge her problem. Her parents are just as reluctant to bring her drinking into the open. Her mother is retreating into the world of her youth, gradually losing touch with reality. Her engineer father escapes into his job. Scoppettone provides a vivid and dramatic rendering of one of the most serious and fastest-growing teenage problems in the country. In the course of this novel, Geri slowly and painfully realizes that she is an alcoholic and recognizes that the road to recovery must be traveled one step at a time. Sandra Scoppettone says, "I am a recovered alcoholic and that is what led me to write this book."

Ages 11 up

Suggestions for the Classroom

1. Write a letter from Geri Peters to the students in your school.

2. Select quotes to discuss and/or to respond to in writing.

3. Write a summary of this book from Geri's mother's perspective. From her father's perspective.

4. Read and discuss other books on alcoholism such as *Something's Wrong at My House* by Katherine Leiner and *Alcohol: What It Is and What It Does* by Judith Seixas.

5. Call your local drug awareness council and request a speaker to talk about alcoholism.

6. Write a report on alcoholism. Interview schoolmates, teachers, principal, and/or parents.

7. Write a "How to Avoid Alcoholism" handbook for your schoolmates.

- **Gay males**
- **Drama**
- **Death**

Trying Hard to Hear You

An American Library Association Best Book for Young Adults

The narrator, sixteen-year-old Camilla, tells of a crucial summer in the lives of her friends. Her close-knit summer theatre group learns that two of its male members are gay. This discovery leads to heartbreak and terror, a time that reveals the group in all its strengths and weaknesses. Scoppettone examines the underlying prejudice that some teenagers harbor toward lesbians and gays. She also deals with relationships between the African American and white communities and between Camilla and those around her. Teenage as well as adult characters are well developed and the plot threads are skillfully interwoven. Camilla gradually educates herself and comes to a more enlightened view of homosexuality. Sandra Scoppettone wrote this book because, ". . . during the summer of 1973, I directed a production of 'Anything Goes' with about sixty teenagers. The kids and an incident and the fact that I'm a lesbian led me to write this book." Warning: Negative portrayal of one of the characters who is fat, and an unfortunate portrayal of African American women as not able to figure out they are being conned by a character who predicts the gender of their unborn children mar what is otherwise an excellent book.

Ages 12 up

Suggestions for the Classroom

1. Camilla made some important discoveries during her sixteenth summer. Create an essay she might have written titled "What I Learned Last Summer."

2. Write several journal entries for the character of your choice.

3. Analyze the way Janet is portrayed. Is fat oppression any more justified than oppression based on race, age, gender, sexual orientation, religion, national origin, color, or disability? Describe Janet in a fat-positive way.

4. Analyze the way African American women are portrayed when Harlan predicts the gender of their unborn babies. Discuss and rewrite the portrayal.

5. Check your library for books for young adults about lesbians and gays. Talk to your teacher or media director about ordering some of the books listed in this guide. Why is it important that all groups be represented in the library collection?

6. Survey relatives, friends, and school personnel about their attitudes toward lesbians and gays. Write an editorial evaluating the results.

7. Analyze prejudice. Why do you think it exists? What can you do to eradicate it? Make an action plan. Encourage your friends to join you.

8. For a list of related resources, see page 82.

Virginia Driving Hawk Sneve

Lakota (1933–)

Birthday: February 21
Contact: Holiday House
40 East 49th Street
New York, New York 10017

". . . I strive to be honest and accurate about the Native American experience portrayed in my work. In so doing, I hope to dispel stereotypes and to show my reading audience that Native Americans have a proud past, a viable present, and a hopeful future."
(Personal Communication)

Books by Virginia Driving Hawk Sneve

***The Chichi Hoohoo Bogeyman*. Illustrated by Nadema Agard. Holiday, 1975; University of Nebraska Press, 1993.**

***Completing the Circle*. University of Nebraska Press, 1995.**

***Dancing Teepees: Poems by American Indian Youth*. Illustrated by Stephen Gammell. Holiday, 1989; 1991.**

***Daughters of Dakota*. Sky Carrier Press, 1990.**

***Enduring Wisdom. Sayings from American Indians*. Holiday, forthcoming.**

***Jimmy Yellow Hawk*. Holiday, *1972*.**

***High Elk's Treasure*. Holiday, 1995.**

***The Trickster and the Troll*. University of Nebraska Press, 1997.**

***They Led a Nation*. Brevet Press, 1975.**

***When Thunders Spoke*. Illustrated by Oren Lyons. Holiday, 1974; University of Nebraska Press, 1993.**

***First Americans Series*. All illustrated by Ronald Himler and published by Holiday House:**

- ***The Apaches*. 1997.**
- ***The Navajos*. 1993.**
- ***The Cherokees*. 1996.**
- ***The Nez Perce*. 1994.**
- ***The Cheyennes*. 1996.**
- ***The Seminoles*. 1994.**
- ***The Hopis*. 1995.**
- ***The Sioux*, 1993.**
- ***The Iroquois*. 1995.**

Virginia Driving Hawk Sneve (rhymes with navy) was born and raised on the Rosebud Reservation in South Dakota and is an enrolled member of the Rosebud Sioux tribe. She attended Bureau of Indian Affairs schools on the reservation and graduated from St. Mary's High School for Indian Girls in Springfield, South Dakota in 1950. She received a B.S. (1954) and M.Ed. (1969) in education from South Dakota State University.

She taught junior and senior high school music, English, speech, and drama, and later served as a guidance counselor. She also worked as a television consultant, producer, and writer. She is presently a counselor at Rapid City Central High School and an associate instructor of English for the Ogalala Lakota College.

The recipient of many awards and honors, Sneve was selected for a Distinguished Native American Alumnus Award from South Dakota State University and the Native American Prose Award from the University of Nebraska Press, both in 1992. She holds an honorary doctorate from Dakota Wesleyan University.

Sneve has written numerous books for children and adults, as well as many short stories, poems, articles, and essays. For her, writing is an extension of being a teacher and a counselor. She writes: "To American Indians, the spoken word was sacred. Children listened to their grandparents tell stories, recite ceremonial prayers and chants, and sing lullabies and other tribal songs. The children grew up remembering this music and knew that the act of speaking words gave life to Native American stories, songs, and prayers. Words were chosen carefully and rarely wasted" *(Dancing Teepees).*

- **Gender roles**
- **Invisible spirits**
- **Mixed ancestry**

Ages 8 to 12

The Chichi Hoohoo Bogeyman

While visiting their grandparents, three adventurous cousins disobey their parents and find themselves in a frightening situation. The story opens with strange occurrences that create an undercurrent of tension. Cindy, Mary Jo, and Lori discuss similarities and differences among the Dakota chichi, the Hopi hoohoo, and the Caucasian bogeyman. After they encounter a strange man while exploring an old fort, Lori experiences nightmares and Cindy disappears. It is up to Mary Jo to explain the events of the past few days to their worried parents. All ends well when the mystery of the chichi hoohoo bogeyman is solved. This is an entertaining story featuring strong females protagonists. However, the way Andy Lytton is portrayed in the first four chapters of the book may be offensive to people with similar disabilities and may be misleading to young readers. Unkempt, disabled men are no more or less likely to be pedophiles than neat, well dressed, "normal" men. In fact, research has revealed that most child molesters are male family members.

Suggestions for the Classroom

1. Cindy, Mary Jo, and Lori resented the differences in the way their parents treated them and their brothers. Discuss the restrictions they and other girls often experience and propose gender-fair guidelines to help adults understand this issue.

2. Cindy understood the negative depictions of Native people in the movies. Reread and discuss her reactions on pages 32–34. Discuss the impact her perceptions had on her cousins.

3. Reread and discuss the author's note. Invite youngsters to research the chichi and hoohoo further. Interested youngsters might want to find out if other cultures have similar figures.

Completing the Circle

North American Indian Prose Award

- **Biography**
- **Grandmothers**
- **Women**

In this eloquent tribute to her grandmothers' lives, Virginia Driving Hawk Sneve lovingly interweaves biography with history, poetry, and storytelling. Describing her female ancestors as resourceful, tough, and adaptable, and at once community-minded and fiercely independent, Sneve introduces her grandmothers including her paternal grandmother, Flora Clairmont Driving Hawk, whose gift for storytelling stirred her granddaughter's imagination. Dedicating her book to her granddaughters, Sneve traces her Santee, Teton, and Ponca Sioux heritage from the mid-19th century to the present. This important book includes a detailed family tree, photographs, and an extensive bibliography.

Ages 15 up

Suggestions for the Classroom

1. When Sneve was gathering data for another project, she became aware of the gaps of information about Lakota women. Later, when she began her personal search for her relatives, she again realized that little was known about her grandmothers. Discuss issues of exclusion, erasure, and marginalization. Examine other books for the inclusion of indigenous women's history. As a group, write and send a request that related materials be included in school and public library collections.

2. Sneve used diaries, memoirs, census records, anecdotes, interviews, family records, and her own memories to piece together the stories of her grandmothers. Inspired by her example, encourage interested young women to interview their female elders. Note: Be sensitive to the fact that some young people do not have access to information about their genealogy.

3. Virginia Driving Hawk Sneve researched the material in this book to help her understand how her heritage has influenced her life and writing. How does reading this book and understanding who she is as a person and as a writer strengthen and enrich the connection readers have with her?

4. For more information about women's history, contact the National Women's History Project, 7738 Bell Road, Windsor, CA 95492-8518; 707-838-6000.

Dancing Teepees: Poems of American Indian Youth

- **Poetry**

Virginia Driving Hawk Sneve (rhymes with navy) selected these poems written by Native American youth. (Three of the poems were written by Sneve.) She writes, "Many of the selections have been passed from the old to the young. Others are from contemporary tribal poets (including the anthologist) who, as children, learned to respect the power of the spoken word."

Ages 7 up

Suggestions for the Classroom

1. Choose one of the poems in the book. Respond with one of the following: Write why you chose that poem; Memorize and recite it for your class; Illustrate the poem; Write a response poem; Make a poetry poster featuring the poem you chose.

2. Check out and read other books with poetry by Native American children such as: *Arrows Four* by T. D. Allen, and *Photographs and Poems by Sioux Children from Porcupine Day School.*

3. Read the poems in the book by Sneve. Then write a journal entry that she might have written when she created one of the poems.

4. One of Virginia Driving Hawk Sneve's goals for her writing is to dispel stereotypes. Her books show that Native Americans have a proud past, a viable present, and a hopeful future. Use *How to Tell the Difference: A Guide to Evaluating Children's Books for Anti-Indian Bias* by Beverly Slapin, Doris Seale, and Rosemary Gonzales (Oyate: 510-848-6700) for valuable information about evaluating books.

- **Tradition and change**
- **Tricksters**
- **Folklore**

Ages 8 up

The Trickster and the Troll

Iktomi, a Lakota trickster, and Troll, from Norse mythology find solace in their unlikely friendship when their humans experience disruption, dislocation, and destruction. Combining elements from her Lakota heritage and her husband's Norwegian background, Virginia Driving Hawk Sneve weaves a thought-inspiring tapestry of two cultures. In perhaps her most imaginative work to date, she has written a powerful history of her people. Readable, entertaining, the book is filled with humor, love, loss, heartache, and hope. Includes glossaries of Lakota and Norwegian terms.

Suggestions for the Classroom

1. This is an excellent example of a children's book that is appropriate for high school students and even adults. The story brings alive important events in Lakota and United States history, adding texture and richness, and exploring multiple levels of what happened. Natural extensions include art, storytelling, writing, and music.

2. Iktomi and Troll are ancient and timeless beings who represent their respective cultures. Discuss their differences and similarities and the developments in their friendship. Examine the changes Iktomi, Troll, and their humans experienced.

3. Sneve examines this period in history from multiple perspectives. The European invaders did not stop to consider the immensity of the losses and grief that abandoning their own cultures and destroying other cultures would bring. Discuss the impact this time of upheaval and cultural disintegration and denial had on Iktomi, Troll, and their humans.

4. Reread and discuss the author's note. Sneve writes that her children, when young, called themselves Sioux-wegian. She dedicated the book to her grandchildren. Discuss her motivations for writing her books and her contributions to cross-cultural understanding and respect.

- **Tradition and change**
- **Grandfathers**

Ages 10 up

When Thunders Spoke

Norman Two Bull, the third generation of his family to live on a Dakota reservation, spends his fifteenth summer exploring the contrasts between the old ways and the new. Encouraged by his grandfather, he makes a perilous climb to the top of a sacred butte where he finds an ancient relic with unusual powers. This haunting story examines generational, cultural, gender, family, and religious conflicts. Note: The illustration selected for the cover of the recent edition of the book depicts Norman killing a rattlesnake in self-defense. This violent image is not indicative of the tone of the book.

Suggestions for the Classroom

1. This book is sure to stimulate lively discussions about a number of issues. Encourage youngsters to generate a list of questions such as: Should the Two Bulls pursue the proposal to set up an agate quarry? What role might the tribal council play in getting the trading post owner to treat the Native children with respect? How might Sarah Two Bull's membership in the women's group help her to become more independent? How might Norman reconcile the complexities presented to him by his relatives and community members?

2. Reread and discuss the prologue. Sneve writes, "Today the ways of the past have been forgotten by many or contemptuously called superstitions." (p. 14). What impact might books like this one have on attitudes toward traditions?

3. Select other quotes for discussions such as Sitting Bull's words: "When you find something good in the white man's road, pick it up. When you find something bad, or that turns out bad, drop it and leave it alone." (p. 76).

Yoshiko Uchida

Deborah Storms

Japanese American (1921–1992)

"Just because you're different from other people doesn't mean you're not as good or that you have to dislike yourself . . . don't ever be ashamed of who you are. Just be the best person you can. Believe in your own worth." (Jar of Dreams, *p. 125)*

"I hope to give young Asians a sense of their own history. At the same time, I want to dispel the stereotypic image still held by many non-Asians about the Japanese Americans and write about them as real people." *(Margaret K. McElderry Books Brochure)*

Books by Yoshiko Uchida

The Best Bad Thing. **A Margaret K. McElderry Book/Atheneum, 1983; Macmillan, 1986.**

The Birthday Visitor. **Scribner, 1975.**

The Bracelet. **Illustrated by Joanna Yardley. Putnam, 1993.**

The Dancing Kettle. **Illustrated by Richard C. Jones. Harcourt Brace, 1949; Creative Arts Books, 1986.**

Desert Exile: The Uprooting of a Japanese-American Family. **University of Washington Press, 1982.**

The Forever Christmas Tree. **Charles Scribner, 1963.**

The Full Circle. **Friendship Press, 1957.**

The Happiest Ending. **A Margaret K. McElderry Book/Atheneum, 1985.**

Hisako's Mysteries. **Charles Scribner, 1969.**

In-Between Miya. **Charles Scribner, 1967.**

The Invisible Thread. **Julian Messner, 1991.**

A Jar of Dreams. **A Margaret K. McElderry Book/Atheneum, 1981; Macmillan, 1985.**

Journey Home. **A Margaret K. McElderry Book/Atheneum, 1978.**

Journey to Topaz. **Charles Scribner's Sons, 1971; Creative Arts Book Company, 1985.**

The Magic Listening Cap. **Harcourt Brace, 1955; Creative Arts Book Company, 1987.**

Makoto, the Smallest Boy. **Thomas Y. Crowell, 1970.**

The Magic Purse. **Illustrated by Keiko Narahashi. Macmillan, 1993.**

Mik and the Prowler. **Harcourt Brace, 1960.**

New Friends for Susan. **Charles Scribner, 1951.**

Picture Bride. **Northland Press, 1987.**

The Promised Year. **Harcourt Brace, 1959.**

Rokubei and the Thousand Rice Bowls. **Charles Scribner, 1962.**

The Rooster Who Understood Japanese. **Illustrated by Charles Robinson. Charles Scribner's Sons, 1976.**

Samurai of Gold Hill. **Creative Arts Book Company, 1985.**

The Sea of Gold. **Illustrated by Marianne Yamaguchi. Creative Arts Book Company, 1988.**

Sumi and the Goat and the Tokyo Express. **Charles Scribner, 1969.**

Sumi's Prize. **Charles Scribner, 1964.**

Sumi's Special Happening. **Charles Scribner, 1966.**

Tabi: Journey Through Time. **United Methodist Publishing, 1984.**

Takao and Grandfather's Sword. **Harcourt Brace, 1958.**

The Two Foolish Cats. **Illustrated by Margot Zemach. A Margaret K. McElderry Book/Macmillan, 1987.**

The Wise Old Woman. **Illustrated by Martin Springett. A Margaret K. McElderry Book/Macmillan, 1994.**

Yoshiko Uchida was born November 24, 1921 in Alameda, California. Her mother, Iku Umegaki Uchida, a poet, and her father, Dwight Takashi Uchida, a businessperson, were born in Japan and came to the United States as young adults. Uchida's mother loved books and their house was filled with them. She often read Japanese stories to her two daughters. She was a deeply caring and giving person. "Don't ever be indifferent; indifference is the worst fault of all," she told her daughters (personal communication).

Uchida was interested in books and writing from a very early age. She started writing stories when she was ten. Being the child of frugal immigrant parents, she wrote her stories on brown wrapping paper which she cut up and bound into booklets. Uchida was a saver and kept these booklets until her death in 1992. The first is titled "Jimmy Chipmunk and His Friends: A Short Story for Small Children."

As a child, Uchida not only wrote stories but kept a journal which she also saved. She recorded special events such as the day she got her dog and the sad day he died of distemper. In her journal, she drew a tombstone for him and decorated it with floral wreaths. She preserved the joy and sadness of special times in her life by writing about them.

Uchida experienced the rejection and alienation felt by many Japanese people who grew up in the United States. Although her family gave her much love and security, she longed to be accepted by the outside community. When she was ten, her family took a trip to Connecticut and the experience of being perceived as a foreigner was very painful. As an adolescent, she still believed in the melting pot; she perceived integration into white American society as the way to overcome the rejection she had experienced in so many aspects of her life.

Uchida was busy studying for her final exams at the University of California when war between Japan and the United States was declared. She and her family were among 120,000 West Coast Japanese Americans who were uprooted from their homes and imprisoned in concentration camps by the United States government. The Uchidas were sent to live in a horse stall at Tanforan Race Track and then moved to Topaz, a bleak concentration camp in the desert in Utah. Uchida has written about this horrific experience in several of her books including her autobiographies, *Desert Exile: The Uprooting of a Japanese-American Family* and *The Invisible Thread.*

Finally in 1976, President Gerald Ford announced that not only was the evacuation wrong, but Japanese Americans were and are loyal Americans. In 1983, the Commission of Wartime Relocation and Internment established by the United States Congress concluded that a grave injustice was done to Japanese Americans and that the causes of the uprooting were race prejudice, war hysteria, and a failure of leadership. In 1988, a Redress Bill was passed by Congress to mitigate some of the massive financial losses suffered by Japanese Americans. And so, many years after the tragic wartime uprooting, the country finally acknowledged that it had made a terrible mistake. But it came too late for most of the Issei (first generation) Japanese Americans who, like Uchida's parents, were deceased, and too late for many Nisei (second generation) also.

Uchida graduated with honors from the University of California with a B.A. in English, Philosophy, and History. She earned an M.A. in Education from Smith College, Northhampton, Massachusetts. She taught elementary school at Topaz and in Philadelphia. She was a full-time writer most of the time after that.

In 1952, Uchida was awarded a fellowship to study in Japan. "My experience in Japan was as positive and restorative as the uprooting and imprisonment had been negative and depleting. I came home aware of a new dimension to myself as a Japanese American and with new respect and admiration for the culture that had made my parents what they were. The circle was complete . . . . I am proud to be a Japanese American and am secure in that knowledge of myself" (*Something About the Author,* Volume 53, p. 155).

Yoshiko Uchida died in June, 1992 at the Alta Medical Center in Berkeley, California. A gifted writer, she wrote over thirty books from 1949 to 1991 and won many honors and awards. Her lively, beautiful books are a very special gift to young readers and to everyone interested in children's literature. She gave her readers a sense of hope, affirmation, and purpose. She felt that people need the sense of continuity that comes from knowing about the past. She reinforced the pride of young Japanese Americans and gave them a profound remembrance of their history and culture. Her superb books portray the pain of rejection, the spirit of determination, and love of self and others. Her body of work constitutes a significant contribution to the world of literature for young readers.

". . . I want each new generation of Americans to know what once happened in our democracy. I want them to love and cherish the freedom that can be snatched away so quickly, even by their own country. Most of all, I ask them to be vigilant, so that such a tragedy will never happen to any group of people in America again" (*Desert Exile*).

"I want to celebrate our common humanity, for I feel the basic elements of humanity are present in all our strivings" (Margaret K. McElderry Books brochure).

For more information about Yoshiko Uchida, see her autobiographies: *Desert Exile: The Uprooting of a Japanese-American Family* and *The Invisible Thread: An Autobiography.*

The Best Bad Thing

American Library Association Notable Book
Junior Literary Guild Book
***Best Books of the Year Lists* School Library Journal**
Notable Children's Master Reading List for William Allen White Award
California Recommended Reading List
Master Reading List—Iowa Children's Choice Award

- **U.S. history**
- **Depression Era**

In this second book in the Rinko trilogy (*A Jar of Dreams, The Best Bad Thing, The Happiest Ending*), Yoshiko Uchida continues the engaging story of the Tsujimuras, a Japanese American family living in California during the Depression Era of the 1930s. Twelve-year-old Rinko spends a dreaded month in East Oakland helping widowed Mrs. Hata and her two pesky sons. Rinko learns again (as she did with her Aunt Waka in *A Jar of Dreams*) not to prejudge people—people are not always what they seem. She ends up having an interesting month after all—one in which she continues to grow in her ability to understand and help people. Uchida again skillfully develops each character as a unique, interesting, complex, and multi-dimensional person. She expertly combines the stimulating with the reassuring, and balances heavy and light in both plot and character development.

Ages 9 up

Suggestions for the Classroom

1. Read *A Jar of Dreams* before reading this book. Later, read the third book in the trilogy, *The Happiest Ending.*

2. Rinko's neighbor, Mrs. Sugarman, said Mama was a combination of pure mercy and moxie. Discuss the meaning of that statement. Have you ever helped someone who needed help? Write about your experiences.

3. Has something you dreaded doing turned out to be different than you thought it would be? Write a story telling about it.

4. Make a list of qualities Rinko would have used to describe Mrs. Hata at the beginning of the book. Then make a list for the end of the book. Compare the two lists. What did Rinko learn about people? She had a similar experience with Aunt Waka in *A Jar of Dreams.* Has this ever happened to you? Write a story describing your experiences. What lesson does this teach us? (Don't prejudge people.) Discuss.

5. Summarize this book using the Good News/Bad News motif. Example: "I didn't get to go to the movies but I did get to go out to the countryside." Make a list of bad things that happened. How did the characters cope with each of these problems? What was the "best" bad thing?

6. Choose a quote to write about such as: "It's not always easy to make a life for yourself in a strange land. Sometimes . . . often, you're afraid, and you close yourself off and shut people out."

- **Internment of Japanese Americans**
- **U.S. history**
- **World War II**
- **Friendship**
- **Keepsakes**

Ages 6 up

The Bracelet

New York Times Book Review *Best Illustrated Children's Book*

Drawing upon her own experiences as a Japanese American during World War II, Yoshiko Uchida wrote this poignant book about friendship, memory, and loss. *The Bracelet* is the tenderly illustrated story of how seven-year-old Emi's life changed forever when she and her family are uprooted from their home in Berkeley and taken away to an internment camp. Just before they leave, her best friend sadly gives her a precious remembrance, a gold bracelet. While settling in to their "apartment" in a horse stall at the Tanforan Racetracks, Emi discovers that she has lost the bracelet. Struggling to understand the betrayal by her country, she worries that without the bracelet, she will forget her best friend. Her mother reassures her, "You don't need a bracelet to remember Laurie any more than we need a photo to remember Papa or our home or all the friends and things we loved and left behind. Those are things we carry in our hearts and take with us no matter where we are sent." An Afterword provides historical context for this sensitive introduction to a tragic chapter in United States history.

Suggestions for the Classroom

1. If Emi had kept a journal, what might she have written during this difficult time in her life?

2. Even though this book is about a painful subject, Yoshiko Uchida left readers with a sense of hope. Examine the book for the ways she accomplishes this. Discuss.

3. Read *Naomi's Road* by Joy Kogawa (see page 135). Naomi, in Canada, and Emi, in the United States, had similar experiences during the war. If they could have written letters to each other, what might they have said?

4. Reread and discuss the Afterword. (Yoshiko Uchida's parents died long before the U.S. government belatedly made symbolic restitution to those Japanese Americans whose civil rights had been abrogated. Uchida lived only four more years.)

The Dancing Kettle and Other Japanese Folk Tales

• Folktales (Japanese)

These fourteen folktales, retold by Yoshiko Uchida, will delight both children and adults. These stories were told to Uchida during her childhood and she has retold them with authenticity and humor. They reflect the universal human traits of goodness and kindness and of greed and folly. The book includes a glossary and a guide to pronunciation.

Ages 7 up

Suggestions for the Classroom

1. Divide the class into groups. Have each group choose one of the folktales to present to the class through drama, storytelling, illustration, or filmstrip.

2. Read other Japanese folk tales such as those by Yoshiko Uchida featured in this chapter. Set up a center in your classroom on folktales. Invite youngsters to write and illustrate folktales of their own. Collect into a class booklet.

Desert Exile: The Uprooting of a Japanese-American Family

• Autobiography
• Internment of Japanese Americans
• U.S. history
• World War II

This moving account is Uchida's personal history of her family's experiences before and during the World War II uprooting and internment of Japanese Americans. She tells with insight and clarity what it was like to be sent by her own government to live in a concentration camp. This "relocation" has since been judged as one of the most shameful episodes in U.S. history. Uchida says, "The ultimate tragedy of that mistake, I believe, was that our government betrayed not only the Japanese people but all Americans, for in its flagrant violation of our Constitution, it damaged the essence of the democratic beliefs on which this country was founded." The U.S. belatedly started trying to make amends, and finally, fifty years later, issued a formal apology, admitted its mistake, and appropriated reparations.

Ages 12 up

Suggestions for the Classroom

1. Read and discuss other books about the internment of Japanese Americans (see page 201).

2. How did Uchida's sense of herself as a Japanese American change? Why?

3. How did some white people try to support Japanese Americans? How did others betray them?

4. Reread the 1976 Executive Order 9066. Discuss and then write a response.

5. Make a list of problems Uchida and her family faced. How did they cope with each problem?

6. What if you and your family were sent to a concentration camp? Write a response.

7. Choose a quote such as the following, and respond: "Don't ever be indifferent . . . Indifference is the worst fault of all." or "Society caused us to feel ashamed of something that should have made us proud."

8. Here is a list of the ten major concentration camps where Japanese Americans were unjustly imprisoned during World War II. Find each on a map: Amache, Colorado (7,318 persons); Gila River, Arizona (13,348 persons); Heart River, Wyoming (10,767 persons); Jerome, Arkansas (8,497 persons); Manzanar, California (10,046 persons); Minidoka, Idaho (9,397 persons); Rohwer, Arkansas (8,475 persons); Tule Lake, California (18,789 persons); Topaz, Utah (8,130 persons); Poston, Arizona (17,814 persons).

9. Reread and discuss the epilogue. Write a response.

- **Arranged marriages**
- **U.S. history**
- **Depression Era**

The Happiest Ending

Junior Literary Guild Selection
Bay Area Book Reviews Award
CCBC Children's Choices
Notable Trade Book in the Field of Social Studies
Iowa Children's Choices Master List
California Recommended Reading List

In this third book of the Rinko trilogy (*A Jar of Dreams, The Best Bad Thing, The Happiest Ending*), Yoshiko Uchida continues the story of the Tsujimuras, a Japanese American family living in California during the Depression Era of the 1930s. Rinko, the indomitable heroine of this trilogy, is a lively narrator. Her perspective is refreshing, absorbing, and noteworthy. In this book, Rinko attempts to intervene in an arranged marriage between Teru, who will be coming from Japan, and a stranger twice her age. Rinko and her family and friends also join forces to help resolve other difficulties—the loss of a boarder's life savings and the sudden break-up of a marriage. Rinko continues to mature in her insight into the complexities of human nature. She discovers hidden strengths in the people around her and begins to recognize that there are many different kinds of love. In this humorous, fast paced conclusion to the trilogy, the engaging protagonist will again delight her readers and teach them much about the commonalities of human experience.

Ages 9 up

Suggestions for the Classroom

1. Write a piece about how Rinko has grown during the trilogy. What has she learned? How has she changed? What will she do differently? What behaviors will she keep?

2. Make a list of experiences that Rinko had that you have also had. What have you learned about the commonalties of human experience?

3. Discuss the ways in which Rinko misjudged Aunt Waka in *Jar of Dreams,* Mrs. Hata in *The Best Bad Thing,* and Mr. Kinjo in *Happiest Ending.* How did they each turn out to be different than she thought?

4. Have you ever admitted to someone that you were wrong about them? Write about what happened.

5. Think about what Rinko has learned about life. Create a recipe for her that expresses her learnings. For example: 1 cup of insight, 2 cups of humor, etc.

6. Find quotes to respond to in writing such as: "I felt all mixed up inside—like I'd dumped everything from my bureau drawer out on my bed and needed to sort things out."

7. What was the "happiest ending"?

8. Write a trilogy of your own. (*The Happiest Ending* is the third book in the Rinko trilogy.)

- **Authors**
- **Autobiography**
- **World War II**

The Invisible Thread: An Autobiography

Children's book author Yoshiko Uchida describes growing up in Berkeley, California as a Nisei (second generation Japanese American), and her family's internment in a Utah concentration camp during World War II. She describes her family, the Japanese American community, the social and political climate of the time, and her early writing experiences. She writes about her school experiences including unhappy days as an outsider in junior and senior high school. She recounts in poignant detail the horrific experiences of being uprooted and incarcerated in concentration camps by her own country. She describes her growth in her understanding of herself from her youth when she was imbued with the melting pot mentality and wanted to be like everyone else, to later in her life when she became aware of new dimensions of herself and developed pride in being a Japanese American. This book is a beautifully written autobiography by a truly outstanding and wonderful person and writer.

Ages 10 up

Suggestions for the Classroom

1. What is the invisible thread? Discuss and/or write about it.

2. When did Uchida write her first book? What was it about? How did Uchida's mother influence her writing? (Her mother, a poet, loved books and read to her often.)

3. How did Uchida feel during her first trip to Japan? How did her feelings change during her second trip to Japan? Why?

4. Why were Uchida's days in junior and senior high school unhappy? What could people do to make sure no one ever feels that way again? Write a response. Make a class list of suggestions.

5. How did Uchida feel about being Japanese American when she was young? How did her feelings change later? What can schools do to help young people who are from diverse cultures? What can you do?

6. Read other books about the uprooting and imprisonment of Japanese Americans during World War II (see page 201). Discuss. How would you feel if your country treated you that way? Write a response. Make a class list of recommendations so that such a tragedy will never happen again.

7. Make a list of problems Uchida, her family, and neighbors faced in the camp. How did they deal with those problems?

8. Read the section regarding the U.S. acknowledgment of the terrible mistake our country made. What other mistakes has our country made? How can we ever begin to mitigate these grave injustices? What can we do to make sure such tragedies will never happen again?

9. What does Uchida mean by "From Mouse to Tiger"? Discuss the titles of her other chapters.

10. What do the Fifth and Fourteenth Amendments to the Constitution say? Discuss.

11. Discuss and/or write responses to quotes such as the following: "Most of all, I ask them to be vigilant, so that such a tragedy will never happen to any group of people in America again."

12. For a list of concentration camps and their locations, see page 195.

A Jar of Dreams

Commonwealth Club of California Medal for Best Juvenile Book by California Author
Notable Children's Trade Book in Field of Social Studies
California Recommended Reading List
Friends of Children and Literature Award

- **Aspirations**
- **Home business**
- **Depression Era**
- **U.S. history**
- **Death of an animal companion**
- **Aunts**

This is the first book in the Rinko trilogy (*A Jar of Dreams, The Best Bad Thing, The Happiest Ending*). Eleven-year-old Rinko, growing up in California during the Depression Era of the 1930s, is made to feel excluded and different because she is Japanese American. Although she, like other children her age, wants to be like everyone else, she begins to realize that she is different *and* a very special and worthy person. This is a touching, yet humorous story of how Rinko finds her strengths and learns to dream her own dreams.

Her Aunt Waka, who is visiting from Japan, plays an important role in helping Rinko and her family deal with the difficulties they face—financial problems, competition for laundry business (threats, slashed tires, violence), and other forms of racism. Uchida has done a beautiful job of telling Rinko's story with dignity, pride, and humor. This is a superb story for demonstrating the pain of rejection, the spirit of determination, and the love of self. Uchida expertly balances tragedy with humor, the intense with the reassuring.

Ages 9 up

Suggestions for the Classroom

1. Has a relative (such as Aunt Waka) helped you deal with problems? Discuss and/or write about how this helped you.

2. What happened to Maxie? Write an obituary for him. Share stories about the deaths of animal companions.

3. Do you have a "jar of dreams"? Write about your hopes and dreams.

4. What qualities helped Rinko cope with the racism she faced?

5. Choose quotes from the story such as the following for discussion and written responses: "Some days I feel so left out, I hate my black hair and Japanese face. . . . And more than anything, I wish I could be like everybody else." or "Just because you're different from other people doesn't mean you're not as good or that you have to dislike yourself. . . . Don't ever be ashamed of who you are. Just be the best person you can. Believe in your own worth."

6. Write a letter from Rinko to Aunt Waka a few weeks after Aunt Waka left.

7. Read the next two books in the Rinko trilogy: *The Best Bad Thing* and *The Happiest Ending.*

- **Internment of Japanese Americans**
- **Concentration camps**
- **Historical fiction**
- **World War II**

Journey Home

Atheneum/Margaret K. McElderry Books
Junior Literary Guild Edition
Children's Choices
Nominated for William Allen White Award
Nene Award
California Young Readers Medal
Special Honor List, International Year of the Child
Notable Children's Trade Book in the Field of Social Studies
Aladdin Paperback Edition
Children's Book of the Year
Nominated for Maud Hart Lovelace Award
California Recommended Reading List

This book is the sequel to *Journey to Topaz.* Yuki and her family are released from a concentration camp where thousands of Japanese Americans were imprisoned during World War II. As they start life anew, they are met with prejudice, hostility, and violence. This is a poignant, candid, and warm story about a tragic, ugly part of United States history. Yuki and her family maintain their hope, dignity, and belief in themselves throughout their ordeal. In addition to winning many awards, the book has been optioned by KCET for PBS television.

Ages 9 up

Suggestions for the Classroom

1. Reread Yuki's nightmare about the dust storm. Then write about a nightmare you had and illustrate it.

2. When Yuki and her family left Topaz Concentration Camp, Yuki thought they would be safe. What bad things happened to them in Salt Lake City and Berkeley?

3. How was Ken different when he returned from the war? For example, he lost the use of his leg and he was depressed and confused—he had an ache inside his soul. What would you do to help your brother or sister if they had a similar experience?

4. What were the three good things that happened in Chapter 5? (Ken was not killed, only wounded in the war; the exclusion order against the Japanese on the West Coast was revoked; and Reverend Wada helped them return to Berkeley.) Discuss.

5. Uncle Oka said, "They are all the same." Are all white people the same? Make a list of the white people who were kind and helpful to Yuki's family. What did they do to help? What would you do to help if you knew some people were being discriminated against?

Journey to Topaz: A Story of the Japanese American Evacuation

ALA Notable Book
Nominated for: Dorothy Canfield Fischer Children's Book Award
Sequoyah Children's Book Award
William Allen White Award
California Recommended Reading Core Title

- **World War II**
- **Internment of Japanese Americans**
- **Concentration camps**
- **Historical fiction**

During World War II, the United States government uprooted 120,000 West Coast Japanese Americans, without hearing or trial, and imprisoned them behind barbed wires. Uchida has based this moving and insightful story on her personal experiences. Eleven-year-old Yuki Sakane's peaceful world is suddenly shattered by the bombing of Pearl Harbor. Her father is taken by the FBI and she, along with her mother and brother, are shipped with thousands of other West Coast Japanese Americans to the horse stalls of Tanforan Racetrack. They are later sent to the desert concentration camp named Topaz. There, they and their new neighbors face illness, crowding, dust storms, tragedy, and many other hardships. This tragic story is told with dignity and sensitivity. The characters are beautifully developed; Yuki is a delightfully optimistic, compassionate person that all readers will love. Don't miss the sequel, *Journey Home.*

Ages 9 up

Suggestions for the Classroom

1. Read Uchida's prologue. Discuss. Read other books about the internment of Japanese Americans (see page 201). Write a statement about your feelings.

2. Discuss Emi's illness. What if Emi had had tuberculosis? Why couldn't Yuki visit her until they found out what was wrong? How did Yuki feel? Has a friend or relative of yours been in the hospital? Write about it.

3. What happened to Mr. Kurihara? (He was shot by the guards while looking for arrowheads.) Pretend you are a newspaper reporter and write an article about his death.

4. Make a list of all the problems Yuki, her relatives, and neighbors faced at Tanforan and Topaz. Discuss how they dealt with these problems.

5. Debate whether or not Ken should have volunteered to serve in the Army. Would you volunteer if your country had treated you the way it treated Ken and his family?

6. Predict what will happen to Yuki's family in Salt Lake City. Then read the sequel, *Journey Home,* to see what happened.

7. What if you had to go to a concentration camp? Make a list of items you would take with you. Write a statement about your feelings.

- **Folklore (Japanese)**

The Magic Listening Cap: More Folk Tales from Japan

Herald Tribune *Honor Book*

California Recommended Reading List

These fourteen folktales, retold and illustrated by Yoshiko Uchida, speak of the universal human condition—of generosity and decency and of greed and cruelty. Told with humor and wisdom and illustrated with charming black and white brush drawings, these stories ring with universal familiarity and help us celebrate our common humanity. The book includes a glossary.

Ages 7 up

Suggestions for the Classroom

1. Set up a center on folktales. Include Uchida's other books: *The Two Foolish Cats, The Dancing Kettle, The Magic Purse,* and *The Sea of Gold,* and *Tales From the Bamboo Grove* by Yoko Kawashima Watkins. For additional titles, see the Subject Index on pages 276–277.

2. Choose one of the folktales. Retell the tale using cartooning. Or write and produce a play or puppet show based on one of the tales.

3. Create a character collage based on the qualities exhibited in the tales such as generosity, greed, wisdom, honesty, etc.

4. Write and illustrate a folktale of your own. Collect into a class booklet.

- **Folklore (Japanese)**

The Magic Purse

After facing many dangers, a poor farmer receives a magic purse that always refills itself with gold. Yoshiko Uchida captured the haunting mood, magic, and imagery in her sensitive retelling of this old tale from Japan. The story is beautifully enhanced by the shimmering watercolor paintings. The farmer bravely faces his own fears as well as the warnings of others to honor a promise. When his kindness is rewarded, he shares his wealth with others.

Ages 5 up

Suggestions for the Classroom

1. This tale lends itself nicely to dramatization. A simple procedure that avoids memorizing lines and rehearsals involves youngsters pantomiming the actions of the characters while the adult reads the story.

2. What do you think the young woman wrote in her letter? As a group, compose the letter as it might have been written.

3. What advice might the farmer give another poor person who longs to take a journey?

- **World War II**
- **Evacuation of Japanese Americans**
- **Immigrants**
- **Arranged marriages**

Picture Bride

Best Books for Teenage List, New York Public Library

This engaging novel traces Hana Omiya's life from the time she left Japan for Oakland, California to marry Taro Takeda in 1917, until 1943 when Taro is killed at the desert concentration camp during World War II. Hana endures many disappointments during those twenty-six years. First, Taro turns out to be reserved and unimaginative with a rundown shop instead of the dynamic, prosperous businessperson he had been portrayed to be. Next, Hana is faced by a hostile white society that causes her to be "... pressed down, apologetic, making herself small and inconspicuous, never able to reach out or to feel completely fulfilled." And one of the most painful denials is the emotional and cultural estrangement of her own daughter. But perhaps worst of all is the cruel treatment by the United States government during World War II. When Hana and other West Coast Japanese Americans are uprooted from their homes and imprisoned in desert concentration camps, Taro is shot by guards while looking for arrowheads. This is a tender, painful, beautifully written novel that tells the story of one early Japanese woman immigrant and the spirit and strength that enabled her to survive. This is a very significant, powerful book.

Ages 13 up

Suggestions for the Classroom

1. Make a list of disillusionments that Hana faced during the twenty-six years this book covers. Choose one to respond to in writing.

2. What if Hana had stayed in Japan? Write a piece telling about how her life might have been different.

3. What if Hana had married Kiyoshi and he had not died? How might her life have been different?

4. What if Hana had decided to remain single? Write a story about her life as a single woman.

5. Research the President's Executive Order 9066. Why weren't German Americans and Italian Americans included?

6. Imagine your family uprooted from your home and sent to a concentration camp. Write a response.

7. Respond to quotes such as the following: "She could never be completely herself. It was as though she were going through life pressed down, apologetic, making herself small and inconspicuous, never able to reach out or to feel completely fulfilled"; or "How could a white person possibly understand the subtleties of the Japanese way of life?"

8. Research arranged marriages. What if your parents arranged a marriage for you? Write a response.

9. Related books: *Journey to Topaz, Journey Home,* and *Desert Exile* by Yoshiko Uchida, *Obasan* and *Naomi's Road* by Joy Kogawa; *Kinenhi: Reflections on Tule Lake* by Tule Lake Committee; *Lost Years: 1942–1946* by Sue Kunitomi Embrey; *Farewell to Manzanar* by Jeanne Houston; *Promises Kept* by Akemi Kikumura; *Through Harsh Winters* by Akomi Kikumura; *Our House Divided* by Tomi Kaizawa Knaefler; *In Search of Hiroshi* by Gene Oishi; *No No Boy* by John Okada; *Ganbare!* by Patsy Kisaku Saiki; *Lucky Come Hawaii* by Jon Shirota; and *Yasui Family of Hood River* by Robert Yasui.

The Rooster Who Understood Japanese

Nominated for Sequoyah Children's Book Award
Nominated for the William Allen White Award

- **Animal companions**
- **Problem Solving**

Miyo enjoys visiting Mrs. Kitamura and her animal companions, especially Mr. Lincoln, the rooster. When a neighbor complains that Mr. Lincoln is disturbing the peace by crowing at 6:00 A.M., Miyo puts her problem solving skills to work. She finds a solution that saves Mr. Lincoln and creates harmony in the neighborhood. Positive images of Miyo's mother as a doctor at University Hospital, of Mrs. Kitamura as being respectful of animals ("She said animals were purer in spirit than most human beings and deserved names that befit their character"), and of Miyo as a capable solver of problems. Also Mrs. Kitamura is portrayed as a flexible person capable of forgiving her crabby neighbor: "Life needs a little stirring up now and then." This is a warm, humorous story that people of all ages will enjoy.

Ages 7 up

Suggestions for the Classroom

1. Where did Mrs. Kitamura find the names for her animal companions? (from a class in American history she took in order to become an American citizen) Who was each animal named after?

2. Choose a character from the story and rewrite the story from her or his perspective. (Don't forget the animals!) Share your stories with the class.

3. Miyo wrote a feature story about Mr. Botts, the school custodian who was retiring. Write a feature story for your class magazine.

4. What might have happened when Mr. Lincoln got to his new home? Write a story about his adventures on the farm. You might want to include a part about when Mrs. Kitamura and Miyo went to visit him.

5. Mrs. Kitamura told Miyo she was a "free spirit." What does that mean? Discuss and/or write about it.

6. Mrs. Kitamura performed the Japanese tea ceremony to help her feel calm and peaceful. Research the tea ceremony. Invite speakers to your class to perform the ceremony.

7. Imagine that one of your animal companions is in trouble. Create a newspaper ad that might solve the problem. Or think of another creative solution to the problem.

- **Historical fiction**
- **Immigrants**
- **Newcomers**

Samurai of Gold Hill

California Commonwealth Club Medal

1869 Japan and California. Twelve-year-old Koichi and his father leave war torn Japan to start a new life in California. They join the Wakamatsu Colony at Gold Hill and attempt to start a tea and silk farm. But in spite of their efforts and those of a few friendly neighbors, the venture fails when hostile miners divert the precious water so that none of it will flow to their land. This book is based on the true story of the first colonists from Japan who came to California. The book includes a glossary and historical information in the author's note.

Ages 9 up

Suggestions for the Classroom

1. Look up Samurai in the glossary. How did Koichi's father's life change?

2. Use a map to trace the route that Koichi traveled from Wakamatsu to Tokyo to Yokohama to San Francisco to Sacramento to Placerville to Gold Hill (near Coloma).

3. Compare life in Wakamatsu to life at Gold Hill. Make a list of the problems the colonists faced in the new land. How did they deal with each of these problems?

4. Discuss the Buddhist beliefs regarding beef and pork. (See the Suggestions for the Classroom for *Much Ado About Aldo* on page 132 for more information on vegetarianism.)

5. Rewrite or tell the story from Okei's point of view. Or write a song or poem she might have written about her new life.

6. Select quotes such as the following to discuss or respond to in writing: ". . . we all have a special place in life, and when we find it, we must accept it."

- **Folktales (Japanese)**

The Sea of Gold and Other Tales From Japan

A California Recommended Reading List Title

This book is a collection of twelve folktales adapted by Uchida. These stories have been told and retold for hundreds of years to the children of Japan. They contain the universal qualities that can be found in folktales the world over. Glossary included.

Ages 7 up

Suggestions for the Classroom

1. Read aloud to children under ten, let older children discover the tales for themselves. Or read one or two to older children to get them started.

2. These tales lend themselves nicely to dramatization; try pantomime while a teacher or student reads the story.

3. Set up a Folktale Center in your classroom or library. Include tales from many cultures. Add student work as the unit progresses.

The Two Foolish Cats

Junior Literary Guild Book

Parent's Choice Honor Book

- **Folklore (Japanese)**
- **Cats**
- **Peace**

This charming new version of an amusing Japanese folktale features two cats who quarrel over who will get the larger portion of food. A wise old monkey settles the dispute in a way that leads the cats to change their ways. "And ever since that day, the two cats never quarreled again, but lived peacefully together at the edge of the dark pine forest." Margot Zemach's watercolor illustrations capture the sly humor of this delightful tale.

All Ages

Suggestions for the Classroom

1. Read other Japanese folktales such as *The Dancing Kettle* and *The Magic Listening Cap* by Yoshiko Uchida and *Tales From the Bamboo Grove* by Yoko Kawashima Watkins. Choose one for a book talk to present to your class.

2. Write a booklet by Big Daizo and Little Suki called "How to Get Along with Others." Illustrate and display in your class book corner.

3. Rewrite the story using the Good News/Bad News format.

4. Write a folktale based on something one of your animal friends did.

The Wise Old Woman

- **Folklore (Japanese)**
- **Elderly people**

A cruel lord decrees that anyone over the age of seventy must be taken into the mountains and left to die because they are no longer useful. However, a young farmer cannot bear to abandon his mother so he hides her in a secret room under their kitchen. When the village is threatened by a powerful conqueror, the wise woman saves the day by performing three seemingly impossible tasks. Henceforth, old people were treated with respect and honor and the villagers lived in peace for all the days of their lives. Yoshiko Uchida has retold this fine Japanese folktale with grace and compassion. This book is a welcome addition to the field of children's literature, which needs more images of strong elderly women.

All Ages

Suggestions for the Classroom

1. Yoshiko Uchida retold many fascinating folktales from Japan. Set up a center featuring these old tales along with tales from other cultures. As you read and share the stories, you will find that they inspire a rich variety of art, drama, and writing extensions.

2. Analyze the portrayal of elderly women in other genres. Discuss ageism and the ways in which it limits people and damages society. What can we do to create a world in which everyone is treated with respect and honor?

Mai Vo-Dinh

Vietnamese American (1933–)

Birthday: November 14
Contact: P.O. Box 211–626
Royal Palm Beach, Florida 33421-1626

"I believe that good illustrations can enrich the mind of a reader, young or old, if they go beyond the routine and the conventional."
(Something About the Author, *Volume 16, p. 273)*

Books by Mai Vo-Dinh

WRITTEN AND ILLUSTRATED

The Toad is the Emperor's Uncle. **Doubleday, 1970.**

ILLUSTRATED

Angel Child, Dragon Child **by Michele Maria Surat. Scholastic, 1983.**

The Brocaded Slipper and Other Vietnamese Tales **by Lynette Dyer Vuong. HarperCollins, 1992.**

First Snow **by Helen Coutant. Alfred A. Knopf, 1974.**

The Gift **by Helen Coutant. Alfred A. Knopf, 1983.**

The Happy Funeral **by Eve Bunting. HarperCollins, 1982.**

The Land I Lost **by Quang Nhuong Huynh. HarperTrophy, 1982; 1986.**

The Miracle of Mindfulness **by Thich Nhat Hanh. Beacon Press, 1988; 1992.**

The Moon Bamboo **by Thich Nhat Hanh. Parallax Press, 1989.**

Sky Legends of Vietnam **by Lynette Dyer Vuong. HarperCollins, 1993.**

The Stone Boy and Other Stories **by Thich Nhat Hanh. Parallax Press, 1995.**

Têt : The New Year **by Kim-Lan Tran. Simon and Schuster, 1993.**

A Thousand Pails of Water **by Ronald Roy. Alfred A. Knopf, 1978.**

Mai Vo-Dinh was born November 14, 1933 in Hue, Vietnam. (In Vietnam, the surname comes first; thus, his name is often written Vo-Dinh Mai.) As a child, Mai often visited a local woodcut artist; he was inspired by the joy the artist exuded while working. He studied at the Lycee of the Hue and then went to Paris to pursue his study of art. He moved to the United States in 1960.

Vo-Dinh is an accomplished writer, translator, and illustrator. He is a professional artist whose works have been widely exhibited to international acclaim. He has illustrated many books and his work has appeared on UNICEF greeting cards. He especially enjoys illustrating with ink or with pencil in combination with elements of his own woodblock prints.

In 1974, Vo-Dinh went back to visit his homeland, Vietnam. He says, "... for Americans, the war had ended, but it was still going on for Vietnamese.... Naturally, the war affected me, an artist, profoundly as it did in other ways all Vietnamese.... If anything, the war between Americans and Vietnamese has reinforced my faith in the miracle of life. It is a faith beyond hope or despair" (*Something About the Author,* Volume 16, p. 273).

In 1964, Mai Vo-Dinh married Helen Coutant, a teacher and writer. He illustrated at least two of her books, *First Snow* and *The Gift.* They have two daughters, Katherine Phuong-Nam and Hannah Linh-Giang.

Mai Vo-Dinh's paintings and woodblock prints have been exhibited in over forty solo shows and in numerous group shows in Asia, Europe, Canada, and throughout the United States. As an author, illustrator, and translator, he has over twenty books to his credit. He is listed in *American Artists, Contemporary Authors* and *Who's Who in American Art.* He has won many awards and honors including the Christopher Award in 1975 and a Literature Program Fellowship from the National Endowment of the Arts in 1984.

Angel Child, Dragon Child

A Reading Rainbow Review Book

A Notable Children's Trade Book in the Field of Social Studies

- **Newcomers**
- **Immigrants**

This is the beautiful, poignant story of Ut (Nguyen Hoa), a Vietnamese newcomer to the United States and of her adjustment to her new country. At first, her classmates cruelly laugh at her and call her names. Most of all, she misses her mother who couldn't afford the trip to the United States yet. When Ut and her sisters first arrive, they are shown in their traditional Vietnamese clothing. As the story unfolds, they begin wearing jeans and t-shirts or spring dresses. The pastel illustrations by Mai Vo-Dinh, along with the text, depict the determined spirits of the newcomers.

All Ages

Suggestions for the Classroom

1. Make a list of problems Ut faced in her new country. How did she cope with each of these problems? How might you feel in a new country?

2. Write a poem that Ut might have written to give to her mother when they were reunited. Use some of the Vietnamese words you learned in this book. Illustrate the poem.

3. What could you do to make a newcomer feel welcome? What would you want people to do for you if you moved to a new country?

4. Read *Ackung's Dream* by Min Paek (see page 175). In what ways were the newcomers alike? Different? In what ways were their classmates alike? Different? Discuss.

5. What can your class or school do to make sure newcomers like Ut do not suffer mistreatment such as name calling? Make a list of ideas and compile into a class booklet.

First Snow

Christopher Award

- **Death**
- **Buddhism**
- **Snow**
- **Newcomers**
- **Grandmothers**

Lien and her family have recently moved from Vietnam to a small New England town in the United States. Lien is eagerly anticipating her first snow. But the cold is weakening her beloved grandmother; one bitterly cold day in mid-December, Lien hears her father say, "Grandmother is dying." Lien wonders, "What does it mean, Grandmother is dying?" With Grandmother's guidance, she searches and finds the answer in the newly fallen snow. Like many

Vietnamese families, Lien's family is Buddhist. One belief of Buddhism is that life and death are but two parts of the same thing. This is a gentle story about the love between a girl and her grandmother and the lesson her grandmother teaches her: that she will change form but will live on in another way. The book has delicate black and white illustrations by Mai Vo-Dinh.

Ages 6 up

Suggestions for the Classroom

1. Discuss the message of the story: Life and death are but two parts of the same thing. When Grandmother dies she will change form but will live on in another form.

2. Helen Coutant and Mai Vo-Dinh believe that many of the ancient ideas and traditions of Buddhism can have meaning for all people. They say that this book might be thought of as a story about death but it is also a story about life. Discuss.

3. Read *The Gift,* also written by Helen Coutant and illustrated by her husband, Mai Vo-Dinh. How are the books similar? Different? How are elderly people depicted in both?

4. Find Vietnam on a map. Then find New England. Estimate how many miles Lien's family moved from their homeland to their new country.

- **Blindness**
- **Friendship**
- **Elderly**
- **Moving**

The Gift

When her family moves, Anna, a Vietnamese American girl, finds it hard to make friends with the other fifth graders. She is very lonely until she looks into the warm, cornflower blue eyes of Nana Marie, an elderly neighbor. The two begin to talk as if they have known each other for years. This is the beginning of a beautiful friendship. But one day, Anna discovers that Nana Marie has suddenly gone blind. After much deliberation, Anna decides on the perfect gift for her dear friend. With sensitivity, Anna promises to describe everything she sees each day. "I'll bring you enough seeing to last forever." This book is lovingly illustrated in black and white by Mai Vo-Dinh.

Ages 6 up

Suggestions for the Classroom

1. What was it about Anna's gift that made it more thoughtful than the ones she had considered earlier?

2. What were some of the special things Nana Marie had that were a history of her life, of her memories stretching over almost a century? Read *The Hundred Penny Box* by Sharon Bell Mathis. (See page 151.) Dramatize a meeting between Nana Marie and Aunt Dew.

3. Discuss the following quote: "All day long Anna had been seeing the world the way Nana Marie had shown her." What did they each give the other?

4. Nana Marie is almost one hundred years old; discuss the way her character is portrayed. Many elderly people are stereotyped in books. Discuss ageism.

5. Study the illustrations by Mai Vo-Dinh. Then look at his illustrations in other books. How would you describe his art to a blind person?

- **Vietnam**
- **Autobiography**
- **Animal companions**

The Land I Lost: Adventures of a Boy in Vietnam

Notable Children's Trade Book in Social Studies

National Council of Teachers of English

Teachers' Choice

An American Library Association Notable Children's Book

Huynh Quang Nhuong, born in Mytho, Vietnam, has written this autobiography about his lost homeland. Upon being graduated from Saigon University with a degree in chemistry, he was drafted into the South Vietnamese army. He was permanently paralyzed by a gunshot wound received on the battlefield, and in 1969 he came to the United States for additional medical treatment. He writes, "... the war disrupted my dreams. The land I love was lost to me forever. These stories are my memories." Illustrated in black and white by Mai Vo-Dinh. Published in five different languages.

Ages 8 up

Suggestions for the Classroom

1. Find Vietnam on a map. Trace and sketch in the details. Interested youngsters might want to find out more about the Vietnam War.

2. What significance might this book have for the illustrator, Mai Vo-Dinh? Study his illustrations. Then look at his illustrations in other books. Discuss his artistic style.

3. Invite each student or group to select a chapter to present to the class through poetry, drama, art, music, etc. Try using some of Mai Vo-Dinh's art techniques.

4. Huynh Quang Nhuong has written a companion volume: *Water Buffalo Days: Growing Up in Vietnam.* Harper Collins, 1999.

Sky Legends of Vietnam

- **Folklore (Vietnam)**
- **Sky observations**

Throughout time, people all over the world have created stories to explain the fascinating cycles of the sun, moon, and stars. Here are six enchanting sky legends that bring to life ancient tales that have been told for centuries. Rich in cultural details, these tales are accompanied by explanatory notes from the author, a pronunciation guide, and striking black-and-white illustrations.

Ages 8 up

Suggestions for the Classroom

1. Vuong writes, "Folklore not only defines a culture but links it to other cultures around it." Read and discuss her other books: *The Brocaded Slipper and Other Vietnamese Tales* and *The Golden Carp and Other Tales from Vietnam.*

2. Set up a Folklore Center. Include folktales from many cultures. (See Subject Index.) Write folktales of your own.

3. Study Mai Vo-Dinh's illustrations. Then create a group mural incorporating all six tales. Use this mural as a backdrop for your Folklore Center.

4. These folktales lend themselves beautifully to being read aloud and dramatized. Pantomime the actions while the stories are being read aloud.

Têt: The New Year

- **Vietnamese New Year**
- **Newcomers**

Ms. Kim, the English language teacher, invites her students to her apartment to celebrate the New Year. But this year is the first Têt away from Vietnam for Huy, one of her students. When he doesn't show up, Ms. Kim calls his father and convinces him to come with his son for the celebration. After all, friends should be with friends to celebrate Têt. Information about customs, traditions, and foods are woven into this gentle story. Glossary included.

Ages 5–10

Suggestions for the Classroom

1. Discuss Huy's behavior before the celebration. How might his feelings change after celebrating the New Year with his teacher and classmates? Why was it important that Ms. Kim and the children make a special effort to include Huy and his father?

2. Discuss the children's favorite memories of Têt and the preparation for this year's celebration.

3. The illustrator, Mai Vo-Dinh, is an internationally acclaimed artist. He has illustrated over twenty books. Study his illustrations closely. How would you describe his art? Try some of his techniques in your next art piece.

4. Mai Vo-Dinh said that he accepts an illustration assignment with delight if the book in question interests him. Why do you think he accepted this assignment?

Alice Walker

Jean Weisinger

African AmerIndian (1944–)

Birthday: February 9
Contact: Harcourt Brace
111 5th Avenue
New York, New York 10003

"It is so clear that you have to cherish everybody . . . every soul is to be cherished, . . . every flower is to bloom." (Alice Walker *by Tony Gentry)*

"I tell people how necessary it is for children not to be ashamed of how their parents sound, not to be ashamed, anywhere in their education, about who they are–it's fatal to being educated."
(North Coast Press, *January, 1998)*

Books by Alice Walker

FOR YOUNG PEOPLE

Finding the Green Stone. **Illustrations by Catherine Deeter. Harcourt Brace Jovanovich, 1991.**

Langston Hughes: American Poet. **Illustrated by Don Miller. Thomas P. Crowell, 1974.**

To Hell With Dying. **Illustrated by Catherine Deeter. Harcourt Brace Jovanovich, 1988; 1993.**

FOR ADULTS

Alice Walker. **Pocket Books, 1989.**

Anything We Love Can be Saved. **Random, 1997; Ballantine, 1998.**

The Color Purple. **Harcourt Brace, 1982; Pocket Books, 1998.**

Everyday Use. **Rutgers University Press, 1994.**

Goodnight, Willie Lee, I'll See You in the Morning. **Harcourt Brace, 1984.**

Her Blue Body Everything We Know. **Harcourt Brace, 1991; 1993.**

Horses Make a Landscape Look More Beautiful. **Harcourt Brace, 1986.**

I Love Myself When I Am Laughing: A Zora Neale Hurston Reader. **(editor). Feminist Press, 1979.**

In Love and Trouble. **Harcourt Brace, 1974.**

In Search of Our Mothers' Gardens. **Harcourt Brace, 1983; 1984.**

Living by the Word. **Harcourt Brace, 1988; 1989.**

Meridian. **Harcourt Brace, 1976; Pocket Books, 1990.**

Once: Poems. **Harcourt Brace, 1976.**

Possessing the Secret of Joy. **Harcourt Brace, 1992; Pocket Books, 1997.**

Revolutionary Petunias and Other Poems. **Harcourt Brace, 1973.**

The Temple of My Familiar. **Harcourt Brace, 1984; Macmillan, 1990. Pocket Books, 1990.**

The Same River Twice. **Simon & Schuster, 1996; 1997; Pocket Books, 1997.**

The Third Life of Grange Copeland. **Harcourt Brace, 1977; Pocket Books, 1991.**

Warrior Marks: Female Genital Mutilation and the Sexual Blinding of Women. **Harcourt Brace, 1993; 1995; Pocket Books, 1993.**

You Can't Keep a Good Woman Down. **Harcourt Brace, 1982.**

Alice Malsenior Walker was born February 9, 1944 in Eatonville, Georgia. She was the eighth and last child of Minnie Tallulah Grant Walker and Willie Lee Walker. She was born into a world of poverty and hardship; her parents were sharecroppers who earned as little as $300 a year working the land owned by a white woman named Meys. Walker's five brothers, two sisters, and parents worked in the fields and milked a large number of cows every morning and night. In addition to going to the fields each day, Walker's mother cooked for her growing family, made all their clothes, planted and tended a large garden, canned vegetables and fruits, made quilts, and somehow found time to tend her flower garden where over fifty kinds of flowers grew.

Her parents were gifted storytellers; they told tales about Brer Rabbit, Tar Baby, and other mythical characters. Her mother also talked about her grandmother, Tallulah, who was mostly Cherokee, and her father told about his great-great-great grandmother Mary Poole, a slave who was forced to walk from Virginia to Georgia, carrying two babies.

Walker started school when she was four years old; she found it to be a wonderful place, full of people who understood her, her family, and their ways. But when she was eight years old, one of her brothers shot her in the eye with a BB gun. Walker lost the sight in that eye and for many years she could not bear to look at herself in the mirror or raise her head to look at anyone else. She walked with her head down and spent her free time reading and writing. When she was fourteen years old, she had an operation that removed the white scar tissue on her eye but the vision in that eye could not be saved.

Walker loved learning and excelled in school; upon graduating first in her high school class and winning a scholarship, she entered Spelman College in nearby Atlanta, Georgia. There, she became involved in the civil rights movement. Two years later, she moved to Sarah Lawrence College in New York. She became a caseworker in the New York City Welfare Department and continued her work for civil rights in the area of voter registration. In 1968, she began teaching Black Studies and lecturing at Jackson State College. She later became a lecturer at Wellesley College and the University of Massachusetts.

Selected as a writer in residence at Tougalou College, Walker soon became a full-time writer. In 1967, she received a Charles Merrill Fellowship and in 1969 a National Foundation of the Arts Award in fiction. She was a consulting editor for *Ms.* and *Freedomways* magazines.

In 1983, after winning many other awards, fellowships, and honors, Walker won the Pulitzer Prize and the American Book Award for her novel, *The Color Purple,* which became a monumental bestseller. A highly gifted writer, she was elevated into modern literature's highest ranks. She has also written three books for young readers, numerous books of poetry, collections of short stories, and several other novels. Walker lives and writes in northern California; she has one daughter, Rebecca.

For more information about Alice Walker, see *The International Dictionary of Women's Biography* and *Alice Walker* by Tony Gentry. An Alice Walker poster is available through Bread and Roses Cultural Project, Inc., 330 West 42nd Street, Floor 7, New York, NY 10036; 800-666-1728.

Finding the Green Stone

- **Siblings**
- **Gems**
- **Friendship**
- **Peace**

Katie and her brother, Johnny, live in a community where everyone has a beautiful, iridescent green stone. One day Johnny loses his stone. Accompanied by Katie, their mother (a doctor), their father (a driver of a pulpwood truck), as well as all the people in the community, Johnny begins searching for the stone. He gradually realizes that he alone can find the green stone—when he recovers the requisite love within his heart. The magnificent illustrations by Catherine Deeter were done in acrylic on Strathmore illustration board.

All Ages

Suggestions for the Classroom

1. Discuss various interpretations of this book. What did Johnny learn? What did he teach us?

2. What mean-spirited things did Johnny do? What was the result? (He lost his green stone.) Dramatize Johnny's apologies to each person. Then write an apology to someone you hurt.

3. Have you ever helped a friend or sibling the way Katie helped Johnny? What happened? How did you feel? How did Katie feel?

4. Have you ever lost something special? Did you find it? How did you feel? Write or tell about it through story, drama, song, or poem.

5. Compare and contrast this book with another picture book by the same author and illustrator: *To Hell with Dying* (see below).

6. This is a unique book. Can you think of any other books that are similar? If so, read them to your class and discuss the similarities and differences.

7. Study Catherine Deeter's paintings. Which is your favorite? Why? Maybe this beautiful book will inspire your next painting.

- **Biography**
- **Poets**
- **Poetry**

Ages 7 up

Langston Hughes: American Poet

Langston Hughes (1902–1967) stayed up all night writing his first poem. When he was in grade school in Lincoln, Illinois he was elected Class Poet. Langston wrote about Black people just as he saw them. He wrote poems, stories, novels, plays, children's books, and history books. By the time he was fifty years old he had become a famous and much loved writer. Walker has written this sensitive biography of a poet who inspired her with love and respect.

Suggestions for the Classroom

1. Set up a Poets and Poetry Center in your classroom. Include posters, books, and pictures of poets. Be sure to include poets from many different cultural groups. Add poems written by the students in your class.

2. Discuss Langston Hughes's life. Make a list of obstacles he faced. Write a poem encouraging oppressed people to carry on.

3. Read Langston Hughes's poems. Then write a poem on a topic of your choice. Print it on large sheets of construction paper. Use for a class bulletin board.

4. Read poems by other African American poets such as Eloise Greenfield, Nikki Giovanni, Gwendolyn Brooks, and Paul Laurence Dunbar. Check the Subject Index for additional poets.

5. Alice Walker is also a poet. Discuss the inspiration she received from Hughes and his life.

- **Dying**
- **Death**
- **Alcoholism**
- **Autobiographical short story**
- **Elderly people**

Ages 12 up

To Hell with Dying

Spanning almost two decades and told from Alice Walker's perspective when she was a graduate student, this reflective autobiographical short story describes the family's warm relationship with their neighbor, Mr. Sweet. "Mr. Sweet was a diabetic and an alcoholic and a guitar player and lived down the road from us on a neglected cotton farm." He was often on the brink of death but when the children came crowding around the bed and threw themselves on the covers and kissed and tickled him, he would revive. On Mr. Sweet's ninetieth birthday, Alice was finishing her doctorate in Massachusetts. When she received a telegram that he was dying, she rushed home, but this time she was not able to save him. "He was like a piece of rare and delicate china that was always being saved from breaking and which finally fell." The large, full color paintings on every other page by Catherine Deeter are rare in a book for young adults.

Suggestions for the Classroom

1. Think about Mr. Sweet's ambitions as a boy. What if he had been a doctor or a lawyer? What obstacles might he have faced? (He was born in 1878.) Write about how his life would have been different if he had pursued one of these careers. Read *Paul Robeson* by Eloise Greenfield to find out more about the barriers an African American person faced as a lawyer at that time.

2. Compose a song that Alice Walker might have sung and played on Mr. Sweet's guitar for him.

3. Write an obituary for Mr. Sweet. Compare perceptions of him and his life.

4. Study Catherine Deeter's illustrations. Do you think that books for young adults should be illustrated? Write an argument for or against.

5. Some people think that the use of "hell" in the title of the book is inappropriate. Debate. Suggest other appropriate titles.

6. Read and discuss books about alcoholism such as *The Late Great Me* by Sandra Scoppettone, *Something's Wrong at My House* by Katherine Leiner, and *Alcohol: What It Is and What It Does* by Judith Seixas. Invite a speaker to talk about alcoholism.

7. Write about the life and death of a human or animal close to you.

8. Read other books by and about Alice Walker. Discuss her writing styles.

9. Read *Alice Walker* by Tony Gentry to find out what was happening in her life while she was writing *To Hell With Dying.*

Mildred Pitts Walter

African American (1922–)

Birthday: September 9

"Writing is a subject that cannot easily be taught. Creativity comes from the soul. The teacher's role is to facilitate that creativity." (Personal Interview)

"Every chance you get, try to seek out people who are different, so you can truly know who you are. You don't really know yourself until you see the differences. You can judge who you are by who you are not." (Personal Interview)

"Teachers must help children be open minded, willing to risk knowing new things." (Personal Interview)

Books by Mildred Pitts Walter

Because We Are. **Lothrop, Lee & Shepard, 1983.**

Brother to the Wind. **Illustrated by Diane and Leo Dillon. Lothrop, Lee & Shepard, 1985.**

Darkness. **Illustrated by Marcia Jameson. Simon & Schuster, 1995.**

The Girl On the Outside. **Lothrop, Lee & Shepard, 1982; Scholastic, 1993.**

Have a Happy. **Illustrated by Carole Byard. Lothrop, Lee & Shepard, 1989; Avon, 1990.**

Justin and the Best Biscuits in the World. **Lothrop, Lee & Shepard, 1986; Avon, 1996; American Printing House for the Blind, 1996.**

Kwanzaa: A Family Affair. **Lothrop, Lee & Shepard, 1995.**

Lillie of Watts: A Birthday Surprise. **Illustrated by Leonora E. Prince. Ritchie, 1969.**

Lillie of Watts Takes a Giant Step. **Illustrated by Bonnie H. Johnson. Doubleday, 1971.**

The Liquid Trap. **Illustrated by John Thompson. Scholastic, 1975.**

Mariah Keeps Cool. **Illustrated by Pat Cummings. Bradbury, 1990; Simon & Schuster, 1990.**

Mariah Loves Rock. **Illustrated by Pat Cummings. Bradbury, 1988; American Printing House for the Blind, 1993.**

Mississippi Challenge. **Bradbury Press, 1992; Simon & Schuster, 1996.**

My Mama Needs Me. **Illustrated by Pat Cummings. Lothrop, Lee & Shepard, 1983.**

Second Daughter: The Story of a Slave Girl. **Scholastic, 1996.**

Suitcase. **Lothrop, Lee & Shepard, 1999.**

Trouble's Child. **Lothrop, Lee & Shepard, 1985.**

Two and Too Much. **Illustrated by Pat Cummings. Bradbury Press, 1990.**

Ty's One-Man Band. **Illustrated by Margot Tomes. Scholastic, 1980; 1984; 1992.**

Mildred Pitts Walter was born September 9, 1922 in Sweetville, Louisiana, the youngest of seven children. Her mother was a beautician and midwife and her father was a log cutter. Mildred remembers summer evenings filled with songs, ring games, storytelling, hand clapping, and folk dancing in her family's yard. They listened to recordings of Ma Rainey, Bessie Smith, and Blind Lemon Jefferson played on a gramophone.

At age four, Walter started accompanying her sisters and brother to the local one-room school. The teacher roomed and boarded with the Pitts family. Walter loved school because it was the only place where she was allowed to get books. (At that time, African Americans were not allowed to use the public library!) Most of the books were discards from the white schools and often were torn with pages missing. Walter has great respect for books and still cannot tear a page from a book or write in it.

Walter and her classmates wrote compositions but there was no creative writing. She was encouraged to give talks and she often stood up and gave an extemporaneous speech. Their teachers, all African Americans, provided many extracurricular activities. Besides basketball, baseball, and calisthenics, the students participated in plays, musicals, choral groups, and oratorical contests. Walter played the part of Sleeping Beauty in the musical by that name when she was in fourth grade.

Even though Walter received support and guidance from her family, school, church, and community, she was separated from the larger community. The Louisiana population was sharply divided along race and color lines. Walter, along with other African American people, were denied services. Even getting a new pair of shoes was an ordeal; they could not go into the store to try on the shoes so they had to buy them and try them on at home. If they didn't fit, they had to go back and forth to the store until they found the right size. Walter remembers settling for the wrong size out of fear of not getting any shoes at all.

Walter went to work the summer she was seven years old as a baby sitter for a three-year-old white girl. She earned her meals and twenty-five cents a week, which was saved to buy her clothes and shoes. Every summer during elementary school, Walter worked in the homes of white people. During high school, she worked two jobs during the summer as well as weekends during the school year.

After graduating from high school second in her class in May of 1940, Walter worked her way through three years of college at Southern University in Scotlandville, Louisiana. Then after a year of working as a shipwright helper on dry dock on the Columbia River, she returned to college. She graduated in the summer class of 1944, with a B.A. in English and social studies, and with practice teaching at the secondary level. Walter later earned her M.A. in education through Antioch College.

Then, with her characteristic courage and sense of adventure, she left the South and moved across the country to Los Angeles where she worked as a personnel clerk and later as a kindergarten teacher. She chose Los Angeles because she had always been fascinated by the city that seemed to stick out into the Pacific Ocean. She was young, healthy, willing to work, and ready to try something new.

She married Earl Lloyd Walter in 1947. Together, they worked with the organization Congress of Racial Equality (CORE). CORE was founded in 1942 in Chicago to ease racial conflicts through nonviolent action. Earl was local chairperson and national vice-chairperson of CORE; he adhered to the tenets of nonviolence in all his relationships, especially within his family. He believed in and practiced gender and racial equality.

As the Congress of Racial Equality became involved in the civil rights movement, Walter participated in many political activities. She walked on the picket line with Martin Luther King, Jr. She became involved in nonviolent actions for equality in housing, jobs, education, and basic rights. Then in June of 1965, Earl died after a six month illness. Walter stayed in Los Angeles with her two sons for five more years before moving to Denver, Colorado in 1970.

As a kindergarten teacher and a book reviewer, Walter was keenly aware of the need for books for young readers about African Americans. This awareness resulted in her first book, *Lillie of Watts: A Birthday Discovery,* which was published in 1969. Thus, her new career as an author was launched! Since then she has written many outstanding books for young people. Each of her books has been written to provide an authentic portrayal of African American experiences. She has written on a wide variety of topics; each book is very different from the others in the collection. In her writing, as in other aspects of her life, she has shown courage and a willingness to try something new.

Some of Mildred Pitts Walter's favorite things are reading, gardening, ice cream, and earth-tone colors. She also has a great enthusiasm for people and places; her travels include trips to China, Africa, Haiti, and the Soviet Union (for the U.S.–U.S.S.R. Peace Walk) as well as travel across the United States. Her home is filled with beautiful art objects from around the world—paintings, carvings, sculptures, etc. She has a lively career as an educational consultant and lecturer and is in demand as a speaker at universities and professional conferences. She has been a consultant at the Western Interstate Commission of Higher Education in Boulder, Colorado and a consultant, teacher, and lecturer at Metropolitan State College in Denver. One of her most recent trips was to Paris where she attended a conference on African American writers.

"Everybody who learns is a teacher and everybody who teaches is a learner. Children can teach adults a lot about becoming less prejudiced, not only about peoples of color but about handicapped people, about old people, and about people who are different in many ways" (personal communication).

"Teachers must not be afraid to look at different cultural patterns within our nation. They have to search beyond what is obvious. They need to delve into writings by Asians, African Americans, Africans, etc. to know many points of view" (personal communication).

For more information about Mildred Pitts Walter, see *Something About the Author Autobiography Series*, Volume 12.

- **Career aspirations**
- **Friendship**
- **Mother-Daughter relationships**
- **Teachers**

Ages 12 up

Because We Are

Seventeen-year-old Emma Walsh, an African American honor student, has been singled out by the teachers at her integrated high school. Held up as an example, Emma feels caught between two cultures. Some of the African American students call her "oreo chick" while some of the teachers encourage her to become part of the mainstream. This pressure leads to a misunderstanding with a white teacher and Emma is transferred to another school, a segregated one. Here she is again an outsider, this time in a different way. Communication problems with her parents, finding new friends, trying to keep her old friends, a racist teacher, and being rejected as a debutante because of the lack of status of her new school due to racism and classism, as well as keeping her grades up and writing a graduation speech keep Emma busy that last semester of high school. As she grows in her ability to listen to her inner self and in her awareness of racism, she begins to find ways to solve her problems. The year ends in triumph as Emma, National Honor Student, recipient of the National Merit Award, and future student of Stanford University, gives her graduation speech.

Suggestions for the Classroom

1. Describe the dilemma Emma was in at Marlborough High. What were her choices? In an ideal world, would she have had to make those choices? Describe this improved world and how it would be different for Emma. What can you do to bring about those changes?

2. Analyze the incident with Ms. Simmons. Why did each person act as they did? What advice would you have for Ms. Simmons? For Emma? For Emma's parents? For the school?

3. Compare and contrast Manning with Marlborough. What advantages and disadvantages did each school have for Emma? If Emma could go back and choose, which school do you think she would choose? Why? In an ideal world, what would her choices be?

4. What if Emma had stayed at Marlborough? Write about what might have happened.

5. Analyze Emma's relationship with Marvin. How do you feel about him taking her to a party where there were drugs without her knowledge? What would you have done?

6. Evaluate the debutante selection process. Write a response.

7. As you read the book, keep a list of the emotions Emma experienced, including humiliation, exhilaration, uncertainty, anguish, rejection, outrage, love, confidence, and satisfaction. Discuss. Keep a list of the emotions you experience. Reflect on the origins of those emotions. Write an analysis.

8. Reread and discuss the racist incidents from Emma's and Allan's childhoods. What do you think should have been done?

9. Examine Mr. Kooner's scramble-for-books practice. Why did he do it? How did Emma try to deal with this situation? What responses did she get from her mother, father, the principal, friends, and classmates? What would you have done? Write about your feelings related to this topic.

10. Racism is often disguised just as Mr. Kooner's was. Write about other examples of racism. How did Mr. Kooner try to get revenge? Did it work? Do you think Mr. Kooner will change the way he teaches? Why or why not?

11. Debate the question: Did the principal know (or care) about the way Mr. Kooner was treating his students? What would you do if you were the principal?

12. What is institutionalized racism? How did the discussions with Allan help Emma understand this?

13. Emma considered Meharry, Howard, and Stanford. Why do you think she chose Stanford? Write a paragraph or chapter about Emma's first semester at Stanford.

14. Analyze Emma's relationship with her mother. How did it change during the book? Why?

15. Analyze the role of the Student Council. What do you think about it? Should it be expanded or stay the same?

16. What can you do to fight racism? See *Taking a Stand Against Racism and Racial Discrimination* on page 165. Make an action plan. Encourage your friends to join you.

17. Write a report on Dr. Charles Drew. Why is his name not a household word? What other names are not household words because of racism? Analyze the behavior of the teacher, another example of covert racism!

Brother to the Wind

Parent's Choice Award for Literature
Notable Children's Trade Book in the Field of Social Studies
National Council of Teachers of English Teacher's Choice

- **Flight**
- **Africa**
- **Wind**
- **Wishes**
- **Magic**
- **Kites**

Emeke, with the help of Good Snake, fulfills his dream of flying. He overcomes ridicule, misunderstanding, and his own self-doubts by following the directions Good Snake gave him to create a special kite and become "brother to the wind." This book is beautifully told and illustrated.

All Ages

Suggestions for the Classroom

1. Make a list of characters who helped Emeke, including Good Snake, Hyena, Elephant, Rhinoceros, Grandmother, and Wind. Now make a list of all who didn't help him, including Turtle, Ndumu, Mongo, Nizam, and Father. Discuss.

2. Did Emeke give up? What advice might he have for you regarding your dreams? Write a poem or recipe. (Example: One cup perseverance, two cups belief in yourself, etc.)

3. Study the illustrations for *Brother to the Wind.* Then create a class mural based on the story.

4. Read other books where Wind has magical powers. (See *Mirandy and Brother Wind* on page 162.) Discuss the differences and similarities in Wind. Then write a story or poem about Wind.

5. See the Subject Iindex for additional books about Flight. Then write a story, song, or poem about flying.

- **Shadows**
- **Colors**
- **Environment**

All Ages

Darkness

This profound book evokes tranquility and joy. Mildred Pitts Walter's reassuring voice calms fears of darkness and encourages an appreciation of the gifts it holds. Her laudatory prose approaches poetry, celebrating the role darkness plays in nature: "Seeds become plants in the darkness of the earth," and "Dark clouds bring refreshing rain." St. Croix artist Marcia Jameson's splendid paintings echo the depth of the text.

Suggestions for the Classroom

1. This is an excellent example of a picture book that is so special, it will appeal to youngsters of all ages. The message is both profound and philosophical and its many layered message will be enjoyed by adults as well.

2. *Darkness* lends itself to several units of study enjoyed by young people including "Shadows," "Constellations," and "Color." In a study of color, feature a different color each day or week. Invite youngsters to bring in items of the featured color and display. These attractive displays often inspire poetry and music.

3. Art is another natural extension for this beautiful book. Invite youngsters to explore the varied dimensions of darkness through paintings, etchings, silhouettes, and papel picado.

- **Desegregation**
- **Historical fiction**
- **Southern states**
- **Civil Rights movement**

The Girl on the Outside

Notable Children's Trade Book in the Field of Social Studies

Christian Science Monitor *Best Book*

A fictional re-creation of the 1957 desegregation of a Little Rock high school as perceived by a white student and an African American student. The African American student, Eva, is one of the first nine students involved in the plan to integrate the schools, a plan that would implement the 1954 *Brown et al. v. Board of Education of Topeka et al.* decision that: "In the field of public education the doctrine of 'separate but equal' has no place. Separate educational facilities are inherently unequal." In her author's note, Mildred Pitts Walter provides the historical framework upon which she based the book. She fictionalized the story to speak directly to teenagers about some of the problems they might face in accepting integration. This is a dramatic and heartrending book.

Ages 12 up

Suggestions for the Classroom

1. What were the advantages of attending Chatman High School? Discuss the "separate but equal" concept.

2. As you read the book, keep a list of emotions experienced by Eva and a list of those experienced by Sophia. Discuss. Write about an emotion that you can strongly identify with.

3. Sophia had information from Burt and Arnold that helped her re-examine the bigotry she had learned from her parents and grandparents. Discuss the process she went through to change. What do you think she will do in the future?

4. What would you have done if you had been in that crowd that spit on Eva?

5. Make a list of the things Eva couldn't do because of the color of her skin. Imagine that you can't try on clothes and shoes or use the public library. Write a response.

6. Sophia had never really "seen" Rod or Ida. Think about the people in your life. Who have you not really seen? Take a fresh look at someone. Write about your new awareness of them as an individual.

7. Analyze Sophia's participation in the "vow." How did she get pulled into the situation? Have you given in to peer pressure? What could you do differently? Write about it.

8. Eva and the others were courageous in joining the historic mission to try to improve the lives of their people. What can you do to improve the lives of all people? Read *Taking a Stand Against Racism and Racial Discrimination* (see page 165). Make an action plan. Encourage your friends and relatives to join you.

9. Burt was a nonracist surrounded by racist relatives and friends. Does one have to believe the bigotry taught by family? Would you have the courage to disagree with someone close to you if they held bigoted beliefs? Write a poem encouraging others to fight for the freedom and liberation of all people.

10. Research the lives of the nine students further. Read *Warriors Don't Cry: A Searing Memoir of the Battle to Integrate Little Rock's Central High School* by Melba Patillo Beals.

11. Try to find more information about Grace Lorch.

12. For more information read "The Little Rock Crisis" in *The Civil Rights Movements in America* (see page 157).

Have A Happy . . .

- **Birthdays**
- **Christmas**
- **Kwanzaa**
- **Woodworking**
- **Unemployment**

Chris's (Christopher Noel Dodd) birthday is December 25 so he often feels that it gets lost in the Christmas shuffle. The year that he turns eleven is the most difficult of all because his father has been unemployed for almost two years. The resulting financial problems put a strain on family interactions. However, Chris takes pride in his skill of making things out of wood. Kwanzaa, a seven-day holiday that begins on December 26 and ends January 1 and celebrates African American history, also gives the family renewed hope and a sense of community. As they celebrate the seven principles of Kwanzaa, one each day, Chris finds the inner strength to overcome his fears. Mildred Pitts Walter has included a Swahili glossary, the seven principles of Kwanzaa, the ritual symbols of Kwanzaa, Swahili greetings, and information about clothing.

Ages 8–12

Suggestions for the Classroom

1. Chris's parents named him Christopher Noel Dodd because he was born on Christmas. Why did your parents choose your name for you?

2. What did Chris do to help his family? How could you help out if your family was having financial problems?

3. Make a list of all the things Chris made with his hands. Make something out of wood to share with the class.

4. Set up a Kwanzaa Center in your classroom. Include *Kwanzaa: A Family Affair* by Mildred Pitts Walter (see page 218).

5. Choose one of the seven principles of Kwanzaa. Plan an activity for your family or class based on that principle.

6. Look in your telephone directory to see if your community has an African American bookstore and/or an African heritage gift shop. If so, invite your family to visit the store with you.

- **Grandfathers**
- **Ranch life**
- **Black cowboys**
- **Gender roles**

Justin and the Best Biscuits in the World

Coretta Scott King Award for Fiction

Ten-year-old Justin, frustrated with trying to do household chores when he doesn't know how, is relieved when his grandfather invites him to his ranch. There, Grandfather teaches him how to make his bed, how to do dishes, and how to make biscuits, as well as about African American history. Justin learns about Black cowboys such as Bill Pickett and Nate Love. He also gains a better understanding about women's and men's work: It doesn't matter who does the work, each person needs to do his or her share the best and most enjoyable way possible. Grandfather also helps Justin realize that it is okay for males of all ages to cry. Justin returns home feeling better about himself and more confident about his chores.

Ages 8–12

Suggestions for the Classroom

1. What did Justin learn? How did he change? Write a short sequel about his first month back home.

2. How does a boy or man make a bed? (the same way a girl or woman makes a bed) Initiate a class discussion or writing activity about gender roles and housework.

3. Reread Grandpa's recipe for biscuits. Then make biscuits for the class. Or design a medal for the best biscuits in the world.

4. Invite youngsters to figure out the ages of the children (Justin 10, Hadiya 12, and Evelyn 15).

5. Read aloud "How We Came to Missouri," followed by discussion or written responses. Make a map showing the journey from the South to Missouri.

6. Look up *palaver.* Why did Grandpa name his horse Palaver? Choose a name for a horse and tell why you chose that name.

7. Name the items displayed at the Festival, including quilts, sweaters, scarves, afghans, photography, woodwork, model airplane, desserts, and vegetables. Illustrate the items.

8. Check out these related resources: Don't Leave Out the Cowboys (videocassette documentary), *Bill Pickett: First Black Rodeo Star* by Sybil Hancock, and *Black Cowboys* by Paul Stewart.

- **Holidays**

Kwanzaa: A Family Affair

Mildred Pitts Walter shares suggestions for Kwanzaa activities, recipes, games, and crafts gathered from thirty years of celebrating this special holiday with her family and friends. Warmly presented with a tone of personal reminiscence, this guidebook includes everything needed to get everyone involved in creating a joyful celebration. Adults and children alike will appreciate the thoughtful bonuses: a suggested reading list, a glossary/pronunciation guide for Swahili terms, and clearly written and illustrated directions for making foods, gifts, and symbols.

Ages 7 up

Suggestions for the Classroom

1. Kwanzaa is *not* an African American celebration of Christmas. It has its own distinct origins, purpose, and traditions.

2. Noting that there are many ways to celebrate Kwanzaa, Walter encourages readers to improvise, to individualize the celebration so that it has special meaning for them. Her book is filled with interesting ideas from which to choose.

3. Invite youngsters to select ideas from the book that are appropriate for the classroom or library. They may choose to work individually or in groups to prepare for the celebration.

4. Invite interested parents to get involved in the preparations. For example, parents enjoy helping youngsters with quilts, handmade books, and cooking projects.

Mariah Keeps Cool

- **Swimming**
- **Diving**
- **Siblings**
- **Step families**
- **Homelessness**
- **Juneteenth**

This book is the sequel to *Mariah Loves Rock*. Mariah's half-sister Denise comes to live with the family. The inevitable conflicts that arise are dealt with honestly and realistically. Mariah and her friends are preparing for a swimming competition with Mariah as the diver. In addition, Mariah plans an unusual surprise birthday party for her sister, Lynn. This party provides a way to collect canned food and clothing for the people at the shelter for the homeless where Lynn volunteers. Mariah is gradually maturing, learning to control her impulsive nature, to deal with disappointments, to compromise, and to understand other people's differences.

Ages 8–12

Suggestions for the Classroom

1. Read *Mariah Loves Rock* before reading this book. Then discuss the ways in which Mariah changed. Analyze the way she handled the change in her family. How might she have handled it if it had happened when she was younger?

2. Write a paragraph written from Denise's perspective. Compare and contrast perceptions of Denise.

3. How did Mariah feel about winning the diving competition? What if she had lost? Write her journal entry both ways, winning and then losing.

4. Write a letter from Mariah to Lorabeth (the racist girl at the pool). Then write a letter back from Lorabeth to Mariah. Do you think that Lorabeth can change? If so, who might help her change? Do you think you could take a position against racism?

5. Lynn volunteered at a shelter for homeless people. Research homelessness. Read *The Homeless* by Laurie Beckleman. Discuss or write about your findings.

6. Plan a way to collect food and/or clothing for homeless people. Possibly have people bring food and/or clothing as their entry "fee" to a school event.

7. When and what is Juneteenth? (June 19, celebration of the emancipation of African Americans in 1863). See the Subject Index for books about Juneteenth.

8. Find out if your community is planning a Juneteenth celebration. Ask your parents if your family can attend. Plan a menu for your family to take.

Mariah Loves Rock

- **Music**
- **Step families**
- **Jealousy**
- **Siblings**

Mariah is a typical fifth grader, concerned about clothes, music, and friends. As school comes to a close her thoughts are on an upcoming performance by her favorite rock star. But she, along with the rest of her family, is confronted with some unexpected changes. Daddy's daughter from his first marriage is coming to live with them. Money is tighter. Will these changes erode or contribute to the family solidarity? This book has watercolor and pencil illustrations by Pat Cummings. Don't miss the sequel, *Mariah Keeps Cool.*

Ages 8–12

Suggestions for the Classroom

1. Make a list of things Mariah and Lynn disagreed about. Then make a list of ways they helped each other. Discuss or write about possible compromises for their disagreements. Roleplay.

2. Cynthia and Lynn shopped at thrift stores. Write about or discuss the reasons someone might do this. Include the following ideas: (1) They may not have enough money to buy new clothes. (2) They may be saving their money to buy something else or to donate to a project. (3) They may like earlier styles. (4) They may not believe in supporting the fashion industry. (5) They may believe in reusing things in order to be ecological. (6) They may want to express their individuality. (7) Other?

3. How did Mariah's feelings about used clothing change? Use quotes to support your answer.

4. Create several journal entries Denise might have written the week before she arrived at the Metcalf's.

5. Write a new chapter about Mariah and Denise getting acquainted. Then read the sequel, *Mariah Keeps Cool.*

6. Pretend that you have a new older sister or brother coming to live at your house. Write a paragraph telling how you would feel. How could you help yourself and other members of your family adjust to this change?

7. Design a room for a new sibling who is coming to live with your family.

- **Civil Rights**
- **U.S. history**
- **Race relations**
- **Mississippi**

Mississippi Challenge

Coretta Scott King Honor Book

Christopher Award

This carefully researched book describes the determined struggle by African Americans for civil rights in Mississippi from the abhorrent days of slavery to the signing of the Voting Rights Act of 1965. With passion and clarity, Walter writes about the Mississippi Challenge, a struggle that lasted more than a century and one that stands out in history as testimony to the determination and strength of a people long kept down by violence and systematic denial of political and economic rights. Speaking through the authentic voices of the people involved wherever possible, Mildred Pitts Walter has written an inspiring, much needed book that includes photographs and an index.

Ages 10 up

Suggestions for the Classroom

1. Using the index, individuals or groups of students might select topics for further research. Share information with the class or team through reports, drama, music, and/or visual arts.

2. Check out biographies of the people presented in the book such as Fannie Lou Hamer, Medgar Evers, and Ida B. Wells. Add to your Mississippi Challenge display or center.

3. Using a map of Mississippi, pinpoint the events chronicled in the book. Add to your Mississippi Challenge bulletin board.

4. Decorate your classroom with the quotes used at the beginning of each chapter. Discuss each quote.

5. Select other quotes from the book and write responses. Share with the class.

6. Math: Using the tables in the book, create math problems for your classmates.

7. Research ADA, CORE, SNCC, COFO, MFDP, NAACP, and SCLC (see index).

8. Check your United States history textbooks to see if any of this information is included. Discuss omission as a form of bias that results in invisibility and distortion. Evaluate. What are authors like Mildred Pitts Walter doing about this problem?

- **Siblings**
- **Jealousy**
- **Babies**

My Mama Needs Me

Coretta Scott King Award for Illustration

A* Reading Rainbow *Review Book

Jason wants to help when his mother brings his new baby sister home from the hospital. When friends invite him to play, he declines, stating, "My Mama needs me." But he becomes confused when his mother and the baby spend so much time sleeping. Children will identify with Jason's feelings—his fear of displacement, his confusion, and his excitement when it is time to help. Helping to bathe the baby and a warm hug from his mother reassure him that he is still loved and needed. Pat Cummings's award winning illustrations are made even more special by the variety in pattern and perspective.

Ages 4–7

Suggestions for the Classroom

1. Make a list of ways Jason could help his mother and new sister.

2. Do you have a younger sibling? Write about your feelings when the baby first arrived. If not, how do you think you might feel?

3. Do you have an older sibling? Write about how they might have felt when you first arrived. Then interview them to see if you were right. Discuss.

4. Create a "Handbook for Older Sisters and Brothers" with advice on how to adjust to a new baby.

6. Study Pat Cummings's illustrations. Then design a quilt for the baby's bed. Design matching curtains.

Second Daughter: The Story of a Slave Girl

- **Historical fiction**
- **Slaves**
- **Massachusetts**
- **Revolutionary War**

Inspired by the 1781 case of Elizabeth Freeman, also known as Mum Bett, a slave who successfully sued for her freedom in Massachusetts, Mildred Pitts Walter has written a fine piece of historical fiction. Narrated by Elizabeth's fictional sister Aissa, the book is rich in period details and personal history. Aissa, whose name means Second Daughter, eloquently describes her unquenchable desire for freedom. Against the backdrop of the Revolutionary War, the slaves face humiliations, harsh working conditions, beatings, killings, and other atrocities. Weaving fact and fiction, Walter has created a powerful tribute to the indomitability of the human spirit.

Ages 11 up

Suggestions for the Classroom

1. Do your history books depict major events from a slave's perspective? Use *Second Daughter* to supplement your study of the Revolutionary War, infusing literature with the social studies curriculum.

2. Reread and discuss the petitions, declarations of rights, and the idea that "all men are created equal." Walter clearly documents that the revolution was a rebellion by white male property owners to protect their own interests.

3. Even though Aissa and Bett were different in many ways, they both yearned to be free. Discuss their differences and similarities and the way they complemented each other.

4. Discuss and respond in writing to quotes such as, "Say yes to freedom, no to bondage and nobody can keep you a slave" p. 125.

5. Reread and discuss the Historical Note. Analyze the choices Walter made in creating this story. For example, why might she have chosen to tell the story through Aissa's voice instead of Bett's?

Trouble's Child

- **Tradition and change**
- **Midwifery**
- **Healing**
- **Grandmothers**
- **Louisiana**
- **Customs**
- **Career Goals**

This is the moving, dramatic story of a young woman's belief in herself and her dreams. Martha struggles to find a way to follow her dream of leaving the island and continuing her education. Her grandmother and the people on the island have other expectations of her. They assume she will follow her grandmother as the island midwife and healer. The pressure that tradition exerts is almost overwhelming and the reader doesn't know which path Martha's life will take until the last pages of the book. This is my favorite of Mildred Pitts Walter's books. Her beautifully-paced writing is spellbinding; I couldn't put the book down. Perfect for the study of tradition and change.

Ages 12 up

Suggestions for the Classroom

1. Why was Martha called "Trouble's Child"? (because she was born during a storm) Discuss.

2. Choose a quote from the book for small group discussions and then write a response. Find another quote and connect it with something in your life.

3. Analyze the pressure put on Martha to get married. Do women who reject marriage "dry up"? Compare Cam's description of the way marriage really was with the picture painted by society.

4. Discuss or write about the connections between what Martha learned from Miss Boudreaux and what she learned from Titay.

5. How does change occur? How might Martha give the people some other ways of thinking about their lives? What do you think the future holds for Martha?

6. Compare the way Martha felt about learning with your attitudes toward learning.

7. Choose one of the traditions on the island and write a paragraph about it. Examples: quilt party or the dance at the fishing festival.

8. See *Bitter Herbs and Honey* by Barbara Cohen on page 55 for a story about a similar conflict between family tradition and desire for education.

- **Siblings**
- **Patience**

Ages 6–10

Two and Too Much

When seven-year-old Brandon volunteers to help his mother get the house ready for a meeting, he isn't prepared for his assignment to take care of his two-year-old sister. Soon little Gina has the house in an uproar. Children with younger siblings will identify with the joys and frustrations humorously captured in this true-to-life story. The amusing illustrations by Pat Cummings are rendered in watercolor, gouache, and colored pencil.

Suggestions for the Classroom

1. Make a list of emotions that Brandon felt during the story. Then write about a time when you felt one of these emotions.

2. Create a list of activities you would use to amuse a younger child.

3. Design a "Helpful Hints" booklet on how to entertain a small child.

4. What do people mean when they talk about "The Terrible Two's"?

5. Rewrite the story from Gina's perspective.

6. Discuss the title *Two and Too Much.* Then make a list of other homophones.

7. Dramatize the meeting that Mother had that evening as the parents swapped stories about their children.

- **Music**
- **Juggling**
- **Dance**
- **Sounds**
- **Musical instruments**

Ages 5–10

Ty's One-Man Band

A* Reading Rainbow *Book

Ty learns about making music from clever Andro, a man who has a peg leg. Using spoons, a comb, a washboard, and a bucket, they provide a concert for the neighborhood. Illustrations by Margot Tomes combine with the text to provide a pleasing story.

Suggestions for the Classroom

1. This story lends itself to dramatization. Try group pantomime while someone reads the story.

2. Create a list of "Fun Things to Do" for the next time Ty has nothing to do.

3. Discuss what might have happened to Andro's leg. Where did he go at the end of the story? Write and illustrate a story about what he might have done the next day.

4. Construct your own musical instruments out of ordinary objects. Check out books from the library for directions. See *Musical Instruments You Can Make* by Phyllis Hayes and *Make Mine Music* by Tom Walther.

5. Practice with your homemade instruments. Get some friends involved. Perform for your class. Encourage your classmates to dance. Try out for your school variety show.

6. Learn to juggle. Read *Juggler* by Caroline Arnold and *Juggling Is For Me* by Nancy Marie Temple. Juggle for your class.

7. Write about a time when your friends or family laughed at your idea and/or didn't believe it would work.

8. Watch the video of *Ty's One-Man Band.*

Yoko Kawashima Watkins

Japanese American (1933–)

Birthday: October 4
Address: 58 Aunt Moll's Ridge Road
Brewster, Massachusetts 02631

"Regardless of race, creed, ability or disability, any one that has the initiative and foresight to set goals and keep them always in front of them, will in time achieve their goals. Some faster than others, but they will all achieve success eventually." (Personal Communication)

"I do not take any of life's gifts for granted. I enjoy the simplest things." (Personal Communication)

Books by Yoko Kawashima Watkins

My Brother, My Sister, and I **(Sequel to *So Far From the Bamboo Grove*). Simon & Schuster, 1994; 1996.**

So Far From the Bamboo Grove. **Lothrop, Lee & Shepard, 1986; Morrow, 1994.**

Tales From the Bamboo Grove. **Illustrated by Jean and Mou-sien Tseng. Simon & Schuster, 1992.**

Yoko Kawashima Watkins was born October 4, 1933 in Korea. Before she learned to read, she went through picture books and made up stories. A family custom was the sharing of experiences and stories after supper. Years later, Watkins recorded some of the folktales told to her by her parents in *Tales From the Bamboo Grove.* Watkins's first story was published when she was in first grade; her father praised her writing, pointing out that she put her honest feelings into her stories.

Although she was born in Korea, Watkins was Japanese; she longed to visit her grandparents in Japan, the homeland she had never seen. 1945 was a dangerous time for Japanese people to be living in northern Korea. More than ever, the Koreans resented the Japanese who had taken over their country and ruled it as their own. Suddenly the threat of war forced Watkins, her mother, and sister to leave their home. In her autobiographical novel, *So Far From the Bamboo Grove,* Watkins tells vividly what happened in the months that followed. During an air raid attack, she suffered a shrapnel wound on her chest and the fragments of metal embedded in her right ear resulted in the loss of hearing in that ear. Watkins, her mother, and sister walked 45 miles to Seoul. Eventually they reached Japan and settled in Kyoto, but illness and hardship continued to plague them. Watkins's mother died at the train station and her sister was disabled.

As Watkins grew older she learned English and worked as a typist and translator at a United States Air Force Base to support her sister. At the base, Watkins met an American who later became her husband. They subsequently moved to the United States and lived in Minnesota, Wisconsin, and Oregon before settling in Massachusetts.

Watkins's struggle to record the nightmare of her escape from the war resulted in her much acclaimed first novel, *So Far From the Bamboo Grove.* The sequel, *My Brother, My Sister and I,* is the harrowing and inspirational story of how she and her siblings lived as refugees in post World War II Japan.

Watkins has received many honors and awards including the 1998 *Literary Lights for Children Achievement Award* and selection as Japanese American of the Year in 1988 by the Iowa City schools. Her hobbies include reading, sewing, needlepoint, woodcut printing, and gardening. She is accomplished in the Japanese Way of the Tea and likes to share the tea ceremony with others. She continues to write and has spoken at many schools and universities.

Genuinely interested in people, Watkins characterizes herself as someone who finds joy in even the simplest of things in life. When she gets frustrated with writing (mostly with the language limitations of translating her work from Japanese to English), she perseveres by "... I vacuum my whole house violently (smile). I take a hot bath. After changing into fresh clothes, I perform The Way of the Tea, known as the Tea Ceremony. While performing, I put my thoughts on the seven beautiful virtues. There is no more stress, and I am ready to challenge my work" (personal communication).

My Brother, My Sister, and I

- **World War II**
- **Autobiographical novel**
- **Japan**
- **Refugees**

Sequel to *So Far From the Bamboo Grove.* This is the poignant story of how Yoko and her siblings survived as refugees in post World War II Japan. Although they face enormous hardships, their love for each other, their resourcefulness and perseverance, and their hope for a better future enable them to survive. Yoko Kawashima Watkins's first-person narrative is beautifully direct; she skillfully builds suspense and draws the reader into the story. The memoir ends with an emotional reunion with their POW father during which they must tell him that their mother died six years earlier. The Afterword covers the years from 1952 to 1994. Fans and friends of Yoko Kawashima Watkins are hoping that she will write another sequel about these years.

Ages 10 up

Suggestions for the Classroom

1. "we are at the bottom of the bottom ..." What qualities did each of the Kawashimas possess that enabled them to cope with the hardships they encountered?

2. Analyze the behavior of Yoko's classmates and Yoko's reactions. Discuss passages such as, "What do the other girls know about being hungry, homeless, and missing someone they love so much?" Today, Watkins writes, "I do not take any of life's gifts for granted. I enjoy the simplest things." This is an opportunity to analyze economic class, an important issue that is often ignored in discussions of oppressions.

3. When the Kawashima's were accused of arson, theft, and murder, how did their resolve help solve the case? This part of the book reads like a mystery. Predict the outcome before the case is solved.

4. Even though Yoko was an outcast, she managed to establish friendships. Discuss her friendships with Mr. Naido and the Minatos.

5. Choose a character and write a paragraph from her or his perspective. Compare and discuss perceptions.

- World War II
- Korea
- Autobiographical novel
- Japan
- Refugees
- Death

So Far From the Bamboo Grove

An American Library Association Notable Book
Parents' Choice Award for Literature
National Council of Teachers of English, Teacher's Choice Book
School Library Journal Best Book of the Year
Judy Lopez Memorial Award for Work of Literary Excellence

An autobiographical novel in which eleven-year-old Yoko escapes from Korea to Japan with her mother and sister near the end of World War II. 1945 was a dangerous time for a Japanese family to be living in northern Korea. The Koreans resented the Japanese who had taken over their country and ruled it as their own. Stationed in North Korea, Yoko and her family lead a peaceful life until the North Korean Communist army begins to advance. Suddenly they must flee for their lives, running on foot at night, crowding into railroad cars, always lacking water and food, always in fear. This is Watkins's poignant story of their escape and struggle for survival. Tragic, spellbinding, inspirational! This is a significant World War II refugee story. Be sure to read the sequel: *My Brother, My Sister, and I.*

Ages 10 up

Suggestions for the Classroom

1. Discuss each of the ordeals Yoko, Ko, and their mother endured during their escape. Write about Yoko's losses, including her grandparents and Mother dying, her loss of home, hearing loss in one ear, her father's fate is unknown, etc.

2. Using the map in the front of the book, trace the route Yoko, Ko, and their mother took. (Nanam to Seoul to Pusan across Korean Strait and Tsushima Strait to Fukuoko to Kyoto.)

3. How was Yoko treated by the other students? How did she react? Have you ever been ridiculed? Have you ever ridiculed someone? What happened? Respond in writing.

4. Yoko wrote about the way her classmates treated her for the essay contest. Write an essay that you think might be similar to the one she wrote.

5. Before reading the sequel, *My Brother, My Sister, and I,* predict what will happen after their reunion with Hideyo.

6. Read *Year of Impossible Goodbyes* by Sook Nyul Choi (see page 51). Discuss the similarities of the ordeals of both families. What might Yoko and Sook say to each other now? How might they feel reading each other's books? How have their lives in the United States been similar? Different?

- Folktales (Japanese)

Tales From the Bamboo Grove

This is a charming collection of six Japanese folktales. The introduction by the author provides insight into each folktale as well as into the significance they held for her family. It was the Kawashima family custom to share experiences and stories after supper each evening. Watkins's parents would tell the children folktales from the villages of northern Japan. These folktales provided comfort for Yoko's parents who lived so far from their homeland; the family spent many years in northeastern Korea where Mr. Kawashima worked as a Japanese government official. The tales delighted Yoko, her sister, and brother; they also taught them the importance of love, morals, history, wisdom, and peace.

All Ages

Suggestions for the Classroom

1. These folktales lend themselves beautifully to being read aloud. The teacher or a student might read one story a day followed by discussion, dramatization, and/or an art activity.

2. "Monkey and Crab" works especially well for dramatization. While the teacher or a student reads the story, invite youngsters to pantomime the main parts and repeat lines such as "Hurry and shoot out," "Hurry and ripen," and "Let us harvest." This happily involves everyone. Conclude the story by pantomiming the Tea of Peace.

3. Set up a Folktale Center in your classroom. Check the Subject Index for titles of folktales from diverse cultures. Invite youngsters to write and illustrate folktales of their own and add them to the Folktale Center. They might want to create a new tale about Monkey or another character in the book.

4. Create a class mural which incorporates all six folktales. Place this mural on the bulletin board behind your Folktale Center.

Camille Yarbrough

African American (1934–)

Birthday: January 8
Contact: African American Traditions Workshop
246 West 137th Street
New York, New York 10030

"When I got problems, the get-up gift send me seein dreams. I can see me doin my best, things that astound the world. And when I'm doin my best, a feelin come over me. Ooh, I feel right warm and bright all over myself. I call it the shimmershine feelin." (The Shimmershine Queens)

Books by Camille Yarbrough

Cornrows. Illustrated by Carole Byard. Coward-McCann, 1979; Putnam, 1997.

A Little Tree Growin' in the Shade. Illustrated by Tyrone Geter. Putnam, 1996.

The Shimmershine Queens. Putnam, 1989; 1996.

Tamika and the Wisdom Rings. Illustrated by Anna Rich. Random, 1994.

Watch Hour. Putnam, forthcoming.

Camille Yarbrough was born in 1934 in Chicago. In addition to writing, she has been an actress, composer, singer, teacher, community activist, and dancer. She has appeared on television and in the theater in a number of roles. She was a member of both the New York and the touring companies of "To Be Young, Gifted and Black." The recording of her songs and dialogues, "The Iron Pot Cooker," has received excellent reviews. Yarbrough was awarded a Jazz Folk Ethnic Performance Fellowship by the National Endowment of the Arts. She received a "Woman of the Month" citation from Essence Magazine in 1979. In 1975, she was named Griot of the Year by the Griot Society of New York. (A griot is a traditional roving poet, musician, and storyteller of Western Africa.) She was awarded the Ida B. Wells Award by the United African Movement and the Unity Award in Media.

Now living in New York City, Yarbrough is a Professor of African Dance and Diaspora in the African Studies Department of City College. She teaches "The Harlem Community" and "Beginners African Dance." She also teaches at African Poetry Theatre, a writing workshop in Queens. She was selected by popular radio host Gery Byrd to be his regular replacement on his Global Black Experience radio show. Yarbrough lectures at colleges and for organizations around the country. Her vibrant books for young readers focus on African American history, culture, identity, and pride.

Cornrows

- **Cornrows**
- **Hairstyles**
- **Grandmothers**
- **Tradition**
- **History**
- **Slavery**

Dedicated to her parents "who did what they could in their day, in their way to pass on to their children the spirit of what could be, would be tomorrow," Yarbrough has written an inspiring book. She explains how cornrow hairstyles are a symbol of courage, honor, wisdom, love, and strength for African people. She tells about the slaver ships that took the people away from their homes, but the "spirit of the symbol is not changed by time, place, class or fame, and not even by hate or shame." She braids in the names of many African Americans, weaving history lessons into this poetic, beautiful story. This special book is lovingly illustrated by Carole Byard.

Ages 7 up

Suggestions for the Classroom

1. What did Mama and Great Grammaw do to teach the children about their heritage? Why? What terrible thing happened? (African people were kidnapped and taken away from their homes on slaver ships.) Read *Many Thousand Gone* by Virginia Hamilton for more information about slavery, resistance to slavery, and freedom.

2. How did cornrows get that name? (They were named after the rows of corn in the cornfields where the slaves worked.) What do they symbolize? (courage, honor, wisdom, and strength)

3. Set up a center in your classroom with biographies of the people listed toward the end of the book and other African Americans. (See the biography series about African American people written by Patricia McKissack on page 159.) Invite each student or group to choose one person to research and share either through book talks or written reports.

4. This is an excellent book to read aloud and to discuss as you are reading. Use it to supplement your history textbook(s).

A Little Tree Growin' in the Shade

- **Cultural Identity**
- **History**
- **Music**
- **Slavery**

At a family gathering at a concert in the park, Sister and Brother are treated to a stirring history lesson. They learn how their people came to be enslaved, how they managed to retain their cultural identity despite the many hardships they suffered, and how they regained their freedom. The informative text is alive with poetic language accompanied by clapping, humming, singing, and drumming.

Ages 7 up

Suggestions for the Classroom

1. Follow the tree symbol throughout the story. After rereading the dedication page, discuss the tenacity of the little tree to keep growing despite many hardships.

2. The songs took a great variety of forms. Inspired by the list of genres on page 27, invite youngsters to explore one or more in their next written piece.

3. The poetic text begs to be read aloud. Discuss the use of alliterative and onomatopoeic language.

- **Internalized racism**
- **Mother/Daughter relationships**
- **Drama**
- **Peer pressure**
- **Self-confidence**
- **Elderly**

Ages 9 up

The Shimmershine Queens

A Booklist Editors' Choice

Encouraged by her Great Cousin Seatta's explanation of how internalized racism can hold you down, ten-year-old Angie works to build her self confidence and pride. She starts speaking up in class, defending herself, and gradually perceiving her own beauty. She struggles to deal with her mother's depression, her parents' separation, and her cruel, unruly classmates. With the support of her best friend and her drama teacher, she nurtures that glow you feel when you feel good about yourself—that shimmershine feeling, the get-up gift passed down from one's ancestors. Yarbrough has done an excellent job of describing the feelings of rejection, frustration, and hope experienced by a ten-year-old African American girl. This is one of the best books I have found for describing internalized racism, when people start believing some of the lies that have been told about their people. This book is written in beautiful Africanized English.

Suggestions for the Classroom

1. What is the shimmershine feeling? (the glow you feel when you feel good about yourself) How did this information change Angie's life? What did Angie do when she felt discouraged? What can you do? Write a "How to Feel Good About Yourself" booklet.

2. Compare how you feel when you feel discouraged with how you feel when you have the shimmershine feeling. Make a list for each feeling (individual or group lists). Example: *Discouraged*: Ready to give up; Unsure; *Shimmershine*: Ready to try; Confident.

3. What is internalized racism? (when people start believing some of the lies that have been told about their people) (See Great Aunt Seatta's explanation in Chapter 1.) Discuss.

4. What if Angie didn't have a relative to encourage her? What books might she read to help her understand the discrimination her people have suffered and/or to inspire her to ignore the lies told about African descent people. Who might she ask for advice?

5. How did Angie change from the beginning to the end of the book? Write a letter she might write to her niece some day encouraging her to believe in herself.

6. How did drama help Angie? Write about a subject or activity that helps you bring out your best self.

- **Drug Abuse**
- **Death**
- **Self-esteem**

Ages 8–12

Tamika and the Wisdom Rings

Eight-year-old Tamika lives in an urban apartment complex where her parents and community members have implemented important programs to build self-esteem. In the weekly meetings of the Sweet Fruit of the African Family Tree Club, Tamika and her friends learn African dances, write poetry, and decorate the walls of the Community Room with their art. When her father is murdered by drug dealers, Tamika finds strength in her family, friends, herself, and the wisdom rings. This easy-to-read chapter book deals honestly with the painful realities of vandalism, drugs, and senseless violence.

Suggestions for the Classroom

1. Camille Yarbrough wrote this about Tamika and her friends: "They're strong. They're bright. And even though their surroundings might seem hopeless, they are full of hope." Yarbrough's books are filled with suggestions for ways adults can help African American youngsters build strong identities and positive self-concepts.

2. What did each of the wisdom rings represent? How did they help Tamika and Ronnie cope with the death of their father?

3. Discuss the self-esteem programs including: Motto, Say What You Feel, Call and Response, Bundle of Sticks, and Wisdom Rings.

4. The "somebody said somebody said" rule is a useful one for everyone. Discuss including it in the list of rules for your group.

Paul Yee

Chinese Canadian (1956–)

Birthday: October 1

Address: c/o Groundwood Books
585 Bloor Street West, 2nd Floor
Toronto, Ontario M6G 1K5, Canada
416-537-2501

"Writing became part of rediscovering my roots and defining what being Chinese Canadian means today. . . . I believe we need to have Chinese Canadian people and their feelings and stories appear in print because it lets readers who are Chinese Canadian know that their life situations are shared by others. They can grow spiritually and creatively from seeing themselves and their people portrayed in stories."
(Canadian Children's Book Centre Brochure)

Books by Paul Yee

***The Boy in the Attic.* Illustrated by Gu Xiong. Douglas & McIntyre, 1998.**

***Breakaway.* Douglas & McIntyre, 1994.**

***The Curses of Third Uncle.* James Larimer & Company, 1986.**

***Ghost Train.* Illustrated by Harvey Chan. Douglas & McIntyre, 1996.**

***Roses Sing on New Snow.* Illustrated by Harvey Chan. Macmillan, 1991; Simon & Schuster, 1992.**

***Saltwater City: An Illustrated History of the Chinese in Vancouver.* University of Washington Press, 1989.**

***Tales From Gold Mountain: Stories of the Chinese in the New World.* Illustrated by Simon Ng. Macmillan, 1989; Simon & Schuster, 1990.**

***Teach Me to Fly, Skyfighter.* James Larimer & Company, 1983.**

Paul Yee was born October 1, 1956 near Naicam, Saskatchewan, Canada. When Yee was about two, his brother and he were taken to Vancouver's Chinatown, British Columbia where he grew up. Yee read a lot as a child because there was no television at home. He was embarrassed because everyone else at school had a TV. He liked to read adventures and mysteries, and he read the Hardy Boys mysteries quickly, anxious to find out how the stories ended.

As a child, Yee never imagined himself as a writer. Eventually, he studied Canadian history and literature at the University of British Columbia. His studies taught him how powerful the printed word is. "It made real on paper the everyday realities and feelings of life that zipped by without making immediate sense" (Canadian Children's Book Centre brochure).

As Yee was going through college, he began to discover himself as a Chinese Canadian. When he started learning about the history of the Chinese people in Canada, he realized how little he knew about himself and his people. So he started speaking Chinese again and doing volunteer work in Chinatown in Vancouver. For the first time in his life, he began to feel that he belonged to a community.

Yee wrote poetry at first because it allowed him to express personal feelings and moods very quickly. He moved on to stories because they allowed him to write about the people for whom he cared. Writing about people "made them last for ever." He writes about Chinese Canadians for children and for adults because they are the people he knows best. His ideas for writing come from research into history, from memories of people and places known, and from his own imagination. Yee enjoys getting feedback on his writing because "writing is essentially a very lonely occupation: you have to do most of it by yourself" (Canadian Children's Book Centre brochure).

He feels that ". . . if celebrating diversity and reducing prejudice is going to be meaningful, people need profound, often painful re-evaluation of their own beliefs and attitudes. It is painful because it means understanding privilege and power, as to who possesses it and who does not, in order to see how we as a nation, a community of communities, will ensure true equality of opportunity" (personal communication).

The Boy in the Attic

- **Moving**
- **Newcomers**
- **Immigrants**
- **Ghosts**

Seven-year-old Kai-ming Wong has just moved with his family from their village in China to a large city in North America. Faced with a new language, unfamiliar customs, and the newness of city life, Kai-ming feels lost until he discovers a mysterious boy from another era living in the attic of his house. Aided by a magic black butterfly, the two boys overcome language, culture, and time barriers and become friends. This evocative ghost story reminds us that friendship, wherever it is found, is precious and has the power to heal and transform.

Ages 7 up

Suggestions for the Classroom

1. Topics for discussion and writing include: the magic of the black butterfly; the courage required to change and grow; similarities and differences between the two boys; the challenges of moving to a new country; and author Paul Yee's use of the ghost motif in this book and his earlier book, *Ghost Train* (see page 234).

2. For related books, see Immigrants in the Subject Index. Also, an excellent resource for adults is *The Inner World of the Immigrant Child* by Cristina Igoa.

Breakaway

- **Soccer**
- **Depression Era**
- **Chinatown Vancouver**
- **Internalized racism**
- **Gender bias**

In this powerful novel, Yee explores the prejudice and hardships experienced by a Chinese family in Vancouver during the Depression. Eighteen-year-old Kwok-Ken Wong dreams of escaping the family farm by attending university on a soccer scholarship. Yee explores a number of compelling themes and issues including: racism, internalized racism, gender bias, poverty, tradition and change, struggle to create identity, career aspirations, group solidarity, and family expectations.

Ages 10 up

Suggestions for the Classroom

1. Discuss each of the themes and issues above. Choose a character and address these issues from her or his perspective. For example, what might Ying have written in her journal about the way her parents discriminated against her and favored her brother?

2. Examine the series of awakenings Kwok experienced that enabled him to perceive the racism against his people. How did he begin to dismantle his own internalized racism?

3. Analyze the forms gender bias took in this story. How did each character feel about favoritism toward male children? Find quotes to support your answer.

- **Uncles**
- **History**
- **China**
- **Death**
- **Gender issues**

Ages 9 up

The Curses of Third Uncle

Set in Vancouver in the early 1900s, this is a story of intrigue, courage, betrayal, and hardship. The author dedicated the book to his aunt, Lillian Ho Wong (1895–1985), whose memories inspired the book. Fourteen-year-old Chinese Canadian Lillian Ho sets out to find her father and save her family. Her fiery determination and sleuthing skills make her an admirable protagonist. The reader learns much about the history of Canada and China, as well as about family strengths and betrayals. As Lillian's perceptions of China change, the reader becomes more aware that life in any country has its advantages and disadvantages.

Suggestions for the Classroom

1. Analyze the prejudice Lillian suffered as a female. Make a list of all the obstacles she faced. How did she deal with each? What if she learns to fly? Write a sequel where she can jump to rooftops.

2. How did Lillian's attitude toward China change? Why?

3. Create a song or poem for Lillian Ho, the heroine of the year.

- **Railroad**
- **Art**
- **Death**
- **Ghosts**
- **Disabilities**

Ages 7 up

Ghost Train

Amelia Frances Howard-Gibbon Award

Ruth Schwartz Award

Governor General's Literary Award

When her father is forced by poverty to leave China and seek work building a railroad in North America, Choon-yi makes her living selling her paintings in the market. Finally the day arrives when he writes and asks her to join him. But when she arrives she discovers that he has been killed in an accident. Choon-yi's artistic gifts provide the means by which the spirits of her father and other Chinese workers finally find their way home.

Suggestions for the Classroom

1. This powerful book is an excellent example of a picture book that is appropriate for both young children and adolescents. Older children will be able to grasp the historical significance of the story while enjoying the magical elements.

2. Choon-yi was born with one arm. Discuss the reactions of those around her and the impact this had on her life.

3. Discuss the role Chinese immigrants played in building the railroads in Canada and the U. S. Read *The Iron Moonhunter* by Kathleen Chang and *Dragons's Gate* by Laurence Yep (see page 243).

4. The role art plays in this story is a very powerful one. With encouragement, it is sure to inspire youngsters to explore new aspects of their artistic endeavors.

Roses Sing on New Snow: A Delicious Tale

Ruth Schwartz Award

- **Culinary arts**
- **Gender roles**

Maylin cooked in her father's restaurant every day of the week, every week of the year. Even though his restaurant was well known throughout the New World for its fine food, Maylin's father made sure that she didn't get credit for her culinary skills. He told everyone that his two sons did the cooking. However, when the Governor of South China visited the New World, Maylin was finally recognized, not only as an excellent chef but as a very wise, special person.

Ages 6 up

Suggestions for the Classroom

1. Discuss the way that Maylin's father treated her. How might this story be different if it took place now? What options might Maylin have now that she didn't have in the early 1900s? Discuss prejudice toward females and the form it took in this story.

2. Write a letter from Maylin to her father. Then write a response from her father to her.

3. Analyze the way Maylin's father and brothers are depicted. Are fat people lazy? Older students might want to research the ways in which fat people have been oppressed.

Tales From Gold Mountain: Stories of the Chinese in the New World

British Columbia Book Prize

National IODE Award

Mr. Christie's Honour List

Parents' Choice Honour

- **Folktales**
- **Chinese Canadians**
- **Canada**
- **Immigrants**
- **Newcomers**
- **History**

This collection of eight stories is based on the turbulent and courageous history of Chinese immigrants to the "New World." The tales reflect the perseverance of the Chinese who overcame many obstacles to build a place for themselves in their new home. Rich traditions combine with frontier life to give us tales that are humorous, sad, romantic, and inspiring. The dramatic paintings are by award winning illustrator Simon Ng.

Ages 8 up

Suggestions for the Classroom

1. Read one tale a day, followed by discussion and/or an art or creative dramatics activity.

2. Each student chooses one story. The class divides into groups based on their choices and works in groups to present the stories to the class; choose pantomime, readers theatre, skits, etc. Props are encouraged. Create a class mural based on the stories in the book to serve as a background for the presentations.

3. Reread and discuss the Afterword. "The Chinese have been in North America for over one hundred and forty years, but even today they are seen as foreigners and newcomers." Respond in writing or with a group discussion.

- **Kites**
- **Kung fu**
- **Soccer**
- **Child abuse**
- **Immigrants**
- **English as a Second Language**
- **Gender roles**

Ages 8 up

Teach Me to Fly, Skyfighter and Other Stories

This is a collection of four stories with background information about and photographs of Chinese Canadian history in Vancouver. The four stories are centered around the lives and activities of four fifth graders: Sharon Fong (a Canadian born Chinese, English speaking), Samson Wong (a Chinese immigrant from Hong Kong), John Chin (a Chinese immigrant from a farming village in China), and Christine Johnson (a white girl from the housing projects). Each has a story written from her or his perspective. This format is an excellent way to examine the similarities and differences between individual Chinese Canadian children.

Suggestions for the Classroom

1. Analyze the differences and similarities among the four children. Discuss stereotypes and how this book helps combat stereotypes of Chinese children; of girls.

2. Discuss the topics dealt with in the book, including child abuse, immigrants, glasses, Kung fu, soccer, kites, and gender bias in sports. Choose one to write about.

Lawrence Yep

K. Yep

Chinese American (1948–)

Birthday: June 14
Contact: HarperCollins Publishers
10 East 53rd Street
New York, New York 10022

"... I often felt like a changeling. I felt not only inadequate but incomplete—like a puzzle with several key pieces missing."
(The Lost Garden, *p. 12)*

"When I was a kid there were no books about Chinese Americans so the books that were real to me were the science fiction and fantasy books where real kids go to another world where they have to learn another culture and another language, adjusting and adapting. That was something I did every time I got on and off the school bus."
(Personal Communication)

Books by Laurence Yep

American Dragons: Twenty-Five Asian American Voices. **HarperCollins Children's Books, 1993.**

The Boy Who Swallowed Snakes. **Illustrated by Jean and Mou-Sien Tseng. Scholastic, 1994.**

Bug Boy. **Hyperion, forthcoming.**

Butterfly Boy. **Illustrated by Jeanne M. Lee. Farrar Straus & Giroux, 1993.**

The Case of the Goblin Pearls: Chinatown Mystery # 1. **HarperCollins, 1997.**

The Case of the Lion Dance: Chinatown Mystery # 2. **HarperCollins, 1998.**

Child of the Owl. **HarperCollins, 1977.**

The City of Dragons. **Illustrated by Jean and Mou-Sien Tseng. Scholastic, 1995.**

The Cook's Family. **Putnam, 1998.**

Curse of the Squirrel. **Random House, 1987.**

Dragon Cauldron. **HarperCollins, 1991.**

Dragon of the Lost Sea. **HarperCollins Children's Books, 1982.**

The Dragon Prince: A Chinese Beauty and the Beast Tale. **Illustrated by Kam Mak. HarperCollins, 1997.**

Dragon's Gate. **HarperCollins, 1993.**

Dragon Steel. **HarperCollins, 1985.**

Dragon War. **HarperCollins, 1992.**

Dragon's Gate. **HarperCollins, 1993.**

Dragonwings. **HarperCollins, 1975.**

The Ghost Fox. **Illustrated by Jean and Mou-Sien Tseng. Scholastic, 1994.**

Hiroshima: A Novella. **Scholastic, 1995.**

The Junior Thunder Lord. **Illustrated by Robert Van Nutt. BridgeWater Books, 1994.**

The Khan's Daughter: A Mongolian Folktale. **Illustrated by Jean and Mou-sien Tseng. Scholastic, 1997.**

Kind Hearts and Gentle Monsters. **Harper & Row, 1982.**

The Imp That Ate My Homework. **HarperCollins, 1998.**

The Lost Garden: Memoirs. **Julian Messner, 1991.**

The Man Who Tricked a Ghost. **Illustrated by Isadore Seltzer. BridgeWater Books, 1993.**

Mountain Light. **HarperCollins, 1985; 1997.**

The Rainbow People. **Illustrated by David Wiesner. HarperCollins, 1989.**

Sea Glass. **Harper and Row, 1979.**

The Serpent's Children. **HarperCollins, 1984.**

The Shell Woman and the King: A Chinese Folktale. **Illustrated by Yang Ming-Yi. Dial Books, 1993.**

Star Fisher. **Morrow Junior Books, 1991.**

Star Trek: Shadow Lord. **Simon & Schuster, 1985.**

Sweetwater. **Illustrated by Julia Noonan. HarperCollins, 1973.**

Thief of Hearts. **HarperTrophy, 1995.**

Tiger Woman. **Illustrated by Robert Roth. BridgeWater Books, 1995.**

Tongues of Jade. **Illustrated by David Wiesner. HarperCollins, 1991.**

Tree of Dreams: Ten Tales from the Garden of Night. **Illustrated by Isadore Seltzer. Bridgewater Books, 1995.**

Laurence Yep was born June 14, 1948 in San Francisco. His parents owned a corner grocery store where Laurence helped out by stocking the shelves when he was young and figuring out the prices of the stock when he was older. Laurence has described this and other childhood experiences in his memoirs, *The Lost Garden.*

Yep grew up in an African American neighborhood and commuted to a bilingual Catholic school in Chinatown. ". . . I did not confront White American culture until high school. Approaching that culture as something of a stranger, I have been fascinated by all its aspects . . . specifically pursuing the figure of the 'stranger' both in my studies and my writing." Many of Yep's books have dealt with the role of the outsider. Often his protagonists have defied tradition and some have searched for their connection to it.

Yep felt like an outsider in his family of athletic people and in his neighborhood. "I was the Chinese American raised in a Black neighborhood, a child who had been too American to fit into Chinatown and too Chinese to fit in elsewhere. I was the clumsy son of the athletic family, the grandson of a Chinese grandmother who spoke more of West Virginia than of China." Yep also has asthma, which added to his feeling of otherness. This experience as the outsider is poignantly expressed in many of his books and this is one of their strengths that makes them such important reading for young people who may be having similar feelings, and for others in understanding those feelings.

"In the 1950s, few people wanted to be strange and different—let alone foreign. . . . At a time when so many children are now proud of their ethnic heritage, I'm ashamed to say that when I was a child, I didn't want to be Chinese. To be Chinese in San Francisco simply brought trouble. It took me years to realize that I was Chinese whether I wanted to be or not. And it is something I had to learn to accept: to know its strengths and understand its weaknesses. It's something that is a part of me from the deepest levels of my soul to my most common, everyday actions."

After attending Marquette University in Milwaukee, Wisconsin, Yep graduated from the University of California at Santa Cruz and later earned his doctorate in English from the State University of New York in Buffalo, New York. He lives in northern California and is married to Joanne Ryder, who is an editor and writer.

Yep never intended to be a writer; he planned to be a chemist. However at eighteen, when his first science fiction short story was published and he was paid a penny a word, he was bitten by the submission bug so he kept on sending in stories. He has written many books for young readers, earning numerous honors and awards. Yep finds writing to be very satisfying. He has taught creative writing at the university level and has many helpful ideas about how to develop the art of writing. "The best writing is bringing out the specialness of ordinary things. Don't wait for inspiration; open up a window to your imagination" (personal communication)

Yep has a talent for stepping into the shoes of his family and friends when he writes. Many of his books are based on the lives of people close to him: his father in *Dragonwings,* his mother in *Star Fisher,* his grandmother in *Serpent's Children, Mountain Light* and *Child of the Owl,* and himself in *Sea Glass.*

One of Yep's most significant gifts to his readers is his willingness and ability to explore the pain of being the "other" which he does with great insight, sensitivity, and humor. He skillfully guides his protagonists (and readers) through the turmoils of rejection and exclusion toward acceptance and love of self. And he is able to accomplish all this while giving us fascinating, profound stories that are a joy to read!

A sound filmstrip "Meet the Newbery Author: Laurence Yep" is available through American School Publishers. For more information about Laurence Yep, see his autobiography, *The Lost Garden* and *Presenting Laurence Yep* by Dianne Johnson-Feelings. Twayne Young Adult Author Series. Macmillan, 1995.

American Dragons: Twenty-Five Asian American Voices

- **Short stories**
- **Poetry**
- **Plays**
- **People of mixed ancestry**

This compelling anthology includes short stories, poems, and excerpts from plays by Asian Americans whose families came from China, Japan, Korea, Thailand, Tibet, and Vietnam. The contributors include published authors like Maxine Hong Kingston, Janice Mirikitani, Darrell Lum, and Bill Wu as well as original pieces by emerging writers.

Ages 12 up

Suggestions for the Classroom

1. "If there is one animal that is synonymous with Asian mythology and art—and the heart—it is the dragon" (preface). Examine these pieces and Yep's other books for the dragon motif. How do the inner dragons impact the Hopescape?

2. These pieces invite written response. Provide a variety of options from which to choose. Share the results with the large group.

3. After rereading and discussing the preface and afterword, invite youngsters to explore other work by these American Dragons.

Butterfly Boy

- **Butterflies**
- **Environment**
- **Observation**

Drawn from the writings of Chuang Tzu, the fourth century B.C. philosopher sometimes called the Butterfly Philosopher, this delightful prose poem tells the story of a boy who dreams he is a butterfly. As a butterfly, he dreams he is a boy. And sometimes he forgets whether he is a boy or butterfly. It matters not that people make fun of him, get angry with him, or praise him, for he does not care what others think. In Jeanne M. Lee's sumptuous paintings, the butterfly's interpretations appear in delicate insets, superimposed on the pages. An exquisite combination of text, art, and design, this captivating book pays tribute to natural beauty and inner serenity.

All Ages

Suggestions for the Classroom

1. This is a fine example of a picture book that is so special that it is appropriate for use with both young and older children.

2. After enjoying the book for its own beauty, use it in discussions about peer pressure. The Butterfly Boy is his own person, one who cares nothing about praise or insults.

3. With its tribute to nature and its refreshing perspective, this book lends itself perfectly to use with a science unit on observation. It will inspire youngsters to examine closely and to challenge assumptions.

4. See page 137 for more information about Jeanne M. Lee, the illustrator of *Butterfly Boy*.

- **Mystery**
- **San Francisco Chinatown**
- **Sweatshops**
- **Aunts**

Ages 11 up

The Case of the Goblin Pearls: Chinatown Mystery # 1

In the first installment of a new mystery series, twelve-year-old Lily Lew and her resourceful Auntie Tiger Lil join forces to solve the theft of the Goblin Pearls. As this hilarious mystery unwinds, Yep touches on a number of themes and issues: the multiplicity of experiences, beliefs, lifestyles, and communities among Chinese people; the influence of a strong, assertive aunt on a young girl's self-concept; racism in the movie industry; the complexities and contradictions of class upward mobility; and the exploitation of sweatshop workers.

Suggestions for the Classroom

1. Reread and discuss the Preface. Yep notes that this series is "... an attempt to define what I like best and least in Chinatown." Although the book is obviously designed to entertain, there is more to the story. Examine and discuss the issues listed above.

2. Lily made some important discoveries about herself. Examine her personal and social growth: "I just went spinning along in the shadows, afraid to try anything" (p. 13); She had "never given her heritage a thought" (p. 99). "All my life I had sat on the sidelines" (p. 126).

3. Discuss Yep's stereotype-breaking portrayal of Aunt Lil, a plump actor in her sixties. Examine her influence on her niece.

- **Chinatown**
- **Grandmothers**
- **Tradition and change**
- **San Francisco**

Ages 11 up

Child of the Owl

Boston Globe–Horn Book *Fiction Award*
American Library Association Notable Children's Book
Jane Addams Children's Book Award
School Library Journal *Best Children's Books*

Twelve-year-old Casey has been waiting all her life for the day when her compulsive gambler father hits it big. But when he ends up in the hospital, Casey is sent to live with her grandmother in Chinatown (San Francisco). At first Casey feels lost in Chinatown. Her life experiences have not prepared her for the Chinese school, the noisy crowds, and learning the Chinese language. Gradually she begins to find her roots as her Grandmother tells her about the mother Casey never knew, about her true Chinese name, and about the family's owl charm. And Casey, at last, begins to understand and celebrate her Chineseness. Note: This book contains some earthy language. Don't miss the sequel, *Thief of Hearts.*

Suggestions for the Classroom

1. Read the Owl Story aloud. Discuss. Predict what significance it will have in Casey's life.

2. As the story unfolds, Casey learned more about the history of Chinese Americans. In what ways did her feelings about Chinatown and herself change? Why?

3. How did Casey feel about her Chinese name? What does it mean? How did she feel about the name "Casey"?

4. Discuss Casey's feelings about her roots. Do you think Casey might have chosen to go to Chinatown earlier if she had known? Discuss. What did you learn about Chinatown?

5. How were Paw Paw and Casey alike? Different? How were Casey and Jeannie alike? Different? Why did Casey want to be like them? What advice did Paw Paw have for Casey about this? (Be yourself.) Discuss.

6. Read and discuss the Afterword. Discuss Yep's reasons for writing this book.

7. Who did you think the thief was? Why? How did Casey feel? Paw Paw? You? Discuss. Would you have forgiven your father? Why or why not?

8. Select quotes such as the following to discuss or respond to in writing: "... it was like there had always been this person inside of me that I had never been able to name and describe ... and now I not only knew her name but I could tell part of her story."

The City of Dragons

- **Appearance**
- **Dragons**
- **Giants**

Combining classic folktale traditions with his own imagination and inspirations from his childhood, Laurence Yep created this appealing original tale about a boy with a face so sad, nobody wants to look at him. When he runs away with a caravan of giants to the city of dragons, he finally finds a place where his face is appreciated. Vibrant watercolors combine authentic scenes of ancient China with a fascinating assortment of magical beings.

All Ages

Suggestions for the Classroom

1. *The City of Dragons* is a good example of a picture book that is appropriate not only for young children but for older ones as well. Once they get past the "baby book" putdowns, they will be delighted with books like this one. (Many of them secretly miss the old days when they could openly enjoy picture books.)

2. This story cleverly points out the mistake of judging a book by its cover or people by their appearance. It is sure to spark discussions about valuing everyone for the content of their character.

3. Laurence Yep has written a number of books about dragons, a topic that intrigues many youngsters. Gather together all of these books for a Dragon Fest. They are sure to elicit stimulating discussions, imaginative writing, fanciful art, and lively creative dramatics.

The Curse of the Squirrel

- **Hunting**
- **Kindness to animals**
- **Vegetarianism**

A giant squirrel convinces Farmer Johnson and his hunting dogs to change their ways. This humorous story follows Howie, the "best" hunting dog, through his transformation into a kindly vegetarian. Yep says, "... I finally achieved an old ambition to write a horror story of my own. But instead of being frightened, I got to laugh a lot."

Ages 7 up

Suggestions for the Classroom

1. Dramatize a discussion between Howie and his brother, Willie.

2. Read Yep's dedication (to Simon, who doesn't eat anything that can have fun). Discuss.

3. Yep said that he always wanted to write a horror story but when he wrote this book, instead of being frightened, he laughed a lot. Discuss. Try mixing humor with another genre.

4. Check out and read books on vegetarianism. Write a short report or give a book talk. See the following resources: Books: *Good For Me* by Marilyn Burns; *Diet and Nutrition* by Brian Ward; *Much Ado About Aldo* by Johanna Hurwitz; *Charlotte's Web* by E. B. White; *Vegetarian Children* by Sharon Yntema; *The Complete Guide and Cookbook for Raising Your Child as a Vegetarian* by Nina & Michael Shandler; Magazines: *PETA Kids* (People for the Ethical Treatment of Animals); P.O. Box 42516, Washington, D.C. 20015, (subscription with tax deductible donation)

5. Make a list of well known vegetarians. (See *Much Ado About Aldo* on page 132 for a list of vegetarians.) Interview a vegetarian. Report back to your class. Or invite a vegetarian to speak to your class.

6. Explain what this term means: "A Cruelty-Free Diet" (a diet that does not cause cruelty to any animal). Discuss.

- **Fantasy**
- **Dragons**
- **Myth**
- **Magic**
- **Chinese folklore**
- **Death**
- **Self-sacrifice**

SHIMMER SERIES:
Dragon of the Lost Sea
Dragon Steel
Dragon Cauldron
Dragon War

Ages 12 up

Dragon Cauldron

This is the third book in the Shimmer Series. Shimmer, the dragon, continues her quest to restore her clan's lost sea home. With the help of Civet, the reformed river spirit, Monkey, a wizard, and the two young humans, Indigo and Thorn, Shimmer faces many obstacles. She seeks the assistance of the fabled Snail Woman and the powerful Smith in repairing the cauldron. But in their journey, they unwittingly unleash a terrible evil, the Nameless One, strongest of the wicked kings from the past. Based on Chinese myths, these characters will find a special place in fantasy lovers' hearts. Be prepared for many unexpected turns of events, especially concerning sacrifices made by Civet and Thorn. Although Shimmer comes very close to success, she is forced to postpone her mission to fight the Nameless One, who is assisted by her brother, Pomfret.

Suggestions for the Classroom

1. Read *Dragon of the Lost Sea* and *Dragon Steel* before reading this book. Predict what will happen in each new book in the series.

2. How would you feel if you lost your magic? Respond with a journal entry, a skit, or a pantomime.

3. Discuss the switch in this third book in the series to Monkey's voice. (The first two were told in Shimmer's voice.)

4. Write an obituary for Civet and/or Thorn.

5. Respond in writing to quotes such as the following: "The past has a way of being more real than the present."

6. Create illustrations of the crypt, the nets, the avalanche, the cavern, the dog, the island, the Butcher's camp, the excavation site, or the cauldron. These might be combined into a mural.

- **Fantasy**
- **Magic**
- **Dragons**
- **Environment**
- **Myth**
- **Chinese folklore**

SHIMMER SERIES:
Dragon of the Lost Sea
Dragon Steel
Dragon Cauldron
Dragon War

Ages 12 up

Dragon of the Lost Sea

An American Library Association Notable Children's Book
International Reading Association: 100 Favorite Paperbacks
A Charlotte Zolotow Book

This book is the first in the Shimmer series. Shimmer, an exiled dragon princess, has spent centuries wandering, disguised in various human forms, searching for ways to restore her beloved lost sea/home. Civet, a powerful river spirit, stole the Dragon Clan's sea and imprisoned it in a pebble. Against her better judgment, Shimmer decides to rescue a thirteen-year-old human boy, Thorn, and to allow him to accompany her on her quest. This novel, based on Chinese myths, is an exciting fantasy full of courage, magic, and paradoxes. Dragons are a national Chinese symbol of life, strength, courage, and royalty.

Suggestions for the Classroom

1. Compare Shimmer's attitude toward humans at the beginning of the book with how she felt at the end of the book. Why did her attitude change? Make a list of quotes to support your theory.

2. Discuss the reason(s) Shimmer was exiled from her home.

3. Compare Shimmer's attitude toward Civet at the beginning of the book with how she feels at the end. Use quotes. Ana-

lyze the reasons for Civet's behavior. Debate whether or not you feel it was justified.

4. Write at least four journal entries for one of the characters in the book. Compile these and share with classmates. How were your perceptions similar? Different?

5. Start a Shimmer mural. Add to it as you read each book in the series.

6. Make a list of magic objects used in the book. Adapt these or create new magic objects in a story of your own.

Dragon's Gate

Newbery Honor Book

- **Historical fiction**
- **Railroads**
- **Exploitation of workers**

This is the third book in the trilogy, with *The Serpent's Children* and *Mountain Light.* In this stirring novel, Cassia's sixteen-year-old adopted son, Otter, travels from his home in Kwangtung Province, China to the Sierra Mountains in California in 1867. There he joins his adoptive father, Squeaky; his hero, Uncle Foxfire; and thousands of other Chinese men who are working on the transcontinental railroad. As they struggle to survive brutal working conditions, starvation, frostbite, explosions, and avalanches, Otter tries to reconcile his ideals with harsh reality. This is a powerful survival story/social history that examines the universal concerns of identity, equality, family loyalty, and ethnic conflict with honor and humor. Yep's carefully researched details combined with his lively storytelling skills have resulted in an extraordinary book.

Ages 10 up

Suggestions for the Classroom

1. One of Yep's most significant gifts to his readers is his willingness and ability to explore the pain of being the outsider which he does with insight, sensitivity, and humor. Examine each of the outsiders in this trilogy and trace their growth through the turmoils of rejection and exclusion toward acceptance and love of self.

2. Cassia, the protagonist in the first book in this trilogy, was admired by many readers for her wisdom, tenacity, resiliency, and compassion. Compare and contrast her roles in each of the books.

3. Otter was devastated to discover that his Uncle Foxfire was not the hero he remembered. Examine the changes in his perceptions of his uncle. In what ways did these changes parallel his vision for the Great Work?

4. Conversations in Chinese are set in plain type while those in English are presented in italics. How does this typographic technique help the reader understand the linguistic shifts required of bilingual people?

5. Examine the events that drove Otter to undertake the desperate mission to save the camp from an avalanche. What impact did this event have on his life?

6. Respond in writing to quotes such as: "fear was like a mole living inside me, its claws scrabbling deeper and deeper into my mind" (p. 171).

7. Reread and discuss the Afterword. Discuss each of the hardships faced by the workers.

8. Both *Dragonwings* and *Dragon's Gate* won Newbery Honor Awards. Compare and contrast the writing, settings, characterizations, and plots of the two books. Which of Yep's other books would you nominate for awards?

- **Fantasy**
- **Magic**
- **Dragons**
- **Environment**
- **Myth**
- **Chinese folklore**
- **War**

SHIMMER SERIES:
Dragon of the Lost Sea
Dragon Steel
Dragon Cauldron
Dragon War

Ages 12 up

Dragon Steel

This is the second book in the Shimmer Series. Shimmer, the dragon princess, and her human companion, Thorn, continue their quest to return Shimmer's clan to its ancestral home. However, they return to find the dragons at war with the humans. Shimmer's clan has been enslaved by her Uncle Sambar, the High King, and forced to work in underwater volcano steel mines to help prepare for the war. With the help of Thorn and a new human companion, Indigo, Shimmer faces the challenges of trying to lead her clan to freedom. But they are met with treachery, jealousy, and more magic. This fantasy of magicians, dungeons, and sea monsters is full of swashbuckling adventure, daring acrobatics, and soul-searching growth.

Suggestions for the Classroom

1. Discuss the four symbols of dragon power. (bowl, mirror, cloud and pearl) Add illustrations to your Shimmer mural.

2. Compare and contrast the three outcasts' (Shimmer, Indigo, and Civet) search for their homes. Why isn't Thorn also searching for his home?

3. Find several quotes describing Shimmer's feelings about her leadership role. Analyze how her feelings change during the story.

4. Discuss the quote regarding history, ". . . history is like a great beast that one either learned how to ride or got trampled by."

5. Create new ways to express the following quotes: "Dreams can change mud into gold." "Sometimes dreams make people rise above their own selfish interests." "Sometimes the worst curse is to find your dream."

6. In what ways did Thorn's perception of Indigo change? Why? Write two journal entries he might have written, one when he first met her, and one toward the end of the book.

7. What does the book say about the environment? What recommendations might Shimmer have for taking good care of the earth?

- **Newcomers**
- **Poverty**
- **Father-Son relationship**
- **Flight**
- **Inventions**
- **Historical fiction**
- **Tradition and change**
- **Earthquake**
- **Immigrants**

Dragonwings

Newbery Honor Book
IRA Children's Book Award
American Library Association Notable Children's Books
School Library Journal ***Best of the Best Children's Books***
National Council for the Social Studies Carter G. Woodson Award
Notable Children's Trade Books in Social Studies
International Reading Association/Children's Book Council Children's Choice

The setting for this fine book is San Francisco in 1903–1910. Yep wrote this "historical fantasy" inspired by a newspaper account of a Chinese immigrant who invented a biplane in 1909. It is a marvelous story of high adventure, a magnificently written tribute to the spirit and perseverance of Chinese immigrants. Eight-year-old Moon Shadow sails from China in 1903 to join his father, Windrider, in the United States. Although Moon Shadow has never met his father, he soon grows to respect and love him. Windrider, who works with relatives in a laundry, is a man of genius with a dream of flying. Together they endure the racism of the whites (demons), the ridicule of the other Chinese, and poverty to make their dreams come true. This book is unique in its portrayal of early 20th century San Francisco, including the earthquake, from a young immigrant's perspective.

Ages 12 up

Suggestions for the Classroom

1. What happened to Moon Shadow's grandfather? (He was lynched.) Discuss the impact this had on Moon Shadow. What did Moon Shadow call the white people? (Demons) Why?

2. Think about the welcome party for Moon Rider. What gifts did he receive? What was different about the present from his father? ("Something for your soul": a kite)

3. Read the story of the Imperial Dragon aloud. Discuss. What was unique about Windrider? Why did he want to fly?

4. What were some of the problems that Chinese immigrants faced in the U.S. in the early 1900s? Include racism, poverty, separation from loved ones, loss of homeland, ridicule, new language and new culture. How did some of the characters react to these problems? (Lefty—gambling, Black Dog—drugs, most of the characters worked harder and persevered.)

5. Compare Miss Whitlaw's and Windrider's views of dragons. Discuss. Moon Shadow decided to try to reeducate Miss Whitlaw about dragons. How did he go about this? Was he successful? What did he learn in the process?

6. What happened to change everything? Check out and read books about earthquakes. See if you can find information about the San Francisco earthquakes of 1906 and 1989. What changes did the earthquake bring for Moon Shadow, his relatives, the Whitlaws, and other San Franciscans?

7. Discuss quotes such as the following: "... if life seems awfully petty most of the time, every now and then there is something noble and beautiful and almost pure that lifts us suddenly out of the pettiness and lets us share in it a little."

8. What were some of the Dragon tests? (flight of Dragonwings, earthquake, poverty, Black Dog's attacks, etc.) Discuss each test.

9. Laurence Yep was commissioned by the Berkeley Repertory Theatre to adapt *Dragonwings* for the stage; the play opened at his old grammar school on the same stage where he had once performed. How do you think Yep felt on opening night? Think about what is involved in adapting a novel for the stage. Dramatize *Dragonwings* for your team or school. (It is available in *Theatre for Young Audiences* edited by Lowell Swortzell.)

The Ghost Fox

Child Study Children's Book Committee Children's Book of the Year

- **Folklore**
- **Ghosts**

In this suspenseful chapter book, Little Lee struggles to save his mother's spirit from a dangerous fox spirit which has assumed human form. Yep adapted this tale from a Chinese classic collected in the seventeenth century by a Chinese scholar. Full-page black-and-white illustrations.

Ages 8–11

Suggestions for the Classroom

1. This fast-paced story is perfect for youngsters who are ready to exercise their skills on chapter books but who are not ready for longer novels. They will enjoy reading and discussing this story about tenacity and courage.

2. Goodness triumphs over evil is a common theme in folklore. After enjoying this tale, invite interested youngsters to write, illustrate, and share tales of their own.

Hiroshima: A Novella

- Atomic bomb
- Japan
- World War II

Ages 9 up

Based on authentic accounts written by survivors, Yep describes the dropping of the atomic bomb on Hiroshima, Japan on August 6, 1945. Through present-tense narration that juxtaposes the experiences of a composite twelve-year-old survivor and the men on the bomber, Yep traces the events of that fateful day. Sachi survived but was badly burned; she later became one of twenty-five "Hiroshima Maidens" who was flown to the United States for plastic surgery as a gesture of goodwill. Complete with a bibliography, *Hiroshima* ends with observations on the destructive potential of nuclear warfare and some of the efforts being made toward disarmament.

Suggestions for the Classroom

1. Fifty years later, the bombing is still the focus of controversy. As with any material that might be perceived as controversial, teachers should read the book carefully and inform their supervisors before introducing it to young children. However, do not avoid it because the material is sensitive; it is too important for young people to not know about.

2. Discuss Yep's motivation for writing this book. (He dedicated it to the memory of Yoshiko Uchida. He noted that he was haunted by photos of the Hiroshima victims for many years. He wrote this book as an "attempt to understand what happened to them.")

3. This is a significant book that will start classroom discussions across the curriculum. Readers of all ages will also be interested in related picture books: *My Hiroshima* by Junko Morimoto; *Hiroshima No Pika* by Toshi Maruki; *Sadako* by Eleanor Coerr; and *Shin's Tricycle* by Tatsuharu Kodama.

The Junior Thunder Lord

- Folklore: China
- Droughts
- Weather

Ages 6 to 8

When Yue was a child, he learned an important lesson: "Those at the top should help those at the bottom." Years later when he follows this advice, it not only saves his life but rescues his homeland from a terrible drought. This humorous seventeenth century tale of kindness rewarded is retold through crisp language and lively illustrations. However, the facial features of all but the main characters lack individuality.

Suggestions for the Classroom

1. Kindness rewarded is a basic theme in folklore. After enjoying this story, examine other tales for variations on this theme. For example, read and discuss the title story in *The Ch'i-Lin Purse.* See page 138.

2. One of the cardinal rules in illustrations is to provide variation in the basic features of all the characters. Examine and discuss the faces of the supporting cast in this book.

3. After enjoying the book, take time to discuss Bear Face, who as an outsider, was unfamiliar with local etiquette. Discuss the importance of not judging people by their appearance or customs.

The Khan's Daughter: A Mongolian Folktale

• Folklore (Mongolia)

Yep's humorous retelling of this tale features antihero Möngke, a shepherd who seeks to marry Borte, the Khan's assertive daughter. Unconventional characters, splendid watercolor paintings, frightful monsters, and dramatic folkloric narrative provide an entertaining adventure.

Ages 5–8

Suggestions for the Classroom

1. Compare and contrast this refreshing tale with other stories where the characters are more conventional.

2. Borte and Möngke lived as equals for the rest of their lives. What qualities did they each possess that created this kind of relationship?

3. Discuss the special features throughout the book such as the title written in Mongolian characters on the copyright page and the Mongolian horse-head cello on the title page and last page.

The Lost Garden

• Autobiography
• Authors

Yep describes how he grew up as a Chinese American in San Francisco and how he celebrates his family and his ethnic heritage through his writing. Yep often felt like an outsider and is now able to express this pain with tremendous insight, humor, and sensitivity. One of his most significant gifts to his readers is his willingness and ability to explore the feelings of the "other" and to guide his protagonists (and readers) through the resulting turmoil toward acceptance and love of self.

Ages 10 up

Suggestions for the Classroom

1. Discuss the ways in which Yep felt different. How has he celebrated this difference in his writings? How has writing helped him understand himself?

2. Yep has based several of his books on the lives of family members. (See the biography of Yep in this chapter.) Discuss. Write a story about someone close to you.

3. Does your library have Yep's books? If not, write a letter to your media director, requesting that they be purchased. Which of his books are your favorites? Why? How does knowing about his life help you understand and appreciate his writing?

4. Analyze the following: A teacher takes many classes in children's literature, yet she has never heard of many authors from parallel cultures such as Laurence Yep. (Exclusion is one of the most insidious forms of bias.) Do you have any recommendations for instructors of children's literature classes?

Mountain Light

• Tradition and change
• Historical fiction: China
• Death
• War
• Gold Rush

In this second book in the trilogy *(The Serpent's Children, Mountain Light,* and *Dragon's Gate),* Cassia teams up with Squeaky Lau even though they are from feuding clans. United in their dedication to the revolution against the Manchu Dynasty, they teach each other valuable life lessons. The last third of the book is devoted to Squeaky's journey to the Land of the Golden Mountain where he joins the gold seekers in California.

Ages 10 up

Suggestions for the Classroom

1. What did Cassia and Squeaky learn from each other? How did they each use these new skills in confronting new challenges?

2. Trace the source of the feud between the Youngs and Laus. Explore the theme of Scarcity and the impact it had on all the misunderstandings, feuds, uprisings, and wars.

3. The Strangers were scapegoated just like many other groups throughout history. Analyze the forms scapegoating took in this saga.

4. Yep often writes about outcasts. Examine each outcast in this book and the ways in which they worked together and against each other.

- **Folktales (Chinese American)**

The Rainbow People

Boston Globe–Horn Book *Honor Award for Nonfiction*
American Library Association Notable Children's Book
Children's Editors' Choices (ALA Booklist)
Horn Book *Fanfare Honor List*
Notable Children's Trade Books in Social Studies

Twenty folktales told by Chinese American immigrants and collected for a 1930s WPA project are retold by Laurence Yep. They maintain the pungency and richness of their origins. Arranged by theme: tricksters, fools, virtues and vices, in Chinese America, and love. Yep says in the introduction, "They are strategies for living." They offered consolation and hope, and expressed loneliness, anger, fear, and love.

Ages 8 up

Suggestions for the Classroom

1. Read other Chinese American folktales such as *Tongues of Jade,* also by Laurence Yep. Read folktales from many cultures. See Folklore in the Subject Index.

2. Divide into groups. Each group selects a tale and decides on a creative way to present it to the class. Examples: drama, filmstrip, mural, storytelling, etc.

3. Select a quote to respond to in writing such as: "Don't fill the jar when it's cracked." ". . . you can do the wrong things for the right reasons."

4. Write and illustrate a folktale. Collect these into a class or team collection and publish. Add this original book to your library.

- **Ballet**
- **Footbinding**
- **Gender roles**
- **Grandmothers**
- **People of mixed ancestry**
- **San Francisco**

Ribbons

Eleven-year-old Robin Lee, whose life passion is ballet, grudgingly agrees to temporarily give up dance lessons so her family can afford to bring Grandmother over from Hong Kong. Determined to maintain her dance skills, Robin practices in the garage, not admitting to herself the damage the cement floor and the increasingly tight toe shoes is doing to her feet. Her resentment grows when Grandmother takes over her room and favors her little brother. But when she discovers that Grandmother's feet were long ago bound in accordance with traditional Chinese custom, her hostility is transformed into compassion and love. This absorbing story incorporates a number of significant themes and topics: bridging cultural and generational gaps, fighting for one's dreams, determination to transcend pain, the connection between dancers' feet and footbinding, personal sacrifice for the benefit of family, favoritism toward male children, interracial families, and the meaning of beauty. (Sequel: *The Cook's Family.* Putnam, 1998.)

Ages 9 up

Suggestions for the Classroom

1. Invite youngsters to explore one of the themes listed above through their choice of written forms.

2. Throughout the book, Robin tried to find ways to communicate her love for ballet. Find and discuss quotes such as "Dance is my life." (p. 48). How did this passion affect her relationships with each family member, her friends, and herself?

3. Examine the behaviors and issues that led to the chasm between Robin and Grandmother. In what ways did they misjudge each other? How did this change?

4. Reread and discuss the Afterword. To augment the information about footbinding in the appended bibliography, read another book by Yep: *The Serpent's Children.* See below.

The Serpent's Children

- **Tradition and change**
- **Historical fiction: China**
- **Footbinding**
- **Death**
- **Father-Daughter relationship**
- **Father-Son relationship**
- **Legend**

The first book in the trilogy: *The Serpent's Children, Mountain Light,* and *Dragon's Gate.* In nineteenth-century China, young Cassia fights against poverty, footbinding, bandits, drought, famine, and ideological conflicts between her brother and father to protect her family. Set in China's Kwangtung's Province, this is a majestic tale full of legend, adventure, sorrow, and humor. Cassia, the indomitable heroine, is the "serpent's child." According to legend, once a serpent sets her mind on something, she doesn't give up. Cassia is eight years old when her father goes to war against the British invaders and when her mother dies. When her father returns, injured and bitter, he trains Cassia and her brother, Foxfire, to carry on the work—the task of freeing China from both British and Manchu domination. Cassia, determined to keep her promise to her dying mother to take care of Father and Foxfire, demonstrates all the qualities of the serpent's child: wisdom, strength, humor, wit, tenacity, resiliency, adaptability, and compassion. An intriguing portrait of a remarkable young woman who defies tradition, of family crises, and of a culture at the crossroads, this is the kind of book you will stay up late to finish. It is one of my favorite books by Laurence Yep.

Ages 10 up

Suggestions for the Classroom

1. How did Cassia feel about being the "serpent's child"? What does it mean to be the serpent's child? How did it impact her life? How might her life have been different if she had not been the serpent's child?

2. What were some of the challenges Cassia faced including the death of her mother, injured/bitter father, ideological conflicts between her father and brother, poverty, footbinding, bandits, drought, and famine? How did she deal with each of these problems? Choose one of the problems and write about it from Cassia's perspective.

3. Research footbinding. How did Cassia feel about footbinding? (Cassia's valiant battle with, and victory over her relatives is one of the most inspiring passages I have ever read; hopefully it will encourage young women to fight against abusive traditions!) Write several journal entries that Cassia might have written during and after this struggle. What advice might she have for others facing similar situations?

4. Read other books set in nineteenth century China. Can you find any other books with strong female characters? Why do you think this is such a rare book?

5. Omission is one of the most insidious forms of bias. Discuss omission in terms of this book. (Notice that many of Laurence Yep's other books have won numerous awards. Perhaps this book didn't sell as many copies as some of the others. Why? Have strong heroines been a priority in children's literature? Is this changing? Think about Casey in *Child of the Owl.*)

6. What do you think Cassia will do next? Write a short sequel telling about an event in her life in a few years. Remember her serpent qualities and her promise to her dying mother. Then read the sequels *Mountain Light* and *Dragon's Gate.*

• Folklore: China

Ages 6 up

The Shell Woman and the King: A Chinese Folktale

Shell must perform three seemingly impossible tasks or she will be forced to marry the king and her husband will be beheaded. Filled with life and death drama, this eighteenth century tale is retold through lively prose and beautiful watercolors. Note: This book contains several grisly scenes.

Suggestions for the Classroom

1. A brave and resourceful woman, Shell outwitted the greedy king. Examine other folktales for images of strong females. Discuss stereotyping of females in folklore.

2. Older students might enjoy debating whether or not folktales for young children should retain their violent aspects such as the amputation of the arm and the burning of the villain.

• Moving
• Newcomers
• Mother-Daughter relationship
• Friendship
• Tradition and change

Ages 10 up

The Star Fisher

This beautifully written book is based on the experiences of Laurence Yep's relatives in 1927, in West Virginia. When sixteen-year-old Joan Lee and her parents, sister, and brother move from Ohio to West Virginia to open a laundry, they are, at first, met with close-mindedness and even hostility. In this heart-felt, humorous novel, Joan tells about her struggles within the family, as well as in the community. At school, she is excluded until she finds Berniece, who is also an outsider in a different way. At home, the challenge is about combining the family's traditional Chinese heritage with their American identities. Joan, born in the United States, and her mother struggle to communicate across the generation and culture chasms. Gradually, they find ways to bridge the gaps. At a church auction, Mrs. Lee's apple pie breaks down some of the barriers; customers start to bring clothes to the family laundry. Joan finds new friends and keeps her friendship with Berniece. This is an important novel about growing up Chinese American, following your dreams, and learning how to "fish for the stars."

Suggestions for the Classroom

1. When Papa was upset, what did he do? (wrote poetry) Discuss each of the frustrating and humiliating things that happened. Write a poem that Papa might have written after one of these incidents.

2. Conversations in Chinese are set in plain type while those in English are presented in italics. How does this typographic technique demonstrate the linguistic shifts bilingual people must make?

3. Describe Joan's first day at school (Chapter 6). Have you ever felt like an outsider? Write about your experiences and how you felt. What can you do to make sure this doesn't happen to someone else?

4. What did Joan learn from Berniece about families? What advice might Joan have for Berniece about her family? Berniece for Joan?

5. Discuss Joan's relationship with her mother. What pressures did they have? What advice might they each have?

6. Give examples of the racism the Lees faced including signs painted on fence, no customers, exclusion at school, condescension at grocery store, sign in appliance store window, name calling, no one would bid on Mrs. Lee's pie, etc. How did the Lee family cope with each? What would you have done? What can you do to prevent such racism?

7. Select quotes such as the following to discuss and/or respond to in writing: "It's funny how there are levels and levels of prejudice in the world." "... [don't] let a lot of silly prejudices blindfold you."

8. What special significance does West Virginia have for Laurence Yep? Why did he make a special trip there before writing this book?

Sweetwater

This is Yep's first book. It is the haunting story of a boy and his people and their valiant efforts to save their way of life. Thirteen-year-old Tyree is a descendent of the first colonists sent from Earth to the star, Harmony. The music-loving boy lives in a commune with other colonists who remained in the original half-flooded city of Old Sion. Amadeus is the greatest Argan songmaster on the planet. He teaches Tyree all he can about music and gives Tyree's blind sister an awesome treasure that enables her to save her family'slife when the old city is invaded by hydras and sea dragons. This fascinating science fiction story will enchant readers with its evocation of believable details concerning a future civilization. Caley's blindness is presented with sensitivity for the most part.

- **Music**
- **Oceans**
- **Blindness**
- **Future**
- **Science fiction**
- **Cities**

Ages 10 up

Suggestions for the Classroom

1. This is Yep's first book. Read his other books. How is *Sweetwater* different from his other books?

2. What is it about *Sweetwater* that makes it such a unique book? Write a review of the book that might appear in a catalog of literature for young readers.

3. Discuss the author's handling of Caley's blindness. Rewrite parts of the story from Caley's perspective. Or write a sequel with Caley as the main character.

4. Music plays an integral role in this story. Compose a song that Amadeus or Tyree might have played on their flutes.

5. Design and construct a future city. Write a science fiction story about it.

6. What if you found yourself on a distant star in the future? Describe your life. Illustrate.

- **San Francisco Chinatown**
- **Grandmothers**
- **Identity**
- **People of mixed ancestry**
- **Stealing**

Ages 9 up

Thief of Hearts

In this long awaited sequel to Yep's superb *Child of the Owl,* Casey has grown up, married a Caucasian, moved fifty miles south of Chinatown, and become a psychologist. This engaging novel focuses on her adolescent daughter, Stacy and her issues of identity as a mixed-race child. Stacy has seldom thought about herself as a Chinese American until she is assigned to help Hong Ch'un, a reluctant immigrant from China. When Hong Ch'un is falsely accused of petty thievery at school and Stacy is labeled a "half-breed" for defending her, Hong Ch'un runs away and Stacy suffers an identity crisis. Stacy, accompanied by her mother and great-grandmother, lovable ninety-year-old Tai-Paw (Paw-Paw in *Child of the Owl),* search for Hong Ch'un in Chinatown. Casey and Tai-Paw find old friends and memories and Stacy makes significant discoveries about her heritage. Returning home with Hong Ch'un, Tai-Paw and Stacy make plans to catch the real thief. With warmth and humor, this page-turning novel touches on issues of peer pressure, mixed-race identity, intergenerational communication, judging people on appearance, and racial stereotyping.

Suggestions for the Classroom

1. *Child of the Owl* was published eighteen years before *Thief of Hearts.* After reading both books discuss the changes in Casey, Tai-Paw, and Chinatown. Compare and contrast the two books.

2. Reread and discuss the two stories within stories, each told by Tai-Paw, and each providing the title and motif for its respective book.

3. Examine the story from the perspective of each character. For example, think about the events from Karen's perspective. Discuss peer pressure and explore ways to resist its damaging effects.

4. Reread and discuss the Afterword. Discuss Yep's motivation for exploring the issues raised in *Thief of Hearts.* See the Subject Index for other books about issues related to mixed-race identity.

Ages 8 up

Tongues of Jade

This companion volume to *The Rainbow People* includes twenty-one folktales retold by Laurence Yep. Stories about spirit people, farmers, sages, fools, poets, kings, and demons provided an anchor for Chinese Americans to their homeland.

Suggestions for the Classroom

See *The Rainbow People* on page 248.

Tree of Dreams: Ten Tales from the Garden of Night

- **Dreams**
- **Folklore**

Drawing on the connection between dreams and folklore, Yep retells ten engaging stories from Brazil, China, Greece, India, Japan, and Senegal. Between his poetic preface and an informative afterword, Yep introduces a parade of fascinating characters and entertaining plots.

Ages 8 up

Suggestions for the Classroom

1. Reread and discuss the Preface. Yep states that dreaming is a bond that unites us beyond language, custom, geography, and time. As you read these tales, analyze the universal phenomenon of dreams.

2. The format of this book lends itself to illustration. Starting with the silhouette of a large tree, invite youngsters to nestle images among the branches, a badger here, a cricket there.

3. Invite interested youngsters to write about and illustrate their dreams. Add these to the branches of the tree. Other natural extensions include map study and drama.

Appendices

Assessment Plan

Multicultural Education Program Assessment

Teacher

1. The classroom environment celebrates diversity: race, gender, ethnicity, age, socioeconomic class, sexual orientation, disabilities, native languages, color, religion, national origin.

___books ___films/filmstrips/videos
___posters ___computer software
___pictures ___records/tapes
___games/puzzles ___musical instruments
___art activities ___movement/dance
___author units ___other__________

2. **Curriculum:** The curriculum reflects multiple perspectives.

3. **Pedagogy:** Teachers modify their teaching in ways that will facilitate the academic and affective growth of students from diverse groups.

4. **Learning Styles:** Teachers utilize activities that will enhance the growth of students with a wide variety of learning styles.

5. **Content:** Teachers use examples and content from a wide variety of cultures.

6. **Knowledge Construction:** Teachers help students investigate and understand the implicit perspectives and assumptions within each discipline and how this influences the ways that knowledge is constructed.

7. **Speakers/Resource People:** The people who visit the school and help in the classroom represent diverse cultures.

8. **Reflective Self-Analysis:** Teachers are aware of the potential for subtle bias in the following behaviors and modify their actions to provide a culture-fair learning environment.

_____ Who do we call on?
_____ Who do we listen to?
_____ Who do we praise?
_____ Who do we help?
_____ Who do we choose as helpers?
_____ Who do we initiate interaction with?
_____ Length of time for a response?
_____ To whom do we give detailed explanations?
_____ To whom do we give the benefit of the doubt?
_____ Expectations (Self-fulfilling prophecy)
_____ Body Language
_____ Who do we look directly at? (Eye contact with teachers is not appropriate in some cultures.)

9. **Other** ______________________

Multicultural Education Program Assessment

Principal/Building

1. Empowering School Culture: Grouping, labeling, discipline, and general school practices; sports, music, art, and extra-curricular activities; office, custodial, food, transportation personnel; and the interactions of staff and students create a school culture that empowers students, staff, and parents from all groups.

2. Building personnel are aware of and follow the District Multicultural Education Policy.

3. The racial/ethnic compositions of staff and student populations are in balance.

4. Staff Development: Inservices on Multicultural Education have been provided for all personnel.

5. Staff Appraisal: Appraisal guidelines include information regarding equity awareness of all groups.

6. Media: The Media Center includes an ample number of materials about all groups for all grade levels. These materials were selected for their sensitivity to all groups. Each genre (example: biography) is in balance with the materials available in the field.

7. Bilingual Materials: Bilingual materials are available for each of the language groups represented in the school.

8. Assessment: Assessment tools, practices, and decisions reflect an awareness of cultural and language bias in assessment materials. Alternative authentic assessments are used.

9. Assemblies/Programs: Performers, consultants, speakers, authors, etc. are representative of diverse groups. Students involved in plays and programs represent all the groups present in the school.

10. Special Education: Students involved in Gifted/Talented, Learning Disabilities, and other special programs are representative of the diverse groups in the school. (Gender/Racial Balance)

11. Calendar: The school calendar includes information about ethnic holidays and special days. There is an awareness in scheduling special events and tests so that the students, parents, and staff involved are not forced to choose between their culture and their education.

12. Curriculum Committees: There is a Multicultural Education Committee. Other committees are working on integrating the curricula with Multicultural Education.

13. Language Diversity: The school encourages and supports dialect and language diversity.

14. Other ____________________

Multicultural Education Program Assessment

Parents

1. Parent Organizations: The Parent/Teacher Organization and other parent groups include members from each of the groups represented in the community. Committees such as the Principal Selection Committee include representatives from each of the racial/ethnic groups in the school/community.

2. Feedback from parents representing all groups is considered when making decisions.

3. Language interpreters are available for all groups needing them during conferences and meetings.

4. All parents are welcome in the school and are encouraged to become involved in school activities.

5. Other ____________________

District

1. The district has a Multicultural Education Policy.

2. The Multicultural Education Policy includes:

___students
___curriculum
___race
___religion
___language
___age
___gender
___disabilities
___parents
___sexual orientation
___color
___other____________________
___personnel
___assessment tools
___national origin
___staff development

3. The district has a Multicultural Education Advisor or Coordinator.

4. The district has a Multicultural Education Task Force or Advisory Board. The members of this group represent the diverse groups present in the district.

5. Personnel groups including teachers, mental health, and administrators are in balance with the racial and ethnic composition of the student population.

6. **Staff Development:** Inservices have been provided or are planned for all district employees.

7. **District Committees:** The members of district committees represent the diverse groups present in the school community.

8. **Board of Education:** The members of the Board of Education represent the diverse groups present in the school community.

9. **Professional Information Services:** The materials and information available reflect an awareness of the importance of Multicultural Education.

10. Other ____________________________

APPENDIX 2

Optional Activities

These activities may be used with any of the author units. Of course, the major goal of the author units will be to enjoy fine literature; however, teachers, librarians, and parents might choose to extend the literary experience by selecting some of these activities or some of the specific activities listed with each book. Many adults will encourage individual youngsters or groups of youngsters to choose among the activities and to create some of their own.

1. **SETTING THE STAGE:** Set up an author center or author corner. Include a photograph of the author, a display of her/his books, posters, realia, maps, a bulletin board, etc. Add student work as it is completed. Youngsters enjoy being involved in the planning of these author units. They might write to the publisher requesting materials such as posters featuring the author's books. Encourage them to take leadership roles in setting up the centers, creating the bulletin boards, and planning the activities.

2. **COMPLETE WORKS:** Provide an overview of the complete works of the author. As you read a book, discuss it within the context of the complete collection.

3. **AUTHORS AS INDIVIDUAL PEOPLE AND AS WRITERS:** Study the author's life. Personalize the author units by focusing on the author's motivation for writing as a career and for writing each book. Why did the author write this particular book? Why did s/he choose this writing style? These illustrations? These words? How has the author's writing style or choice of genres changed? Youngsters enjoy exploring the experiences that shaped the authors' lives and thinking and inspired them to share their joys, struggles, defeats, and triumphs with their readers. Seemingly minor connections often hold great significance for people of all ages. Even adults get excited when they have the same birthday or grew up in the same area as an author. These personal connections establish stronger and longer lasting ties with the author.

4. **LITERATURE LOGS/RESPONSE JOURNALS:** Youngsters may respond in writing to the selection read each day or week. These journals may be ongoing all year or semester. Long or shorter journals may be kept for each author or book. Encourage a wide variety of responses such as poems, letters, thoughts, feelings, illustrations, etc. Students may share these journals with partners, groups, or the class. These may also be used for self evaluation and/or teacher assessment.

5. **PERSPECTIVE:** Compare and contrast the perspectives in books with similar themes. Discuss or rewrite the story from the perspectives of selected characters. Perhaps each student or group of students could choose characters and present the book from a variety of perspectives.

6. **QUOTES:** Select or encourage youngsters to select quotes from the books for discussion and/or written response. Use a quote from a book for the caption of a bulletin board.

7. **PREDICTIONS:** Predict what will happen in the book, on the next page, in the next chapter, and/or in a sequel. These predictions may be written in the literature logs and/or discussed.

8. **DEDICATION PAGE:** Discuss and/or respond in writing to the dedication page. What additional information does it give us about the author? Encourage youngsters to create a dedication page for the next book they write.

9. CHARACTER LETTERS: Youngsters or leaders might write a letter from one of the characters in the book to the class introducing, motivating, summarizing, embellishing, etc. Or one character could write to another character (within books or from book to book).

10. LETTERS: Youngsters enjoy writing letters to the authors. Addresses for most authors are included with their chapter. Many authors are too busy to respond to each letter individually but they might write a note to a class, school, or library.

11. AUTHOR VISITS: Invite an author to visit your school or library. Contact the publisher to arrange the visit. Because of budget and scheduling constraints, many schools team up with another school, library, bookstore, or conference.

12. CONFERENCE CALLS: Arrange to make a conference call from your class to the author. Youngsters will enjoy reading the author's books and preparing questions in advance. The call might be taped and listened to again later.

13. INTERVIEWS: Role play a possible interview with the author or a character from the book. Or pretend that one character is interviewing another character.

14. RECIPES: Write individual or class recipes based on the book's message such as "A Recipe for Friendship" or "A Recipe for Combating Prejudice." Display on the bulletin board featuring the author.

15. TRAVEL: Plan an imaginary or real trip to the places featured in the book. Write for travel brochures, study maps to plot your route, develop and budget, and plan an itinerary, etc.

16. NEWSLETTERS: Include items from author units in your class, school, or library newsletter. Youngsters enjoy interviewing authors and writing about these intriguing discussions.

17. DRAMA: Youngsters love to create and perform in plays, puppet shows, pantomime, skits, dance, etc. based on the book or a collection of books.

18. BOOK TALKS: Invite youngsters to prepare short Book Talks to introduce and inspire others to read the books they recommend. These may be done a few at a time whenever you have a few minutes or during an assigned time. Students may also do extra Book Talks for extra credit.

19. BOOK REPORTS: Find creative ways to make book reports more fun! *Book Report Forms* by Evan-Moor offers a number of innovative ideas.

20. BOOK BOXES: Combine art and book reports. Students cover a box with paper and then decorate it with words, drawings, cut-outs, etc. that represent the book. The book boxes may hold items or tasks related to the book. These items may be used to dramatize the book or other students might write questions or comments about the book and put them in the boxes. Arrange for a Book Box Exhibit with boxes created by several groups displayed.

21. AUTHOR BOXES: Do the same as Activity 20 but with the focus on the author.

22. BOOK BUTTONS: Youngsters love to design buttons to wear! Directions: If you don't have a button maker, students may cut out a circle on construction paper and another on tagboard. Decorate with book title, author, illustrator, and pictures. Glue the construction paper to the cardboard. Tape a safety pin on the back. Wear these during Book Talks, Book Reports, Book Fairs, etc.

23. BOOK RIBBONS: Invite youngsters to design ribbons to advertise their favorite books. Display on bulletin boards, around the room, halls, or library to encourage others to read the books.

24. BOOKMARKS: Design bookmarks to go with selected books.

25. CHARACTER BOARD: For each character in a book or series of books, make a five-to-seven-inch-high paper figure. Place these figures on a chart depicting the roles played in the book. Print their names above each. Below each, write some of their personality traits.

26. CHARACTER CUTOUTS: Enlarge pictures of characters onto a large piece of paper. Cut out and use to start a bulletin board. Students then add words describing the characters printed on colorful strips of paper and other illustrations to the bulletin board.

27. CHARACTER GROWTH: To demonstrate the growth and changes in a character within a book or within a series, a student roleplays the character at each stage of her/his development. (Example: The Rinko trilogy by Yoshiko Uchida: *Jar of Dreams, Best Bad Thing,* and *The Happiest Ending.*)

28. ART: Study the art techniques used in the book. Research. Then experiment with those techniques. Add the results to the Author Center.

29. COLLAGE: Create individual or group collages portraying aspects from a book, a collection of books, and/or the author's life.

30. BOOK HUNT: Hide a book and create a coded message to help others find the book. Perhaps one student or group of students could be in charge of this activity each day or week.

31. TIME LINE: Make a time line for the events in a book, a series of books, or the author's life.

32. SEQUENCE CARDS: (created by youngsters and/or adults) On each of four or five cards, write a word or sentence, or draw a picture showing something that happened in the book. Youngsters may work individually or in groups to put the cards in order. Add these to the Author center.

33. CLASS BOOKLET: Collect all the work done by the youngsters related to a book or author into a class booklet. Display.

34. BOARD GAMES: Youngsters create board games based on the events in a book. These may be used in a variety of ways, including during free time and indoor recesses.

35. BIRTHDAYS: On an author's birthday, declare that day "_______ Day." (Example: October 18 is Joyce Hansen Day.) Have a read-a-thon featuring the author's books. Also, students might design cards and/or write letters to the authors. Students will be interested in which authors have birthdays on the same day as theirs.

36. DIORAMAS: Students create dioramas based on the author, book, or a series of books.

37. POP-UP BOOKS: An optional activity for talented youngsters. Create a pop-up book based on the book being read.

38. MAPPING AND WEBBING: At first, make the character maps or semantic maps together as a large group. Gradually, youngsters will be ready to create their own or to work together in small groups.

39. CARTOONING: Create cartoons based on the events in a book or as a sequel to a book.

40. ADVICE BOX: Invite youngsters to write letters from or to the characters in the books, asking for advice. Periodically, the teacher or students read these letters to the class and they respond in writing, with discussion, or by role-playing.

41. MOBILES: Design a mobile to introduce, promote, or represent a book or author.

42. RECOMMENDATIONS: Write a letter to the school media director recommending a book or series of books for purchase.

43. BOOK JACKETS: Youngsters might design new book jackets for the books.

44. DIARY: Youngsters might pretend that they are one of the characters in a book. They prepare a diary that the character might have kept during the beginning, middle, end, and/or the most significant parts of the story. This activity enables young people to identify more closely with the character.

45. SURVEY: Invite youngsters to check your public and/or school library to see which of the books by selected authors are included. Make a checklist or graph. Students might want to check how many books about an ethnic group are included. Evaluate the results and discuss ways to respond.

46. PLACE MATS: Pretend that an author or several authors are coming for lunch. Design place mats to honor your guests. Use fabric, yarn, etc. (This would make a great culminating activity at the end of the year or semester to review all the authors studied.) This activity was inspired by *The Dinner Party* by Judy Chicago which features a place setting for each of thirty-nine women from history.

47. AUTHOR QUILT OR MURAL: Quilts and murals make good culminating activities. A quilt might feature one square per author.

48. AUTHOR OR CHARACTER PARTY: At the end of the semester or year, each student dresses as their favorite character or author. They each give a short talk from the perspective of the author or character, using the voice, gestures, and props they think appropriate. Videotape these talks. The next day watch the video and serve refreshments provided by the students, inspired by the books represented. This video might also be used to introduce the author units to another group or shown at community events such as Parents' Night.

49. RIDDLES: Youngsters enjoy creating riddles based on the books or authors studied. This activity is excellent for review. For example: "I'm thinking of a book about a cakewalk." Answer: *Mirandy and Brother Wind.*

50. THEMES: The subject index includes a wide variety of themes, genres, and topics to facilitate infusing literature across the curriculum.

51. REVIEW BULLETIN BOARD: Invite youngsters to create and display cut-outs of all the characters from all the books read during the semester or year.

52. BOOK JAMBOREE: Invite youngsters to sit in a circle. Put all the books from a unit in the middle of the circle. Students select books for a final short browse and then they each share one or two comments about the book. This is an excellent review activity.

53. BOOK FAIR: This school-wide or library event is similar to the familiar Science Fair. Once a year, all the projects created by the youngsters are displayed. Parents, community members, and other youngsters will enjoy the wide variety of projects.

54. ASSESSMENT: Youngsters might write tasks or questions that could be included in the evaluation of the author unit. Encourage high level questions that stimulate thinking rather than recall of details.

55. ASSESSMENT: (Pre- and Post-) Invite individuals (any age) to make a list of all the authors that they can think of. Evaluate together as a group or individually. Did they include authors from diverse groups? Which groups were included? Excluded? What recommendations do the members of the group have for improving this situation? What recommendations do youngsters have for books to be purchased?

56. ASSESSMENT: Library Checkout: Are books available that represent diverse groups? Are youngsters requesting and checking out books representing diverse groups?

57. ASSESSMENT PLAN: For additional information on assessment, please see the Assessment Plan in Appendix 1 on page 257.

Author Birthdays

January

Minfong Ho 1-7-51
Camille Yarbrough 1-8-34

February

Shonto Begay 2-7-54
Alice Walker 2-9-44
Ignatia Broker 2-14-19
Virginia Driving Hawk Sneve 2-21-33
Sharon Bell Mathis 2-26-37

March

Virginia Hamilton 3-12-36
Barbara Cohen 3-15-32

May

Nancy Garden 5-15-38
Eloise Greenfield 5-17-29
Jeanne M. Lee 5-17-43
Dia Cha 5-19-62

June

Sandra Scoppettone 6-1-36
Joy Kogawa 6-6-35
Nikki Giovanni 6-7-43
Laurence Yep 6-14-48
Vivian Sheldon Epstein 6-21-41
Min Paek 6-28-50

August

Patricia McKissack 8-9-44
George Littlechild 8-16-58

September

Mildred Pitts Walter 9-9-22
Carmen Lomas Garza 9-12-48

October

Paul Yee 10-1-56
Yoko Kawashima Watkins 10-4-33
Faith Ringgold 10-8-30
Johanna Hurwitz 10-9-37
Joseph Bruchac 10-16-42
Joyce Hansen 10-18-42
Rudolfo Anaya 10-30-37

November

Nicholasa Mohr 11-1-38
Bette Bao Lord 11-3-38
Pat Cummings 11-9-50
Mai Vo-Dinh 11-14-33
Yoshiko Uchida 11-24-21

December

Anilú Bernardo 12-1-49
George Ancona 12-4-29

Multicultural Calendar

January
1st Mochitsuki Day (Japanese)
6th Three King's Day (Puerto Rican)
15th Martin Luther King, Jr.'s Birthday
Chinese/Korean/Vietnamese New Year (varies)

February
African American History Month
Sisterhood/Brotherhood Week (varies)
5th Constitution Day (Mexican)
Purim (Jewish) (varies)
15th Susan B. Anthony's Birthday
15th Nirvana Day (Mahayana Buddhism)
Shivaratri (Hindu) (varies)

March
Women's History Month
Pesach (Passover) (Jewish) (varies)
3rd Girls Day (Japanese)
4th Two Trung Sisters Day (Vietnamese)
5th Boys Day (Japanese)
8th International Women's Day
22nd Emancipation Day (Puerto Rican)
26th Kuhio Day (Hawaiian)
31st César Chávez Day

April
1st International Children's Book Day
Earth Month
5th Ching Ming Festival (Chinese)
8th Buddha Day
13th Vaisakhi (Sikh)
17th Verranzano Day (Italian)
21st Festival of Ridvan (Baha'i)
29th Hung Vuong (Vietnamese)

May
Asian American Heritage Month
2nd Holocaust Memorial Day
5th Cinco de Mayo (Mexican)
5th Children's Day (Japanese)
24th Women's International Disarmament Day
28th Dragon Boat Festival (Chinese)

June
6th Memorial Day (Korean)
11th Kamehameha Day (Hawaiian)
19th Juneteenth Day (African American)
29th Green Corn Dance (Seminole)
Lesbian/Gay Pride Month

July
15th Bon (Mahayana Buddhism)
21st Hopi Niman Dance Day
25th Constitution Day (Puerto Rican)

August
6th Hiroshima Day
9th Nagasaki Day
15th National Day (Korean American)
26th Women's Equality Day
30th Sunrise Dance Day (Native American)

September
Rosh Hashanah (Jewish) (varies)
Yom Kippur (Jewish) (varies)
Sukkot (Jewish) (varies)
Maulud-un-Nabi (Muslim) (varies)
8th Cherokee National Day
15th Respect for Aged Day (Japanese)
16th Mexican Independence Day
18th International Day of Peace
28th & 29th American Indian Day

October
Hispanic Heritage Month
1st World Vegetarian Day
11th National Lesbian/Gay Coming Out Day
12th Day of the Race (Latino/a)
16th World Food Day
24th United Nations Day
28th Czechoslavak Independence Day
Dussehra (Hindu) (varies)
Pavarana (Theravada Buddhism)
Kanname Festival (Shinto) (varies)

November
1st & 2nd Days of the Dead (Latino/a)
15 International Day of the Indian
Children's Book Week (varies)
Latin American Week (varies)
Niiname Festival (Shinto)
Native People Day of Mourning (varies)

December
Chanukah (Jewish) (varies)
5th Discovery Day (Haitian)
10th Human Rights Day
15th Navidades (Puerto Rican)
16th Posadas (Mexican)
26th to Jan. 1st Kwanzaa (African American)

APPENDIX 5 ◆

Resources for Educators, Librarians, and Parents

Books

Day, Frances Ann. *Latina and Latino Voices in Literature for Children & Teenagers.* Heinemann, 1997

———. *Lesbian and Gay Voices: An Annotated Bibliography and Guide to Literature for Children and Young Adults.* Greenwood, 2000.

Derman-Sparks, Louise. *Anti-Bias Curriculum: Tools for Empowering Young Children. National Association for the Education of Young Children,* 1989.

Ioga, Cristina. *The Inner World of the Immigrant Child.* St. Martin's Press, 1995.

Kruse, Ginny Moore, and Kathleen T. Horning. *Multicultural Literature for Children and Young Adults.* Cooperative Children's Book Center, 4290 Helen C. White Hall, University of Wisconsin, 600 North Park Street, Madison, WI 53706. 608-263-3720.

Loewen, J. W. *Lies My Teacher Told Me: Everything Your American History Textbook Got Wrong.* New Press, 1995.

Mathias, Barbara and Mary Ann French. *Forty Ways to Raise a Nonracist Child.* HarperPerennial, 1996.

McCann, Donnarae and Gloria Woodard. *The Black American in Books for Children: Readings in Racism.* 2nd ed. Metuchen, NJ: Scarecrow Press, 1985.

Miller-Lachmann, Lyn. *Our Family, Our Friends, Our World.* R. R. Bowker, 1992.

Muse, Daphne (ed.) *The New Press Guide to Multicultural Resources for Young Readers.* New Press, 1997.

Rochman, Hazel. *Against Borders: Promoting Books for a Multicultural World.* Booklist/ALA Books Publication, 1993.

Rollock, Barbara. *Black Authors and Illustrators of Children's Books: A Biographical Dictionary.* Garland, 1992.

Sims, Rudine. *Shadow and Substance: Afro-American Experience in Contemporary Children's Fiction.* 2nd ed. Chicago: NCTE/ALA, 1982.

Slapin, Beverly; Doris Seale, and Rosemary Gonzales. *How to Tell the Difference: A Guide to Evaluating Children's Books for Anti-Indian Bias.* Oyate, 1996. 2702 Mathews St., Berkeley CA 94702 (510) 848-6700.

Slapin, Beverly and Doris Seale. *Through Indian Eyes: The Native Experience in Books for Children.* New Society Publishers, 1992.

Trotter, Tamara and Joycelyn Allen. *Talking Justice: 602 Ways to Build and Promote Racial Harmony.* R & E Publishers, 1992.

Catalogs

AACP Asian American Curriculum Project. P. O. Box 1587, San Mateo, CA 94401 (800)874-2242.

Arte Público Press. University of Houston, Houston, TX 77204-2090 (800) 633-2783.

AWAIR. Arab World & Islamic Resources. 2137 Rose St., Berkeley, CA 94709 (510) 704-0517.

Bread and Roses. (Poster & Videos) 330 W. 42 St. 15th Floor, New York, NY 10036. (212) 631-4565.

Children's Book Press, 6400 Hollis Street, Suite 4, Emeryville, CA 94608. (510) 655-3395.

Del Sol Books. 29257 Bassett Rd., Westlake, OH 44145 (888) 335-7651.

Lee and Low. 95 Madison Avenue, New York, NY 10016 (888) 320-3395.

National Women's History Project, 7738 Bell Road, Windsor, CA 95492-8518 (707) 838-6000.

Oyate. Books by Native Authors. 2702 Mathews St., Berkeley CA 94702 (510) 848-6700.

Pan Asian Publications. 29564 Union City Clvd., Union City, CA 94587 (800) 909-8088.

Illustrator Index

Agard, Nadema
The Chichi Hoohoo Bogeyman 188
Ancona, George See author/illustrator unit 15
Andreasen, Don
Eagle Song 36

Baca, Maria
Maya's Children 13
Barnett, Moneta
Me and Neesie 95
Begay, Shonto See author/illustrator unit 23
Brodsky, Beverly
Gooseberries to Oranges 58
Here Come the Purim Players 58
Brooks, Kevin
Window Wishing 45
Byard, Carole
Africa Dream 90
Cornrows 229
Grandmama's Joy 92

Calvin, James
Talk About a Family 98
Cha, Chue and Nhia Thao
Dia's Story Cloth 47
Chan, Harvey
Ghost Train 234
Roses Sing on New Snow 235
Clay, Wil
213 Valentines 64
Cook, Scott
Nettie Jo's Friends 163
Cooper, Floyd
Grandpa's Face 93
Jaguarundi 106
Ma Dear's Aprons 160
Cuffari, Richard
Thank You, Jackie Robinson 64
Cummings, Pat See author/illustrator unit 66

Deeter, Catherine
Finding the Green Stone 209
To Hell With Dying 210
Deraney, Michael J.
Molly's Pilgrim 61
Yussel's Prayer 65
Dillon, Diane and Leo
Brother to the Wind 215
Her Stories 104
Honey, I Love 93
Hundred Penny Box 151
Many Thousand Gone 108
The People Could Fly 111
Dugan, Karen
Halmoni and the Picnic 51
Yunmi and Halmoni's Trip 52

Epstein, Vivian Sheldon See author/illustrator unit 73

Fadden, John Kahionhes
Keepers Series 38
Feelings, Tom
Daydreamers 91
Ferguson, Amos
Under the Sunday Tree 98
Ford, George
Ego-tripping 87
Paul Robeson 96
Frimer, Linda Spaner Dayan
In Honour of Our Grandmothers 144

Gammell, Stephen
Dancing Teepees 189
Garza, Carmen Lomas See author/illustrator unit 83
Geter, Tyrone
The Little Tree Growin' in the Shade 229
Gilchrist, Jan Spivey
First Pink Light 92
For the Love of the Game 92
Nathaniel Talking 95
Night on Neighborhood Street 95
Red Dog, Blue Fly 152
Gutierrez, Rudy
All for the Better 169
The Magic Shell 171
Old Letivia and the Mountain of Sorrows 172

Halpern, Joan
The Carp in the Bathtub 55
Hamanaka, Sheila
Class President 130
Teacher's Pet 133
Hewitson, Jennifer
Brother Rabbit: A Cambodian Tale 122

Ho, Kwoncjan
Sing to the Dawn 125
Hu, Ying-Hwa
The Best Older Sister 49

Isadora, Rachel
Flossie and the Fox 159

Jacob, Murc
The Boy Who Lived with the Bears 35
Jameson, Marcia
Darkness 216
Jones, Jan Naimo
Make a Wish, Molly 60
Jones, Richard C.
The Dancing Kettle 195

Kellogg, Steven
Abby 43

Lee, Jeanne M. See author/illustrator unit 137
Littlechild, George See author/illustrator unit 142
Locker, Thomas
Between Earth and Sky 34
The Earth Under Sky Bear's Feet 36
Thirteen Moons on Turtle's Back 41
Lyons, Oren
When Thunders Spoke 190

Martins, George
Spin a Soft Black Song 88
Martorell, Antonio
The Song of el Coquí 173
Meade, Holly
Hush! A Thai Lullaby 123
Miller, Don
Langston Hughes, American Poet 210
Morin, Paul
Fox Song 37
Moser, Barry
In the Beginning 106
When Birds Could Talk & Bats Could Sing 112
A Ring of Tricksters 112

Narahashi, Keiko
The Magic Purse 200
Ng, Simon
Tales From Gold Mountain 235
Noonan, Julia
Sweetwater 251

Paek, Min See author/illustrator unit 174
Pinkney, Brian
The Dark-Thirty 158
Pinkney, Jerry
Drylongso 104
Mary McLeod Bethune 94
Mirandy and Brother Wind 162
Pinkney, Myles
Can You Imagine? 157

Rich, Anna
Tamika and the Wisdom Rings 230
Ringgold, Faith See author/illustrator unit 179
Robinson, Charles
The Rooster Who Understood Japanese 201

Sandoval, Richard C.
Farolitos of Christmas 12
Schutzer, Dena
A Million Fish 162
Seltzer, Isadore
Tree of Dreams 253
Shimin, Symeon
Zeely 113
Simont, Marc
In the Year of the Boar and Jackie Robinson 149
Springett, Martin
The Wise Old Woman 203
Steptoe, John
She Come Bringing Me That Little Baby Girl 97

Tomes, Margot
Ty's One-Man Band 222

Tseng, Mou-sien and Jean
The City of Dragons 241
The Ghost Fox 245
The Khan's Daughter 247
Maples in the Mist 124
The Two Brothers 126

Uchida, Yoshiko
The Magic Listening Cap 200

Valdez, Jaime
Cuentos: Tales from the Hispanic Southwest 12
Van Camp, Richard
A Man Called Raven 145
What's the Most Beautiful Thing You Know About Horses? 147
Van Nutt, Robert
The Junior Thunder Lord 246
Van Wright, Cornelius
The Best Older Sister 49
Vo-Dinh, Mai See author/illustrator unit 204
Vojtech, Anna
The First Strawberries 37

Wiesner, David
The Rainbow People 248
Tongues of Jade 252
Word, Carol
Keepers of the Earth 38

Xiong, Gu
The Boy in the Attic 233

Yang, Ming-Yi
The Shell Woman and the King 250
Yardley, Joanna
The Bracelet 194

Zemach, Margot
The Two Foolish Cats 203

Title Index

Abby 43
ABCs of What a Girl Can Be 74
Africa Dream 90
African-American Inventors 156
African-American Scientists 156
Aekyung's Dream 175
Aldo Applesauce 128
Aldo Ice Cream 129
Aldo Peanut Butter 129
All for the Better 169
American Dragons 239
The Anaya Reader 10
Angel Child, Dragon Child 205
Anne Frank: Life in Hiding 130
Annie On My Mind 79
Anthony Burns: The Defeat and Triumph of a Fugitive Slave 102
Aunt Harriet's Underground Railroad in the Sky 180

Ba-Nam 138
Because We Are 214
The Best Bad Thing 193
The Best Older Sister 49
Between Earth and Sky 34
Between Two Fires: Black Soldiers in the Civil War 116
Bitter Herbs and Honey 55
Bless Me, Ultima 11
Bonjour, Lonnie 181
Bowman's Store 35
The Boy in the Attic 233
The Boy Who Lived with the Bears 35
Booker T. Washington: Leader and Educator 159
Bracelet, The 194
Breakaway 233
Breaking Ground, Breaking Silence 117
Brother Rabbit: A Cambodian Tale 122
Brother to the Wind 215
Butterfly Boy 239

Can You Imagine? 157
The Captive 117
Carousel 67
Carp in the Bathtub, The 55
Carter G. Woodson: The Father of Black History 159
The Case of the Goblin Pearls 240
The Chichi Hoohoo Bogeyman 188
Child of the Owl 240
Childtimes: A Three-Generation Memoir 91
Ch'i-lin Purse, The 138
Chilly Stomach 43
Christmas Revolution, The 56
C is for City 68
City of Dragons 241
Civil Rights Movement in America: From 1865 to the Present 157
Class President 130
The Clay Marble 122
Clean Your Room, Harvey Moon 68
C.L.O.U.D.S. 69
Coasting 56
Completing the Circle 189
Constance Stumbles 158
Cornrows 229
Cousins 103
Cuentos Chicanos: A Short Story Anthology 11
Cuentos: Tales From Hispanic Southwest 12
Curse of the Squirrel 241
Curses of Third Uncle 234

Dancing Kettle and Other Japanese Folktales, The 195
Dancing Teepees: Poems by American Indian Youth 189
Darkness 216
Dark-Thirty: Southern Tales of the Supernatural, The 158
Daydreamers 91
Desert Exile 195
Dia's Story Cloth 47
Dinner at Aunt Connie's House 181
Dragon Cauldron 242
Dragon of the Lost Sea 242
Dragon's Gate 243
Dragon Steel 244
Dragonwings 244
A Dream Come True 131
Drylongso 104

Eagle Song 36
Earth Daughter: Alicia of Ácoma Pueblo 17
The Earth Under Sky Bear's Feet 36
Echoes of the White Giraffe 49
Ego-Tripping 87

Family Pictures/Cuadros de Familia 84

Faraway Summer 131
Farolitos of Christmas: A New Mexico Christmas Story 12
Fat Jack 57
Felita 170
Fiesta U.S.A. 18
Finding the Green Stone 209
First Pink Light 92
First Snow 205
First Strawberries: A Cherokee Story, The 37
Fitting In 28
Flossie & the Fox 159
Folk Stories of the Hmong 47
Fox Song 37
For the Love of the Game 92
Frederick Douglass: Leader Against Slavery 159
Frederick Douglass: The Black Lion 159

Gathering of Pearls 50
The Genie in a Jar 87
George Washington Carver: The Peanut Scientist 159
The Ghost Fox 245
Ghost Train 234
Gift, The 206
Gift-Giver, The 118
Girl On the Outside 216
Going Home 170
Good Moon Rising 80
Gooseberries to Oranges 58
Grandmama's Joy 92
Grandpa's Face 93
Great African American Series 159

Halmoni and the Picnic 51
Handtalk: An ABC of Finger Spelling & Sign Language 18
Handtalk Birthday: A Number & Story Book in Sign Language 18
Handtalk School 18
Handtalk Zoo 18
Happiest Ending, The 196
Happy Endings Are All Alike 184
Have a Happy 217
Heart of Aztlan 13
Here Come the Purim Players 58
Her Stories 104
Hiroshima 246
History of Colorado for Children 75
History of Colorado's Women for Young People 75
History of Women Artists for Children 75
History of Women for Children 76
History of Women in Science for Young People 77
Honey, I Love 93
House of Dies Drear, The 105
How the Birch Tree Got Its Stripes 144
How the Mouse Got Brown Teeth 144
Hundred Penny Box 151
Hush! A Thai Lullaby 123

Ida B. Wells-Barnett: A Voice Against Violence 159
In Honour of Our Grandmothers 144
I Need a Lunch Box 44
In My Family/En mi familia 84
Innkeeper's Daughter 59
In Nueva York 171
In the Beginning: Creation Stories from Around the World 106
In the Year of the Boar and Jackie Robinson 149
Invisible Thread: An Autobiography, The 196
I Thought My Soul Would Rise and Fly 118

Jaguarundi 106
Jar of Dreams, A 197
Jesse Owens: Olympic Star 159
Jimmy Lee Did It 69
Journey Back, The 177
Journey Home 198
Journey to Topaz 199
Jumping Off to Freedom 28
The Junior Thunder Lord 246
Just Us Women 44
Justin and the Best Biscuits in the World 218

Keepers of Life 38
Keepers of the Animals 38
Keepers of the Earth 38
Keepers of the Night 38
Khan's Daughter, The 247
Kia Tanisha Drives Her Car 93
King of the Seventh Grade 59
Koya DeLaney and the Good Girl Blues 94
Kwanzaa: A Family Affair 218

Land I Lost, The 206
Langston Hughes: American Poet 210
Langston Hughes: Great American Poet 159
Lark in the Morning 81
Lasting Echoes 38
Late Great Me, The 185
Legend of the Li River 139
Legend of the Milky Way 139
Listen for the Fig Tree 151
Little Tree Growin' in the Shade, The 229
Long Hard Journey: The Story of the Pullman Porter 160
Long Way Home, The 60
Loves Me, Loves Me Not 29
Lost Garden: Laurence Yep 247
Louis Armstrong: Jazz Musician 159

Madam C. J. Walker: Self-Made Millionaire 159
Ma Dear's Aprons 160
Magic Listening Cap 200
Magical Adventures of Pretty Pearl, The 107
The Magic Purse 200
The Magic Shell 171
Ma'ii and Cousin Horned Toad: A Traditional Navajo Story 24
Make a Wish, Molly 60
A Man Called Raven 145
Many Thousand Gone: African Americans from Slavery to Freedom 108
Maples in the Mist 124
Mariah Keeps Cool 219
Mariah Loves Rock 219
Marian Anderson: A Great Singer 159
Martin Luther King, Jr.: Man of Peace 159
Mary Church Terrell: Leader for Equality 159
Mary McLeod Bethune 94
Mary McLeod Bethune: A Great American Educator 161
Mary McLeod Bethune: A Great Teacher 159
Maya's Children: The Story of La Llorona 13
M.C. Higgins, the Great 108
Me and Neesie 95
Messy Bessey Series 161
Million Fish . . . More or Less, A 162
Mirandy and Brother Wind 162
Mississippi Challenge 220
Molly's Pilgrim 61
Mom Can't See Me 19
Mom's Best Friend 19
Monkey-Monkey's Trick 162
Mountain Light 247
Much Ado About Aldo 132
Mud Pony: A Traditional Skidi Pawnee Tale 25
My Aunt Came Back 70
My Brother, My Sister, and I 225
My Dream of Martin Luther King 182
My Mama Needs Me 220
Mystery of Drear House, The 110

Naomi's Road 135
Nathaniel Talking 95
Native American Book of Change 26
Native American Book of Knowledge 26
Native American Book of Life 26
Native American Book of Wisdom 26
Navajo: Visions and Voices Across the Mesa 25
Nettie Jo's Friends 163
Night Flying Woman: An Ojibway Narrative 31
Night on Neighborhood Street 95
Nilda 172

Obasan 136
Old Letivia and the Mountain of Sorrow 172
Once I Was a Plum Tree 132
Orphan Game, The 62
Out From This Place 119
Over Here It's Different: Carolina's Story 19

Pablo Remembers: The Fiesta of the Day of the Dead 20
Paul Laurence Dunbar: A Poet to Remember 163
Paul Robeson 96
Paul Robeson: A Voice to Remember 159
Paul Robeson: The Life and Times of a Free Black Man 110
People Could Fly: American Black Folktales, The 111
People Like Us 62
Petey Moroni's Camp Runamok Diary 70
A Picture of Freedom 164
Picture Bride 200
A Piece of My Heart 85
The Piñata Maker/El Piñatero 21
Powwow 21

Rainbow People, The 248
Rebels Against Slavery: American Slave Revolts 164
Red Dog, Blue Fly: Football Poems 152
Ribbons 248
Rice Without Rain 124
A Ring of Tricksters 112
Rooster Who Understood Japanese, The 201
Roots of Survival 39
Rosa Parks 96
Roses Sing On New Snow: A Delicious Tale 235
Run Away Home 165
Running Girl 152

Samurai of Gold Hill 202
Satchel Paige: The Best Arm in Baseball 159
Sea of Gold and Other Tales From Japan 202
Second Daughter: The Story of a Slave Girl 221
Serpent's Children, The 249
She Come Bringing Me That Little Baby Girl 97
The Shell Woman and the King 250
Shimmershine Queens, The 230
Sidewalk Story 153
Silent Lotus 140
Sing to the Dawn 125
Sister 97
Sky Legends of Vietnam 207
So Far From the Bamboo Grove 226
Sojourner Truth: A Voice for Freedom 159
The Song of el Coqui 173
The Song of Mu Lan 140
Spin a Soft Black Song 88
Star Fisher, The 250
Storm in the Night 70
Survival This Way 40
Sweetwater 251

Taking a Stand Against Racism and Racial Discrimination 165
Tales From Gold Mountain 235
Tales From the Bamboo Grove 226
Talk About a Family 98
Talking With Artists Volume One 71
Talking with Artists: Volume Two 71
Tamika and the Wisdom Rings 230
Tar Beach 182
Teacher's Pet 133
Teach Me to Fly, Skyfighter 236
Teacup Full of Roses 153
Tell Me a Tale: A Book About Storytelling 40
Tell Us Your Secret 63
Têt: The New Year 207
Thank You, Jackie Robinson 64
Thief of Hearts 252
Thirteen Moons on Turtle's Back 41
This Land is My Land 145
Toad is the Uncle of Heaven 141
To Hell With Dying 210
Tongues of Jade 252
Tortuga 14
Tree of Dreams 253
The Trickster and the Troll 190
Trouble's Child 221
Trying Hard to Hear You 186
Two and Too Much 222
Two Brothers, The 126
Two Foolish Cats, The 203
213 Valentines 64
Ty's One-Man Band 222

Under the Sunday Tree 98
Upstairs Room, The 178

Vacation Time 88

We Are All Related 146
What's the Most Beautiful Thing You Know About Horses? 147
When Birds Could Talk & Bats Could Sing 112
When Thunders Spoke 190
Which Way Freedom? 119
Who Is Who? 166
Willie Bea and the Time the Martians Landed 113
Willie's Not the Hugging Kind 72
Window Wishing 45
Wise Old Woman, The 203
Women of Hope 120

Year of Impossible Goodbyes 51
Yellow Bird and Me 120
Young, Black, and Determined 167
Yunmi and Halmoni's Trip 52
Yussel's Prayer: Yom Kippur 65

Zeely 113
Zora Neale Hurston: Writer and Storyteller 159

Subject Index

ABOLITIONISTS
Anthony Burns 102
Aunt Harriet's Underground Railroad in the Sky 180
Between Two Fires 116
House of Dies Drear 105
Many Thousand Gone 108
Mystery of Drear House 110
A Picture of Freedom 164
Rebels Against Slavery 164
Sojourner Truth 159

ÁCOMA INDIANS
Earth Daughter 17

ACTORS
Also see Drama 276
Good Moon Rising 80
Grandpa's Face 93
Paul Robeson 96, 110, 159
Also see Camille Yarbrough 228

ADOPTION
Abby 43
Bonjour, Lonnie 181
Dragon's Gate 243
Mountain Light 247
Native American Book of Wisdom 26
Orphan Game 62

AGING (See Elderly People 276)

AFRICA
Africa Dream 90
Brother to the Wind 215
Captive, The 117
Cornrows 229
Little Tree Growin' in the Shade, The 229

ALABAMA
Run Away Home 165

ALCOHOLISM
In Honour of Our Grandmothers 144
Late Great Me 185
Listen for the Fig Tree 151
This Land Is My Land 145
To Hell with Dying 210

ALL HALLOWS EVE
ALL SAINTS DAY
ALL SOULS DAY
Pablo Remembers 20

ALPHABET BOOKS
ABCs of What a Girl Can Be 74
C is for City 68
Handtalk: An ABC of Finger Spelling & Sign Language 18

ANIMAL COMPANIONS
Aldo Peanut Butter 129
Bowman's Store 35
Carp in the Bathtub 55
Curse of the Squirrel 241
Jar of Dreams 197
Land I Lost 206
Mom's Best Friend 19
Much Ado About Aldo 132
Rooster Who Understood Japanese 201
Run Away Home 165
Storm in the Night 70
Teacher's Pet 133

ANIMAL RIGHTS
Curse of the Squirrel 241
Jaguarundi 106
Man Called Raven, A 145
Much Ado About Aldo 132

APPACHE
Run Away Home 165

APPALACHIAN MOUNTAINS
Appalachian Elders 86
M. C. Higgins, the Great 108

APPEARANCE
Aekyung's Dream 175
Ba-Nam 138
City of Dragons, The 241
Fat Jack 57
Happy Endings Are All Alike 184

ARCHAEOLOGY
Breaking Ground, Breaking Silence 117

ART & ARTISTS
Also see Illustrator Index 267
C.L.O.U.D.S 69
Cornrows 229
Darkness 216
Dia's Story Cloth 47
Dinner at Aunt Connie's House 181

Earth Daughter 17
Family Pictures 84
Folk Stories of the Hmong 47
Ghost Train 234
Have a Happy 217
History of Women Artists for Children 75
In Honour of Our Grandmothers 144
In My Family 84
Navajo: Visions and Voices Across the Mesa 25
Piece of My Heart, A 85
Talking With Artists 71
Tar Beach 182
This Land Is My Land 145
We Are All Related 146

ASTHMA
Mary McLeod Bethune 94,159, 161
Faith Ringgold 179
Laurence Yep 237

ATHLETES (See Sports 282)

ATOMIC BOMBS
Hiroshima 246

AUNTS
Case of the Goblin Pearls, The 240
Hundred Penny Box 151
Jar of Dreams 197
Just Us Women 44
My Aunt Came Back 70
Naomi's Road 135
Obasan 136

AUTHORSHIP & WRITING
Also see Diaries 275
Bowman's Store (Joseph Bruchac) 35
Can You Imagine? (Patricia McKissack) 157
A Dream Come True (Johanna Hurwitz) 131
Invisible Thread, The (Yoshiko Uchida) 196
Lost Garden (Laurence Yep) 247
Survival This Way 40
Tell Us Your Secret 63
Young, Black, and Determined (Lorraine Hansberry) 167
Zora Neale Hurston 159

AUTHORS & CO-AUTHORS
Ahenakew, Freda 142
Alexander, Sally Hobart 16
Barrett, Joyce Durham 68
Caduto, Michael 32
Charlip, Remy 16
Cohen, Caron Lee 23
Coutant, Helen 204
Fang, Linda 137
Gottfriedson, Garry 142
Huynh, Quang Nhuong 204
Jameson, Cynthia 66
Little, Lessie Jones 89
Livo, Norma 46
McKissack, Fredrick 154
Miller, Mary Beth 16
Ros, Saphan 121
Schneider, Reisa Smiley 142
Stolz, Mary 66
Surat, Michele Maria 204
Tran, Kim Lan 204
Vuong, Lynette Dyer 204
White Deer of Autumn 23

AUTOBIOGRAPHICAL FICTION
In the Year of the Boar and Jackie Robinson 149
Innkeeper's Daughter 59
Naomi's Road 135
Obasan 136
Tar Beach 182
Tortuga 14

AUTOBIOGRAPHY & AUTOBIOGRAPHICAL NOVELS
Bowman's Store 35
Can You Imagine? 157
Childtimes 91
Desert Exile 195
Dia's Story Cloth 47
Dream Come True, A 131
Echoes of the White Giraffe 49
Family Pictures 84
In My Family 84
Invisible Thread, The 196
Journey Back, The 177
Land I Lost, The 206
Lost Garden, The 247
My Brother, My Sister, and I 225
A Piece of My Heart 85
So Far From the Bamboo Grove 226
This Land Is My Land 145
To Hell with Dying 210
Upstairs Room, The 178
Year of Impossible Goodbyes 51

BABIES
Also see Board Books 274
Abby 43
The Best Older Sister 49
Hush! A Thai Lullaby 123
My Mama Needs Me 220
She Come Bringing Me That Little Baby Girl 97
Two and Too Much 222

BAHAMAS
Under the Sunday Tree 98

BALLET
Ribbons 248
Silent Lotus 140

BAR MITZVAH, BAT MITZVAH
King of the Seventh Grade 59
People Like Us 62

BASEBALL
In the Year of the Boar and Jackie Robinson 149
Satchel Paige: The Best Arm in Baseball 159
Thank You, Jackie Robinson 64

BEACHES
Orphan Game 62

BILINGUAL
CHINESE: *Maples in the Mist 124*
Song of Mu Lan, The 140
KOREAN: *Aekyung's Dream 175*
SPANISH: *Cuentos 12*
Family Pictures 84
In My Family 84
Piñata Maker, The 21
MANY LANGUAGES: *We Are All Related 146*

BIOGRAPHY
Also see Autobiography 273
All for the Better 169
Anne Frank: Life in Hiding 130
Anthony Burns: The Defeat and Triumph of a Fugitive Slave 102
Booker T. Washington: Leader and Educator 159
Carter G. Woodson: The Father of Black History 159
Completing the Circle 189
Dinner at Aunt Connie's House 181
Earth Daughter 17
Frederick Douglass 159
George Washington Carver 159
History of Women Artists 75
History of Women in Science for Young People 77
Ida B. Wells-Barnett 159
Jesse Owens 159
Langston Hughes 159, 210
Louis Armstrong 159
Madam C. J. Walker 159
Marian Anderson 159
Martin Luther King, Jr.159
Mary Church Terrell 159
Mary McLeod Bethune 94, 159, 161
My Dream of Martin Luther King 182
Over Here It's Different 19
Paul Laurence Dunbar 163
Paul Robeson 96, 110, 159
Ralph Bunche: Peacemaker 159
Rebels Against Slavery 164

Rosa Parks 96
Satchel Paige 159
Sojourner Truth 159
Talking With Artists 71
Women of Hope 120
Young, Black, and Determined 167
Zora Neale Hurston 159

BIRTHDAYS
Also see Author Birthday Chart 263
Aldo Ice Cream 129
Best Older Sister, The 49
Carousel 67
Handtalk Birthday 18
Have a Happy 217
Make a Wish, Molly 60
Messy Bessey's Birthday Sleepover 161

BLINDNESS
Dragon's Gate 243
Gift , The 206
Mom Can't See Me 19
Mom's Best Friend 19
Sweetwater 251

BOARD BOOKS
Big Friend, Little Friend 89
I Make Music 89
Kia Tanisha 89
Kia Tanisha Drives Her Car 93
My Aunt Came Back 70
My Doll, Keshia 90

BOUND FEET
Ribbons 248
Serpent's Children, The 249

BUDDHISM
First Snow 205
Sing to the Dawn 125
Two Brothers, The 126

CAKEWALK
Family Pictures 84
Mirandy and Brother Wind 162

CAMBODIA
Brother Rabbit: A Cambodian Tale 122
Clay Marble, The 122
Silent Lotus 140
Two Brothers, The 126

CANADA
Breakaway 233
Curses of Third Uncle 234
Ghost Train 234
In Honour of Our Grandmothers 144
Naomi's Road 135
Obasan 136
Tales From Gold Mountain 235
Teach Me to Fly, Skyfighter 236
This Land is My Land 145
What's the Most Beautiful Thing You Know About Horses? 147

CANCER
Good Moon Rising 80
Long Way Home, The 60

CAREERS
ABCs of What a Girl Can Be 74
African American Inventors 156
African American Scientists 156
Because We Are 214
Bitter Herbs and Honey 55
Bless Me, Ultima 11
Breakaway 233
Breaking Ground, Breaking Silence 117
Coasting 56
History of Women Artists for Children 75
History of Women for Children 76
History of Women in Science for Young People 77
I Thought My Soul Would Rise and Fly 118
Jar of Dreams 197
Loves Me, Loves Me Not 29
Ribbons 248
Silent Lotus 140
Sing to the Dawn 125
Teacup Full of Roses 153
Trouble's Child 221
Young, Black, and Determined 167

CATS
Aldo Applesauce 128
Storm in the Night 70
Two Foolish Cats 203

CEMETERIES
Ba-Nam 138
Breaking Ground, Breaking Silence 117
Pablo Remembers 20
Window Wishing 45

CHILD ABUSE
Chilly Stomach 43
Lark in the Morning 81
Teach Me to Fly, Skyfighter 236

CHINA
Butterfly Boy 239
City of Dragons 241
Dragons' Gate 243
Ghost Fox, The 245
Ghost Train 234
In the Year of the Boar and Jackie Robinson 149
The Junior Thunder Lord 246
Maples in the Mist 124
Mountain Light 247
Rainbow People, The 248
Serpent's Children, The 249
Song of Mu Lan, The 140
Tongues of Jade 252

CHINATOWN, SAN FRANCISCO
Child of the Owl 240
Lost Garden , The 247
Ribbons 248
Thief of Hearts 252

CHINATOWN, VANCOUVER
Breakaway 233
Curses of Third Uncle , The 204
Teach Me to Fly 236

CHRISTMAS
Bells of Christmas, The 99
Christmas Revolution 56
Farolitos of Christmas 12

CITIES
C is for City 68
Sweetwater 251
Aso see New York City; Chinatown, San Francisco; Chinatown, Vancouver

CIVIL RIGHTS
Between Two Fires: Black Soldiers in the Civil War 116
Breaking Ground, Breaking Silence 117
Civil Rights Movement in America 157
Frederick Douglass 159
Girl on the Outside 216
I Thought My Soul Would Rise and Fly 118
Martin Luther King, Jr. 159
Mississippi Challenge 220
My Dream of Martin Luther King 182
Paul Robeson 96, 110, 159
Picture of Freedom, A 164
Rebels Against Slavery 164
Rosa Parks 96
Taking a Stand Against Racism and Racial Discrimination 165
Young, Black, and Determined 167

CIVIL WAR (U. S.)
Between Two Fires: Black Soldiers in the Civil War 116
I Thought My Soul Would Rise and Fly 118
Out From This Place 119
Rebels Against Slavery 164
Which Way Freedom 119

CLOUDS
C.L.O.U.D.S. 69

COLORADO
History of Colorado for Children 75
History of Colorado's Women for Young People 75

COLORS
Darkness 216

CONFLICT RESOLUTION
Eagle Song 36

CONSERVATION (See Ecology 276)

CONSTELLATIONS
Legend of the Milky Way 139
Sky Legends of Vietnam 207

CONSTITUTION
Anthony Burns: The Defeat and Triumph of a Fugitive Slave 102
Civil Rights Movement in America 157
I Thought My Soul Would Rise and Fly 118
Second Daughter 221
Taking a Stand Against Racism and Racial Discrimination 165

COWBOYS & COWGIRLS
Justin and the Best Biscuits in the World 218

CREATION STORIES
In the Beginning 106
Native American Book of Knowledge 26

CUBA
See Anilú Bernardo's chapter 27

CURANDERAS
Bless Me, Ultima 11
Old Letivia and the Mountain of Sorrow 172

DANCE
Family Pictures 84
Mirandy & Brother Wind 162
Powwow 21
Ribbons 248
Silent Lotus 140
Ty's One-Man Band 222

DAY OF THE DEAD
Fiesta U.S.A. 18
Pablo Remembers 20

DEAFNESS
Handtalk Series 18

DEATH AND DYING
Of Animals
Carp in the Bathtub 55
Jar of Dreams 197
Mom's Best Friend 19
A Picture of Freedom 164
Run Away Home 165
Of Humans
Bless Me, Ultima 11
Bowman's Store 35
The Clay Marble 122
Cousins 103
Curses of Third Uncle, The 234
Dragon Cauldron 242
Dragon's Gate 243
Felita 170
First Snow 205
Fox Song 37
Gathering of Pearls 50
Ghost Train 245
Good Moon Rising 80
Listen for the Fig Tree 151
Mountain Light 247
Native American Book of Wisdom 26
Nilda 172
Pablo Remembers 20
Picture of Freedom, A 164
Rice Without Rain 124
Sister 97
So Far From the Bamboo Grove 226
Tamika and the Wisdom Rings 230
Teacup Full of Roses 153
Thank You, Jackie Robinson 64
To Hell With Dying 210
Trying Hard to Hear You 186
Which Way Freedom? 119

DEPRESSION ERA
All for the Better 169
Best Bad Thing 193
Breakaway 233
Happiest Ending 196
Jar of Dreams 197

DESEGREGATION
Girl on the Outside 216

DIARY / JOURNAL
Anne Frank: Life in Hiding 130
Faraway Summer 131
I Thought My Soul Would Rise and Fly 118
A Picture of Freedom 164
Running Girl 152

DISABILITIES
Also see Alcoholism 272
Artificial Leg
Ty's One-Man Band 222
Asthma
Mary McLeod Bethune 159, 161
Faith Ringgold 179
Laurence Yep 237
Blindness
Dragon's Gate 243
Gift, The 206
Listen For the Fig Tree 151
Mom Can't See Me 19
Mom's Best Friend 19
Sweetwater 251
Bound Feet
Ribbons 248
Deafness
Handtalk Series 18
Silent Lotus 140
Diabetes
To Hell With Dying 210
Dyslexia
Yellow Bird and Me 120
Hearing Loss
Handtalk Series 18
Yoko Kawashima Watkins 224
Multiple
The Chichi Hoohoo Bogeyman 188
One Arm
Ghost Train 234
Paralysis
Land I Lost, The 206
Tortuga 14
Stutter
I Thought My Soul Would Rise and Fly 118

DIVORCE
Because We Are 214
Talk About a Family 98

DOGS
Aldo Peanut Butter 129
Bowman's Store 35
Jar of Dreams 197
Mom's Best Friend 19
Run Away Home 165

DOMESTIC WORKERS
Ma Dear's Aprons 160

DOMINICAN REPUBLIC
The Magic Shell 171
Over Here It's Different 19

DRAGONS
American Dragons 239
The City of Dragons 241
Dragon Cauldron 242
Dragon of the Lost Sea 242
Dragon Steel 244
Dragonwings 244

DRAMA, THEATRE
American Dragons 239
Anaya Reader, The 10
Christmas Revolution 56
Dragonwings 244
Fat Jack 57
Good Moon Rising 80
Grandpa's Face 93
Here Come the Purim Players 58
Long Way Home 60
Paul Robeson 96, 110, 159
Shimmershine Queens 230
Trying Hard to Hear You 186
Yellow Bird and Me 120
Young, Black, and Determined 167

DREAMS
Also see Careers 274
Aekyung's Dream 175
Africa Dream 90
Bless Me, Ultima 11
Carousel 67
Daydreamers 91
Ghost Train 234
My Dream of Martin Luther King 182
Night Flying Woman 31
Tar Beach 182
Tree of Dreams 253

DROUGHT
Drylongso 104
Junior Thunder Lord,The 246
Rice Without Rain 124
Toad is the Uncle of Heaven 141

DRUG ABUSE
Because We Are 214
Dragon's Gate 243
Dragonwings 244
Tamika and the Wisdom Rings 230
Teacup Full of Roses 153

DYSLEXIA
Yellow Bird and Me 120

EARTHQUAKE
Dragonwings 244

ECOLOGY, ENVIRONMENT
Between Earth and Sky 34
Butterfly Boy 239
Dragon of the Lost Sea 242
Dragon Steel 244
Drylongso 104
Earth Daughter 17
In Honour of Our Grandmothers 144
Keepers Series 38
M. C. Higgins, the Great 108
Native American Book of Wisdom 26
Navajo: Visions and Voices Across the Mesa 25
Sweetwater 251

ELDERLY PEOPLE
Also see Grandfathers & Grandmothers 277
Aldo Ice Cream 129
Ba-Nam 138
Bowman's Store 35
Child of the Owl 240
First Snow 205
Fox Song 37
Gift, The 206
Hundred Penny Box 151
Ribbons 248
Shimmershine Queens 230
Thief of Hearts 252
To Hell With Dying 210
Wise Old Woman, The 203

ENDANGERED ANIMALS
Jaguarundi 106

ENGLISH AS A SECOND LANGUAGE
Also see Bilingual 273
Aekyung's Dream 175
Fitting In 28
Gathering of Pearls 50
Halmoni and the Picnic 51
In the Year of the Boar and Jackie Robinson 149
Molly's Pilgrim 61
Over Here It's Different 19
Teach Me to Fly, Skyfighter 236

ENVIRONMENT (See Ecology 276)

EUTHANASIA
Tortuga 14

EVICTION
Sidewalk Story 153

EXTRATERRESTRIAL BEINGS
Willie Bea and the Time the Martians Landed 113

FARM LIFE
Breakaway 233
Faraway Summer 131
Picture of Freedom,A 164
Rice Without Rain 124
Willie Bea and the Time the Martians Landed 113
Zeely 113

FATHER-DAUGHTER RELATIONSHIP
Carousel 67
Child of the Owl 240
Serpent's Children, The 249

FATHER-SON RELATIONSHIP
Bowman's Store 35
Breakaway 233
Dragon's Gate 243
Dragonwings 244
Eagle Song 36
Serpent's Children, The 249

FAT OPPRESSION
Fat Jack 57
Long Way Home, The 60
Roses Sing on New Snow 235
Trying Hard to Hear You 186

FANTASY
Magical Adventures of Pretty Pearl 107
Shimmer Series 242-244

FEAR
Ba-Nam 138
Jumping Off to Freedom 28
Mountain Light 247
Storm in the Night 70

FIESTAS
Fiesta U.S.A. 18
Pablo Remembers 20

FISH
Aldo Ice Cream 129
Bless Me, Ultima 11
Carp in the Bathtub 55

FLIGHT
Aunt Harriet's Underground Railroad in the Sky 180
Best Bad Thing 193
Brother to the Wind 215
Dragonwings 244
People Could Fly, The 111
Shimmer Series 242-244
Tar Beach 182
Teach Me to Fly, Skyfighter 236

FOLKLORE
Between Earth and Sky 34
Boy Who Lived with the Bears, The 35
Brother Rabbit: A Cambodian Tale 122
Ch'i-lin Purse,The 138
Cuentos 12
Dancing Kettle 195
Earth Under Sky Bear's Feet,The 36
Folk Stories of the Hmong 47
Ghost Fox,The 245
Her Stories 104
In the Beginning 106
Junior Thunder Lord, The 246
Khan's Daughter, The 247

Legend of the Li River 139
Legend of the Milky Way 139
Magic Listening Cap 200
Magic Purse, The 200
Ma'ii and Cousin Horned Toad 24
Monkey-Monkey's Trick 162
Mud Pony: A Traditional Skidi Pawnee Tale 25
Old Letivia and the Mountain of Sorrow 172
People Could Fly: American Black Folktales 111
Rainbow People, The 248
Ring of Tricksters, A 112
Sea of Gold 202
Shell Woman and the King, The 250
Sky Legends of Vietnam 207
Song of el Coqui, The 173
Tales From Gold Mountain 235
Tales From the Bamboo Grove 226
Toad is the Uncle of Heaven 141
Tongues of Jade 252
Tree of Dreams 253
Trickster and the Troll, The 190
Two Brothers, The 126
Two Foolish Cats 203
When Birds Could Talk and Bats Could Sing 112
Wise Old Woman, The 203

FOOD
Faraway Summer 131
First Strawberries, The 37
Justin and the Best Biscuits 218
Make a Wish, Molly 60
Much Ado About Aldo 132
Native American Book of Life 26
Rice Without Rain 124
Roses Sing On New Snow 235

FOOTBALL
Red Dog, Blue Fly: Football Poems 152

FREEMAN, ELIZABETH
Second Daughter 221

FROGS
Song of el Coqui, The 173

FUGITIVE SLAVES
Anthony Burns 102
Between Two Fires 116
Many Thousand Gone 108
Out From This Place 119
Picture of Freedom, A 164
Rebels Against Slavery 164
Which Way Freedom? 119

FUTURE
Sweetwater 251

GAY MALES
Trying Hard to Hear You 186

GEMS
Child of the Owl 241
City of Dragons, The 241
Finding the Green Stone 209
Mountain Light 247
When Thunders Spoke 190

GENDER ROLES
ABCs of What a Girl Can Be 74
Bitter Herbs and Honey 55
Breakaway 233
"Breaking Tradition" in American Dragons 239
Chichi Hoohoo Bogeyman, The 188
Clay Marble, The 122
Completing the Cirlce 189
Curses of Third Uncle 234
Gathering of Pearls 50
Her Stories 104
History of Colorado's Women for Young People 75
History of Women Artists for Children 75
History of Women for Children 76
History of Women in Science for Young People 77
Justin and the Best Biscuits in the World 218
Khan's Daughter,The 247
Mountain Light 247
Over Here It's Different 19
Ribbons 248
Rice Without Rain 124
Roots of Survival 39
Roses Sing On New Snow 235
Sing to the Dawn 125
Song of Mu Lan, The 140
Teach Me to Fly, Skyfighter 236
Trouble's Child 231
When Thunders Spoke 190
"Who's Hu?" in American Dragons 239

GHOSTS
Boy in the Attic,The 233
Dark-Thirty, The 158
Ghost Fox, The 245
Ghost Train 234

GIFTED & TALENTED
213 Valentines 64
"Who's Hu?" in American Dragons 239
Young, Black, and Determined 167

GOLD RUSH
Mountain Light 247

GRANDFATHERS
Bowman's Store 35
Farolitos of Christmas 12
Grandpa's Face 93
Justin and the Best Biscuits in the World 218
Late Great Me 185
People Like Us 62
Storm in the Night 70
When Thunders Spoke 190
Window Wishing 45

GRANDMOTHERS
Best Older Sister, The 49
Bowman's Store 35
Child of the Owl 240
Completing the Circle 189
Cornrows 229
Cousins 103
Felita 170
First Snow 205
Fitting In 28
Fox Song 37
Grandmama's Joy 92
Halmoni and the Picnic 51
Hundred Penny Box 151
In Honour of Our Grandmothers 144
People Like Us 62
Ribbons 248
Thief of Hearts 252
Trouble's Child 221
Yunmi and Halmoni's Trip 52

GREAT WALL OF CHINA
Legend of the Li River 139

HALLOWEEN
Willie Bea and the Time the Martians Landed 113

HANUKKAH
Christmas Revolution 56
Also see Multicultural Calendar 264

HARLEM RENAISSANCE
Bonjour, Lonnie 181
Shimmy Shimmy Shimmy Like My Sister Kate 86

HEALING
Bless Me, Ultima 11
Loves Me, Loves Me Not 29
Native American Book of Wisdom 26
Old Letivia and the Mountain of Sorrows 192
Second Daughter 221
Trouble's Child 221

HEARING LOSS
Also see Deafness 275
Yoko Kawashima Watkins 224

HISTORICAL FICTION
Bracelet, The 194
Captive, The 117

Clay Marble, The 122
Dragon's Gate 243
Girl on the Outside 216
I Thought My Soul Would Rise and Fly 118
Journey Home 198
Journey to Topaz 199
Mountain Light 247
Out From This Place 119
Picture Bride 200
Rice Without Rain 124
Run Away Home 165
Samurai of Gold Hill 202
Second Daughter 221
Serpent's Children, The 249
Which Way Freedom? 119

HMONG
Dia's Story Cloth 47
Folk Stories of the Hmong 47

HOGS
Breakaway 233
Zeely 113

HOLIDAYS (See specific holidays)
Also see Multicultural Calendar 264

HOLLAND (See Netherlands) 279

HOLOCAUST
Anne Frank: Life in Hiding 130
In Honour of Our Grandmothers 144
Journey Back 177
Tell Us Your Secret 63
Upstairs Room 178

HOMOSEXUALITY
Gay Males
Trying Hard to Hear You 186
Lesbianism
Annie on My Mind 79
Good Moon Rising 80
Happy Endings Are All Alike 184
Lark in the Morning 81

HORSES
Justin and the Best Biscuits in the World 218
Mud Pony: A Traditional Skidi Pawnee Tale 25
Picture of Freedom, A 164
What's the Most Beautiful Thing You Know About Horses? 147

HOSPITALS
Tortuga 14

HOUSEWORK
Ma Dear's Aprons 160
Picture of Freedom, A 164

ILLNESS
Also see Death & Dying
Farolitos of Christmas 12
Fat Jack (mental illness) 57
Late Great Me (mental illness) 185
Long Way Home (cancer) 60
Tortuga 14

IMMIGRANTS
Also see Newcomers 280
Aekyung's Dream 175
Angel Child, Dragon Child 205
Bitter Herbs and Honey 55
Boy in the Attic, The 233
Dia's Story Cloth 47
Dragonwings 244
Fitting In 28
Folk Stories of the Hmong 47
Gooseberries to Oranges 58
In the Year of the Boar and Jackie Robinson 149
Make a Wish, Molly 60
Magic Shell, The 171
Molly's Pilgrim 61
Over Here It's Different 19
Picture Bride 200
Ribbons 248
Samurai of Gold Hill 202
Tales From Gold Mountain 235
Teach Me to Fly, Skyfighter 236
Thief of Hearts 252

IMMORTALITY
Maya's Children 13

INCEST
Chilly Stomach 43

INDIGENOUS PEOPLES (See Native Peoples) 279

INTERGENERATIONAL RELATIONSHIPS
Loves Me, Loves Me Not 29
Also see Grandmothers and Grandfathers 277

INTERNALIZED RACISM
Bowman's Store 35
Breakaway 233
Shimmershine Queens 230

INVENTIONS AND INVENTORS
African American Inventors 156
Dragonwings 244
The Farolitos of Christmas 12
George Washington Carver 159

IROQUOIS
The Boy Who Lived with the Bears 35
Eagle Song 36
Roots of Survival 39

JAPAN
Dancing Kettle 195
Hiroshima 246
Magic Listening Cap 200
My Brother, My Sister, and I 225
Sea of Gold 202
So Far From the Bamboo Grove 226
Tales From the Bamboo Grove 226
Two Foolish Cats 203
Wise Old Woman, The 203

JEALOUSY
Best Older Sister, The 49
I Need a Lunch Box 44
Mariah Loves Rock 219
My Mama Needs Me 220
She Come Bringing Me That Little Baby Girl 97
Sing to the Dawn 125
Yunmi and Halmoni's Trip 52

JEWISH HOLIDAYS (See specific holidays)
Also see multicultural calendar 264

JOURNAL (See Diary) 275

JUNETEENTH
Many Thousand Gone 108
Mariah Keeps Cool 219

KEEPSAKES
Bracelet, The 194
Gift, The 206
Hundred Penny Box 151
Ma Dear's Aprons 160
Thief of Hearts 252

KMER
Clay Marble, The 122
Silent Lotus 140

KITES
Best Bad Thing 193
Brother to the Wind 215
Dragonwings 244
Teach Me to Fly, Skyfighter 236

KOREA
Aekyung's Dream 175
Echoes of the White Giraffe 49
So Far From the Bamboo Grove 226
Year of Impossible Goodbyes 51
Yunmi and Halmoni's Trip 52

KWANZAA
Have a Happy 217
Kwanzaa: A Family Affair 218
Listen for the Fig Tree 151

LA LLORONA
Maya's Children 13

LANGUAGE
(See English as a Second Language) 276
(See Bilingual) 273

LAOS
Dia's Story Cloth 47
Folk Stories of the Hmong 47

LAS POSADAS
Fiesta U.S.A. 18

LAWYERS
Anthony Burns: The Defeat and Triumph of a Fugitive Slave 102
Happy Endings Are All Alike 184
Paul Robeson 96, 110, 159

LEADERSHIP
Annie On My Mind 79
Class President 130
Good Moon Rising 80
Heart of Aztlan 13
Lasting Echoes 38
Rebels Against Slavery 164

LEARNING DISABILITIES
Yellow Bird and Me 120

LEGENDS (See Myths)

LESBIANISM
Annie On My Mind 79
Good Moon Rising 80
Happy Endings Are All Alike 184
Lark in the Morning 81

LOS MATACHINES
Fiesta U.S.A. 18

MAGIC
Brother to the Wind 215
City of Dragons, The 241
Her Stories 104
Magical Adventures of Pretty Pearl 107
Magic Purse, The 200
Magic Shell, The 171
Shimmer Series 242-244
The Two Brothers 126

MARRIAGE (Arranged)
Happiest Ending 196
Picture Bride 200

MASSACHUSETTS
Second Daughter 221

MEXICO
Maya's Children 13
Pablo Remembers 20
Piñata Maker, The 21

MILKY WAY
Legend of the Milky Way 139
Sky Legends of Vietnam 207
Story of the Milky Way, The 33

MISSISSIPPI
Mississippi Challenge 220

MINES & MINING
M. C. Higgins, the Great 108
Mountain Light 247

MIXED ANCESTRY
American Dragons 239
Bonjour, Lonnie 181
Bowman's Store 35
Chichi Hoohoo Bogeyman, The 188
Fox Song 37
Ribbons 248
Thief of Hearts 252
We Are All Related 146
What's the Most Beautiful Thing You Know About Horses? 147

MONGOLIA
The Khan's Daughter 247

MOON
Sky Legends of Vietnam 207
Thirteen Moons on Turtle's Back 41

MOTHER/DAUGHTER RELATIONSHIPS
Because We Are 214
Innkeeper's Daughter 59
Late Great Me 185
Make a Wish, Molly 60
Mom Can't See Me 19
Nilda 172
Running Girl 152
Shimmershine Queens, The 230
Star Fisher 250
Thief of Hearts 252

MOTHER/SON RELATIONSHIPS
Ma Dear's Aprons 160

MOVING
All for the Better 169
Aldo Applesauce 128
Boy in the Attic, The 233
Eagle Song 36
Felita 170
Heart of Aztlan 13
In the Year of the Boar and Jackie Robinson 149
Magic Shell, The 171
Star Fisher 250

MUSIC & MUSICAL INSTRUMENTS
Hush! A Thai Lullaby 123
Koya DeLaney and the Good Girl Blues 94
Little Tree Growin' in the Shade, The 229
Louis Armstrong: Jazz Musician 159
Mariah Loves Rock 219
Marian Anderson: A Great Singer 159
Naomi's Road 135
Obasan 136
Paul Robeson 96, 110, 159
Song of el Coqui, The 173
Sweetwater 251
Ty's One-Man Band 222

MYSTERY
Case of the Goblin Pearls, The 240
House of Dies Drear 105
Mystery of Drear House 110
Petey Moroni's Camp Runamok Diary 70

MYTHS/LEGENDS
Between Earth and Sky 34
How the Birch Tree Got Its Stripes 144
How the Mouse Got Brown Teeth 144
In the Beginning 106
Keepers Series 38
Legend of the Li River 139
Legend of the Milky Way 139
Magical Adventures of Pretty Pearl 107
Ma'ii and Cousin Horned Toad 24
Roots of Survival 41
Thirteen Moons on Turtle's Back 41

NATIVE PEOPLES
Earth Daughter 17
Run Away Home 165
Also see the following Author Units:
Shonto Begay 23
Ignatia Broker 30
Joseph Bruchac 32
George Littlechild 142
Virginia Driving Hawk Sneve 187

NEEDLEWORK
Aunt Harriet's Underground Railroad in the Sky 180
Dia's Story Cloth 47
Folk Stories of the Hmong 47
Tar Beach 182

NETHERLANDS
Anne Frank: Life in Hiding 130
Journey Back, The 177
Upstairs Room 178

NEWCOMERS
Aekyung's Dream 175
Aldo Applesauce 128
Angel Child, Dragon Child 205
Bitter Herbs and Honey 55
Boy in the Attic , The 233
Dragon's Gate 243
Dragonwings 244
Eagle Song 36
Faraway Summer 131
First Snow 205
Fitting In 28
Gathering of Pearls 50
Halmoni and the Picnic 51
Heart of Aztlan 13
In the Year of the Boar and Jackie Robinson 149
Make a Wish, Molly 60
Magic Shell, The 171
Molly's Pilgrim 61
Mountain Light 247
Over Here It's Different 19
Picture Bride 200
Ribbons 248
Samurai of Gold Hill 202
Tales From Gold Mountain 235
Teach Me to Fly, Skyfighter 236
Têt: The New Year 207
Thief of Hearts 252
Yunmi and Halmoni's Trip 52

NEW MEXICO
Bless Me, Ultima 11
Cuentos: Tales From the Hispanic Southwest 12
Earth Daughter 17
Farolitos of Christmas 12
Heart of Aztlan 13
Tortuga 14

NEW YORK CITY
Breaking Ground, Breaking Silence 117
C.L.O.U.D.S. 69
Carousel 67
Coasting 56
Felita 170
Gift Giver, The 118
In Nueva York 171
Magic Shell, The 171
Nilda 172
Once I Was a Plum Tree 132
Tar Beach 182
Yellow Bird and Me 120

NON-VIOLENCE
Felita 170
Ida B. Wells-Barnett: A Voice Against Violence 159
Martin Luther King, Jr. 159

OCEANS
Shimmer Series 242-244
Sweetwater 251

ORAL TRADITION (See Storytelling)

ORATORS
Frederick Douglass 159
Lasting Echoes 38
Martin Luther King, Jr. 159
Paul Robeson 96, 110, 159
Sojourner Truth: A Voice for Freedom 159

OUTDOOR EDUCATION
Between Earth and Sky 34
Keepers Series 38
Thirteen Moons on Turtle's Back 41

PARALYSIS
The Land I Lost 206
Tortuga 14

PARIS
Bonjour, Lonnie 181

PASSOVER
Carp in the Bathtub 55
Make a Wish, Molly 60
Once I Was a Plum Tree 132

PEACE
Clay Marble, The 122
Eagle Song 36
Finding the Green Stone 209
Martin Luther King, Jr. 159
Ralph J. Bunche 159
Roots of Survival 39
Two Foolish Cats 203

PEER PRESSURE
Fitting In 28
Gift Giver, The 118
Make a Wish, Molly 60
Thief of Hearts 252
Yellow Bird and Me 120

PETS (See Animal Companions) 272

PHOTOGRAPHY
(See George Ancona's chapter) 15

PLAYS (See Drama) 276

PINATA
Family Pictures 84
The Piñata Maker 21

POETRY
American Dragons 239
C is for City 70
Clean Your Room, Harvey Moon 68
Dancing Teepees 189
For the Love of the Game 92
The Earth Under Sky Bear's Feet 36
Genie in a Jar 87
Honey , I Love 93
Hush! A Thai Lullaby 123
In Honour of Our Grandmothers 144
Jimmy Lee Did It 69
Maples in the Mist 124
Nathaniel Talking 95
Navajo: Visions and Voices Across the Mesa 25
Night on Neighborhood Street 95
Red Dog, Blue Fly: Football Poems 152
Song of Mu Lan, The 140
Spin a Soft Black Song 88
Survival This Way 40
Thirteen Moons on Turtle's Back 41
Under the Sunday Tree 98

POETS
Joseph Bruchac 32
Pat Cummings 66
Paul Laurence Dunbar 163
Nikki Giovanni 86
Garry Gottfriedson 144
Eloise Greenfield 89
Langston Hughes 159, 210
Joy Kogawa 134
Sharon Bell Mathis 150
Reisa Smiley Schneider 144
Virginia Driving Hawk Sneve 187
Alice Walker 208

POTTERY
Earth Daughter 17

POWWOW
Powwow 21

PUERTO RICO and PUERTO RICAN AMERICANS
Class President 131
Also see Nicholasa Mohr's chapter 168

PULLMAN PORTERS
A Long Hard Journey 160

PURIM
Here Come the Purim Players 58

QUILTS
Aunt Harriet and the Underground Railroad in the Sky 180
Kwanzaa: A Family Affair 218
Tar Beach 182

RABBITS
Brother Rabbit: A Cambodian Tale 122
A Ring of Tricksters 112

RAILROADS (see TRAINS) 282

RAINFOREST
Jaguarundi 106

RAPE
Happy Endings Are All Alike 184

RAVENS
A Man Called Raven 145

RECONSTRUCTION ERA
The Civil Rights Movement in America 159
I Thought My Soul Would Rise and Fly 118
Out from This Place 119

REFUGEES
Clay Marble, The 122
Dia's Story Cloth 47
Echoes of the White Giraffe 49
Jumping Off to Freedom 28
My Brother, My Sister, and I 225
So Far From the Bamboo Grove 226
Year of Impossible Goodbyes 51

REVOLUTIONARY WAR
Second Daughter 221

ROCKY MOUNTAIN REGION (See Colorado) 275

RUNAWAY SLAVES (See Fugitive Slaves) 277

RUNAWAYS
Lark in the Morning 81
Run Away Home 165
Thief of Hearts 252

RUNNING
Running Girl 152

SAMURAI
Samurai of Gold Hill 202

SAN FRANCISCO
See Laurence Yep's Chapter 237

SCHOOL
Also see Teachers 282
Annie On My Mind 79
Because We Are 214
Class President 130
Eagle Song 36
Echoes of the White Giraffe 49
Fitting In 28
Gathering of Pearls 50
Good Moon Rising 80
Handtalk School 18
In the Year of the Boar and Jackie Robinson 149
I Need a Lunch Box 44
I Thought My Soul Would Rise and Fly 118
Me and Neesie 95
Molly's Pilgrim 61
My Brother, My Sister, and I 225
Native American Book of Wisdom 26
Shimmershine Queens, The 230
Sing to the Dawn 125
So Far From the Bamboo Grove 226
Teacher's Pet 133
Thief of Hearts 252
This Land Is My Land 145
213 Valentines 64
Yellow Bird and Me 120

SCIENCE (See Clouds, Constellations, Drought, Earthquake, Ecology, Fish, Flight, Gems, Inventions, Kites, Oceans, Seasons, Sky Observations, Stars, Sounds, Technology, Trains, Trees, Weather, Wind)

SCIENTISTS
African American Scientists 156
George Washington Carver 159
History of Women in Science for Young People 77
Women of Hope 120

SCIENCE FICTION
C.L.O.U.D.S. 69
Curse of the Squirrel 241
Sweetwater 251

SEASONS
Thirteen Moons on Turtle's Back 41

SEDER
Once I Was a Plum Tree 132

SEXISM (See Gender Roles) 277

SEXUAL ABUSE
Chilly Stomach 43
"Dana's Eyes" in American Dragons 239
Happy Endings Are All Alike 184

SHADOWS
Darkness 216
Keepers of the Night 38

SHAKESPEARE
Fat Jack 57
Long Way Home 60

SHORT STORIES
American Dragons 239
The Anaya Reader 10
Cuentos Chicanos 11
Fitting In 28

SIGN LANGUAGE
Handtalk Series 18

SKY OBSERVATIONS
Also see Stars 282
C.L.O.U.D.S. 69
Earth Under Sky Bear's Feet, The 36
Keepers of the Night 38
Legend of the Milky Way 139
Sky Legends of Vietnam 207

SLAVERY
Anthony Burns 102
Breaking Ground, Breaking Silence 116
Captive, The 117
Cornrows 229
Dark-Thirty, The 158
Frederick Douglass 159
I Thought My Soul Would Rise and Fly 118
Little Tree Growin' in the Shade, The 229
Mary McLeod Bethune 94, 159, 161
Out From This Place 119
Picture of Freedom, A 164
Rebels Against Slavery: American Slave Revolts 164
Second Daughter 221
Song of el Coqui, The 173
Which Way Freedom? 119

SOCCER
Breakaway 233
Teach Me to Fly, Skyfighter 236

SOCIOECONOMIC CLASS
Bowman's Store 35
Faraway Summer 131
Loves Me, Loves Me Not 29
Rice Without Rain 124
213 Valentines 64
Yussel's Prayer 65

SOUTH CAROLINA
I Thought My Soul Would Rise and Fly 118

SOUNDS Also see Music 279
Storm in the Night 70
Ty's One-Man Band 222

SOUTH (Southern United States)
Between Two Fires 116
Dark-Thirty, The 158
Girl on the Outside 216

I Thought My Soul Would Rise and Fly 118
Ma Dear's Aprons 160
Many Thousand Gone 108
Mississippi Challenge 220
Out From This Place 119
People Could Fly, The 111
Picture of Freedom, A 164
Rebels Against Slavery 164
Run Away Home 165
Trouble's Child 221
Which Way Freedom? 119

SOUTH DAKOTA
See Virginia Driving Hawk Sneve's Chapter 187

SOUTHWEST (U. S.)
See books by Rudolfo Anaya 9

SPANISH LANGUAGE
Bendiceme, Ultima 11
Cuentos 12
El Piñatero 21
El regalo magico 171
Fiesta U.S.A. 18
Family Pictures 84
In My Family 84
La canción del coquí 173
La Vieja Letivia y el monte de los pesares 172
Pablo Recuerda 20

SPEAKERS, SPEECH
(See Orators) 280

SPIRITUALITY
Bless Me, Ultima 11
Native American Book of Wisdom 26

SPORTS
Bowman's Store 35
Breakaway 233
For the Love of the Game 92
In the Year of the Boar and Jackie Robinson 149
Jesse Owens: Olympic Star 159
Mariah Keeps Cool 219
Red Dog, Blue Fly: Football Poems 152
Running Girl 152
Satchel Paige: The Best Arm in Baseball 159
Teach Me to Fly, Skyfighter 236
Thank You, Jackie Robinson 64
Ty's One-Man Band 222

STARS
Earth Under Sky Bear's Feet, The 36
Keepers of the Night 38
Legend of the Milky Way 139
Sky Legends of Vietnam 207
Star Fisher 250

STORYTELLING
See Joseph Bruchac's chapter 30
Can You Imagine? 157
Folk Stories of the Hmong 47
Little Tree Growin' in the Shade, The 229
Night Flying Woman 31
Ring of Tricksters, A 112
Tell Me A Tale 40
Zora Neale Hurston 159

SUKKOS
Molly's Pilgrim 61

SUPERNATURAL
City of Dragons, The 241
Dark-Thirty, The 158

SWEATSHOPS
Case of the Goblin Pearls, The 240

TALL TALES
Million Fish . . . More or Less, A 162

TEACHERS & EDUCATORS
Annie On My Mind 79
Because We Are 214
Booker T. Washington 159
Class President 130
Desert Exile 195
Good Moon Rising 80
Handtalk School 18
Invisible Thread 196
I Thought My Soul Would Rise and Fly 118
Lost Garden 247
Mary McLeod Bethune 94, 259, 161
Native American Book of Wisdom 26
Teacher's Pet 133
213 Valentines 64
Yellow Bird and Me 120

TECHNOLOGY
African American Inventors 156
African American Scientists 156
Dragon's Gate 243
Heart of Aztlan 13
History of Women in Science 77

TêT
Têt: The New Year 207

TEXAS
Family Pictures 84
In My Family 84

TEXTILES (See Needlework) 279

THAILAND
Dia's Story Cloth 47
Folk Stories of the Hmong 47
Hush! A Thai Lullaby 123
Rice Without Rain 124
Sing to the Dawn 125

THANH-MINH DAY (Vietnamese Memorial Day)
Ba-Nam 138

THANKSGIVING
Molly's Pilgrim 61

THEATER (See Drama) 276

THREE KINGS' DAY
Fiesta U.S.A. 18

TRACK AND FIELD
Running Girl 152

TRADITION AND CHANGE
Bitter Herbs and Honey 55
Child of the Owl 240
Childtimes 91
Cornrows 229
Dragon's Gate 243
Dragonwings 244
Family Pictures 84
Farolitos of Christmas 12
Gathering of Pearls 50
Halmoni and the Picnic 51
Hundred Penny Box 151
In My Family 84
Mirandy and Brother Wind 162
Mountain Light 247
Navajo: Visions and Voices Across the Mesa 25
Native American Book of Life 26
Picture Bride 200
Piece of My Heart, A 85
Powwow 21
Ribbons 248
Rice Without Rain 124
Sing to the Dawn 125
Thief of Hearts 252
Trickster and the Troll, The 190
Trouble's Child 221
When Thunders Spoke 190

TRAINS
Dragon's Gate 243
Ghost Train 234
Long Hard Journey, A 160

TRAVEL
Africa Dream 90
Going Home 170
Just Us Women 44
Mountain Light 247

My Aunt Came Back 70
Yunmi and Halmoni's Trip 52

TREES
How the Birch Tree Got Its Stripes 144

TRICKSTERS
Brother Rabbit: A Cambodian Tale 120
Her Stories 104
Ma'ii and Cousin Horned Toad 24
Ring of Tricksters, A 112
Trickster and the Troll, A 190

TUBMAN, HARRIET
Aunt Harriet's Underground Railroad in the Sky 180
Between Two Fires 116
Honey, I Love 93
Many Thousand Gone 108
Rebels Against Slavery 164

TURTLES
Old Letivia and the Mountain of Sorrows 172
Thirteen Moons on Turtle's Back 41

TWINS
Christmas Revolution 56
Long Way Home 60
Orphan Game 62
Who Is Who? 166

UNCLES
Between Earth and Sky 34
Curses of Third Uncle, The 234
Dragon's Gate 243

UNDERGROUND RAILROAD
Aunt Harriet's Underground Railroad in the Sky 180
House of Dies Drear 105
Many Thousand Gone 108
Mystery of Drear House 110
A Picture of Freedom 164
Rebels Against Slavery 164

UNITED STATES HISTORY
Also see Civil War and World War II
Also see Biography
Breaking Ground, Breaking Silence 117
Captive, The 117
Civil Rights Movement 157
Dinner at Aunt Connie's House 181
Dragon's Gate 243
I Thought My Soul Would Rise and Fly 118
Lasting Echoes 38
My Dream of Martin Luther King 182
Native People, Native Way Series 26
Picture of Freedom, A 164
Rebels Against Slavery 164
Roots of Survival 39
Second Daughter 221
Taking a Stand Against Racism and Racial Discrimination 165

VALENTINE'S DAY
213 Valentines 64

VEGETARIANISM
Aldo Applesauce 128
Aldo Ice Cream 129
Aldo Peanut Butter 129
Curse of the Squirrel 241
Much Ado About Aldo 132

VERMONT
Faraway Summer 131

VIETNAM
See Mai Vo-Dinh's Chapter 204
Also see Dia Cha's chapter 46

VIRGINIA
Picture of Freedom, A 164

WAR
Also See Civil War and World Wars
Clay Marble, The 122
Dia's Story Cloth 47
Hiroshima 246
Mountain Light 247
Second Daughter 221
Serpent's Children, The 249
Song of Mu Lan, The 140

WEATHER
Ba-Nam 138
Brother to the Wind 215
C.L.O.U.D.S. 69
Junior Thunder Lord, The 246
Mirandy and Brother Wind 162
Storm in the Night 70
Toad is the Uncle of Heaven 141

WIND
Brother to the Wind 215
Mirandy and Brother Wind 162
Old Letivia and the Mountain of Sorrows 172

WISHES
Brother to the Wind 215
Window Wishing 45

WOMEN
Also see Biography 273
ABCs of What a Girl Can Be 74
All for the Better 169
Completing the Circle 189
Dinner at Aunt Connie's House 181
Her Stories 104
History of Colorado's Women for Young People 75
History of Women Artists for Children 75
History of Women for Children 76
History of Women in Science for Young People 77
Just Us Women 44
Picture Bride 200
Serpent's Children, The 249
Sing to the Dawn 125
Song of Mu Lan, The 140
Wise Old Woman, The 203
Women of Hope 120
Young, Black, and Determined 167

WORLD WAR I
Bonjour, Lonnie 181

WORLD WAR II
Anne Frank: Life in Hiding 130
Bonjour, Lonnie 181
Bracelet, The 194
Desert Exile 195
Hiroshima 246
In Honour of Our Grandmothers 144
Invisible Thread 196
Journey Back 177
Journey Home 198
Journey to Topaz 199
My Brother, My Sister, and I 225
Naomi's Road 135
Obasan 136
Once I Was a Plum Tree 132
Picture Bride 200
So Far From the Bamboo Grove 226
Upstairs Room 178
Year of Impossible Goodbyes 51

YOM KIPPUR
Yussel's Prayer 65

لی کا چینی نیا سال

Li's Chinese New Year

Fang Wang
Illustrated by Jennifer Corfield

Urdu translation by Qamar Zamani

Mantra Lingua

چینی نئے سال سے ایک ہفتہ پہلے لی کی کلاس نے چین میں نئے سال
پر کی جانے والی پریڈ کی فلم دیکھی۔ اِس میں رقص کرتے ہوئے لوگ تھے جنہوں
نے شیروں کے رنگین نقاب پہن رکھے تھے اور موسیقی کی دُھن پر ناچ رہے تھے۔

The week before Chinese New Year, Li's class watched a film of a New Year's parade in China. There were lion dancers carrying the huge mask of a colourful lion, making it move with the music.

''ہم ایک خاص اسمبلی کر رہے ہیں جس میں چینی نئے سال کی تقریب ہوگی۔'' مس گرین نے کہا

''میں چاہتی ہوں کہ تم سب اپنے اس پسندیدہ جانور کی نقاب بناؤ جو چینی سماوی دائرے میں شامل ہے۔''

لی کو نقاب بنانے کا بہت شوق تھا۔ مس خان نے سب بچوں کو گھر لے جانے کے لئے ٹشو پیپر اور چمکدار کارڈ دیئے۔۔۔

لیکن لی کون سا جانور بنائے گا؟

"We're having a special assembly to celebrate Chinese New Year," said Miss Green. "I'd like each of you to make a mask of your favourite animal from the Chinese zodiac."

Li loved making masks. Miss Khan gave out tissue paper and shiny card for the children to take home — but what animal would Li make?

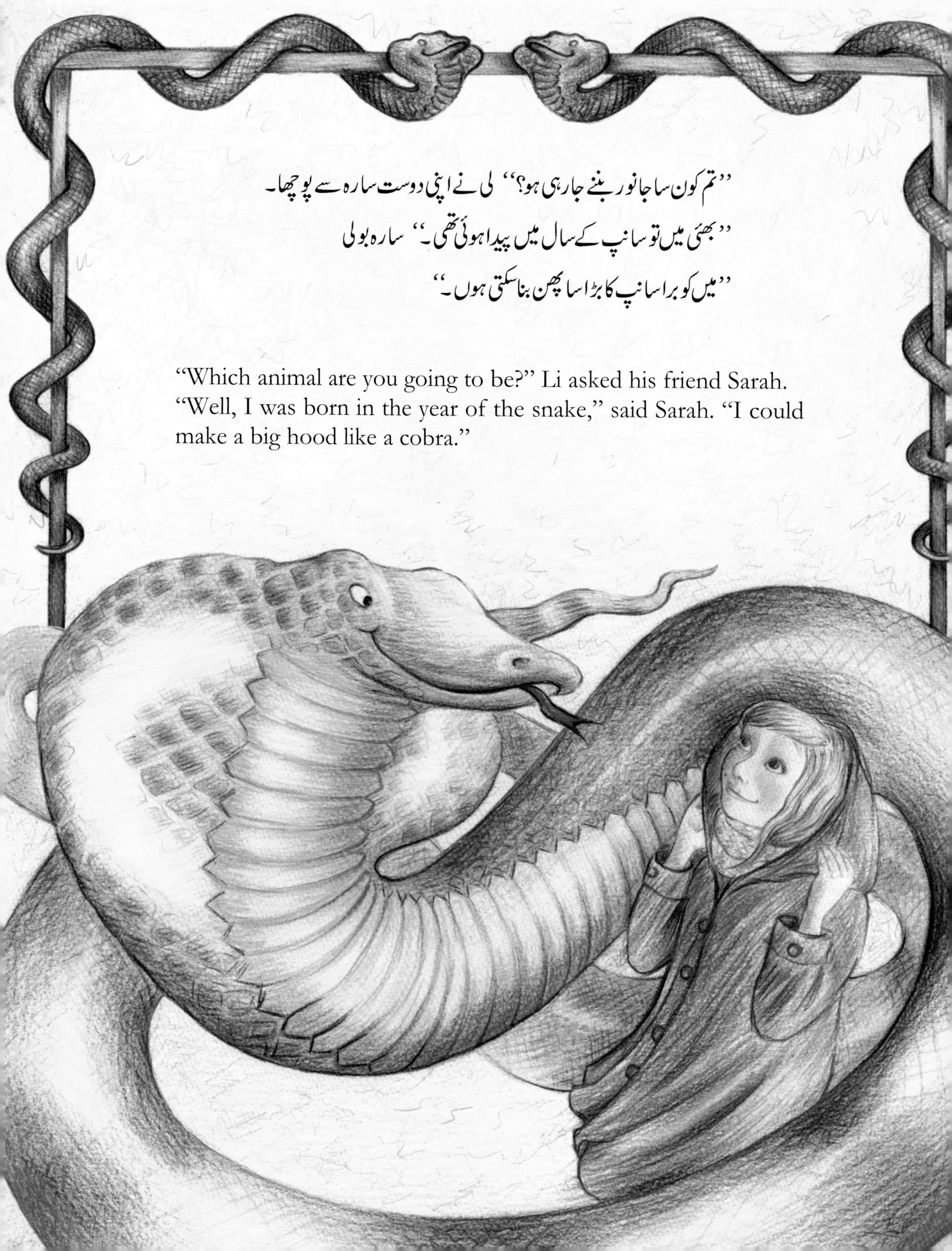

”تم کون سا جانور بننے جا رہی ہو؟“ لی نے اپنی دوست سارہ سے پوچھا۔
”بھئی میں تو سانپ کے سال میں پیدا ہوئی تھی۔“ سارہ بولی
”میں کوبرا سانپ کا بڑا سا پھن بنا سکتی ہوں۔“

"Which animal are you going to be?" Li asked his friend Sarah. "Well, I was born in the year of the snake," said Sarah. "I could make a big hood like a cobra."

لیکن لی کی آدھی کلاس سانپ ہی تھی۔ وہ اِن سے مختلف رہنا چاہتا تھا۔
''اچھا تم لکی کی طرح کا ایک کتا بن جاؤ،'' سارہ نے ہنس کر کہا۔
لکی نے اپنی بھیگی، بھیگی بھوری آنکھیں اُٹھا کر لی کو دیکھا۔ لی کو یقین تھا
کہ وہ اِس سے زیادہ دلچسپ جانور اپنے نئے سال کی نقاب کے لئے تلاش کر سکتا ہے۔

But half of Li's class were snakes. He wanted to be something different.
"Well you could be a dog like Lucky," Sarah laughed.
Lucky looked up at Li with soppy, brown eyes. Li was sure he could find a more exciting animal for his New Year mask.

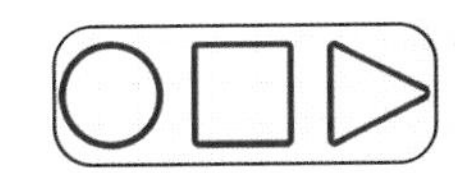

’’شاید تم ایک اژدھا بن سکتے ہو،‘‘ امّی نے نئے سال کے سرخ لمبے جھنڈے دیوار پر لٹکاتے ہوئے مشورہ دیا۔
’’ایک بڑا سا سرخ اژدھا تمام بُری روحوں کو بھگا دے گا اور خوش قسمتی کا پیغام دے گا۔ اگر بہت سال پہلے لوگ ایک بڑا سا اژدھا بنا کر خوفناک جانور لی این کو ڈرانے کے لئے اِس میں سے آتشبازی نہ چھوڑتے تو یہ نئے سال کی تقریب بھی نہیں منائی جاتی!‘‘

"Perhaps you could be a dragon," suggested Mum, as she hung the red New Year's banners. "A big, red dragon would scare away bad spirits and bring good luck. There wouldn't even be a Chinese New Year if people hadn't made a huge dragon and let off fireworks to scare away the monster Nian, many years ago!"

”لیکن میں اسکول کی پریڈ میں اژدھا بننے جا رہا ہوں، اور میں نہیں چاہتا کہ لی میری نقل کرے۔
ہمیشہ کی طرح،“ لی کے بڑے بھائی چین نے کہا۔
”خیر میں اژدھا بننا ہی نہیں چاہتا“ لی نے کہا حالانکہ دل میں اُس کو تھوڑی سی مایوسی ہوئی تھی۔
”تم ایک بندر بن سکتے ہو۔ تب تمہیں نقاب کی بالکل ضرورت نہیں پڑے گی،“ چین نے چپکے سے کہا تاکہ امّی نہ سن لیں۔

"But I'm going to be a dragon in the school parade and I don't want
Li copying me — as usual," said Li's big brother Chen.
"I don't want to be a dragon anyway," said Li, although secretly he
was a bit disappointed.
"You can be a monkey — then you won't need a mask at all,"
Chen said under his breath so that Mum couldn't hear.

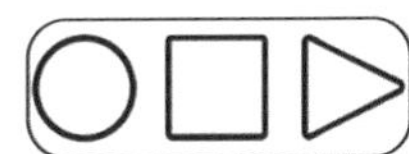

''ہوسکتا ہے میں ایک بڑا سا طاقتور بیل بن جاؤں،'' لی نے اپنے بھائی کی بات کی پرواہ نہ کرتے ہوئے کہا
''ہمارا نیا کزن بھی تو ایک بیل ہوگا۔''
''ہاں اگر وہ نئے سال کی شام تک پیدا ہوگیا۔ ورنہ وہ میری طرح ایک شیر ہوگا۔ سب سے بہترین جانور!''
''خیر میں بے وقوف شیر کا نقاب تو بنانے سے رہا،'' لی نے غصّے سے کہا۔

"Maybe I'll be a big, strong ox," said Li, ignoring his brother. "Our new cousin's going to be an ox."
"Only if it's born before New Year's Eve. Otherwise it'll be a tiger like me — the best animal!"
"Well I'm not going to make a stupid tiger mask," said Li crossly.

''جھگڑا کرنا بند کرو اور آ کر میری مدد کرو،'' امّی نے بڑے کمرے سے پکارا۔
''نانی نے چین سے خوبصورت لالٹین اور کاغذ کی بنی مختلف شکلیں بھیجی ہیں۔ لی کیا تم اُن کو ٹانگ سکتے ہو؟''
اُنہوں نے چین کے ہاتھ میں ایک جھاڑو پکڑا دی۔ ''اور ہمیں پورے گھر میں جھاڑو دینی ہے تاکہ بُری
قسمت یہاں سے باہر پھینک دی جائے۔''
''اوہ امّی، کیا یہ کرنا ضروری ہے؟'' چین نے ٹھنڈی سانس بھری۔

"Stop arguing and come and help me," Mum called from the hall. "Granny has sent beautiful lanterns and paper cutouts all the way from China. Can you put them up, Li?" She handed Chen a broom, "And we've got to sweep the whole house to clear away bad luck."
"Oh Mum, do I have to?" Chen groaned.

نئے سال کا دن آ گیا اور ساتھ میں دادا بھی آ گئے۔
وہ اپنی پسندیدہ کرسی پر بیٹھ گئے اور لی اور چین کو اُس زبردست دوڑ کی کہانی سنائی۔

New Year’s day arrived, and so did Grandpa.
He sat in his favourite chair and told Li and Chen
the story of the great race.

”پورے سماوی دائرے کا سب سے عقل مند جانور چوہا ہے،“ دادا نے کہا۔
”جب تمام جانور نئے سال کو اپنے نام سے شروع کرنے کا مقابلہ کر رہے
تھے تو چالاک چوہا کود کر بیل کی پیٹھ پر چڑھ گیا، پھر اُچک کر اُس کے سر
پر پہنچ گیا اور اِس طرح وہ دوڑ کے اختتام پر سب سے آگے تھا۔“
”یہ تو چالاکی ہے،“ لی چیخا ”بیل کو جیتنا چاہئے تھا!“

"The cleverest animal in the whole zodiac is the rat," said Grandpa.
"When the animals competed to have the new year named after them, cunning Rat jumped on Ox's back, hopped over his head and reached the finishing line first."
"That's cheating," shouted Li. "Ox should have won!"

”دادا جان آپ کون سا جانور ہیں؟“ چین نے پوچھا۔
”ظاہر ہے میں چوہا ہوں! محنتی اور پُرکشش۔ ہم چوہوں میں سب سے بہتر خوبیاں ہوتی ہیں۔“
”دادی جان کون سا جانور تھیں؟“ لی نے پوچھا۔
”وہ ایک خرگوش تھیں“ دادا جان نے اُداسی سے مسکرا کر کہا ”مہربان، دلکش اور باوقار۔“
”کیا آپ اُن کی کمی محسوس کرتے ہیں؟“ لی نے پوچھا۔

"What animal are you Grandpa?" asked Chen.
"I'm a rat, of course! Hardworking and charming — we rats have all the best qualities."
"What animal was Grandma?" asked Li.
"She was a rabbit," Grandpa said, with a sad smile, "kind, graceful and elegant."
"Do you miss her?" Li asked.

"یہ تو احمقانہ سوال ہے،" چین نے کہا۔

"نہیں یہ بہت اچھا سوال ہے۔" دادا جان بولے "میں اُن کو بہت یاد کرتا ہوں اور اُن کے متعلق باتیں کرنا چاہتا ہوں۔
میں نئے سال کے تیسرے دن تم کو اُن کے متعلق اور بھی باتیں بتاؤں گا کیونکہ اُس دن ہم اپنے عزیزوں کو یاد کرتے ہیں۔"

"اچھا، اَب تم دونوں آؤ، آٹے کی گولیاں بنانے کا وقت ہو گیا ہے،" امّی نے دروازے پر آ کر کہا۔

"That's a silly question," said Chen.
"No, it's a good question," said Grandpa. "I miss her very much, and I like to talk about her. I'll tell you more about her on the third day of Chinese New Year when we remember loved ones."
Mum appeared in the doorway. "Okay, you two, it's time to make some dumplings."

امّی اور ابّا صبح سے باورچی خانے کے چکر لگا رہے تھے۔ جب لی نے وہ تمام مزیدار کھانے
دیکھے جو شام کے لئے تیار کئے گئے تھے تو اُس کے پیٹ میں چوہے دوڑنے لگے۔
وہاں پر کوفتے تھے، مرغی اور مچھلی کے لمبے قتلے، اور بھاپ میں پکی ہوئی روٹی۔
گوشت کے لمبے سموسے تو بہت لذیذ لگ رہے تھے۔

Mum and Dad had been in and out of the kitchen since very early in the morning. Li's stomach growled when he saw all the different dishes ready for the evening. There were meatballs, chicken and fish strips, and steamed bread. The lamb rolls looked delicious.

امّی نے گوشت کا بنا مسالہ اور آٹا نکالا۔ اُنہوں نے پھرتی سے وہ مسالہ ایک کوفتے کی شکل میں ڈھال لیا۔
لی نے اُن کی نقل کرنے کی کوشش کی لیکن اُس کے کوفتے ہر شکل اور سائز کے تھے۔ ''گھبراؤ مت''
امّی نے کہا ''وہ بھی اتنے ہی مزیدار ہوں گے۔ اچھا اَب آنکھیں بند کرو۔''
اور اُنہوں نے ایک کوفتے میں چپکے سے ایک سکّہ ڈال دیا۔

Mum brought out the meat stuffing and flour. She quickly shaped some stuffing into a neat ball. Li tried to copy her, but his dumplings were all shapes and sizes. “Don’t worry,” said Mum, “they’ll taste just as good. Now close your eyes,” and she slipped a coin into one of the dumplings.

''کنگ ہے فیٹ چھوئے، سب کے لئے!'' ابّا نے اُس شام کہا۔
''نیا سال مبارک ہو!'' لی اور چین نے چلّا کر کہا۔
لی نے اتنا کھایا کہ اُسے لگا اُس کا پیٹ پھٹ جائے گا۔ شاید بہترین جانور وہ ہے جو سب سے زیادہ کھا سکتا ہے،'' اُس نے رائے دی۔
''سب سے زیادہ کھانے والا جانور تو شاید سُور ہے،'' امّی نے کہا۔
لی کو چین کے ہنسنے کی آواز آئی اور اُس نے فیصلہ کر لیا کہ وہ سُور کی نقاب نہیں بنائے گا۔
''ہاں تو، کچھ لوگوں کو یقین یہ ہے سماوی دائرے کے جانوروں کو ہر سال کے لئے نام اُس وقت دیئے گئے جب اُنہوں نے شہنشاہ کی ضیافت میں شرکت کی،'' ابّا نے کہا۔
''باقی سب جانور بھی مدعو کئے گئے تھے لیکن وہ اتنی دور سفر کرنے میں سُستی کر گئے۔''
ایک دم لی کو اپنے کوفتے میں کچھ چمکدار چیز نظر آئی۔ ''مجھے وہ مبارک سکّہ مل گیا،'' وہ چلّایا۔

"Kung Hey Fat Choy, everyone!" said Dad at dinner that evening.
"Happy New Year!" shouted Li and Chen.
Li ate until he thought he would burst. "Maybe the best animal is the one that can eat the most," he suggested.
"The biggest eater is probably the pig," said Mum.
Li heard Chen giggle and decided not to make a pig mask.
"Well, some people believe that the twelve zodiac animals each had a year named after them for attending the emperor's feast," said Dad. "The other animals were all invited, but they were too lazy to make the journey."
Suddenly Li noticed something shiny in his dumpling. "I found the lucky coin," he cried.

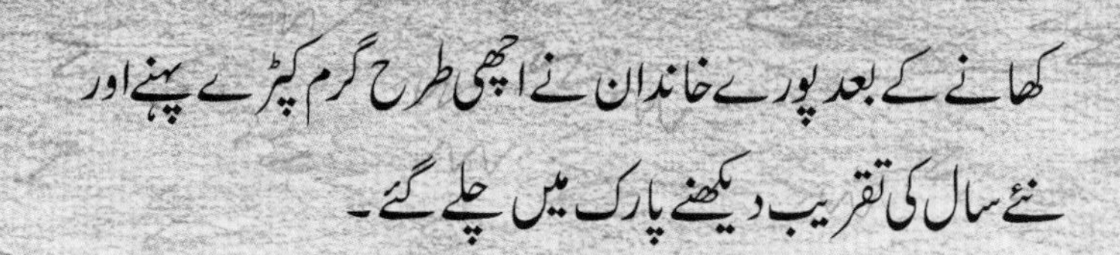

کھانے کے بعد پورے خاندان نے اچھی طرح گرم کپڑے پہنے اور
نئے سال کی تقریب دیکھنے پارک میں چلے گئے۔

After dinner, the family wrapped up warm and went to the park to watch the New Year's celebrations.

لی کی دوست سارہ وہاں اپنے امّی ابّا کے ساتھ آئی تھی اور اُنہوں نے ساتھ ساتھ وہ حیرت انگیز اژدھے کا ڈانس دیکھا
اور اُس کے بعد آتشبازی کی انتہائی دلفریب نمائش دیکھی۔
لی کو یقین تھا کہ اُس نے آتشبازی میں کچھ سماوی دائرے کے جانوروں کی شکلیں بھی دیکھیں۔
لیکن دراصل تو ایسا نہیں تھا۔ کیا خیال ہے؟

Li's friend Sarah was there with her mum and dad, and together they watched the spectacular dragon dances and the fantastic firework display.
Li was sure he could see some of the animals from the Chinese zodiac in the fireworks, but he couldn't really, could he?

اگلا دن کیلنڈس تھا، یعنی نئے سال کا پہلا دن۔ لی کو اپنے پلنگ پر نئے کپڑے ملے جو نئی شروعات کی نمائندگی کرتے ہیں۔

''اُٹھو، سُست الوجود! چلو امّی ابّا کو نئے سال کی مبارک باد دیں!'' اُس نے چین کے بستر پر کودتے ہوئے کہا۔

''تمھیں تو ایک مرغا ہونا چاہئے تھا'' چین نے جمائی لیتے ہوئے کہا۔ ''تمہارے ہوتے ہوئے کسی کو الارم کلاک کی کیا ضرورت ہے!''

The next day was Kalends, the first day of the New Year. Li found new clothes on his bed, bought specially to represent new beginnings.

"Wake up, sleepyhead! Let's go and wish Mum and Dad a Happy New Year!" he said, jumping on the end of Chen's bed.

"You should be a rooster," Chen said, yawning. "Who needs an alarm clock with you around!"

ناشتے کے وقت امّی نے دو چھوٹے سرخ رنگ کے لفافے نکالے جن پر سنہرے الفاظ میں کچھ لکھا تھا، ایک چین کے لئے
اور ایک لی کے لئے تھا۔ لفافوں میں جو سکّے تھے وہ جفت نمبر بناتے تھے اور یہ خوش نصیبی کی علامت ہے۔
''ایک اور اچھی خبر بھی ہے'' امّی نے کہا جبکہ لی یہ منصوبہ بنا رہا تھا کہ اُن پیسوں کو کس طرح خرچ کرنا ہے۔
''تمہاری ایک نئی کزن پیدا ہوئی ہے۔ مے فین اور انکل ٹائی کے یہاں بچے کی پیدائش ہوئی ہے۔''

At breakfast, Mum took out two small red packets covered with golden words, one for Chen and one for Li. The coins in each packet added up to an even number: a lucky sign.
"There's more good news too," said Mum, as Li planned what to do with his money. "You have a new cousin — Mei-Fen and Uncle Tai have a new baby."

”تو وہ ایک شیر ہے یا بیل؟“ یوآن نے پوچھا۔
”وہ ایک ننھی بچی ہے،“ امّی نے کہا۔ ”اور وہ بیل کا سال ختم ہونے سے کچھ منٹ پہلے ہی پیدا ہوئی ہے۔“
”مجھے معلوم تھا کہ وہ بیل ہی ہوگی،“ لی نے نہایت مسکرا کر کہا۔

“So is it a tiger or an ox then?” asked Chen.
“*She* is a little girl,” said Mum, “and she was born in the last few minutes of the year of the ox.”
“I knew she’d be an ox,” said Li, with a big smile.

لی کو دراصل اُس کی پرواہ نہیں تھی کہ اُس کی کزن کون سا جانور تھی۔
اور اُسے ابھی تک یہ بھی نہیں معلوم تھا کہ اُس کو کون سی نقاب بنانا ہے۔ اُس نے ایک دو بنانے کی کوشش بھی کی لیکن کوئی بھی ٹھیک نہ لگی۔
''لی، چلو اَب خوش ہو جاؤ'' ابّا نے کہا ''دیکھو دادا جان تمہارے لئے کیا لائے ہیں۔''
داد جان کے ہاتھ میں دو خوبصورت جانوروں کی شکل کی پتنگیں تھیں۔

Li didn't really mind what animal his cousin was. And he still didn't know what mask to make. He had tried to make a few, but none turned out right.
"Cheer up, Li," said Dad. "Look what Grandpa has brought."
Grandpa was carrying two beautiful, animal-shaped kites.

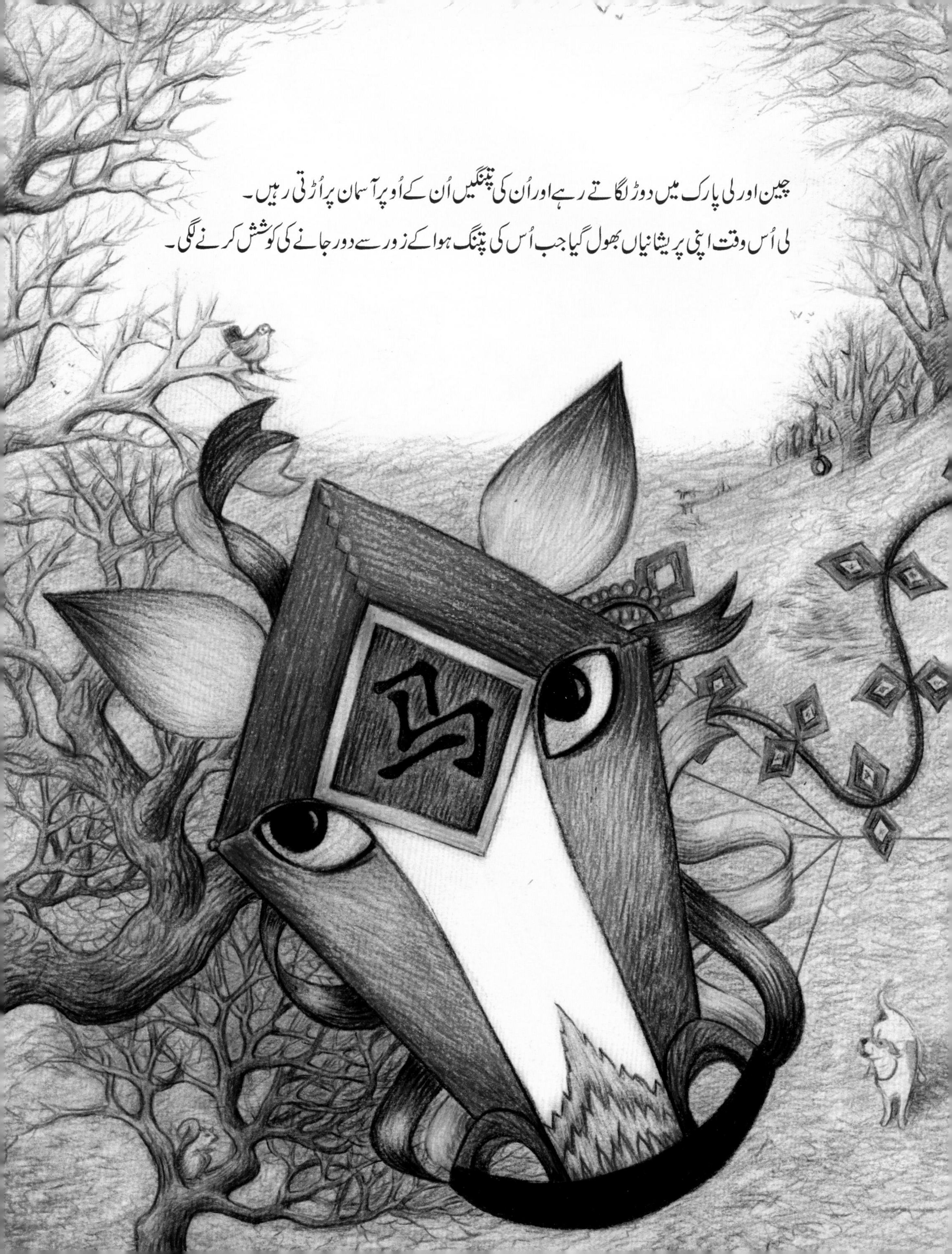

چین اور لی پارک میں دوڑ لگاتے رہے اور اُن کی پتنگیں اُن کے اُوپر آسمان پر اُڑتی رہیں۔
لی اُس وقت اپنی پریشانیاں بھول گیا جب اُس کی پتنگ ہوا کے زور سے دور جانے کی کوشش کرنے لگی۔

Chen and Li raced through the park with their new kites soaring above them. Li forgot about his worries as he felt the kite tugging on the string, trying to fly away.

دوسرے دن اسکول جانے سے پہلے لی کچھ اُداس تھا۔ اُس کی بہت خواہش تھی کہ وہ اسکول کی اسمبلی میں حصّہ لے۔
لیکن وہ اکیلا نہیں تھا بہت سے بچے یہ فیصلہ نہیں کر سکے کہ کون سا نقاب بنائیں۔

Before school the next day, Li felt sad. He really wanted to be in the school assembly. But he wasn't the only one who couldn't decide what mask to make.

کھیل کے وقفے کے دوران لی، طارق، جیک اور سمیرا سب مس گرین سے بات کرنے کے لئے گئے۔
''پریشان مت ہو'' اُنہوں نے کہا ''میرے پاس ایک بہت زبردست منصوبہ ہے۔
مجھے اسمبلی کے ایک خاص حصّے کے لئے کچھ کام کرنے والے بچے چاہیئے ہیں۔
ہمارے پاس سماوی دائروں والے بہت سے خوبصورت جانور تو نہیں لیکن ہمیں ضرورت ہوگی کچھ۔۔۔''

At break time, Li, Tariq, Jack and Samira all went to talk to Miss Green.
"Don't worry," she said, "I have the perfect plan. I need some volunteers for an extra special part of the assembly. We already have lots of lovely Chinese zodiac animals, but..."

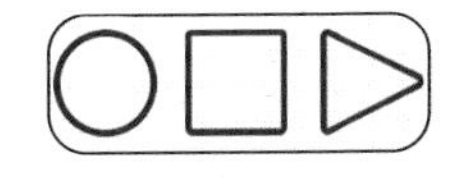

”۔۔۔اژدھے کا رقص کرنے والوں کی!“

“...we still need some dragon dancers!”

Hei Fat Choi!

鼠
Rat
2008
Charming
Popular

牛
Ox
2009
Patient
Logical

龙
Dragon
2012
Energetic
Confident

蛇
Snake
2013
Wise

猴
Monkey
2016
Ambitious
Cheeky

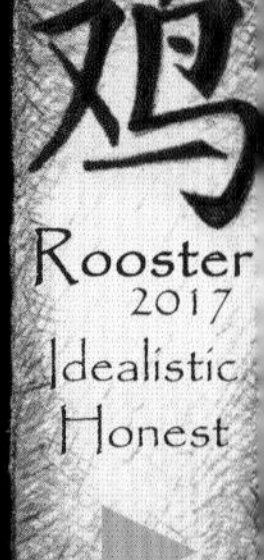
鸡
Rooster
2017
Idealistic
Honest

虎
Tiger
2010
Romantic
Brave

兔
Rabbit
2011
Lucky
Tidy

马
Horse
2014
Dynamic
Cheerful

羊
Ram
2015
Sincere
Artistic

狗
Dog
2018
Alert
Loyal

猪
Pig
2019
Happy
Outspoken

MASK MAKING
paints
brush
pen
scissors
card
string
paper plate
tape
Use your Talking Pen to choose a character then follow the 3 stages of instructions to make a mask and celebrate your chosen year.
choose your character
Tiger
Rabbit
Dragon
Tiger 2010
Rabbit 2011
Dragon 2012
Stage 1
Stage 2
Stage 3
Story mode
Origins of the Chinese Zodiac